CHICAGO UNION STATION

RAILROADS PAST AND PRESENT

GEORGE M. SMERK AND H. ROGER GRANT, EDITORS

INDIANA UNIVERSITY PRESS

Fred Ash

CHICAGO UNION STATION

This book is a publication of

Indiana University Press

Office of Scholarly Publishing

Herman B Wells Library 350

1320 East 10th Street

Bloomington, Indiana 47405 USA

iupress.indiana.edu

The paper used in this publication meets the
minimum requirements of the American
National Standard for Information
Sciences—Permanence of Paper for Printed
Library Materials, ANSI Z39.48–1992.

Manufactured in the United States of America

Library of Congress Cataloging-in-Publication Data.

Names: Ash, Fred, author.
Title: Chicago Union Station / Fred Ash.
Description: 1st edition. | Bloomington, Indiana :
Indiana University Press,
[2018] | Series: Railroads past and present | Includes
bibliographical references and index.
Identifiers: LCCN 2017060511 (print) | LCCN
2017040253 (ebook) | ISBN
9780253029157 (e-book) | ISBN 9780253027290
(cloth : alk. paper)
Subjects: LCSH: Union Station (Chicago, Ill.)
—History. | Railroad stations—Illinois—Chicago
—History. | Railroad
stations—Illinois—Chicago—Pictorial works. |
Railroads—Illinois—Chicago—Passenger traffic. |
LCGFT: Illustrated works.
Classification: LCC TF302.C48 (print) | LCC TF302.
C48 A84 2018 (ebook) | DDC
385.3/140977311—dc23

LC record available at https://lccn.loc.
gov/2017060511

ISBN 978-0-253-02729-0 (cloth)
ISBN 978-0-253-02915-7 (ebook)

1 2 3 4 5 23 22 21 20 19 18

CONTENTS

ACKNOWLEDGMENTS

THE AUTHOR IS RESPONSIBLE FOR ALL ERRORS of fact or interpretation. While he tended his manuscript, his wife Martha Ash and daughter Karolina Ash ably looked after him. This book would not have been possible without their support, and it is dedicated to them. The genesis of this work came from suggestions by Curtis Katz and Charles Stats. Greatly aiding the research and providing editorial criticism were Chris Baer of the Hagley Museum and Library, Greg Ames of the John W. Barriger III National Railroad Library, the late Ed DeRouin, the late Stanley Brandt, Roger Grant, Darrel Babek, Bob Johnson, Dave Leider, and Bill Shapotkin. Marc Magliori of Amtrak facilitated procurement of intellectual property. Dennis McClendon was an invaluable resource on Chicago history and an infallible proofreader, in addition to his cartographic expertise.

Chicago is blessed with tremendous research facilities and patient staff members at the Burnham Library of the Art Institute of Chicago, the Newberry Library, the Chicago History Museum, the Harold Washington branch of the Chicago Public Library, and the Northwestern University Transportation Center Library. Thank you to their staff. Gerald Austiff of the Metropolitan Water Reclamation District and architect Lucien LaGrange were unstinting with their time and assistance. Linda Oblack, Peggy Solic, Ashley Runyon, Rachel Rosolina, and Peter Froelich of Indiana University Press sagely advised on the nuances of the publications business. Brian Cudahy and John Spychalski provided suggestions and corrections critical to the manuscript. Jim Cappio's diligence as copy editor is especially appreciated.

CHICAGO UNION STATION

INTRODUCTION: THE CONTINENTAL DIVIDE

MORE THAN A CENTURY BEFORE AMERICA'S AIRLINES made it the hub of their systems, Chicago was already the nation's transportation center. From the foot of Lake Michigan, lines of steel radiated through the prairies, and over these thin bands rode the abundance of a rich land. The rails carried the people who farmed it, who worked in its factories, and who built its towns. All points of the compass and all American cities of importance were directly connected by trains or by through cars to one of Chicago's six intercity passenger terminals.

Just as today's O'Hare Field is more important than Midway Airport, Chicago Union Station overshadowed its five crosstown rivals: Central, Dearborn, LaSalle Street, Grand Central, and Madison Street stations. From Union Station passengers could reach the major cities on the Atlantic, Pacific, and Gulf coasts and the countless villages and towns in between. Chicago Union Station was and is the nexus of routes over which commuters travel from leafy suburban bedroom communities into the city. You can still catch any number of intercity and suburban trains from Union Station, unlike many of the great railroad stations built in this nation. It was always in a class by itself; no other Chicago depot operated twenty-four hours a day; none had such monumental architecture; none connected so many places. In sum, none of Chicago's other depots compared to Union Station.

The history of Chicago is the history of its railroads. The city and the railroad network grew up together and any study of one's ascendance must look at the other. Chicago came to dominate the trade of the Midwest because of its railroads, and from early in its history it was known with justification as the "Railroad Capital of the World." The railroads and Chicago both remain important, but modern narratives overlook their linkage except when discussing their early development. This book is an inquiry into the continuing relationship between the railroad corporations and the city—in particular their competing visions for one crucially important piece of Chicago real estate.

Chicago Union Station's site has been continually owned and occupied by a series of successor corporations for fifteen decades. Over this time, both its function and its neighborhood evolved remarkably. Originally the site was important in the movement of carload and break-bulk freight, a business on which the city developed. It later specialized in the movement of intercity mail and passengers. Today, it serves primarily as a portal by which commuters from remote residential areas enter the downtown office district. These changes correspond to a transformation in the public view of the station's owners. Local government originally looked to the railroads as development partners but came to distrust the giant corporations that developed. The public then sought to limit and even to remove the railway terminal it once encouraged. As the importance of the railroads waned, public antagonism abated. Now, the partnership is reborn as transit-oriented development has become a key public policy.

The railroad industry's decline resulted in benign neglect of both the station and public transport in general. It reached the point where Union Station appeared nonviable at least for a period. Faced with the simultaneous decline and possible demise of both commuter and intercity rail service, governments rediscovered their linkage to their city's development. Public policy came full circle.

Railroad stations by their nature are both public space and private property. A study of Chicago Union Station illuminates how different generations weighed the dilemmas arising from this duality. Railroad managers defended unfettered ownership rights, while politicians and reformers advocated greater obligation. More than most enterprises, the public views railroad companies as a linchpin for economic or social reform. Railroad corporations thus became unwilling facilitators of broad urban planning schemes.

For railroads, the need to efficiently use expensive center city real estate remains a constant. Chicago Union Station, like other railroad terminals, may be thought of as a building, but it encompasses yards, tracks, and ancillary structures that cover a swath of land nearly two miles long. The term "station" is used in both senses in this book. These massive landholdings were acquired at such great cost that it affected their owners' relationships with local governments, with other corporations, and with the public. It even directly affected the owners' corporate governance and the way their trains operated. This land retains significant

value—but value now derived from the vitality of the downtown real estate market it helped create, rather than as an asset used in a profitable railroad operation.

At their peak, Chicago's six stations, together with their ancillary yards, roundhouses, postal facilities, express houses, and tracks, comprised a several-hundred-acre tract surrounding downtown. This isolated the business district from rest of the city and even from Lake Michigan's shore. These facilities covered two and one-half times the area of the business district, profoundly shaping the development of Chicago's Loop and the city. A passenger who walked out of the station would, in all likelihood, join the throng moving toward the business district, an area where, within blocks of the depot, rents rose to among the highest in the nation. Until recent times, however, if that same passenger walked west, they would literally be on the other side of the tracks, a world of cheap bars and flophouses. Union Station was the division point between radically different urban neighborhoods, and for decades it delineated the most extreme change in property values in the world. Likewise, the depot served as a line of demarcation in the workaday world of the suburbanites. Each morning Chicago's office workers depart their leafy residential tranquility for the concentrated sights and sounds of the city. Union Station separates those worlds.

Chicago Union Station has always been more than the center point of its city, and it deserves acknowledgment as a unique pivot for its region and the nation. This can be readily confirmed by looking at a railroad timetable. Most show Chicago as point of origin, especially for westward-traveling trains. One column of each table shows mileage as measured from Union Station. On many lines, these measurements were made concrete, literally, by the erection of cement mileposts indicating the distance from Chicago Union Station. Such markers spanned half the continent. Union Station, moreover, has been and remains a watershed for the nation's passenger rail traffic. With minor exceptions it has always been a true terminal. No passenger trains transit the station to other destinations. A passenger traveling from the eastern to the western areas of our county, therefore, must change trains in Chicago. It is the true continental divide.

Chicago Union Station's genesis came when the horse and the canal boat were the railroad's only transportation rivals. Its current buildings and tracks were built when railroads and streetcars were the city's primary transport modes. That it survives in the era of automobiles and airplanes testifies to its vitality. Its operation spanned periods that saw the Chicago region transformed from a blue-collar industrial powerhouse to a white-collar dynamo. It adapted and survived.

Union Station remains a great railroad terminal, a vital crossroads for travelers, and a gateway for its hometown. Its peers have fallen to the wrecking ball or have adapted to other uses, but Chicago's premier depot soldiers on. Commuters continue their daily rush past its grandeur and Amtrak passengers patiently queue by trackside gates awaiting travel adventure. They testify to the vision of long-forgotten men who shaped both this building and a great city.

CHAPTER ONE
HUMBLE BEGINNINGS

LAMENTATION

What had he gotten himself into? Ankle deep in turgid marsh water, William Butler Ogden surveyed the plot of land for which he had forsaken prominence, fortune, and security. His wealthy brother-in-law, Charles Butler, had been persuasive—seemingly too persuasive—in talking his young relative into seeking glory on the American frontier. Butler and his friends paid a fortune, $100,000, for property the size of a small farm. This land elsewhere would cost less than $150 and it stretched the imagination to call it land. Purchased in the dry summer prior to Ogden's arrival in the wet spring of 1835, much of it was now marsh. The sole Chicago asset of Butler and Ogden's enterprise, the American Land Company, was a windswept 182-acre tract of virgin sand drift.[1] Scrub and weeds grew from its undulating dunes and stagnant pools collected in the intervening hollows. Ogden found it hard to imagine a worse property. Like the sandy lakeshore extending a hundred miles in each direction, it was unsuitable for crops and had no timber, no stone, not even sod to construct a shelter. These were only the first of his problems.

As with all real estate, the Land Company's property value derived from its location, but Ogden must have had second thoughts about that as well. Located north of an outpost huddled around a log-walled stockade, it was separated from both by a stillwater stream. The village appeared smaller than its reputed population of 4,000. Lack of local capital combined with the expense of importing construction materials meant that there were few buildings. Residents slept a dozen to a room, often two or three to a bed. As a result, flea and chigger bites tormented Ogden as he paced the sandy wasteland the morning after his arrival. His friends seemingly paid more for their landholdings than the entire village of Chicago was worth.

The justification for the village was the feeble river of like name that flowed into Lake Michigan. The Chicago River, however, also gave Ogden pause. Even with the season's freshets, the diminutive stream sat languidly. Without a current sufficient to scour a path through the dunes, it was evident that the recently dredged channel would soon silt back to even lesser prominence. This channel was the lifeline that allowed steamboats, like the one that brought Ogden from Buffalo, a Chicago berth. The port, in turn, promised to make the American Land Company's river frontage an attractive investment. But could this feeble creek support the Land Company's lofty ambition?

Lake Michigan's western shore had better anchorages than Chicago. Chicago, however, had a plan—no more than a dream really—for a canal from its meager stream westward to the Illinois

River. A waterway to crest the divide between the Great Lakes and the Mississippi watersheds, the era's principal travel arteries, was a glimmering prospect. There were signs, albeit faint ones, that this canal might soon be more than tavern talk. Chartered to great fanfare, the Illinois and Michigan Canal Company was nevertheless far from a reality. Its proposed route looked short and easy, but canals by their nature were enormously expensive projects. Fortunately, canal company stocks and bonds were popular investments. In fact, they were one of the few marketable securities in which an individual could invest. A canal connecting the unsettled frontier to a minor lakeside village, however, was speculative by any standard.

To jump-start the enterprise, the federal government gave I&M canal commissioners a land grant that included the best part of their port, a knoll next to Fort Dearborn on the south bank of the Chicago River. Ogden arrived just as they prepared to subdivide and sell the town lots needed to finance the long-dreamed-of ditch between watersheds. This presented Ogden with a dilemma. At once canal lots came to market whose value vastly exceeded all property previously sold in the region. They were superior to the Land Company's north side lots if for no other reason than that they were drier. They also enjoyed existing wharfage and were near the fort whose soldiers provided the only local market. On the other hand, if Ogden prevailed on settlers, against the odds, to buy his company's land, I&M Canal Company land sales could suffer. That jeopardized the financial underpinnings of the very project upon which the future of his enterprise depended.

Ogden seemingly abandoned a prosperous future to settle in the rude West. He was the son of a Revolutionary War officer rewarded for his service with land in then-remote Walden, New York. The father prospered in lumber, which he sent down the nearby Delaware River to Philadelphia. He built a sawmill, soon joined by a gristmill and then by several woolen mills that carded and pulled local fleece. The mills created Ogden family wealth and their specialized machinery gave William an early education as a millwright.[2] Young William next studied law until age sixteen, when his father died. Abandoning his studies, he and his brothers took control of the family businesses and multiplied their profits. At twenty-three, his life took a dramatic turn at the urging of his oldest sister's husband.

Charles Butler came from wealth and influence, including a brother who was US attorney general. His own rise to prominence and fortune came after he studied law under Albany's pre-eminent attorney, Martin Van Buren. Entering his own practice, he devised a financial plan that allowed upstate New York farmers to buy property from the original Dutch land companies. This endeavor was backed by mortgages from the New York Life Insurance and Trust Company, the first financial services company established in the nation's future banking center.[3]

Butler was a key member of the Albany Regency, Van Buren's faction of Jacksonian Democrats that dominated New York politics. He persuaded Regency leaders to have Ogden represent his district in the 1834 election. Ogden espoused many Jacksonian ideals, but Regency support was pragmatic. Party leaders, including Butler, had investments in the proposed New York and Erie Railroad. They needed loyal votes to procure state aid for their enterprise, one of the largest railroad projects in the world. An instant insider, Ogden simultaneously learned politics and railroad finance.

Ogden confirmed Butler's confidence. The young legislator's sole speech praised the necessary legislation and helped enact a previously rejected bill. After less than a year in the legislature, however, Butler pushed Ogden to undertake another task, the management of land investments. Butler formed the American Land Company, which bought frontier tracts. Arthur Bronson, whose family founded and controlled the New York Life Insurance and Trust Company, was a Land Company cofounder. Ogden became both a shareholder and the company's Chicago agent. Capitalized at $1 million, the company allowed its stockholders to purchase shares in a portfolio of holdings rather than speculate on one location. It owned farmland in Ohio, timber tracts in Michigan, and plantations in several southern states. It developed town lots in Toledo and Evansville, both canal terminals like Chicago. It was Chicago, however, that became its premier investment.

Ogden arrived in Chicago fresh from his legislative resignation. Although he had bought and sold forestland, he had little experience with town lots. Nevertheless, he quickly induced his wealthy backers to add a further $15,000 to their original $100,000 Chicago investment and proceeded to grade streets, improve drainage, and build model buildings. Ogden then followed Butler's earlier model, forgoing quick profits by providing credit to prospective buyers. The concept of improving raw land before subdividing it was relatively novel for the cash-starved frontier, and when combined with easy financing, it proved an effective sales stimulant. Ogden turned the canal company's nationally publicized land sale to his advantage, for it attracted prospective settlers and spectators to Chicago. Once they saw the American Land Company's well-drained lots on graded streets, many purchased them as the superior product. The company sold nearly one-third of its Chicago holdings, more than recouped its original investment, and guaranteed itself an income stream from future installment payments.

Despite initial reservations, Ogden stayed in Chicago to collect these installments and to further the business. By 1837, he not only managed the American Land Company office but was agent for nearly one hundred other eastern investors. Selling property to these absentee landholders, he then performed on-site duties for a nominal fee. He contracted for the erection of buildings, arranged leases, collected rents, paid taxes, and generally acted as property manager and trustee. Because he routinely counseled clients about other local investments, handled their cash, and provided them with extensive news about frontier business conditions, his moneyed investors saw him as a valued investment adviser. One byproduct, however, was that from the town's first days absentee landlords held large sections of its land. At the same time, Ogden continued to sell land on credit to local buyers, hired them as laborers, and advised land purchasers about taxes or other legal matters. Local inhabitants thus viewed him as their banker, their attorney, and their employer. Despite potential conflicts of interest, Ogden melded these roles to his advantage. Pioneer businessmen and eastern speculators alike viewed him as one of their own.

WILLIAM OGDEN AND THE ASCENT OF A CITY

The Town of Chicago had been born on August 12, 1833, when twenty-eight voters ratified a charter and elected five trustees. These soldiers and settlers had been the vanguard of settlement that followed completion of the Erie Canal. That project shifted the nation's east-west transportation corridor away from the

Ohio River to the Great Lakes. In turn, the Illinois and Michigan Canal Company promised to extend this route westward. The I&M commissioners, Ogden, and other speculators platted streets and town lots bordering the harbor where canal and lake boats were to meet, literally placing Chicago on the map.

So begins our story, which centers upon the contentious relationship between a city and one of its largest absentee property owners, a railroad company. First, however, we must understand the legal foundation of this relationship. Chicago's original charter from the state of Illinois was frustratingly vague as to the legal powers granted the village.[4] Charter revisions in 1835 and 1837 dealt with immediate shortcomings and the later revisions elevated Chicago to the status of a city. City charters were less restrictive than those for towns and villages, as the latter were thought to be too small to have educated and effective trustees. No charter in Illinois allowed a municipality to issue bonds to finance canals, railroads, or other private corporations. Nor could cities levy taxes to commercial enterprises. In 1837, however, an Illinois statute did allow cities to issue debt instruments and scrip for their own account.[5]

Local governments could "invest surplus funds" from a municipal bond sale as they saw fit, but the full faith and credit of the city supported the debt and eventually bond proceeds had to support a valid municipal project. "Eventually" never came in some cases and this was a loophole large enough to drive a train through. Illinois towns used the statute's vagaries to purchase blocks of securities in fledgling private ventures. Municipal bonds purportedly created public works, but everyone winked at their true intent, which often was to induce businesses to locate in the newly indebted town. Loophole or not, Chicago's

political climate prevented municipal investment in the railroad or turnpike schemes that proliferated in the era. From their city's earliest days, Chicagoans had a single-minded conviction of their locational superiority. Railways, they knew, had to come to them. Unlike many towns, Chicago's government never gave cash subsidies or donated large parcels of property to railroad enterprises. By contrast, Wisconsin law allowed Milwaukee to issue bonds in support of eight railroad companies.[6]

Like most frontier communities, fledgling Chicago had problem enough funding its own explosive growth, let alone financing region-wide projects. Property taxes were the city's dominant revenue source, but their take was meager. By definition, revenues from property taxes lag city growth, so they barely covered Chicago's day-to-day needs and were woefully insufficient to fund improvements. Underwriting tax-supported municipal securities for public sale was itself relatively novel. It did not take hold until the issuance of New York City's general obligation bonds of 1848.[7] Banks could lend money, but they were few in number and even after they formed locally, their thin capitalization was insufficient to meet staggering municipal needs. In a now-famous incident, the only major bank in Illinois, the State Bank in Shawneetown, turned down the city's loan application because it believed Chicago would never amount to much. To cover its bills, the city paid creditors with scrip in one-, two-, and three-dollar denominations. These non-interest-bearing bills traded locally and were redeemable only with the collection of the semiannual tax levy. They nevertheless established the city's ability to issue debt, and more importantly to repay it.

The 1837 city charter concentrated political power with the mayor. Previously, authority vested jointly among the aldermen.[8]

The new arrangement fostered partisan politics and pushed William Butler Ogden toward political office. With the support of the city's leading newspaper, John Wentworth's *Chicago Democrat*, Ogden became the first mayor on May 3, 1837. His opponents painted him as a "transient speculator," but he won convincingly by a vote of 489–217. Summer of that year saw a financial panic grip the nation, with ruinous consequences for both Ogden and Chicago. The Illinois legislature, whose prescription for municipalities prohibited corporate investment, had never taken its own medicine. Like other states, its guarantee stood behind a staggering amount of bonds used to finance an ill-conceived network of canals, turnpikes, and railroads. Dizzying growth in the national economy created a desperate need for infrastructure, then known as "internal improvements." Less developed areas of America such as Illinois, however, built transportation projects in advance of demand.

These projects soon defaulted on their bonds. Their original plan anticipated earnings sufficient to pay debt, but many enterprises failed before they opened. Upon default, the interest and scheduled principal payments on these "improvement bonds" became payable from each state's general fund—debt that by definition was repayable from taxes. In many cases the bonds accelerated upon default; that is, *all* principal became due at once. State governments simply lacked the cash for redemptions. Since governments were the only large-scale enterprises in the frontier economy, their embarrassment caused the entire commercial sector to collapse. Banks had purchased bonds bearing the full faith and credit of state governments because they sought an ultraconservative investment. Perversely, the default of these seemingly sound state bonds ruined the strongest banks.

Throughout America, there were calls to repudiate crushing state debts, especially from the Jacksonians who first elected Ogden to the New York legislature.

Ogden had his own problems because the speculators to whom he sold land on credit also defaulted. Cash from land sales evaporated at the very moment that local governments hiked property taxes to raise money for their own spiraling needs. Hounded by his own creditors, he defiantly retorted to his fellow citizens that their governments should not "commit the folly of proclaiming their own dishonor."[9] To press his point that state and local debts must be repaid, Ogden turned his back on the Jacksonians. A later commentator dryly noted that he was "not much of a partisan." He amply demonstrated this during his lifetime, as four different political parties were to nominate him for office. His mayoral duties, of course, were secondary to the time he spent on commerce, and his business affairs held up surprisingly well during the financial panic. Local debtors supported him for defending their honor, while eastern bondholders had every incentive to agree with his platform. Despite the severity and longevity of this depression, his correspondents continued to send Ogden funds to invest.

Ogden's involvement in transportation projects grew from his belief that Chicago's geographic advantage, in and of itself, was insufficient to assure its growth. He personally built over one hundred miles of streets and two bridges in Chicago. Later he applied the development principles he honed selling city lots to the entire region. He formed a lake steamship company in 1836 and as early as 1840 held construction contracts for several portions of the I&M Canal. The steamship company was decidedly unprofitable, and it is questionable whether direct gain was even a goal of the canal contracts. Ogden hitched his wagon to Chicago's rising star, and while he couldn't move heaven to promote his adopted city, he most certainly moved a lot of earth.

Ogden was the incorporator, promoter, and largest shareholder of Chicago's first railroad, the Galena and Chicago Union (the "Galena"). The fact that Galena received top billing in the corporate title was no mistake, as the lead mining center was then the larger of the two cities. The charter for a rail line connecting them came in 1836, concurrent with the legislature's passage of a charter for the Illinois and Michigan Canal Company. The railroad charter was a sop to get populous Galena's support for a canal in which the town had no real interest. This initial railroad attempt and a second effort failed before Ogden became involved. His task was to resurrect a moribund project.

The railroad surveyed a line to Galena in September 1847 while Ogden vainly tried to interest his correspondents in its securities. On paper, the new rail route seemed to have great prospects. The 1846 repeal of the Corn Laws in Great Britain materially pushed up demand and prices for the grains that were to be the railroad's primary commodity. Ogden raised enough money locally to run the survey westward from a wharf on the north branch of the Chicago River. This pier was crucial because traffic patterns on this rail line would be similar to those of a canal; freight and passengers to and from the prairie would transload to lake schooners. Seven miles of track were put under construction in fall 1847, but it was a shoestring affair. Within the city limits, oak rails had a scant band of secondhand strap iron nailed on top, all spiked without intervening ties directly to the plank-road street. By December of 1848, the line reached a point near the Des Plaines River, but only after Ogden personally carried the stock subscription books by horseback throughout northern Illinois.[10]

April 5, 1848 saw the Galena and Chicago Union's board authorize construction of its first depot in Chicago. Completed that fall, the small one-story frame structure accommodated freight and provided office space. Structures contemporary with this depot survive today and their construction suggests that the railroad did not use the economical balloon-frame design, a relatively recent invention common in early Chicago. Rather, they used traditional heavy-timber post-and-lintel framing.[11] The depot was south of Kinzie Street and east of Canal Street. It had an east-west axis with an entrance near West Water Street, which once ran along the riverbank. Tracks ran along the south side of the depot. Passenger accommodation at the station and aboard trains, if any, was crude. The Pioneer, the line's first locomotive, entered service on October 24, 1848, but the railroad's first passenger car did not arrive until July 3, 1849. City aldermen, fearful that steam locomotives would spew fire-starting cinders, forbade the use of engines within the city limits. The first trains into the Galena depot were thus drawn by horses.[12] In 1849, the depot received an addition that tripled its freight-house space and provided two stories for passengers and offices at its east end. From this depot, the Galena headed into a sea of prairie grass that began even before the town's nearby edge.

Another prairie line became a feeder to the Galena railroad in September 1850. The Aurora Branch, later known as the Chicago, Burlington and Quincy (the "Burlington"), ran from present-day West Chicago to the burgeoning Fox River community of Aurora. This fledgling line was to develop into a major railroad system with its own route into Chicago, but initially it reached

Chicago's first depot was built in 1848 by the Galena & Chicago Union. It only consisted of the single-story part of the building at the left side of this illustration. The two-story addition on its east end is commonly mislabeled as the first station, but this was an addition built the following year.

the Galena's humble Chicago depot by running thirty miles over the latter's track. With the success of his first railroad project and a rebound of the national economy, Ogden advised investors such as Edward Russell, a retired clipper ship merchant from Connecticut, to expand beyond real estate. Actually, Russell eased into railroad investments in a familiar way. Russell and Ogden sold the new Chicago and Milwaukee (today's Metra UP North line) depot and wharfside lands in early 1854.[13] In payment, they received bonds—and, as was a common pattern, stock to sweeten the deal. Ogden struck a similar agreement with the Illinois and Wisconsin Railroad (today's Metra UP Northwest line), a broad-gauge route that was proposed to run inland toward the Wisconsin border.[14] Both railroads built stations on the west bank of the Chicago River immediately north of the Galena depot. This land had considerable value and thus securities tendered for payment were substantial. Another of Ogden's correspondents could not come to terms with the railroads on the price for a slender strip of land between these depots. The I&W had to pay an extortionate rent of $1000 per year for the right to cross it.

Even before the Galena laid its first rail, Ogden and Butler purchased the moribund Indiana charter of the Buffalo and Mississippi Railroad. The B&M was an Indiana corporation that lacked any legal right to build or operate in other states, but the Galena's Illinois charter conveniently allowed it to build to the state line. That railroad's board rebuffed Ogden regarding a plan to connect the two railroads.

The Michigan Southern Railroad was smaller and financially weaker than its rival, the Michigan Central. Lacking cash, it purchased the B&M charter for stock and Butler took a seat on its board. When the established Michigan Central heard that its brash rival intended to head to Chicago, it quickly cast aside its original doubts and decided to go there as well. A track-laying race across Indiana commenced and any doubts about Chicago's ascendance vanished.[15]

The Michigan-based railroads employed identical strategies to enter the blossoming metropolis: partnership with a locally chartered corporation. Land speculation was Chicago's chief industry and thus building lines into the city promised to be expensive. For their part, the eastern railroads had assets locals lacked: capital access plus a corps of experienced surveyors, engineers, and lawyers. Outsiders, however, needed political muscle and a scarce commodity—an Illinois charter.

On January 3, 1851, William B. Ogden wrote to the Michigan Southern with an offer to have the Galena build to the Indiana state line. Two days later, he was removed as president of the railroad. Late in 1851, the Michigan Southern found its Illinois ally when it agreed to aid the proposed Chicago and Rock Island Railroad in constructing an arrow-straight line southward from the heart of the city that would then veer to its western terminus.

Shortly after formation of the Michigan Southern–Rock Island alliance, the Michigan Central and Illinois Central Railroads concocted a similar joint venture to survey a route from the state line to the west bank of the Chicago River. Much of this alignment later became the route used by others to reach the future site of Union Station. In this instance, however, the city of Chicago induced the companies to abandon their survey and instead build along the lakeshore.

Eastern connections provided by the Michigan rail lines were catalysts for a revolutionary transformation. They promised to reduce Chicago–New York shipment times to two days year round from the previous summer-only transit of three weeks. Meanwhile, their westward connections funneled grain into Chicago. From this central point, cereals could be efficiently marketed and transshipped to eastern US and European points. The telegraph lines that accompanied the eastern railroads allowed split-second communication between grain buyers and sellers. Chicago was the point where the information and distribution networks merged.

A THIRD WAY EAST

Charles Butler and William Ogden reaped fortunes from the astronomic appreciation of their Chicago real estate in addition to their American Land Company holdings. They invested the proceeds in railroad securities and other ventures. By March of 1851, for example, Butler consolidated several Wisconsin lines to form the Rock River Valley Union Railroad. However, the investment that is central to our story is Ogden's involvement in the Ft. Wayne and Chicago Railroad. Fort Wayne, Indiana, was a prosperous canal town. Its local merchants wanted to ensure its prominence with railroad connections radiating at right angles from the canal.[16] The first organizational meeting for such a project was held in Warsaw, Indiana, on September 14, 1852. Chicagoans invested in the project from the beginning, but they never saw Fort Wayne as its terminal. Rather, they sought to link it with other planned railroads to provide another connection between Chicago and the eastern seaboard. The *Tribune*'s first mention of the railroad stated, "it will give us direct connection with Pittsburg, Philadelphia, Baltimore, and the South-Eastern cities, and compete at our doors with other railroads—thus lessening the cost of transportation."[17] By December 1852, the railroad surveyed the line and the *Tribune* reported, "the Company has succeeded in securing excellent depot grounds in Chicago."[18] In fact, the company did not purchase Chicago property until June 23, 1853, when it entered into contracts with Ogden's clients Amasa Wright and Samuel Russell.[19]

An ordinance passed February 13, 1854 allowed the Ft. Wayne to build a single track in any street west of Clark Street. Only five such streets were on the plats, and for the most part their only physical manifestation consisted of surveyors' stakes pounded into the sodden prairie. Like previous Chicago ordinances, this one required the railway to use horse power, to grade and plank the street for wagon traffic, and to obtain the consent of adjoining landowners. The act's vague geographic boundaries raised local ire, but this latitude prevented individual landowners from holding the company hostage. The problem of a dissenting owner extracting a high price was well known to the person whose signature graced the draft ordinance: William Butler Ogden. He did not join the Ft. Wayne board, however, until the following November.[20]

The public considered right-of-way gifts a subsidy requiring reciprocal nonmonetary consideration, such as the prohibition on locomotive-hauled trains. Alternatively, the company could purchase land or exercise its power of eminent domain. The poorly capitalized Ft. Wayne seemingly had little choice, and the *Tribune*, among others, thought the cost of private land acquisition was "an insuperable obstacle . . . so great that it cannot be thought of."[21] This belief was based on the fourfold appreciation of land values since the Michigan Southern purchased its properties. Chicago citizens were confident their gift would be accepted, strings attached. To their surprise, railroad executives left town without accepting their offer.

Many Chicagoans doubted the Ft. Wayne railroad would build into the city. They suspected that the Cincinnati, Peru, and Chicago Railway (the "Cincinnati") would be the first road from the southeast. This not-yet-built line already had a contract with the Michigan Southern to bring its traffic into Chicago from a planned junction at Plymouth, Indiana.[22] Another agreement already existed for the Cincinnati line to carry the Ft. Wayne's traffic westward from their intended union at Valparaiso. The conventional wisdom held that, by use of existing tracks, there was no need for new railroads to build into Chicago. Snide comments about the Ft. Wayne's intention to build toward Chicago became common.

Doubts about the Ft. Wayne proved unfounded. In February of 1855, Ogden forwarded the official "Report of the Chief Engineer of the Fort Wayne and Chicago Railroad" to the *Tribune*, which published it in its entirety. Half the text related to the importance of Chicago, while it barely mentioned Fort Wayne.[23] Word became action two months later when the railroad acquired more land for a West Side Chicago terminal. This was a transaction with Ogden's original railway affiliation. Previously, on April 10, 1854, the Galena acquired a potential competitor, the Chicago, St. Charles, and Mississippi Airline Railway (the "Airline") for $600,000. By some accounts, the Airline's formation was for the sole purpose of a sale to the Galena.[24] It laid twelve miles of track parallel to the Galena, but it never opened for business. Other observers stated that the Galena's desire to purchase the Airline stemmed from the fact that the "Pioneer Road" [the Galena] had a "not very secret alliance" with the Michigan Central Railroad. Its antagonist, the Michigan Southern, helped promote the Airline but lost control, giving its rival an opportunity. In any event, the Galena thwarted a would-be competitor and obtained the Airline's terminal grounds on the south branch of the Chicago River, a fifty-acre plot.[25] Due to the run-up in real estate values, this land may have been more valuable than the Airline's other assets combined. To help pay for its purchase, the Galena immediately sold the Ft. Wayne sixteen acres, a plot sufficient for a roundhouse and car shop. The Galena, however, retained the Airline's valuable riverside wharf. Within two years, the Ft. Wayne sold half its Airline acreage for a smart profit to the Chicago, Burlington and Quincy, the former Aurora Branch Railroad. The gain from this sale was the Ft. Wayne's principal income, as only a small amount of track near its namesake town was open to business.

The Ft. Wayne had $1.2 million in paid capital and issued $500,000 in bonds. This was about half the amount necessary to finish the entire road, and all work was at its east end. G. W. Balley, a director of the Ft. Wayne's eastern connection, the Ohio and Pennsylvania Railroad, also had a Chicago-area construction contract with the Illinois Central. When the Illinois Central work finished, he planned to turn his men to the Ft. Wayne's line from Plymouth, Indiana to Chicago. This line was touted as "remarkably free from curves, with low grades, allowing it to be worked at the highest speeds."[26] Construction stopped, however, due to another economic storm. The national business climate turned troublesome, this time exaggerated in Chicago by a cholera epidemic during the hot summer of 1854. Little commerce was done as businessmen fled with their families. In-migration ceased entirely.

The downturn caught William Butler Ogden at an especially vulnerable time. His guarantee stood behind a contract for the Illinois and Wisconsin Railroad to purchase $1.5 million in iron rails, and that railroad defaulted on payments. Ogden's correspondents offered him cash to redeem his obligations, but he met the crushing debt on his own. He sold and mortgaged property, often at a loss. He collected receivables and hustled business in every form imaginable. Ogden saw what his detractors and creditors did not—opportunity in catastrophe. Nevertheless, with cholera rampant and business moribund, he left for an eighteen-month tour of Europe. There, he expanded his network of financial correspondents in new directions.

Before embarking on his grand tour, Ogden took I&W bonds that bore an extravagant 10 percent coupon as collateral for his guarantee. After the railroad suspended all interest payments, he accrued an even larger stake in its debt at a substantial discount. He was able to convert this speculation into a seemingly more secure investment on March 15, 1855, when the I&W reorganized and consolidated with the Rock River Valley Union Railroad. His holdings in the consolidated firm were actually larger than those of his brother-in law, founder of the more established RRVU. To casual observers it appeared a strange merger, for the I&W had only thirty-nine miles of track running northwest from Chicago. The RRVU had twenty-nine miles southward from Fond du Lac, Wisconsin. A gap of 108 miles separated the divisions of the newly named Chicago, St. Paul and Fond du Lac Railroad (the "Fond du Lac"). Even had they met, they would have had different track gauges.

From their earlier deals, Ogden and Butler knew the value of owning railroad charters in adjoining states. Moreover, while the area between their lines had little population, the endpoints—Wisconsin's Fox River valley and the area surrounding Chicago—were well settled with prosperous farms clamoring for a better way to move their produce to market. Surely similar land in undeveloped central Wisconsin held an even greater prospect, and due to a lucrative federal land grant awarded the railway, farmland values could directly finance the new railroad. Ogden's Chicago real estate office soon became the railroad's land sales office. When the economy briefly rebounded, the new Fond du Lac railroad converted its Chicago-area lines, originally built with six-foot-wide tracks, to standard gauge. Construction resumed and the lines linked near Gainesville, Wisconsin.

The new route failed to prosper, for America again fell into depression in 1857. The financial crisis had international causes, but a 50 percent decline in wheat prices was the local source of distress. The Fond du Lac was bankrupt and it struggled through June 2, 1859, when the court sold it to its bondholders, who formed the Chicago and North Western Railway to take

ownership. By that action, Ogden's bonds converted to stock. He now controlled a railroad with little debt serving a region with bright prospects.

Although Ogden spent most of the 1850s protecting his position in the railroads running northwest from Chicago, he was also active in resurrecting the Ft. Wayne. Charles Butler later eulogized, "On the organization of the Ft. Wayne and Chicago Company in 1853, he became a director and has, we believe, always continued his active interest in that enterprise. The line to Pittsburgh then embraced three distinct companies, all weak and all engaged, with limited means and credit, in the work of construction. He regarded a trunk line under one management, from Chicago to Pittsburgh, as essential to a valuable business connection."[27]

By the spring of 1856, these separate but end-to-end railroads connected central Indiana and Ohio with Pittsburgh using a common track gauge of four feet, ten inches, the standard for central and southern Ohio. Ogden became one of only two Ft. Wayne incorporators to ascend to the board when the three lines consolidated into the Pittsburgh, Ft. Wayne, and Chicago Railroad. Another party interested in the company was the Pennsylvania Railroad, which completed its own Philadelphia-to-Pittsburgh main line in 1854. It sent the Ft. Wayne "chair" rail from its New Portage Railroad over the Allegheny Mountains. This English metals design had been obsolete in America for over a decade. The eastern railroad also invested $239,000 in cash, its president J. Edgar Thomson joined the fledgling company's board, and it financed the Ft. Wayne by allowing it to pay for the used rail in bonds. One of the era's most dynamic individuals, Thomson—like

William B. Ogden represented east coast moneyed interests from his first days in Chicago, but they would not finance his first railroad venture.

Ogden—sought long-term gain over immediate profits in an era when many craved a quick fortune through self-serving construction contracts or stock manipulation. His appointment to the board may have been the most valuable of the Pennsylvania's contributions.

Despite a business downturn, the Ft. Wayne arranged a tentative Chicago link when it reached Plymouth in the summer of 1856. There it connected with the Peru and LaPorte Railroad, the locally financed portion of the planned Cincinnati route. As envisioned years before, this connection led to a second junction with the Michigan Southern. Passengers needed to change cars to complete their westward journey, but traffic soared. The *Tribune* opined, "The Ft. Wayne road owns very valuable Depot grounds in Chicago, as well as an excellent route." It neglected to mention that the cobbled-together route did not connect with the company's Chicago property.

The three railroads consummated their marriage on July 31, 1856, although the westernmost 85 miles of the 463-mile line from Chicago to Pittsburgh were incomplete. The remaining construction would cost $2.8 million, which promised to push the total debt up to $13 million.[28] Three months before the first meeting of the consolidated railroad's board, it had already printed a bond circular looking for $3.5 million in additional debt.[29] Even with this foresight, it missed a brief uptick in the economy, and the bonds went unsold. This was just as well, as a downturn turned into a major panic. The October failure of Pittsburgh banks holding the railroad's deposits forced it to default on its existing bonds.[30] At the same time, fifteen railroads operating in Illinois with $181 million in outstanding debt had to make assignments to their creditors. The established Michigan Central saw its stock price drop from $88 a share the previous year to $9. Even the strong Galena saw shares drop from $119 to $54.

THE RAILROAD CAPITAL

As the Ft. Wayne pushed toward completion, significant changes occurred in its western terminal city and the surrounding region. Unlike the first railroads to enter Chicago, the Ft. Wayne sought connections with an established rail network. In 1854, a track linking many railroads had been built within the city limits. Known as the St. Charles Airline, its route followed the easternmost portion of a similarly named earlier company. No legal connection existed between these companies, for unique among railroads the new line had no corporate charter. Rather, it was a partnership with four railroads as equal owners. Its major purpose was to allow Burlington trains to come off the Galena's tracks (actually the "original" Airline tracks) on their way to the Burlington's new terminal at the Illinois Central's depot on Lake Street east of Michigan Avenue. In addition to the Illinois Central and Michigan Central on the lakefront, the new Airline also connected with the Chicago and Rock Island and the Michigan Southern. It therefore connected all lines in the city except the Chicago and Milwaukee and the Fond du Lac Railroads. This did not sit well with the latter's majority owner, William Ogden.

Today the interline exchange of freight cars between companies is crucial, but at the time transloading freight between companies was key to success. As late as 1855, there was a proposal to connect the various railway depots in town by canal. Warehouses, elevators, and lumberyards dominated the riverfront because they remained reliant on waterborne commerce. Like the Great Lakes schooners and Illinois River flatboats that preceded them, trains allowed access to distant markets. Rail tariffs were higher than water rates, but trains allowed quick postharvest shipment. In turn, this allowed farmers to receive payment before their spring planting. Rail transit also reduced spoilage and shrinkage, which were the bane of waterborne trade.

Chicago's geographic attributes helped it become a transshipment center. In particular, the languid Chicago River lacked steep embankments. This lowered transfer and warehouse costs since, unlike in Saint Louis or Cincinnati, Chicago freight transfers dispensed with the brigades of stevedores required to heave sacks up and down a steep levee. Another innovation allowed Chicago merchants to eliminate the expensive sacks for grain transfer.[31] The grain elevator, an improvement that first arose in 1842 in Buffalo, arrived in Chicago only six years later. Originally horse-powered, its utility soon improved with the application of steam engine lifts. Great lifting power allowed Chicago elevators to reach truly mammoth proportions. The Munger, Armour and Dole elevator of 1861 could handle 40,000 bushels per hour and unload a boxcar in six minutes.[32] In 1854, when the Crimean War blocked traditional ports for shipment of Ukrainian grain, Chicago passed Odessa as the world's largest grain port and its trade continued to rise. The closure of western markets to Ukrainian wheat again made the American grain business lucrative.

Trade in grain, the system of elevator receipts, and a standardized grading system revolutionized more than agriculture. As historian William Cronon noted,

> Chicagoans began to discover that a grain elevator had much in common with a bank. Farmers and shippers took their wheat or corn to an elevator operator as if they were taking gold or silver to a banker. After depositing the grain in a bin, the original

owner accepted a receipt that they could redeem in much the same way that they could redeem a check or banknote for precious metal. Instead of completing a sale by redeeming the receipt, and turning over the physical grain to a purchaser, the original owner simply turned over the receipt itself. The elevators effectively created a new form of money, secured not by gold, but by grain.[33]

Liquidity was a dire need because the frontier was remarkably deficient in coinage. To fill this void, banks throughout the nation issued currency, but nearly all of it traded at discount. Each note floated with public perceptions of its worth. Weak firms known as "wildcatters" often floated the most notes and this currency could become worthless overnight. Barter thus remained as common as cash purchase. Chicago grain receipts were, in essence, collateralized warehouse notes, and merchants preferred them to bank notes. This sound addition to the money supply provided Chicago with a competitive advantage vis-à-vis other cities and its multiplier effect spurred even greater growth. Grain-based capital provided the funds to invest in the construction of more elevators and slips along the Chicago River. The Galena's wharf, purchased as part of the St. Charles Airline, became one of the city's largest concentrations of elevators, which were among the nation's largest buildings.

The Chicago River's south branch also became central to another trade dominated by Chicago. Prairie farmers and merchants needed wood from the virgin forests of Wisconsin and Michigan for the homes and stores blossoming across the treeless plains. Near the junction of the two branches of the river, stacks of drying lumber dominated the skyline. After 1854, much of this trade moved to the river's bank south of Twenty-Second Street.

A British visitor noted, "The timber yards are a considerable part of the city's surface, there appearing to be enough boards and planks piled up to supply a half dozen states." That was precisely its market, as waves of settlement rolled across Chicago's unforested hinterland. The city was also the entry point for immigrants lured by promises of cheap prairie land. Upon arrival, however, many Old World craftsmen decided that farming held fewer opportunities than did the lakeside metropolis. As a result, skilled tradespeople were abundant in Chicago from an early date. In particular, carpenters and cabinetmakers settled near the West Side lumber market. So did ironworkers who relied on the related charcoal market and tanners who relied on tannin derived from waste tree bark.

Mercantile business grew with the city's population, and railroad connections to the east provided another stimulant. Before the railroad, water and land transportation ceased half the year. Year-round rail transportation meant that retailers no longer had to carry inventory that sat unsold until next season. Nor did stores need to retain staff during previously fallow periods since rural shoppers could now travel to the city year round. Low-cost access to eastern suppliers and year-round operation allowed Chicago merchants to undercut prices and thus dominate Midwest trade. As a result, Chicago's population surged, doubling every three years for decades. From 4,470 in 1840 it rose to 29,963 at the next census. By 1855, Chicago boasted 83,509 souls. In midwinter of that year, Chicago saw fifty-eight passenger and thirty-eight freight trains each day. With the opening of the navigation that year, freight poured in for reshipment on 443 side-paddle steamers, 409 propellers, 119 barques, 439 brigs, 3,049 schooners and 70 sloops.

Nowhere was the ascendance of Chicago better symbolized than in one of its railroad depots. By 1856, the Michigan Central and its local affiliate, the Illinois Central, erected Great Central Station, a massive limestone structure. Built on an expansive landfill near the mouth of the Chicago River, it featured an impressive arched train shed spanning multiple tracks. The station was among the largest buildings in the American West, matched only by Chicago's massive grain elevators. Surprisingly for a city less than twenty years old, it was also among the world's largest train stations. It had the second largest single-span train-shed roof in the world, after New Street Station in Birmingham, England.[34] At the depot, visitors saw technologies largely absent from the American frontier: indoor plumbing and gas illumination.

Twin Michigan lines already linked the city to the eastern seaboard, but the public eagerly anticipated the Ft. Wayne line and its eastward connections. Part of its allure was the wider four-foot, ten-inch track gauge, not previously found in Chicago but shared with a network of Indiana and Ohio railways.[35] It also promised a connection to Philadelphia, the nation's second largest city and the great trade rival of New York City. Local aspirations, however, hinged on the belief that increased competition would lower rates. This was somewhat naive. The railway companies across the Allegheny Mountains had met in 1854, "with a view of agreeing upon general principles which should govern Railroad Companies competing for the same trade, and preventing ruinous competition."[36] In other words, they agreed to fix rates, a practice then perfectly legal. While this agreement ultimately proved unstable and ineffective, it promised rate stability and an increase to every railroad's profit. It also stimulated the companies to find nonprice means to differentiate

Great Central Depot on the lakefront was the envy of the western states and prompted competitors of its owners, the Illinois Central and Michigan Central railroads, to plan equally imposing Chicago passenger terminals.

COURTESY OF THE AUTHOR

their services. Companies advertised faster, comfortable trains and the scenic wonders of their routes. Impressive, convenient depots also provided a competitive advantage. Passengers provided a substantial proportion of each railroad's income. Substantial buildings denoted reliability and safety, in addition to providing superior comfort to entraining passengers. Extravagant depots and expensive real estate were thus seen as effective business promotions.

SEASON OF STAGNATED ENTERPRISE

To Ft. Wayne managers a structure like the Great Central Depot was only a dream. First they had to complete their line, and on November 17, 1856, they procured an amendment to the original city ordinance to allow a line along Stewart Avenue and Beach Streets from Sixteenth Street to Harrison Street. It was a bold proclamation, for financial panic again gripped the nation. The railroad appealed to owners of property adjacent to the proposed

The era's most talented railroad manager was J. Edgar Thomson of the Pennsylvania Railroad.

line for help. After the railroad pledged to build its depot nearby, neighbors promised to contribute $75,000.[37] A bird's-eye-view lithograph of this period shows a long, massive building, either a warehouse or a depot, along the west bank of the Chicago River near the proposed rail line.[38] The drawing, however, showed expected rather than actual development. In all likelihood, only wooden shops populated the area. Given apparent land values, the extravagant local contribution was staggering. In the previous

decade, however, boldness rewarded speculators. In eight years, the collective value of all land in Chicago had grown ninetyfold, from $1.4 million in 1848 to $126 million in 1856. The area west of the river in 1856 was the hottest market in town. Property values doubled in five years due to the extension of plank roads into the area.[39]

Money contributed by West Division speculators went into the general coffers of the railroad company without evident progress. J. Edgar Thomson, president of the Pennsylvania Railroad, became so frustrated with the Ft. Wayne's inability to consummate its last link that he appointed himself chief engineer of the Chicago extension. The Pennsylvania's own line across its namesake state had just been completed, but the *American Railroad Journal* rightly stated, "there is scarcely a railroad company in the United States that occupies the same position."[40] The confident and competent Thomson was a major factor in that success. Everyone believed he would quickly push the railroad toward Chicago despite the expansive marshlands that hindered its construction. The problems, however, were not of an engineering nature. It was a period a contemporary commentator called "this season of stagnated railway enterprise."[41]

THE ALTON CONNECTION

The Joliet and Chicago Railroad (the "Joliet"), like its contemporary the Ft. Wayne and Chicago, received its charter amid the optimism of 1854. It too had difficulty raising funds and was one link in a longer scheme, the final connection in a route to Saint Louis. The Joliet's southern partner, initially known as the Chicago and Mississippi, reorganized as the Chicago, Alton and St. Louis in February of 1855. It was to be popularly known as the Alton for nearly one hundred years (it and its successors will be called "the Alton" here).

The Alton had a line from Joliet to Springfield and consolidated with another that pushed it to the Mississippi River town of Alton. The Illinois legislature denied any railroad the right to terminate opposite Saint Louis, Missouri, but promoted state interests by issuing three railroad charters running to Alton, a bit upstream. The largest of the three, the Chicago and Mississippi,

came under the management of Henry Dwight, whose interest was in plundering the railroad's treasury rather that in building a solid company. Its charter allowed it to build to Chicago, but it was too weak to do so within the stipulated time, forfeiting a valuable franchise. What should have been one of the strongest lines in the Midwest failed to reach either of its logical terminals. At the north end, it contracted with the Chicago and Rock Island to allow downstate passenger trains to run between Joliet and Chicago. It could use the Rock Island's Van Buren Street depot; on July 31, 1854, the first train departed Alton for Chicago.

The Alton's friendly relationship with the Rock Island resulted from the intervention of a third railroad. The Michigan Southern and Northern Indiana ("MS&NI") Railroads had come under the control of a syndicate headed by Brooklyn bankers Edwin and Elisha Litchfield. Charles Butler remained an influential member of that group. The MS&NI lent the Alton used rail to complete its line and it retained a large Chicago and Rock Island stake from its earlier financing of that firm. The Alton appeared headed for a similar orbit.

The Alton's Rock Island arrangement was thankfully short-lived, as the contract allowed the new line neither through freight nor local Chicago-Joliet passenger service. In July 1855 the Alton concocted an alternative Chicago route. The new Joliet & Northern (the "J&N") allowed Alton trains to run forty miles due east to a connection with the Illinois Central. From there, trains traveled to the Illinois Central's Great Central Depot. Litchfield and Dwight interests soon engaged in a vicious duel for control of the Alton. To the south, the Litchfields and Butler gained control of the contested railway's Alton–Saint Louis connection. This placed Dwight's road in a deadly grip. Rerouting trains over the

J&N and IC minimized this pressure. The Illinois Central and its partner, the Michigan Central, were more than happy to tweak the rival Litchfield group. They even allowed the Alton use of their Chicago freight houses. Alas, the Alton's alliance with the J&N and IC also proved unstable. The IC made downstate connections with an east-west railroad to carry its own passengers to Saint Louis—competing with its tenant, the Alton.[42] The IC's downstate connection was another line controlled by the Litchfields and Butler.

The Joliet, promoted by Lockport merchants, promised to solve the Alton's problems. Despite local enthusiasm, its prospects as an independent had always been rather dim. Its endpoints, Joliet and Chicago, after all, were already connected by two rail routes plus the Illinois and Michigan Canal. As a result, the Joliet had a long gestation, even as the shortest link in an otherwise complete route between the Midwest's largest cities. Its February 15, 1855, charter actually mandated that its tracks start at the Alton's depot in Joliet.

The Joliet's ultimate success was the result of one determined man, Illinois Governor Joel Matteson from Joliet, who had also been the force behind the J&N's 1855 completion. His surveyor set both the J&N and the Joliet lines, but the latter's construction only commenced north from Joliet in May of 1857.[43] In the interim, just as the governor left office and to the surprise of nearly everyone, he gained control of the entire Chicago & Mississippi line from Joliet to Alton. His reorganized and renamed St. Louis, Alton and Chicago Railroad, however, remained a broken property. Dwight and his fellow swindlers left it with three overlapping mortgages, unpaid workers, and an overabundance of other debts. These debtors were hostile to each other and toward the company.

Matteson enlisted two rising stars to run his enterprises. Roswell Mason, former construction chief of the Illinois Central, became general manager of the completed Alton line. Mason's protégé, Timothy B. Blackstone, became the Joliet's chief engineer. Born in Branford, Connecticut in 1829, Blackstone demonstrated a considerable aptitude at mathematics during his public school education. At age eighteen he became a rodman surveying the New York and New Haven Railroad, serving under Roswell Mason, then that line's chief engineer. Blackstone became assistant engineer of the Stockbridge and Pittsfield before his nineteenth birthday.[44] In May of 1851, he came to Illinois at Mason's request to build the Illinois Central line between Bloomington and Dixon, a difficult section traversing the Illinois River valley. Steep slopes there required the construction of inclined planes in addition to a major bridge over the river and the adjacent I&M canal. On the isolated Illinois prairie Blackstone learned how to manage a truly large-scale enterprise.[45] He, in turn, attracted other talented engineers, notably Octave Chanute, who was to build rail lines throughout the nation and who much later became an aviation pioneer. Blackstone was much in demand as a contractor for rail line construction. In the process, he amassed a modest fortune, met locally prominent businessmen, and made important political connections. Among the lines he constructed were portions of Alton predecessors.

Both Blackstone and Mason were substantial investors in the Joliet. Unsurprisingly, Blackstone soon became its president. While the Alton struggled, however, it remained unhappy with its Chicago access, changing stations again in July 1856 by moving back to the Rock Island depot.[46]

Despite little ability to finance its short line of track, the Joliet always talked of joining the Ft. Wayne in a joint depot. As prospects improved during 1857, it used its scarce capital to purchase a half interest in the Ft. Wayne's unfinished south branch bridge and the line northward to Van Buren Street.[47] Cozy relations between the Alton and the Joliet railroads soon became apparent. On March 18, 1858, Alton passenger cars formed the new line's first train from Joliet into Chicago. Two brass bands provided festive notes for a trip marred by several derailments before the train terminated on the far side of the South Branch Bridge.[48] Completion of the bridge on April 1 allowed Joliet trains to run to Canal and Van Buren Streets.[49] Given the impassable condition of local streets, this site proved relatively distant from the business district. Even in older parts of town, where the black mud was planked over, jets of muck greeted the passage of heavy wagons. Ft. Wayne trains were not to arrive at Van Buren Street for several months.

As noted with the Ft. Wayne, the fact that any railroad could push to Chicago was remarkable given the Panic of 1857 and the depression that followed. The suspension of specie payments by New York financial houses caused the failure of one of Chicago's largest banks on August 11. New Yorkers, with justification, blamed the problem on western speculation and the building of railroad lines in advance of traffic. Chicago land values fell by one-half, except for the most valuable plots. Building construction continued, especially in the West Division near the Alton depot, due to continued in-migration. Two-story frame structures sprouted mushroom-like along Canal Street. Occupied at street level by saloons, above they held tenements, boarding houses, and small hotels. A commentator noted, "Thus has been won for that section a rather hard reputation in many respects, and it has been well represented in our police records."[50] Those who ran afoul of the law did not stray far, for the shabby city jail, the "Bridewell," stood immediately across the new Van Buren Street bridge from the depot. Commenting on a jailbreak, a reporter noted, "No prisoner of any self-respect can be expected to stay in Bridewell, we may say, he is lucky if he does not fall out of that rickety establishment by accident."[51]

One reason the railroads accepted the Van Buren Street location for the time being, was the macadamization of Canal Street to that point. The macadam system improved street drainage by layering progressively smaller layers of crushed stone atop one another, with a finish of compacted gravel on top.[52] It was a tremendous improvement over the muck that characterized most city streets, albeit not as sturdy as the expensive brick or wooden block roadways used in the commercial center. Macadam roads were themselves a product of the steam age, inasmuch as the introduction of mechanical crushers lowered the price of gravel.[53]

GRAND PLANS

Public announcement of the pending construction of a "grand union depot" west of the river came on May 7, 1858, as the depression eased. Specifications were drawn for a Union Depot to accommodate the Ft. Wayne, the Chicago and Milwaukee (now the Metra UP North line), the Fond du Lac (now the Metra UP Northwest line), and the Joliet (now the Metra Heritage Corridor). By some accounts, the Galena & Chicago Union and the Michigan Southern also planned to use the depot. While the *Tribune* lamented this period of stagnation, business on lines that planned using the depot remained brisk. The Fond du Lac briefly became a link in the fastest line to Minneapolis; the Joliet was part of the best route to Saint Louis; and population growth in the northern suburbs increased passenger traffic on the Chicago and Milwaukee.

The proposed depot was to be the largest in the West at 250 feet wide and 500 feet long, indeed, it would have been one of the world's largest structures of any type.[54] Its site, however, remained unannounced. Despite existing ordinances setting down rail line locations, the project's colossal size stimulated rivalry between the city's West, South, and North Divisions.[55] Earlier depots saw adjacent land values rise to stratospheric levels, so speculators wanted the project near their holdings. Surely, they thought, the city could compel the railroads to build wherever it dictated.

Public debate was brief, intense, and fruitless, but it nevertheless fatally delayed the railroads' plans and exposed the fault lines among the city's elite. Ogden stayed out of the limelight, while the *Daily Democrat* and the *Tribune* pummeled each other. The squabble centered on John Wentworth, publisher of the *Daily Democrat*, as he jostled to regain lost prominence. Some Chicagoans suspected that Wentworth, a longtime friend of Abraham Lincoln, had a cool allegiance to the newly formed Republican Party. Affluent property owners formed the backbone of this aggressive new party, whose first Illinois meeting had been that spring. Among their number was Judge Ebenezer Peck, a candidate for Congress, long engaged in a blood feud with Wentworth. As a condition of support for his nomination, West Division Republicans extracted a pledge from Peck backing their district for the depot. Ten years earlier Wentworth had printed an attack stating that Peck used graft to land his first legal clerkship.

Afterwards he relentlessly referred to Peck in print as the "midnight clerk." Infuriated, Peck tried to pummel Wentworth with a silver-handled walking stick, but slipped midattack on the muddy street. According to the *Daily Democrat*, the diminutive Peck fell into the lanky Wentworth's arms to his great embarrassment. According to the *Tribune*, Wentworth received a well-deserved caning. This decade-old feud caught the depot controversy in its toxic grip.[56] Wentworth backed a south side location favored by Democratic senator Stephen Douglas. Douglas remained a large landholder in that area and, as the hated author of the proslavery Kansas-Nebraska Act, he was the special target of Republican venom.

The south siders' weapons included an injunction against the bridge across the branch of the Chicago River needed to reach the West Side site. This came only days before the bridge opened, so the delay was more symbolic than threatening. Debate over the depot site, however, postponed the final ordinance needed to push track along the riverbank. In an era of oratory as entertainment, the conflict fostered spirited public meetings. In hindsight, its true significance was that it was one of the first, if not the first, forays by the Republican Party into local Illinois politics.

An ordinance submitted August 6, 1858, addressed the "Pittsburgh, Ft. Wayne and Chicago and the Chicago, St. Paul and Fond du Lac Railroad Companies and such other Railroad Companies as may unite with them." The act allowed the use of West Water Street along the north and south branches of the Chicago River. For a three-block stretch near the business district, it also allowed the use of an alley and Clinton Street to the west. This latter provision somewhat tipped the railroad's hand as to where it hoped to obtain land, for the parallel strips were useless without property in between. The ordinance provided that the railroads could cross public streets—in theory there were twenty-nine crossings, although only ten streets were actually in use. There was one exception to these rights: "that the tracks of said roads at Madison and Randolph Streets, shall be carried under the streets on the approaches to the bridges, and if for these purposes it is necessary to raise the grade of such streets, the same shall be done by and at the expense of said Companies." The ordinance further stipulated that as soon as the grade of Lake, Van Buren, and Kinzie Streets rose, the companies would provide further "tunnels for their tracks." Today such "tunnels" are called viaducts, a word not then in common usage.[57]

Any ordinance stipulating grade separation between streets and a railway was uncommon in America.[58] In effect, it tied together two major engineering works; one public, the other private. The redesign of Canal Street west of the tracks was the linchpin of the project. Plans already existed to raise that street as part of a project known as "high grades and complete sewerage." This system was the work of engineer Ellis Sylvester Chesbrough, from 1855. Previously the designer of Boston's water system, the self-trained Chesbrough recognized that Chicago's soil was too swampy to allow excavation for water and sewer lines. His elegant solution laid utility pipes on top of existing streets and filled them over to create a new grade. Muck mechanically dredged from the adjacent river bottom provided fill, another instance where the application of steam power aided street construction.

This sewerage project, often cited as the first urban sewer system in the United States, was simple but enormously expensive. Chesbrough's grand idea had one flaw: the city had no money. Along each street landholders thus had to vote by a two-thirds majority to collectively tax themselves for this improvement, knowing that they then had to jack up their buildings to the new grade. There were, however, some carrots. Water and gas lines installed next to the sewers brought modern amenities, which in turn increased property values. Nevertheless, it took powerful sponsorship to raise the grade of an entire city. If you were to guess that William Butler Ogden was behind the plan, you begin to understand the local political process. He was one of the three sewerage commissioners who hired Chesbrough.

In the case of Canal Street, raising the level created more opportunities than obstacles. The city had already induced the business district to lift its grade and was desirous of extending the concept north and west of the river. On the North Side, the tracks of the Galena and Chicago Union were one block from the riverbank and there were persistent complaints that standing rail cars blocked bridge approaches. For those already crossing on the swing bridges there were nervous moments whenever a steamer bore down with its whistle signaling the bridge tender. By contrast, the ordinance elevating Canal Street and requiring viaducts over the tracks eliminated such blockades. At the same time, longer approaches promised that cross streets would have gentler bridge ascents. Fortunately, the swing bridges themselves were easily modified. The center piers were simply jacked up and oak cribbing inserted. Despite the expense forced on them, the railroads seemed pleased. They got authorization for their new line and it explicitly provided for locomotive-powered trains—indeed it mandated coal-burning motive power.[59]

Even this simple plan had problems. For a start, much of West Water Street and the nearby alley specified for the tracks did not actually exist. Due to an error in the 1832 survey plat of this section, the city did not own these streets south of Madison, but held only an easement. Property owners therefore had to cede a strip of right of way in the street. Most did so gratefully, recognizing that the value of adjoining land would appreciate. For others, pressing needs outweighed long-term gain. Property near the river was the most valuable West Side land at the time. Owners resented being asked to give away land, to agree to new tax levies, to raise their buildings to the higher street grade, and to have their businesses disrupted while all this transpired. Wharfage had an additional problem since the warehouses located on the wharves created heavy wagon traffic that needed to be at dock level. To retain this business, owners built ramps down from Canal Street. Ramps precluded more profitable use of that land. Because there was a major business contraction in full force, it is not surprising that about one-fifth of the property owners balked. Some demanded up to $8,000 for as little as thirty feet of right of way. Publicly vilified, they nevertheless held out for their big payday.

The railroads did not immediately accept the ordinance seeking minor modifications. This left the door open for political intrigue regarding alternative routes and depot locations. Local meeting halls overflowed nightly for spirited debates. Almost unnoticed in the flood of oratory was the start of a new service by one of the depot's intended users—a business that eventually came to dominate depot operations. In July, the Chicago and Milwaukee began issuing fifty-cent commutation tickets to Waukegan for those buying fifty or more rides.[60] It was Chicago's first commuter fare, albeit on an existing train. Finally, on August 16, 1858, the railroad companies procured their municipal ordinance.

A giant celebration the following night eclipsed the excitement over the proposed depot, when sixty thousand citizens took to the streets for bonfires, carnivals, and fireworks to fete completion of the Atlantic telegraph cable. Highlight of the festivities was a sixty-foot-long transparency illuminating the Revere House, projected from the Ft. Wayne's office on Dearborn and Randolph Street. Celebrating the marriage of the hemispheres, it was signed "Chicago's Great Union Depot, West Side." The *Tribune* fueled speculation about the new depot by claiming, "It will be a rare curiosity and far more useful than the pyramids of Egypt. No ordinary inducement would divert travel from Chicago when, by coming here one could see a larger and more splendid building than the Crystal Palace of New York."[61]

The quest to acquire property sufficient to accommodate the touted two-block-long depot began. Before the month was out the Pennsylvania Railroad's J. Edgar Thomson, "nobly aided by several of our far seeing and patriotic men," toured the West Side for several days. They made several key property purchases, notably a block at Canal and Adams bought from the defunct Chicago Locomotive Works. That firm expired in 1856 after completing only nine engines.[62] Its factory never connected to the rail network it sought to serve; rather, its locomotives moved by oxcart to the nearby Galena tracks. In late August, Canal Street property owners voted to assess themselves for raising its grade with the two-thirds majority required to force compliance by holdouts. Property owners along Madison Street meanwhile voted to macadamize their street from State Street west to the bridge.[63] By mid-September only one property owner still refused to donate the right of way. The city agreed to raise the swing bridges and to install their east bank inclines. The steep angle of that ascent was cause for concern since it set the maximum load for city freight wagons. By one estimate, a four-foot increase in the height of the bridge subtracted 50 percent from the capacity of each dray. This was no small matter, for the Madison Street bridge saw 2,010 teams daily, while the Randolph Street bridge carried 2,845. Respectively, 7,946 and 12,660 pedestrians crossed as well.[64]

Ogden likely aided the Ft. Wayne in the purchase of West Side land, even though his holdings were mostly north and northwest. A respected adviser, he may nevertheless have been less than impartial. During this period, a company's ties to its officers were very close. Major investors often took profits from "their" firm by selling it land, by platting towns, or by awarding themselves lucrative construction contracts. Butler, Wisconsin, and Butler, Indiana are but two examples of the towns platted by Ogden and his associates. By reputation, Ogden was especially forthright, but contemporary standards did not necessarily prohibit businessmen from profiting from inside information.

Actual construction of track to the riverside depot site commenced in secrecy prior to a deadline set in the ordinance. Ogden's creation, the Galena, became his nemesis as it sought to block his new firm from crossing its line toward a connection with eastern lines. Under the direction of Fond du Lac (Chicago and North Western) engineers wagons of materials were staged on a Friday. Their track crews, augmented by those of the Alton and the Ft. Wayne, worked day and night as soon as the courts closed for the weekend and the threat of an injunction ended. Their nightly labors down West Water Street were illuminated using pitch torches and sperm oil lanterns. Work was under way until about six on Sunday morning when a major engineering error was discovered. The city required that a train use the line

prior to a pending deadline, and it was found that the viaducts could not clear a locomotive. A diminutive old secondhand 0-4-0 switcher, the Vulcan, already sat disassembled in company shops, so crews pieced it together without a cab or high smokestack. It edged under the viaduct barely before the midnight deadline. This first train of the C&NW carried no passengers but established possession of the line. C&NW trains, however, continued to use their existing depot.[65]

The Ft. Wayne line pushed westward from Plymouth, Indiana. J. Edgar Thomson had persuaded noted civil engineer John Jarvis out of his Rome, New York retirement. Jarvis had successfully pushed the Michigan Southern across the northern Indiana marshland and he speedily completed the same daunting task for the Ft. Wayne to public acclaim. Public excitement was as great as that accorded the two previous lines running from the east to Chicago, but only after carefully orchestrated fanfare. The railway lavished politicians, dignitaries, and newspaper correspondents with trips to Pittsburgh and seaboard cities. It distributed starry-eyed projections of the benefits to flow from the new line, and as a result, reporters for competing newspapers filed nearly identical stories. The field of public relations hardly existed, but the railroad served up story lines as deftly as it handed out wine, cigars, and oysters. Pittsburgh, the reporters dutifully commented, could flex its industrial muscles because of fifty-cent coal. The same ton cost four to seven dollars in Chicago. They reported that the new line promised similar prosperity for the city on the lake. Note that substantial freight charges would be added for delivery of this cheap energy to Chicago.

Parts of the depot site itself still required purchase and a lively debate ensued as to whether the depot buildings should be north or south of the new Madison Street Bridge. Land to the south cost one-third less, but was farther from the Lake Street commercial district.[66] J. Edgar Thomson returned in early November to make the final choice. Fearful of the renowned executive's power to impose one-sided propositions, locals were anxious over the possible "chicanery of bargain making." However, Thomson charmed Chicagoans and it was stated, "Mr. Thomson's plain, direct, unvarnished mode of treating matters, his high-toned, honorable propositions, left no ground for doubt. A cordial understanding was at once inspired."[67]

With a route already fixed, Thomson had little opportunity to maneuver. But his timing was right and the Ft. Wayne seems to have struck a real bargain. Later analysis of the costs incurred by the three eastern lines that laid tracks from the Indiana-Illinois state line into Chicago shows that the Ft. Wayne's line was relatively economical. The joint Michigan Central/Illinois Central line along the lakefront required a staggering outlay of $1,188,981. By comparison, the Michigan Southern/Rock Island route cost $150,000 for a similar distance. The Ft. Wayne seemingly had a great disadvantage since Chicago real estate values soared after the other railroads entered town. Its entrance into Chicago via twelve miles of Illinois track, however, cost only $121,000. Inclusive of depot lands, a drawbridge over the south branch of the Chicago River, and an expensive wharf, the entire price was $507,000. The newcomer benefited from the fact that in 1858 economic troubles temporarily forced speculators to sell at cut-rate prices. The following year prices fell even more; prime business lots sold for 75 percent of their top asking price, but these were temporary aberrations in an otherwise rising market.

On November 30, Ft. Wayne traffic stopped using the Michigan Southern tracks from Plymouth, but passengers continued to use that railway's Van Buren Street depot. The lines now connected at Englewood, only four miles from the city. For the next month, the Ft. Wayne leased Chicago and Rock Island Railroad tracks from that point. The new route immediately attracted freight traffic because the distance to the Atlantic seaboard via its line to Philadelphia was less than to Boston or New York. Savings were about $4 per ton. Because the standard gauge track into Chicago was an inch and a half narrower that the Ft. Wayne, through traffic likely used "compromise cars" whose wide treads awkwardly traversed both gauges. Nevertheless, the 824-mile route was now the longest in the world under one management, simplifying billing and movement. Ignoring earlier tariff agreements, the competitors fought for freight. Passenger fares remained as before, but Chicago's existing lines made impressive service improvements to counter their new competitor. Both Michigan lines added sleeping cars and put on a third daily trip, making them the only routes from Chicago with more than two departures. With the Ft. Wayne's two scheduled passenger trains, twenty-two trains now departed Chicago each day.

AN EXHAUSTED ARRIVAL

At 7:00 a.m., Christmas Day 1858, guns of the Chicago Light Artillery fired in salute to the first Ft. Wayne train to depart its temporary Chicago passenger station, the Joliet and Chicago depot on Canal Street south of Van Buren Street. The company's annual report for 1859 proudly trumpeted the erection of a dressed-stone freight house at Chicago, but no mention was made of passenger accommodations. Local newspapers were

Published by Jevne & Almini

JUNCTION OF THE CHICAGO RIVER

similarly reticent about passenger facilities, although several spoke of the great volume of freight at the depot. The railroad probably lacked a dedicated passenger building. If a separate depot building existed, it was a modest wood-frame structure. Newspaper ads noted the location of the station, but during this pioneering era, the terms "station" and "depot" often described the act of selling tickets by a company's agent, or the place for doing so, not necessarily a building. Tickets may have been sold at trainside, from the freight house, or at a nearby store. Nonetheless, passenger traffic was heavy from the beginning and within the year the Ft. Wayne operated three daily trains each way.[68] The new line did surprisingly well despite an abysmal business climate. Even without its own Chicago terminal for most of the year the Ft. Wayne line captured nearly a third of 1858's 277,113 passengers to and from the east.

It is unclear if the Ft. Wayne continued to use the same facilities as the Joliet. Newspapers referred to the Alton depot, the Joliet depot, or the Ft. Wayne depot. The title "Union Depot" was never used, although the Alton clearly used the same building as the Joliet. The one and one-half inch difference in track gauge between the Ft. Wayne and the Alton/Joliet certainly complicated matters. While the Ft. Wayne had some cars with compromise wheels, the new rail line along the river was labeled a "compromise track." Specifications for such a track remain a mystery, but there are indications that it was not a particular success.[69] Despite operation from West Van Buren Street and substantial nearby company landholdings, the long-term depot site remained a political hot potato. In March 1859, John Wentworth's *Daily Democrat* renewed its attack on the proposed West Side depot site. This rearguard action may have reflected Wentworth's increasing investment in the Galena. Ogden's Fond du Lac road had been increasingly successful in competition against that road. As his detractors claimed, Wentworth may have seen an opportunity to obstruct the Fond du Lac's physical connection with eastern railroads.

The exertion of building into Chicago depleted the Ft. Wayne. By December 7, 1859, less than a year after their line's completion, it petitioned for receivership. As Charles Butler explained:

In 1859 steps were taken for the appointment of Receivers and a Sequestrator was appointed in Pennsylvania and a Receiver in Ohio. A want of harmony in the several States seemed likely to end in ruinous litigation, and in defeating the project, or at least suspending it indefinitely. This would have involved great losses, not to individuals only, but to counties which had subscribed largely to the stock. At a meeting in Pittsburgh, Ogden succeeded in reconciling the conflicting parties. Receivership

DEPARTURE OF A COLONY OF EMIGRANTS FOR COLORADO.—[SEE PAGE 203.]

with unanimity was tendered to Ogden with a salary of $2500. He refused this offer due to his other duties, but no other name was found acceptable.[70]

On January 17, 1860, Ogden became sole receiver of the Pittsburgh, Ft. Wayne and Chicago Railroad and in October 1861 he reorganized it as the Pittsburgh, Ft. Wayne and Chicago Railway. The Pennsylvania Railroad's small financial stake in the Ft. Wayne remained, with J. Edgar Thomson as president pro tem. Ft. Wayne debt converted to equity during reorganization.[71] At the same time, Ogden leveraged the railroad's expensive Chicago real estate to relieve strain on the enterprise. Free from the encumbrance of its original mortgage, the Ft. Wayne issued $241,500 in Chicago real estate bonds and $126,500 in Chicago bridge bonds. The proceeds repaid expensive bank loans payable upon demand, replacing them with slowly amortizing fixed-rate bonds.[72] With separate mortgages on valuable Chicago parcels, Ogden obtained about 20 percent of the cash he needed to pay the company's trade creditors.

A busy man, Ogden also ran the Chicago and North Western Railway. When this line reached Green Bay in 1861, its fortunes improved materially.[73] Times were not as rosy to the south, where the ailing Alton exchanged freight with its Joliet protégé.

The Joliet still could not provide for through passengers. There was little freight and few passengers, as twenty-six of the Alton's thirty-eight locomotives awaited either repair or the junkman. The Alton entered bankruptcy protection in November of 1859 with fourteen trustees, one of whom was William Butler Ogden. It seems unlikely that Ogden was protecting his own investment. Rather he was the local representative of the Litchfield syndicate.

Commerce remained sluggish, but the summer of 1860 saw unprecedented travel to Chicago, the site of the vitriolic national convention of the Republican Party. It became an intensely personal experience since the rival Democratic presidential candidate was a local son. Stephen Douglas had a large south side acreage and personally knew the local Republican favorite, Abraham Lincoln, from an earlier era when both courted Mary Todd. The mid-May Republican Convention featured special trains on every line into the city. New England and New York delegations came over the Michigan lines at dusk, with nearly 1500 passengers on each train. The Pennsylvania delegation, its rolls swelled by a fourteen-dollar excursion fare, pulled into the Ft. Wayne depot the following morning to a hearty welcome. One car in their train was notable. Built wholly of iron by Merrick,

Hanna and Company of Pittsburgh, it remained on exhibit at the depot during the convention. Because public squares and parks were sadly lacking, the station was the focus of much conventioneering. West Van Buren Street lacked nearly all amenities, but that did not stop the Pennsylvania Republicans from soundly praising their host railroad. As they left the city, they gave three lusty cheers for Lincoln, followed by three for the Ft. Wayne's local agent Dan W. Boss. Boss was a luminary in the rival party.

The ragtag depot buildings became the departure point for local abolitionists as they prepared for the onslaught many feared would follow the election. Ellsworth's Zouaves, a precision militia bedecked in loose-fitting uniforms copied from crack French units in the Crimean conflict, took their drills to audiences throughout the North. They were flamboyantly attired in royal blue jackets with yellow piping and closely set gold buttons over powder-blue blouses and baggy crimson breeches. A red cap, black knapsack, and drab leggings completed their parade dress. Cadets barbered their facial hair into a Vandyke, like the original Zouaves. A reminiscence by cadet Henry Miller described the unit's return on August 14, 1860, after a fund-raising tour of the East: "The train was delayed somewhat by an accident, but all Chicago patiently waited for them at the Alton Depot. When the train came in sight salutes were fired, cannons boomed, bands played, torches were waved by both the 'Wide-Awakes' and the 'Ever-Readies' as in this event the great party spirit of the great political campaign, then in progress, was laid aside. Everyone welcomed 'Our Boys.'"[74]

Neither the embryonic nature of Chicago nor a general lack of settlement elsewhere along the railroad delayed the inauguration of commuter services on the Ft. Wayne. An astute township board in a swampy area south of the city mandated such trains as a condition for granting the railroad a right of way. The railroad complied, with service provided by a curious steam coach. One of three cars built in New Brighton, Pennsylvania, it was a cross between a locomotive and a passenger coach. Painted robin's-egg blue with red trim, it may have been more eye-catching than successful. An excursion using the fifty-seat car went south to Englewood on November 1, 1860, but this novelty reportedly had already been in operation for months.[75]

On November 21, 1860, a station unofficially known as the West Side Union Depot opened in a wooden structure purchased and moved to Canal and Madison Streets.[76] Although several railways proclaimed their intent to use it, only Ft. Wayne trains initially did so. Closer to the Lake Street business district than the Van Buren stop, it too was across the Chicago River from the commercial area. The river's busy use as a harbor magnified this physical separation. When drawbridges swung open to clear passage for boats, they became choke points clogging their streets with vehicles and pedestrians. One slight advantage of the station's Madison Street site was its location next to the city's second iron bridge. Iron was as yet too expensive to be common in bridge construction, but it had the advantage of being considerably lighter than a wooden span. Chicago swing bridges were all hand cranked into position, and a lighter span opened and shut quicker than bulky timber structures.

Not until January 14, 1861 did the West Side Station live up to its title as a union depot, when trains of the Alton entered. Ogden's Chicago and North Western continued in its own depot, even as the Ft. Wayne purchased more land for the terminal. Expansion required little demolition, although the three-story brick foundry of Charles Reassign at Adams Street had to come down. Just as work finished the *Tribune* admitted, "It has long been the pet scheme of leading railroad men and of residents of the West division to bring about a Union enterprise, with a common railroad centre and terminus of similar advantages to that on the Lake Shore. The Chicago and Milwaukee have excellently well located passenger accommodations, which they will probably make permanent. The Galena will likely stay in their present location on North Wells Street."[77]

Another eastern railroad now captured public attention. The Cincinnati and Chicago Airline opened for passenger service on April 1. Later known as the "Panhandle" route, for a portion of its line through that West Virginia appendage, it initially offered service to Dayton, Columbus, Indianapolis, Louisville, and Cincinnati.[78] It intended to make Chicago its terminus as early as 1853, but progress on the diagonal from Cincinnati had been slow. It reached Logansport, a canal town in competition with the city of Fort Wayne, in 1857. Everyone assumed the Ft. Wayne line would be a feeder to the Cincinnati route, but the opposite occurred. It surely deflated Logansport boosters that their line's entry into Chicago used forty miles of rival Ft. Wayne's hometown road from a junction at Valparaiso.

Newspaper articles touting the new railway reinvigorated talk of a planned depot. They specifically stated that "the proposed plan excites the admiration of those who have seen the same. The building will be over 800 feet in length and about 140 feet in width, with passenger and baggage rooms, ticket offices, and all other accommodations necessary. The building, if completed on this plan, will be an ornament to the city, and a great acquisition to the West Side."[79] They stated that the depot design

could accommodate eight companies, including some of their freight business.

In Chicago, the Cincinnati and Chicago Airline entered into a five-year lease on a coal yard abutting the west bank of the river between Randolph and Madison Streets for its freight depot. Despite the area's proximity to the business district and several railroad terminals, it was described as "occupied by high piled stacks of lumber, timber & etcetera, and also by very closely ranged wooden buildings, sheds, outhouses, and workshops."[80] The only substantial building in the district was the six-story marble-front Cochran House, a failed and shuttered hotel that partially burned with five surrounding blocks on September 15, 1859. Half the establishments destroyed were saloons.

Cincinnati passengers used the former Alton depot at Canal and Van Buren Streets. From its first days, however, the public understood that the Cincinnati line intended to use the planned "Grand Union Depot."[81] The route, now known as the Chicago & Great Eastern Railroad (the "Great Eastern"), saved up to twelve hours' travel time to Cincinnati and offered Woodruff sleeping car service. The commercial opportunities of its eastern terminal led to great expectations. Immediate prosperity, however, came from the connection of the increasingly prosperous Upper Midwest with the front lines of the Civil War, which began weeks after this railroad's completion.

WAR OF REBELLION

In an era that glorified armed struggle, the blare of a brass band often signaled troop departures. The first wartime movement through the depot transferred 380 men and a battery from Fort Ridgely, Minnesota, to Washington, DC. At 7:00 p.m., April 16,

1861, their North Western train came directly into the Madison Street depot, where Ft. Wayne had connecting cars. It took two hours to effect the change of trains because a crowd estimated at ten thousand greeted the troops. This is the only recorded use of the Union Depot by the North Western.[82]

The first regiment of US troops raised in Chicago (as opposed to the state militias) was the Hecker Jaegers. Colonel Hecker's farewell address in German noted that he and many of his soldiers had "opposed the despotisms of Europe and [taken] up arms in behalf of Freedom." Escorted from their south side encampment by a company of dragoons and several bands, they followed a newly presented silk regimental flag. Accustomed to drill, the troops made an orderly progress over the Madison Street Bridge to a waiting twelve-car train for Alton.[83]

On May 9, the Great Eastern marked the beginning of twice daily trains from Chicago. That day saw a special excursion celebrating the official opening to the Ohio River at Cincinnati. It traveled the same line then speeding troops to reinforce federal garrisons in that area. Everyone assumed a swift Union victory.

That November, although Union army prospects seemed less assured, a great throng greeted Colonel Mulligan, defender in the Battle of Lexington (Missouri). Six hundred souls left for Joliet to intercept the returning hero. When both special trains returned after dark, several thousand citizens covered the depot grounds. They fired signal rockets and waved torches to an earsplitting cannonade.[84] However, the realities of the war were less glamorous, even in Chicago. Up to a hundred soldiers often squeezed into a single fifty-foot long coach. As the conflict progressed, a few hurried goodbyes, the shuffle of rucksacks, and the clatter of boots on the oak-planked station platform replaced

martial music as the sound of departure. The experiences of Darwin Atwood and his Wisconsin heavy artillery unit were typical: "Arrived Chicago 5 O'clock in the morning. Went to Soldiers Rest for breakfast but not time to eat, as it was not ready and had to partake of our hardtack and arrange to get to Depot in time for cars—6 O'clock Ft. Wayne and Pittsburgh Road—slept on floor of train through Ohio." Atwood was lucky. Other accounts speak of the soldiers riding on flatcars or dirty cattle cars. The worst conditions were those endured by the rebels destined for imprisonment in the nation's second largest prisoner-of-war internment camp, Chicago's Camp Douglas.

Early in the war recruitment was easy thanks to patriotic fervors and high unemployment. Enlistment seemed attractive. Bankruptcies of the Ft. Wayne, Fond du Lac, Alton, and other railroads were hardships shared with other local enterprises as business conditions worsened. So much "wildcat" money was in circulation that consumers tried to pass dubious currency while it still had value. It was noted that "the course of nature is reversed; debtors absolutely pursue their creditors, and creditors as swindlers dodge the sheriff." After a month of hostilities, Chicago railroads and steamship lines jointly agreed on discount rates for bank notes issued as currency. By posting acceptance rates for each bank's notes, they hoped to prevent competitors from covertly cutting rates through better payment terms. Discounts ranged up to 50 percent and many banknotes suddenly became unacceptable. Of sixty-four listed, only six were valued at par.[85]

The root cause of the currency problem was the Illinois banknote law. At the war's outbreak, Illinois banks had $12,320,000 of private currency in circulation. State law required each bank to secure its banknotes by depositing an equal amount of negotiable bonds with the state auditor. Banks purchased these bonds with their deposits, but they then could make an equal amount of loans with their own currency. As borrowers spent loan proceeds, the currency floated in the local economy until redeemed. The problem was a statutory requirement that bonds held as collateral earn interest in excess of 6 percent. Southern bonds tended to have higher coupons than Illinois bonds, so by May 1861, $9,527,500 of the $14 million in bonds held on deposit originated from secessionist states. When these issuers refused to pay interest to Yankee bondholders, the state auditor called for additional, but unobtainable, collateral.[86] As a result, the year 1861 saw 89 of Illinois's 110 banks fail. Not until the military supply contracts of the following year lifted the economy did business regain its footing.

Nonetheless, in July 1861 newspapers reported that foundation work for a planned depot had started at Canal and Madison Streets.[87] By October 17, the *Tribune* stated, "The wharfage is now complete and already several vessels have unshipped their cargos of rails and ties. A network of tracks is being laid down to accommodate the rolling stock of the different lines. Soon the immense area near Madison Street Bridge will be a complete forest of roofs."[88]

In fact, the Ft. Wayne's greatest effort was to build an eighty-by-eight-hundred-foot brick warehouse at the water's edge. By November, work ceased for the season on the passenger station, whose reported dimensions were now 121 by 758 feet.[89] The change in dimensions from earlier reports reflected a shift of the site to south of Madison Street. Substantial warehouses still stood on the originally planned two-block site to the north. Now bulging with war materials, they were impossible to purchase.

It seems remarkable that construction progressed, for it preceded the emergence of its proprietor from bankruptcy. Reorganization of the Ft. Wayne by its bondholders occurred on October 24. William Ogden left the management of the road, but J. Edgar Thomson remained. Things were little better at the Alton, whose able new managers were then in negotiations with creditors. Its formal reorganization came on October 15, 1862. The Chicago and Milwaukee, meanwhile, leased the Galena's original Chicago depot from June 1, 1860, which brought them three blocks closer to the town center.[90] The C&M never stumbled, but until 1863 it controlled only the Illinois portion of its line.

On March 14, 1862, lightning struck the Madison Street depot. At about 1:00 a.m., the Ft. Wayne's passenger agent, Captain H. J. Spaulding, awoke from his quarters in the station and attempted to save ledger books kept in the flaming building. After several successful trips, an air current slammed the door shut, trapping him, and he sustained serious burns before his rescue. Spaulding hovered near death for many days. The damage estimate was $10,000, but this was a bad guess. In the baggage room were three trunks owned by Cyrus McCormick. The Pennsylvania Railroad returned them from Philadelphia to Chicago subject to a twenty-cent dispute over checked baggage charges. They contained silks, diamonds, and gold valued at $5,400 and the lost bags resulted in twenty-three years' legal wrangling.[91]

An early history of Chicago remarked, "The damage to the depot was at once repaired and [it] served the public, after a fashion, for many years . . . with additions and slight improvements."[92] Alton officially stating, "The present passenger depot in this city, which is jointly owned by the Pittsburgh, Ft. Wayne and Chicago road and this company, is *not* respectable for two such corporations, whose business is rapidly increasing. A depot for the accommodation of these two roads should be erected at an early date that should be creditable to say the least of two such companies."[93] A list of company assets showed, however, that the only building the Alton owned was a twelve-by-eighteen-foot tool shed. On May 4, 1862, three daily Great Eastern trains to Cincinnati moved to the Madison Street depot from Van Buren Street. Three railroads now called at the depot.

A notable event at the station occurred at four minutes to 4 p.m. on August 28, 1862. The boiler of Alton engine number eight exploded as the Wilmington accommodation train loaded. Two freight cars between the locomotive and the coach prevented disaster. The crew was inside awaiting orders—remarkably, there were no injuries, although the smokestack rocketed into the baggage room and locomotive parts scattered the landscape.[94]

The same month, Alton finances awaited repair until the railroad was sold to bondholders under a new name, the Chicago and Alton. With this reorganization, William Butler Ogden severed his affiliation with the company. Freed of existing debt, the new company issued securities for improvement and expansion. One such opportunity came on January 1, 1864, when the Alton leased the Joliet for 999 years. Timothy Blackstone joined the Alton board and became its president. He was unable to break the Alton's lease for the Rock Island depot until 1865, but he then shifted all trains to the depot shared with the Ft. Wayne. For a short period, it operated local Joliet trains from one station and through Alton trains from another depot. The railroad stated that 55,460 passengers departed over the road during 1865 and a nearly equal number arrived.

Despite his removal from the helm of the Alton and the Ft. Wayne, William Ogden's empire did not diminish. On April 15, 1862, he was a founding incorporator of the Northern Pacific Railroad. His signature underwrote the petition to Congress requesting a land grant to support its construction from Superior, Wisconsin, to Puget Sound. Nor was that enough to keep him busy, for on November 5 subscription books for the Union Pacific Railway, of which Ogden was the first president, opened in his office at Clark and Lake Street. His biggest railroad coup was still over the horizon, but in the meantime, he confirmed his reputation as the preeminent western railroad developer.

On June 17, 1863, the Chicago and Milwaukee, which ran only to the state line, purchased its Wisconsin alter ego, the Milwaukee and Chicago. While connecting the region's largest cities, the consolidated railroad did not interchange cars at either end. Interline traffic required the drayage and reloading of goods. As a result, Ogden's North Western, which passed well west of Milwaukee, received the agricultural and lumber traffic from the northern part of the state. The location of the North Western's terminal on the north branch of the Chicago River effectively blocked its rival from connecting with lines to the south, although C&M passenger trains ran through to the Galena's old depot. That station was redundant after its owner built a brick depot across the river in the North Side. Upon consolidation of the two Chicago-to-Milwaukee components, the company stated, "the most vigorous efforts will be made to . . . effect a connection in the city with a view of making a grand Union Depot."[95] Ogden had no intention, however, of allowing a competitor access to lucrative interchange traffic. His policy of weakening the Milwaukee line became clearer in 1864 when the North Western purchased a line from Rockford into Kenosha, the latter being a major intermediate point on the C&M.

Meanwhile, traffic on the Ft. Wayne grew threefold over its inaugural year. Business continued to rise through 1865 despite a labor shortage that hindered harvests and limited industrial production. Like many railroads, the Ft. Wayne increasingly switched to coal to fire its locomotives, in part due to insufficient civilian manpower to cut the wood previously used as fuel. Nevertheless, in 1864 the Ft. Wayne-to-Chicago portion of the railroad burned 83,610 cords of wood—or, in the words of one Hoosier commentator (clearly exaggerating), enough to build a wooden pile four feet high and four feet wide between Fort Wayne and Indianapolis.[96]

Traffic into Chicago now necessitated a larger terminal. In 1861, the city vacated Monroe Street between Canal Street and the river. It ceded a similar stretch of Depuyster Street in 1862 and a north-south stretch of Stewart Avenue in 1863. At the time, the Ft. Wayne offered $20,000 toward the construction of a Washington Street tunnel the city hoped to build under the river and the tracks. That was one-fifth of its estimated cost, but the offer was conditional on the city vacating Adams Street between the river and Canal Street. Local property owners rebelled because they wanted a bridge at Adams, and they stated that the value of the vacated street was $250,000. Thwarted, the railroad rearranged its yards even without Adams Street being vacated and ran more tracks across the as yet nonexistent street. As part of that improvement, it jacked up the passenger depot and moved it to the northwest corner of its lot adjacent to the higher Canal Street grade.[97]

William Ogden now engineered a dramatic change in the railroad landscape. On June 2, 1864, his Chicago and North Western acquired the larger Galena and Chicago Union. Popularly called the "Grand Consolidation," Ogden's financial maneuver created an 860-mile system. His syndicate held the majority stake and he was clearly in charge. The implications for a Union Depot in Chicago were clear. The C&NW now had the Galena's original passenger building, the former Fond du Lac train shed, and the fine new east bank depot of the Galena. Of greater importance, it had a Chicago freight belt, the Rockwell Street connection to the St. Charles Airline tracks, which allowed efficient interchange with eastern lines. Ogden now had no need for the joint riverside track with the Ft. Wayne or the planned depot. In an article announcing the Grand Consolidation, the *Tribune* stated that Ogden intended to build his own mammoth passenger terminal on the north side of the river near the lakeshore.[98] His Chicago Dock and Canal Company controlled much of the surrounding real estate. As a bonus, Ogden now evicted his rival, the Chicago and Milwaukee from the leased Galena depot.

THE HIGH PRICE OF VICTORY

The sad finale to the Civil War played out on the evening of May 2, 1865, when the body of Abraham Lincoln moved from the Cook County Courthouse escorted by one thousand torch-carrying mourners. Along the route to the depot, the street grade changes resulted in many wooden sidewalks cheaply carried on trestles above the original city stratum. Now densely crowded with spectators, several collapsed, causing multiple injuries. From the depot, two special trains preceded the funeral train itself. First was an 8:00 p.m. departure for Chicago's delegation to the Springfield funeral. It departed with eleven sleeping cars, notably the Pioneer, George Pullman's elegant creation. A pilot train left the Union Depot at 9:20 p.m. behind Alton engine #40 to ensure a safe route. Finally, the bunting-covered cars of the funeral train itself departed into the darkness.[99] Headed by Alton #57, the railroad's newest locomotive, it pulled one baggage car, several coaches, the presidential carriage, and a final car.

The war was now over, but only after enriching Chicagoans such as cotton speculator Potter Palmer, who invested his profits in real estate. Through astute purchases and flamboyant development, he created the new shopping mecca of State Street, hitherto a narrow, muddy lane. In the years that followed, he built nearly forty marble-front buildings along this thoroughfare, including his namesake hotel and the Field, Leiter and Company department store. The removal of the Board of Trade to a new building at Washington and LaSalle Streets also helped reorient the business district. Formerly oriented east to west on Lake Street, it now ran north to south and its center was closer to the Ft. Wayne Depot.

Like Palmer, many railroad men became immensely wealthy. The Alton and its leader were particularly close-knit. Much of Timothy Blackstone's fortune, however, came from an 1864 investment, when he joined with nine railroads, including the Ft. Wayne and the Alton, to invest in the Union Stock Yard and Transit Company. This 320-acre stockyard site became Chicago's defining enterprise, a distinction it held for ten decades. Immensely wealthy, Blackstone was nonetheless frugal to a fault.[100] In his twenty-nine-year tenure as president of the Alton, he proved incredibly risk averse. The Alton eschewed mergers, built fewer branch lines than its competitors, and made only minimal capital improvements to the Chicago–Saint Louis route whose traffic it dominated. It is perhaps not surprising that its Chicago depot remained modest.

The price of wartime success was high; Chicago inflation during 1863–1864 averaged 80 percent. This in turn fueled the area's first railroad strikes in March and May 1864. It was the cost of the war in human life, however, that was noteworthy. Cook County sent 22,436 soldiers into battle. (Remarkably, the 1860 census had listed only 18,791 voters—noncitizens and in-migration accounted for most enlistees.) Nearly four thousand Chicagoans lost their lives in the conflict.

Talk of a grand new depot continued, but little construction occurred. Terminal yards were barely sufficient for the traffic, while station buildings accreted into a confusing hodgepodge. The brick, hip-roof Ft. Wayne freight house along the river was dominant. Three multistory additions extended it from Madison to Adams Streets with a separate brick annex south of Adams. At viaduct level on Madison Street was a twenty-by-seventeen-foot brick structure called the "Ticket House," but it did not serve passengers. Rather, it marked the start of a half-block-long timber ramp that descended to track level near the freight house. Tracks running northward to connect with the North Western separated that area from the "Passenger House." Travelers entered one-third of a block south of Madison on Canal Street, which now boasted wood-block paving. This seventy-by-twenty-five-foot frame structure contained the waiting rooms. Three stub tracks served this depot from the south. Also south of the Passenger House were four interconnected wood buildings—probably baggage rooms. Another spur track stopped short of this assemblage from a point where all tracks curved eastward toward the twin mainline tracks. Period maps show switches awkwardly located in the middle of Adams Street, which dead-ended at the river.[101] To be sure, east of Canal Street that thoroughfare remained little more than a legal fiction: a "paper street."

The Ft. Wayne was not particularly enthusiastic about its facility, stating, "A passenger house at this terminal has become necessary as [there is] no such commodious or fine building."[102] They estimated the cost of a suitable structure at $250,000. Whatever its shortcomings, there certainly was no want of traffic. A later report stated that iron rails on the joint Ft. Wayne-Alton line needed replacement four times per year, due to punishing overuse and the wobble induced by two gauges of wheels on the compromise track. Steel rails installed in 1870 rectified the problem.[103] Given their then relatively high cost, it was an extravagance indicative of the site's importance. American steel rails had first been rolled only two years previously in a mill financed by the Pennsylvania Railroad and its president, J. Edgar Thomson.[104]

At some point, possibly 1869 when the Adams Street Bridge arose on the same principles as Madison Street, the railroads built a baggage building under that viaduct. It measured twenty by one hundred feet. A sixty-by-thirty-foot express building also arose under Madison Street. Still later, there are reports that two train sheds, one four hundred feet long and the other three hundred feet long, were added to connect this eclectic mix of buildings. These seem to have been simple platform coverings.

Great Eastern passengers used the Ft. Wayne's facilities via connections, but as its lines pushed closer to Chicago it became awkward to use the tracks of a competitor. Great Eastern management became increasingly aggressive after their 1863 purchase of an Illinois charter that existed only on paper, the Galena and Illinois River Railroad. Amended, it allowed an eastern terminal at the Indiana state line rather than Chicago. Their plan for

entry into Chicago was to file condemnation suits against various properties, including half the width of the Ft. Wayne right of way into Chicago. The Ft. Wayne naturally resisted.[105] Concurrently the Great Eastern sought a local ordinance to allow entry into Chicago. On July 15, 1864, it asked the Ft. Wayne for use of its trackage and depot from a new junction in the city, but never received the courtesy of a reply.

On March 6, 1865, the Great Eastern opened its Chicago line, running just outside the city limit. At Sixteenth Street it connected with the North Western's north-south connector between the original Galena line and the Airline. The Great Eastern signed a contract to use this C&NW Rockwell Street line, plus its mainline (which turned at a right angle) into downtown, and the old Galena and Chicago Union depot, on November 25, 1864. The Great Eastern's alignment resulted in a question-mark-shaped route that crossed nearly every rail line radiating from Chicago. Perhaps to advertise its route to the Steel City, the Great Eastern purchased two passenger coaches constructed entirely of that metal. Built in New Brighton, Pennsylvania, they reached Chicago on April 1, 1866 to considerable press.

The Great Eastern had no intention of staying in the leased Galena depot. There was little attraction in paying $75,000 per year to rent an archaic building. On October 8, 1866, an ordinance passed allowing it to build a track parallel to the C&NW, but one block south along Carroll Street. It then erected a small depot at Clinton Street, likely of frame construction. Although there was agitation to require viaducts along the new line similar to those required of the Ft. Wayne, the Carroll Street line was too close to the C&NW Kinzie Street tracks. The city had no legal means to compel the established C&NW to bridge streets over its tracks,

ARRIVAL OF DELEGATES TO THE REPUBLICAN CONVENTION AT CHICAGO.—SKETCHED BY W. B. BAIRD.—[SEE PAGE 362.]

so there was little point in having the adjacent Great Eastern do so. The newcomer agreed, however, to pave and build sewers the length of Carroll Street.[106] A Chicago guidebook stated, "The Company proposes, eventually, to build a fine passenger depot at Carroll Street." The Great Eastern merged into the Columbus, Chicago & Indiana Central in 1868, which, in turn, became part of the Pittsburgh, Cincinnati, Chicago and St. Louis Railway, still known as the Panhandle.[107]

Speculation about another mammoth depot for Chicago was hardly naive, but other railroads were to grab those laurels. In April 1866, the Michigan Southern and Rock Island railroads commenced erection of a stone Italianate colossus at the foot of LaSalle Street. Architect W. W. Boyington planned a three-story façade to front Van Buren Street of "Athens Marble," actually the trade name for Lockport, Illinois, limestone. If anyone doubted the competitive nature of the railroad companies, they had only to read the depot's official announcement, which stated that it would eclipse the Great Central Depot in size and general excellence. The depot opened on December 18 amid calls for construction of a similar edifice for the West Division railroads.

CHAPTER TWO
COMING TOGETHER

NEW PLAYERS ON THE STAGE

The post–Civil War period, dubbed the "Gilded Age" by Mark Twain, witnessed the lavish lifestyles of rapacious railroad managers, merchants, and industrialists. At the same time, fetid tenements spawned embryonic socialist, communist, and anarchist movements. Voluntary welfare societies such as the Red Cross, orphanages, and fraternal groups evolved to bridge the gap, but disparity grew between the have-nots, the middle class, and the rich. Calls for political redistribution of wealth grew, but this remained an alien concept—quite literally. Waves of German immigrants fueled the city's growth and the newcomers brought the radical philosophies that so often caused their rapid departure from their homeland. Income redistribution was their battle cry and the patronage system became its primary vehicle. Urban politicians historically dispensed favors, but the difficulties experienced by a largely rural-born population in finding employment in an industrial landscape accelerated demands. To supply this largesse, politicos exacted extralegal payments from the moneyed. Nobody had more cash or was a better target than the growing railroad corporations.

Crooked politicians were not the only ones looking for deep pockets. Municipal revenues in Illinois derived from the property tax, an assessment against wealth. After the Civil War Chicago was relatively wealthy for the first time. A growing real estate base allowed municipal income to rise even though the state constitution limited both tax rates and the amount of bonded debt. Because municipal debt limits were a function of aggregate property values, rising land values lifted Chicago's bond cap. Desirable works that previously could be funded only by special assessments (and then only with the consent of adjacent property owners) were now fully paid for from general revenues. Because railroads were the largest landowners in town, changes in tax policy affected them disproportionately. Tax policies, in turn, influenced their holdings, their appetite for more land, and their use of property.

In theory, Illinois statutes required uniform property assessment and taxation. Railroad property, however, was unique. An 1849 statute required the assessment of railroad land by the Illinois Auditor of Public Accounts, with revenues payable to the state treasury.[1] This made sense when there were few municipalities. The law changed in 1853 so that railroad, telegraph, and plank-road companies had to record their property with each township assessor. This proved unproductive, and less than two years later the task devolved to each county's board of supervisors.[2] This system prevailed until 1870 when the state enacted a new constitution. Previously, each city and each corporation had a unique charter, but now homogeneous rules replaced separately legislated incorporations.[3] Uniform municipal finance regulation followed in 1872, when the legislature gave broad powers to the Board of Equalization, a body created in 1865 to ensure uniform taxation among the counties. The assessment and collection of taxes on railroad property no longer fell to local government, and the board used valuation methods that differed from any previously used.[4] The new system ignored the market value of individual plots and looked solely to the total earning power of each railroad within the state. Municipalities then received a pro rata share based on the length of the company's track in their jurisdiction. Under this system, expensive urban property had the same taxable value as rural farmland. Municipalities came to lament railroad land purchases, especially if no new track was built. Previously taxable at the commercial rate, railroad land's assessment was now relatively low. Unlike real estate development, a city reaped no taxes from the construction of railroad stations or buildings.

The biggest taxation change came in the financing of streets. Then as now, the public clamored for better pavement, street-lights, sewers, and other improvements. Infrastructure was difficult to fund, however, given exponential growth in police, fire, and sanitation payrolls. Up to this point, capital improvements relied on assessments, a tax on those neighboring properties that directly benefited from a proposed project. Assessments usually provided for construction, but sometimes they provided services. In 1852, for example, the city levied a tax on railroad companies to pay a police officer to patrol downtown depots. More often, assessments provided paving and sewers. This was so common that assessments represented the majority of city council agenda items. Property owners paid levies based on proportional street frontage. Since railroad companies had linear landholdings, they disproportionately bore the cost of street, sewer, and other improvements. Railroads saw little direct benefit from paving adjacent streets and less from sewers. Because assessment district votes required a supermajority, the railroads often held veto power over any planned improvement. The 1858 planking of Lumber Street, parallel to but one block east of the Ft. Wayne, was particularly contentious. At first, the city made no demand against the railroad company, but it bowed to popular pressure. So the city council gerrymandered a special district to get sufficient voter approval. As a result, the railway company paid much of this improvement's cost.

Postwar prosperity allowed for a mixed system of municipal finance. Special assessments and general fund revenues were now sufficient to improve and expand the city. The length of water lines, sewer pipes, and paved streets increased geometrically. Platting and paving streets became so demanding that in 1861 the Bureau of Public Works became the first municipal agency in Illinois with a professional staff. Special assessments continued, but their use peaked in 1870. Thereafter the municipal government relied primarily on general revenues for infrastructure finance, much to the relief of the railroad companies.

The Bureau of Public Works had its own construction staff. Together with the policemen, firemen, inspectors, and clerks, the city now employed a veritable army. The ability of officeholders to appoint friends and supporters to such positions became the centerpiece of local elections. As a result, the political landscape changed with the Civil War. Previously, civic-minded citizens

This 1863 Chicago map shows that the streets formed a grid to which the radial pattern of railroad development struggled to adapt.

COURTESY DENNIS McCLENDON, CHICAGO CARTOGRAPHICS

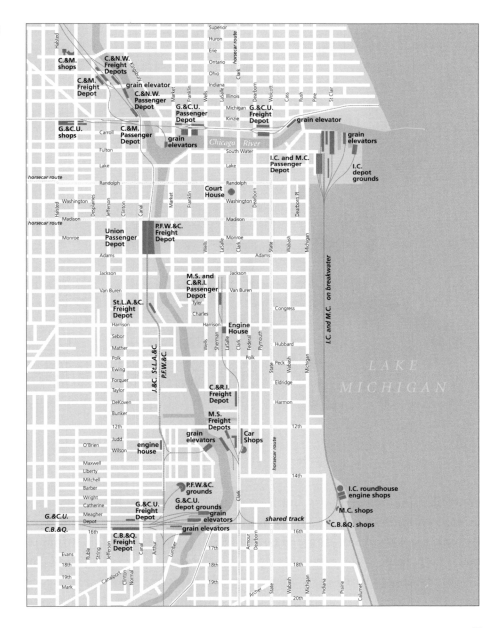

Thomas Scott greatly expanded Pennsylvania Railroad interests outside that railroad's traditional markets, but at a great cost.

COURTESY OF THE AUTHOR

controlled municipal affairs, but they retired from public life or entered military service. At the same time, the city redrew its ward maps to reflect ethnic or parochial interests. So-called machine politics arose, a system in which neighborhood ward bosses distributed patronage. On the plus side, this represented a solution to the provision of social welfare. Aldermen dispensed jobs, made small loans, helped in obtaining permits, and provided other favors. Machine politicians' huge financial demands prompted them to use any means, legal or otherwise, to fund their patronage. Graft became so prevalent that some aldermen posted fee schedules for the passage of ordinances on their office door, and wealthy railroad corporations attracted these grafters like moths to a flame. When railroads needed special privileges, such as the right to lay a sidetrack across a street, bribes greased the path. Colloquially known as "boodle," the cost of graft often exceeded construction expenses.

The first conviction of a Chicago alderman for accepting bribes occurred in 1872, but rampant corruption arose ten years earlier. Central to this new regime were James Hildreth, alderman from 1869 to 1888, and Edward F. Cullerton, alderman from 1872 to 1920. Their faction was known as the "Big Four," but an equally corrupt "Little Four" vied for control. For decades, these groups controlled nearly two-thirds of the aldermanic seats, and if unified their vote was veto proof. Fortunately, machine politics was so local that citywide organization was difficult. Except when united in a play for graft, they focused on neighborhood interests. For larger issues, however, this meant the need for not one but many separate fixes to pass an ordinance. If an ordinance failed to pass, there were no refunds from the minority of politicians who had "demonstrated their loyalty." This was the origin of the cynical Chicago definition of an honest politician as "a man who stays bought." Few politicians met even this low hurdle and with the railroads constantly expanding their industrial tracks, Chicago became an expensive place for business.

RAILROAD CONSOLIDATION

William Ogden remained a large shareholder in the Ft. Wayne and the North Western, but at the age of sixty-three, he began to unwind his affairs in anticipation of retirement. In June of 1868, he resigned the office of president and his board membership at the North Western. His replacement was Henry Keep, a financier whose life rivaled that of the fictional Horatio Alger. Interest in

a joint depot flagged under Keep's brief management and, when he died the following year, talk of a new depot disappeared as his successors solidified their control.[5] A similar evolution occurred at the Ft. Wayne as Ogden's ownership position diluted with the company's sale of additional stock.[6]

In 1869, the Pennsylvania Railroad leased both the Ft. Wayne and the Panhandle. While the Pennsylvania previously aided both companies, absolute control of these properties required goading. The giant Pennsylvania found that it had been over-confident regarding its western connections when it sold its Ft. Wayne securities and used the proceeds to expand the competing Panhandle. They battled each other, resulting in two relatively weak connecting lines. Jay Gould jolted the Pennsylvania awake when his Erie Railroad attempted to acquire both.[7] The Pennsylvania quickly leased them in a defensive action.[8]

Unlike most corporations of the era, no single financier or syndicate controlled the Pennsylvania Railroad. President Thomas Scott, like his predecessor and mentor J. Edgar Thomson, was one of the great personalities of his age and one of the nation's most able managers. Scott owned a personal portfolio of companies with wealthy Philadelphia backers in addition to his primary job, but never had sole control of the Pennsylvania. Because of its widely held shares, it was a truly modern corporation. It had an independent board that relied on a team of hired managers, who worked within a rigid chain of command drawn from military practice. One of the largest firms in the world, it nevertheless could move quickly. In the case of the Ft. Wayne, it moved so fast that it failed to fully inspect the property leased.[9]

The Pennsylvania accrued advantages and disadvantages from system building. Amalgamation into a self-contained system boosted revenues by the retention of through traffic. It simultaneously reduced the number of companies that might be tempted to start a rate war. Despite the Pennsylvania's best efforts and those of the various pools and cartels to which it belonged, however, rates fell. Passenger rates, for example, declined 50 percent between 1849 and 1870. Improvements, such as stronger locomotives, bigger cars, and better roadways all reduced costs. Administrative innovations, such as the line and staff structure, also helped. The savior for a railroad or any other organization with high capital costs, however, was to move more business and thus spread fixed charges over a larger base. Traffic growth was indeed explosive, but even in good times it barely seemed to cover expenses. Moreover, the cost-saving innovations necessary for effective competition proved frightfully expensive. Powerful locomotives, for example, could pull more freight with the same crew, but they required heavier bridges and track. Thomas Scott found that even his prosperous Pennsylvania Railroad strained under the costs of improving its western acquisitions.

With the lease of both the Ft. Wayne and the Panhandle, the Pennsylvania had two Chicago problems. First, it controlled railroads with stations five blocks apart. Tracks connected the depots, but to get cars between them required a double saw-back switch movement. In all likelihood, this complicated operation was rarely attempted. But the real issue was that the Pennsylvania taxed its coffers to their limit to buy weak lines competing with one another. In particular, the Panhandle paid too much for the Great Eastern line to Chicago, a problem compounded by the Pennsylvania paying richly for the Panhandle. The Pennsylvania's rent had to be sufficient to amortize Panhandle and

Ft. Wayne bonds, but its revenues were barely sufficient to cover operating expenses before lease payments. The Pennsylvania's due diligence failure burdened the entire system. On a map, its system looked strong, but the view at track level was less favorable. Poor, lightly built track stood atop an unballasted roadbed. Over this ran dilapidated rolling stock. A better Chicago terminal was a low priority, the Pennsylvania had little money for local improvements, and the lessors were primarily concerned with paying their bonds and a dividend.

In less than five years, the Pennsylvania Railroad's system-building strategy pushed it from a 491-mile operation to more than 6,000 miles of track, or 8 percent of the nation's total. By 1874, its capitalization of $400 million represented 13 percent of the total amount invested in US railroads.[10] As principal western terminal for two of its main lines, Chicago was secure in its position as the system's western gateway. Although less apparent in the Chicago terminal, the Pennsylvania slowly improved the Ft. Wayne and Panhandle routes. Passing track construction, motive power additions, and infrastructure improvements allowed speedier schedules. These came just in time, as traffic growth accelerated. The spread of greenback currency brought liquidity to an economy previously centered on barter, and the commerce of the Midwest that formerly moved downriver now headed east.

With cash, more people could travel and they could afford comfortable accommodations. In July 1867, the Ft. Wayne offered through cars to Jersey City, opposite Manhattan, that included daytime compartments for groups. Night trains featured "Silver Palace" sleeping cars decorated with oiled black walnut interiors accented with gold stenciling and silver lamps.[11] The train was the work of the Central Transportation Company, which represented the interest of all the roads used on the journey: the Central of New Jersey, the Lehigh Valley, the Eastern Pennsylvania, the Lebanon Valley (owned by the Philadelphia and Reading), the Pennsylvania, and the Ft. Wayne.[12] While lavishing luxurious appointments on some trains, the railroad had no money for the fancy depot Chicagoans demanded.[13]

FIRE

October 7, 1871 saw the near destruction by fire of the Ft. Wayne and Alton's station, now commonly known as "Union Depot." This was not the famous conflagration traditionally blamed on the O'Leary cow—that fire started the following day. This prelude incinerated twenty acres of coal and lumberyards along the west bank of the Chicago River. Fighting this fierce fire exhausted the firefighters, contributing to the city's inability to contain the famous blaze that followed. This first fire started at eleven o'clock at night in a planing mill across the street from the original Alton Station at Canal and Van Buren Streets. The *Chicago Tribune* reported,

> In the brief space of twenty minutes, the space between Jackson and Adams and Clinton Streets and the river were all ablaze. On the east side of Canal Street and between it and the Pittsburgh and Ft. Wayne tracks bounded north and south by Adams and Jackson, were several coal and lumber offices, all of which disappeared like tinder. Huge piles—hundreds of tons of anthracite—lay back of these buildings, and the flames at last became so intense as to communicate with the coal and to set it on fire. Up to this time the passage across the Adams Street Bridge had been unrestricted. . . . but at last

the flames reached the Adams Street viaduct. Before any steps could be taken, the sidewalks and railings of the iron viaduct were lapped up and a long, low shed on the northeast corner of Adams and Canal, used as a freight depository by the United States and Adams Express companies, was doomed to destruction. Beyond this shed, to the eastward, stood a large number of passenger coaches of the Pittsburgh and Fort Wayne Railroad, to save which it was necessary to take down the shed, which was successfully accomplished. Had it been otherwise and had these cars taken afire, nothing could have checked these flames, which would have communicated with the freight depot, continuing in their train the passenger buildings, cars, etc. and never stopping until Madison Street.

Fortunately, the open right of way south of the depot formed a void. This firebreak allowed the fire department to position a line of steam pumpers to contain the inferno. The only railroad property directly affected was a shed at Jackson and Canal. Its roof collapsed under the weight of an estimated 150 spectators who climbed atop it for a better view; several were severely crushed. The Adams and United States Express companies were not so fortunate; they lost their freight houses to the flames.

The Great Chicago Fire swept west from the O'Learys' barn at approximately nine o'clock the next evening. Its 137 West DeKoven Street origin was only blocks from the station tracks. A Ft. Wayne train pulled into the depot at ten, shortly after the alarm sounded, and the fire was noticeable to astute passengers. Alton conductor Richard Riley was among the first to spot the fire while awaiting the omnibus that took him to work. Sensing impending tragedy, his superiors telegraphed stations along their

line. From its Bloomington shops, the Alton dispatched the locomotive Major Nolton with the local pumper and its firemen.
The train reached speeds of over seventy miles per hour, but it
arrived in vain after the municipal water supply suffered severe
damage.[14]

Given the depot's wooden construction, it is amazing that
it survived both major conflagrations. Brisk winds caused the
second fire to leap to the eastern riverbank south of the depot.
The area burnt the previous day created a firebreak that prevented
the greater inferno from spreading northward. Thus sheltered,
the depot survived a fire that destroyed 17,450 buildings.

The Ft. Wayne did lose several uninsured but minor out-
buildings. The Alton was not so lucky; it lost its Van Buren Street
freight house, 113 freight cars, and its general office building on
Dearborn Street. Station tracks remained intact and they helped
evacuate an estimated 30,000 people over the next two days.[15]
Five days after the fire and with the city still smoldering, the Ft.
Wayne advertised, "No very large amount of freight can be taken
immediately, but enough to enable parties to raise money from
their Eastern correspondence."

The railroads made hasty repairs before the cruel Chicago
winter without changing the depot layout. Railroads west of the
river were lucky, not just in the preservation of property, but because for months they gained business at the expense of their
east bank competitors. Included in the property losses were the
huge limestone passenger depots of the Illinois Central and the
Rock Island. Obstacles to business, however, remained for the
Panhandle, the Ft. Wayne, and the Alton, as the fire consumed
eight nearby street bridges and three viaducts.

In addition to handling an influx of inbound freight for the
city's reconstruction, the depot yard became the city's new post
office. Before the main post office burned, Postmaster McArthur
successfully removed all of its mail to outlying branches. He
later claimed that not a single letter was lost to fire. In the fire's
aftermath, the postal service kept the mail moving by parking
all of the railway postal cars from a two-hundred-mile radius
in local rail yards to act as temporary quarters. This dismayed
McArthur, for the position of postmaster was a political plum.
Local postmasters essentially ran their offices as businesses and
those that distributed mail originating elsewhere were paid 5
percent of the postage. This was particularly lucrative, and as a
result, collusion between postmasters often resulted in circuitous routings. The separately administered Railway Mail Service eliminated these inefficiencies, at great cost to local office

holders. Now the Chicago postmaster was temporarily cut off entirely from this revenue stream. This arrangement continued until December 20, when a church on Wabash Avenue became the temporary home to the main post office. The use of railway post office cars was again required when the church post office burned on July 14, 1874. The main post office later moved to rented space in the Honore Block. It too burned on January 4, 1879. At the time, newspapers told the public to take mail to Milwaukee Road car #57, parked under the Madison Street bridge, or to Illinois Central car #38, parked at the foot of Randolph Street.[16]

City resources were understandably strained after the Great Fire. Streets needed repair and wooden bridges need replacement, but a city full of hungry people and a fast-approaching winter dictated the need to address more immediate concerns than reconstruction. Late winter relief efforts emptied the municipal treasury.[17] The State of Illinois repurchased $3,000,000 in Illinois and Michigan Canal bonds that the city bought years before. Chicago had made every effort to avoid investments in development projects, but its sole indulgence now saved it financially.[18] The Adams Street Bridge nevertheless took nine months to rebuild, and the unscathed Madison Street span shouldered the flow of men and materials that rebuilt the business district.[19]

NEW TENANTS AND GRAND PLANS

Chicago's post–Great Fire problems centered on the needs of 104,500 homeless survivors. Nonetheless, citizens quickly noted that the destroyed area provided a blank slate on which a new and better city could arise. Commentators recognized, for example, that the rectilinear street grid was not entirely compatible with the radial web of railroad tracks. Nevertheless, the Great Fire never was the accelerant for radical changes to the city's fabric. New streets and buildings, albeit of better construction, simply replaced ruined predecessors. Stringent new building regulations for a "fire district" dictated expensive brick and stone construction. The first to articulate how the city would change was no stranger to the real estate market. In an era of screaming headlines, the *Tribune* provided a nearly full-page editorial entitled only "The Hon. W. B. Ogden's Views." Ogden declared two principles. The first was that the fire district should not require construction that was too expensive, because workers needed affordable housing. This principle accurately predicted the fate of the residential neighborhood south of downtown within the fire district. Workmen there could ill afford to rebuild their cottages, and the area soon devolved to industrial and commercial use. The second half of Ogden's essay discussed the need to provide room for more railroads to enter downtown.[20]

Ogden's prescience regarding more railroad land near downtown only needed to extend until the following year. The 7,400 miles of track built in 1872 were the most of any year in US history. The Chicago, Milwaukee and St. Paul; the Chicago, Danville and Vincennes; the Baltimore and Ohio; and the Chicago and Pacific all entered Chicago. All but the latter, however, used the tracks of established companies for their final lap. The exception, the Chicago and Pacific, had a terminal far from the town center. One realtor noted, "The railroad arteries have hardened into an iron network around downtown."

In April 1872, the Chicago, Milwaukee and St. Paul (the "Milwaukee Road") became a tenant of the Panhandle. For its part, the Milwaukee Road's line from its namesake city had to run inland, away from the populous lakeside communities already served by the North Western. The Milwaukee Road's president, Alexander Mitchell, had briefly been president of the lakefront line when it had been the Chicago and Milwaukee. Ogden thwarted his efforts to absorb it into his own company in 1865. Mitchell now belatedly built his own line to Chicago.

The Milwaukee Road and the Panhandle pinned their hopes on pushing through an ordinance allowing them to occupy all of Carroll Street. The Panhandle already had some track in this street one block south of the North Western's Kinzie Street route, but the new proposal provoked vocal opposition. The North Western saw the Panhandle as aiding its enemy. It purchased land in the path of the proposed line and arranged hostile public meetings. Both sides packed the meeting halls with ruffians, although no violence ensued. Authorization nonetheless was quick and the Panhandle tracks were immediately built. Upon their completion, the Milwaukee Road purchased a one-half interest in the right of way between Western Avenue and Canal Street. There was as yet no easy way to reach the nearby Ft. Wayne depot and the railroads erected a small new station near the river. The North Western could still thwart a direct link because it jointly owned the tracks into the Ft. Wayne depot. While there was a physical connection with the North Western, it was with its former Fond du Lac line, not the ex-Galena line, which paralleled the Milwaukee and Panhandle track.

The Panhandle, now formally known as the Columbus, Chicago and Indianapolis Central, also acquired a less welcome tenant. The Chicago, Danville and Vincennes Railroad (the "CD&V," later the Chicago and Eastern Illinois) came from due south of Chicago. Established railroads considered it an unstable rate cutter, a stigma attached to the Panhandle only a few years before. The northern section of the CD&V opened from Dolton to Momence, Illinois, on October 10, 1869, but it lacked the financial muscle to push further toward Chicago. Surveying their options, its attorneys discovered a defect in the original Chicago and Great Eastern ordinance. The Panhandle line once ran west of the city limit, but now much of it was inside the municipal boundary and subject to local regulation. The problem with the original enabling statute was that it contained no assignment provision whereby successor corporations could assume rights granted the Great Eastern. CD&V lawyers notified the city of this deficiency and asked that any amendment require the Panhandle to grant the CD&V rights into downtown.

On November 18, 1871, the Panhandle—under duress—entered an agreement allowing the CD&V to use its tracks from Dolton to Chicago. The CD&V undoubtedly made liberal gifts to aldermen to insure a favorable vote on their redraft of the Panhandle authorization, but it was an easy decision. The city truly needed another rail line from southern Illinois and Indiana coalfields because the local appetite for coal was nearly insatiable. Forced to take an unwelcome tenant, however, the Panhandle never allowed its renter to build the switches, spurs, or sidetracks needed for freight delivery. The CD&V could transfer freight cars to other lines and it could load and unload passengers on the Panhandle main track. The later practice, however, saw the tenant's trains block movements into its landlord's station. The ordinance allowing it into the city required viaducts at Halsted, Sangamon, Lake, and Madison Streets. In theory, both the CD&V and the Milwaukee Road had to contribute to their erection. In fact, they

remained unbuilt. By December 1872, the Panhandle operated
five trains each way, including an accommodation (commuter)
run to Lansing, Illinois.[21] Traffic grew quickly. A December 1874
tally of passenger trains at Halsted Street listed forty-four on
the North Western, eighteen on the Milwaukee, eighteen on the
Panhandle, and ten on the CD&V.[22]

After the Great Fire, speculative real estate mania again
appeared, with the West Division its epicenter. In one year, the
division's population rose from 160,000 to 214,000 as refugees
sought shelter in hastily built structures of dubious quality. The
shortage of good residential and commercial buildings ignited
tremendous speculation as the price of developed property
doubled and tripled throughout town. As developers scram-
bled to reap their fortunes in the bubble, they neglected one
important fact. The same financial structure applied to all the
properties being built. With inflated values and the standard
five-year mortgage at 8 percent interest, reasonable rents failed
to provide sufficient income. In addition to higher land values,

a bid-up in wages inflated building costs. Bricklayers and carpenters who earned 2–3 dollars a day made 5–10 dollars during the boom. These newly prosperous workers rushed to buy their own cottages, further fueling speculation. By May 1873, the bubble burst as panicked developers simultaneously attempted to dump their properties. Local problems were overshadowed in September, when the banking firm of Jay Cooke & Company collapsed, precipitating a nationwide financial panic and protracted depression. By the bottom of the business cycle in 1877, twenty-one local banks collapsed and investment capital became nonexistent.

Despite the weak economy, a realignment of Chicago railroad properties seemed imminent. Chicago's first terminals were more than shared buildings; they were true alliances, with cross-ownership of the underlying companies. These combinations became unstable, particularly the lakefront alliance that shared Great Central Depot. The Michigan Central and the Chicago, Burlington and Quincy Railroads both sparred with the Illinois Central, which controlled tracks into the station. The IC co-owned the depot itself with the MC, with the Burlington as tenant. Boston capitalists controlled all three companies in the 1850s, but the Illinois Central became increasingly independent as its first-generation managers retired and the initial capitalists' ownership diluted. At the same time, traffic growth meant that each company needed more space. Unfortunately, the lakefront had no adjacent land for expansion. The final blow came when the IC granted the Baltimore and Ohio a route into town against the wishes of the Michigan Central.

The agendas of the intertwined companies started to unwind in 1869, when the IC forced its tenants into a high-stakes lawsuit against the city of Chicago for the right to build a new lakefront terminal. Appalled by their need to operate from a fire-ruined depot, the MC and the Burlington had little faith that they would win a fight to infill the lake. As an alternative, they looked longingly at the West Side's potential. They ordered an appraisal of the Ft. Wayne depot, but their findings were somewhat disturbing.[23] The market value of the West Side depot and approach tracks was found to be:

Property	$28,600
12th Street Viaduct	$25,000
Track, crossings, etc.	$25,000
Structures	$171,350
	$250,000

Twelve years previously, the Ft. Wayne issued $337,133 in bonds for this depot. The disparity may not be as great as it seemed, since the 1874 valuation excluded freight houses. Even in a year of severe depression, however, it seems remarkable that an appraisal would find so little value in the depot property. A contemporary commentator wildly opined that a West Side depot to house both the existing lines and those on the lakefront would cost at least $10 million.

One beneficial byproduct of the IC's efforts came on April 6, 1872, when the state legislature passed "An Act Authorizing the Formation of Union Depots and Stations for Railroads." Three or more railroad corporations, together with other individuals, could now incorporate to own and operate a depot as joint property. Such companies could issue up to $3 million in stock. Even as lakefront depot discussion stalled, the Rock Island and Michigan Southern announced in June 1872 that they were replacing their Van Buren Street station. Less publicly, the Ft. Wayne assembled parcels near the existing station for a four-block-long depot with the Alton, Panhandle, and Milwaukee.[24]

Rumors of a grand new depot for the West Side swirled through 1872, their credence fueled by frequent inspections made by Thomas Scott and other railroad luminaries. A contract did circulate for the construction of a depot large enough to accommodate every railroad in the city, but not a single railroad signed it. February 1873 saw a Panhandle track crew build a connection arching southward toward the Ft. Wayne depot. In the process, the crew attempted to install a switch to the existing line. The North Western responded to the modification of this track, jointly owned with the Ft. Wayne, by obtaining an injunction against an unauthorized connection.[25] The injunction delayed completion for weeks, but soon Panhandle and Milwaukee Road trains rolled unimpeded southward to the Ft. Wayne depot. Throughout the year and into the next, the Ft. Wayne and Alton negotiated with the North Western to bring it into their planned depot. The only railroad to complete a building, however, was CD&V, which built a triangular depot south of the tracks on the arc that swept from the Panhandle's Carroll Street alignment to the Ft. Wayne depot. It lacked a dedicated station track, an indication of its unwanted tenancy. The Panhandle actively tried to rid itself of its lessee, but it was unable to break its contract until the tenant built its own depot, Dearborn Station, in 1881.

Depot plans remained unsettled. On November 28, 1874, William B. Strong, general manager of the Michigan Central, wrote James Joy, president of the Burlington, with a proposal that they move their roads out of the Great Central Depot to a west side station. He stated, "The Northwestern [sic], Milwaukee and St. Paul (the Milwaukee Road) roads have agreed to join the Burlington, the Chicago and Alton, and Ft. Wayne Roads at the depot."[26] The following April, however, he wrote:

> The more I consider the possibility of a Union Station at Madison and Canal the more it seems impossible. First, the street is several feet (in fact both streets) higher than the tracks. It *must* be owing to the viaducts. This will make it necessary to have an inclined plane, so that instead of 24 feet we figured for outside platform, the first track next to Canal Street must be set back not less than 50 feet. *2nd* The width, I am told is but 250˙feet. *3rd* The length is but two blocks, or about 1000 feet —Divide this in the middle for the north and south roads coming into it and you have a depot about the size of our ruined depot.[27]

Strong next presented a brash alternative. He asked Charles Perkins of the Burlington to consider a scheme to build a mammoth new depot at Twenty-Sixth Street for all of the railroads using Union and LaSalle Street depots. Its genesis was a vacant eighty-acre parcel available at distressed prices due to the economic depression. The railroads could build their terminal there and sell excess downtown real estate for a profit. Strong thought the entire downtown area would shift southward by this ploy, but the scheme received little attention from his peers.

In August 1875, President Blackstone of the Alton provided the Burlington with a $700,000 estimate for the cost of a new station on the West Side site. Land for a new coachyard was to cost an additional $300,000. Blackstone indicated that six companies would share the cost of the station: the three original lines plus the Burlington, the Michigan Central, and the Lake Shore and Michigan Southern. Surprisingly, Blackstone excluded the

Panhandle, despite its current use of the depot. Nor did he include the CD&V, the Panhandle's tenant. Blackstone's central role in the negotiations reflected the Alton's transformation from its early failures. By the 1870s, it was the third-largest hauler of corn to the Chicago market, trailing only the far larger Illinois Central and the Burlington. More importantly, at the time it was the largest hauler of coal, the commodity that made the city an industrial powerhouse.

As the depression abated, rumors again circulated that an imposing new depot would arise on the West Side. The *Tribune* stated, "No one can deny, not even the railroads themselves, that the unsightly and dilapidated sheds serving as a union depot were not only a disgrace to the railroads, but to the city, as the smallest towns on any of the lines serving the Madison street depot had better accommodations. The sheds serving as a depot have now become so dilapidated that they cannot serve another year."[28]

It was a shock when the companies responded that they would erect a temporary brick structure for $20,000. They retracted this statement two weeks later after the Ft. Wayne's chief engineer, Felecian Slataper, determined that the cost of a temporary fix would be far higher. In its place, he sketched an innovative $300,000 depot with a two-hundred-foot front on the Adams Street viaduct. Waiting rooms eighty feet wide were to be built at street level with spiral staircases to descend to track level. Passengers would leave the depot by crossing the platform to a Canal Street carriageway whose ramps connected with Madison and Van Buren Streets. The waiting room structure was to be of brick and stone, whose "two wings will be of iron and roofs of corrugated iron and glass . . . [whose] pillars will be highly ornamental." These wings, in all likelihood, consisted of the train sheds north and south of Adams Street.[29]

URBAN WARFARE

After a brief respite in 1877, the economy again spiraled into panic. The railroads, led by the Pennsylvania, responded to the downturn on June 1. The Pennsylvania cut wages by 10 percent and changed work rules to require far greater output per employee. By June 16, workers protested by preventing trains from moving. Beginning as a local action in West Virginia, the stoppages gathered momentum, becoming the first nationwide strike of industrial workers. Tensions escalated into full-scale riots and violence flared in every major eastern city. On July 21, flames engulfed the Pennsylvania Railroad's Pittsburgh buildings, depots, yards, and cars. Without a national labor policy or any precedent for handling such disputes, President Rutherford B. Hayes reacted erratically.[30] Federal troops were dispatched to some cities, but not to others. Nevertheless, this was the nation's first federal intervention in a labor dispute.

Chicagoans scanned their newspapers for news of what came to be known as the Great Strike as its violence migrated westward. Monday, June 23 was tense with anticipation, as everyone knew the railroad employees' grievances. Previous stoppages halted Union Depot trains in a March 1864 strike by the Brotherhood of the Footboard and in May 1867 for an eight-hour-day demonstration.[31] Rioting now seemed a distinct possibility. The North Western retracted a previously announced wage cut, while the Alton, which never reduced wages, canceled all freight trains.[32] That afternoon a crowd of five thousand converged on Market (now Wacker) and Madison Streets across the river from the West Side Depot. The assembly was peaceful, despite the appeals of speakers seeking to inflame the crowd. Socialist, anarchist, and communist activists beseeched the working class to expand the strike into a great blow against capitalism. On the following day, they announced a similar rally, but they had not reckoned with Joseph T. Torrence. The thirty-four-year-old Torrence was a former blacksmith who enlisted as a private in the Ohio infantry as a teenager during the Civil War. After four wounds inflicted at the battle of Perryville, the Army discharged him. When the Confederate raider John Hunt Morgan penetrated the Union lines near Torrence's place of convalescence, he volunteered to chase the rebel force, successfully. Despite some notoriety, Torrence never received a commission during the war. He moved to Chicago, where his knowledge of iron furnace design and operation attracted investors. He founded the successful Chicago Iron Works and the Joliet Steel and Wire Company. His new standing in society and his political connections enabled him to enlist as colonel in the Second Regiment of the Illinois Guard. On the eve of the violent labor strife, he became brigadier, and everyone addressed him as "General" for the remainder of his life.

Tuesday afternoon, Torrence ordered his troops to charge the crowd as it trickled toward the dais erected for the day's speakers. The city previously swung the bridges open to isolate the business district from the industrial west side and, with their exits blocked, the crowd panicked. Several thousand people stampeded into a streetcar tunnel under the river near the Union Depot, where they were crushed to near fainting as police flailed stragglers with their batons. The crowd dispersed, but deprived of a common rallying point, it splintered into over fifty separate mobs. They roamed the city into the following day. Factories closed as the raging throngs of men, women, and children threatened those still working. Looting centered on stores that sold guns or liquor. One crowd attempted to occupy the North Western passenger depot, but it was driven back by policemen wielding truncheons.

"RED WAR" screamed the *Tribune*'s Thursday headline as it detailed the previous evening's carnage. As this hit the newsstands, a mob 1,500 strong attacked the Burlington roundhouse at Sixteenth and Halsted streets. Over the protests of the few railroad employees in the crowd, vandals began to strip parts from switch engines to render them inoperable. Police officers fired on the roundhouse and shots rang out in return. At least four rioters were killed and dozens more injured. One officer died on-site, with ten more wounded. A detachment of twenty officers en route to the scene met an even larger mob on the Halsted Street viaduct spanning the Burlington tracks. The scene was a repeat of the roundhouse, but in addition to casualties among the rioters and police, the dead included innocent bystanders, including a strike-busting Alton conductor riding a streetcar home from work. At day's end, the death toll stood at fifteen.

During Thursday's disturbances, the 11:00 a.m. Ft. Wayne local left on time, but rioters soon boarded and pulled the coupling pins. Conductor Shelter came prepared and he pulled a long-barreled revolver from his coat. With one hand on his pistol, he deftly replaced all of the couplings. He then instructed the engineer to back the train to the depot. As afternoon shadows lengthened, the sound of gunfire crackled toward Union Depot. Public relief was palpable when the Milwaukee Road's afternoon train arrived with a load of federal troops. A second section with more troops followed. They contained the Second and Twenty-Second Regiments ordered to Chicago by General Philip Sheridan. Without actual authorization to dispatch his troops, he nevertheless paraded them conspicuously from the depot and crossed the business district to a lakefront bivouac.[33] The presence of the battle-hardened Twenty-Second illustrated the gravity of the situation. Pulled from the Little Bighorn command, they were the backbone of the force seeking revenge for Custer's defeat the previous summer. The troops never engaged strikers in Chicago, as the violence was already in decline. Torrence received credit for quelling the riots, as he stationed infantry along the length of Halsted Street, paraded cavalry with drawn sabers throughout working-class neighborhoods, and placed grapeshot-loaded cannon at the bridges.[34]

Recent commentary on the Great Strike suggests that the riot's roots were more complex than can be explained by labor grievances.[35] The Great Strike certainly began in reaction to railroad wage cuts, but it evolved into a violent rejection of corporate power. Events certainly transcended employee action; contemporary accounts noted an almost complete absence of railroad workmen in the mobs. Rather, the Great Strike exposed an emotional antirailroad public sentiment. The encroachment of trains into city streets was an issue shared by many riot-torn communities; as historian David Stowell observed, "There is no greater sower of discord in an urban area than a steam locomotive running down a crowded street." Railways increased the perils of everyday life and made impossible such mundane activities as keeping the clothes drying on a line clean. After decades of futile petition against the noxious smoke, injurious disregard for public safety, noise of bells and whistles, and monopolization of scarce urban land, the railways became the target of public wrath.

PLANS FOR A BETTER DEPOT

Events returned to normal, but Union Depot was not improving with age. The *Toledo Blade* contemptuously reported, "The paint has long since been worn off by the action of the weather, and the woodwork on the inside is thickly covered with a deposit of grease and dirt that makes it very variegated in appearance. The floor is covered by a thick, three-ply carpet of tobacco quids."

On February 6, 1879, however, newspaper reports brought hope. They revealed that the Milwaukee Road, Alton, and North Western were meeting in the offices of the Ft. Wayne for discussions dedicated to replacing the "old, dilapidated rookery at the corner of Madison and Canal streets." A week later, however, the headline read, "THOU ART SO NEAR, AND YET SO FAR." The sticking point was the need to relocate the Ft. Wayne freight houses in order to provide room. The *Tribune* announced with poisoned pen,

> The rats and other vermin hold high carnival at their paradise, the so-called depot of the Ft. Wayne, Alton and St. Paul Railroads, all day yesterday on account of the bright prospects of being allowed to continue in their most favored resort for some time longer. They had been in great distress during the week, owing to the reports that the building they have inhabited for so many years, and which offered them conveniences not possible to be found in any other building in the city, was to be torn down. They had already packed their duds, and were ready to leave, when they learned that they would be allowed to continue in the peaceful prospect of their cherished home.[36]

Halsted Street located five blocks west of the depot saw violent confrontations during several periods of labor unrest, especially on its viaduct over the Burlington tracks.

Unknown to the public, on April 30, 1879, George B. Roberts of the Pennsylvania sent a letter to the decidedly independent Ft. Wayne board (because the road was leased, rather than owned), which had to approve construction expenditures. Roberts stated that a new depot was "an absolute necessity" and called for a $608,121 expenditure. The Ft. Wayne board demanded more detail.

What took the parties so long to reach a consensus for operating one of their most important depots? The roller-coaster economy made capital scarce, although a nationwide boom in track construction somewhat belies that point. A change in the Pennsylvania Railroad's senior management had an important bearing on the partners who would occupy the Chicago terminal.[37]

Thomas A. Scott, dynamic president of the Pennsylvania, was in poor health after having failed in his attempt to push the company further west through alliances and purchases. In June of 1880, he retired.[38] Correspondence with the Ft. Wayne suggests his replacement, the cautious George B. Roberts, ran the company's affairs for at least a year before his official ascension. Roberts feared external entanglements and was wary of the companies that sought entrance into the new Chicago depot. Roberts seemingly decided that his railroad was casting its net too wide for tenants. For whatever reason, at the last minute the North Western and the Michigan Central were either excluded or decided not to join in the new depot.

CHAPTER THREE

A DEPOT WORTHY OF CHICAGO

A UNION DEPOT IN MORE THAN NAME

Railroad managers trod delicately as they sought to build the ideal West Side Depot. The need for more land caused them to refrain from public declarations even as grand rumors circulated. Upon denial of these rumors, even more scorn fell on their existing operation. The *Tribune* stated:

> The City of Chicago has a right to insist that railroad companies to which it grants valuable franchises and real privileges shall not support nuisances within the city limits. The citizens . . . have a right to complain of dirty, stinking, badly ventilated, tumbled down shanties that some of these rich corporations continue to maintain and call passenger depots. Probably the worst and most disgraceful of the whole lot is the old rookery at the corner of Canal and Madison streets. It is not as nearly tidy as a thrifty farmer's hog pen and ought to be condemned as a common nuisance.[1]

Against their better judgment, the railroads finally announced their intent. Their change of heart had less to do with a desire to deflect civic scorn than with a competitive threat. The challenger, the Chicago and Western Indiana (the "Western Indiana"), was jointly owned by five railways to bring their trains into the heart of the city. In many ways, the Western Indiana

was the revenge of the CD&V, since renamed the Chicago and Eastern Illinois. It tried for a decade to work with the Panhandle, but its unwilling landlord always denied it comfort. Joining this jilted suitor were the Grand Trunk, which connected to eastern Canada; the Erie, which ran due east to upstate New York; the Monon route to Louisville; and George Gould's Wabash line to St. Louis.[2] Later the powerful Atchison, Topeka and Santa Fe with its California line joined them. The Western Indiana thus promised Chicago another terminal with radiating lines to nearly every compass point. In response, Chicago's entrenched railroads literally went to the barricades. The Ft. Wayne led this opposition, for the upstart's planned route abutted its own line from Sixty-Second Street to downtown, promising to compete en route for the business of every coal yard and factory.

The Ft. Wayne's first line of defense pushed friendly aldermen to encumber the newcomer with a raft of restrictive ordinances, a strategy not without problems. The public wanted new railroads and viaducts over major streets. The latter expense would seriously impair the Western Indiana, but any viaduct also had to span the Ft. Wayne's parallel tracks, a cost thus far avoided. One expense on which neither side stinted was a headlong pursuit of aldermanic votes. In early September, the Western Indiana scored a seeming victory in the city council with an ordinance to allow it to run its tracks. But the ordinance required the railroads to build viaducts wherever and whenever the city might demand. Mayor Harrison publicly supported the new line and then vetoed the franchise amid accusations of demagoguery.

The Western Indiana overcame the mayoral veto and started laying track only to encounter a second line of defense: brawling thugs who disrupted construction. Rivals blocked rail crossings with standing cars, while the new company's switches and rails disappeared into the night. Competitors purchased key parcels, and when the Western Indiana exercised its power of eminent domain it met squadrons of lawyers supported by pliant judges. William T. Stead, who wrote about the city council members in his influential book *If Christ Came to Chicago*, captured the reformers' view of their elected representatives:

> It being expected . . . that the Aldermen will steal, the longer headed, well to do citizens limited . . . the taxing powers of the city. As a result of these expedients, which so severely limited the financial resources of the city, the Aldermen were driven to forage for plunder in other fields. Unfortunately they were too numerous and the pastures to be obtained lay in tempting profusion on every side. The powers of the city, although strictly limited in the levying of taxes, are almost unlimited in relation to the common property of the city. The streets, for instance, have furnished an estate of incalculable value, which could be sold wholesale or retail to the highest bidder.[3]

Shady aldermen were never well regarded in the executive suites, but railroad managers and the public alike knew that when a government was for sale, advantage went to those with cash. Stead recounted the political climate:

A story is told of a very well known boodler in the town, who was at the time a member of the City Council. . . . A railroad corporation was endeavoring to secure a franchise to give it the right of way into the heart of the city. The alderman in question had not been offered, so the story runs, so much for his vote as he deemed it worth. He made an eloquent and impassioned speech against the tyranny of the railroad corporation, dwelt upon the devastation which it would make coming into the city, and he voted against the ordinance. The ordinance was passed, however, and vetoed by the Mayor. It was therefore necessary to secure the necessary two-thirds majority. The gentleman in question was to all appearances unshaken in his opposition. He had previously intimated to the ring that they would have to pay him his price or he would vote to sustain the Mayor's veto. As they made no sign before the debate opened, he took part in it and began a denunciation of the railroad company and expressed his strong determination to defend the rights of the people. While he was speaking, the chief of the ring laid an envelope before him, on the corner of which was written "$1,000." Hastily thrusting it into his breast pocket he continued his speech, when suddenly, to the great amusement of those who were in on the secret, he wound up with the declaration that, notwithstanding his detestation of railroad tyranny, and his reluctance to see the streets interfered with, still, under the present circumstances, seeing the great advantages which would accrue from having another depot in the center of the city, he would vote for the ordinance which he had previously opposed . . . The Alderman was warmly congratulated by his new allies upon his conversion. When the council broke up they crowded him so that he did not have a chance to examine his $1,000. When he returned home that night he said complacently to his wife, as he produced the envelope from his pocket, "See, dear,

I have made $1,000 this day," and handed her the envelope. She opened it and found a $100 bill! The Alderman was sold. His vote was recorded and the ordinance was passed and the boodler was boodled.[4]

Everyone recognized that disruptive tactics could only delay the new line's completion, and that the Western Indiana would declare victory by announcing the construction of a lavish downtown terminal. Rumors flew of modern replacements for the city's other stations. While the press spun sugarplum dreams about fairy-tale depots, competitive response to the Western Indiana actually came in the form of commonsense improvements to train service, not to stations. The most extravagant project was that of the Illinois Central, which built a whole new two-track railroad parallel to its lakefront line and inaugurated a dedicated commuter service. The Rock Island, meanwhile, placed new coaches on its suburban accommodation trains, formerly handled by hand-me-downs from pioneer years.[5] As the Western Indiana inched closer to the commercial district, a fierce rate war erupted. The new line's free omnibus service from its ever-closer end of track prompted the cuts, but they lingered after it reached its downtown goal.

By November 1879, the *Tribune* was confident enough about a new West Side depot that its headline read, "IT'S NO JOKE THIS TIME." Initially the papers knew only that the Ft. Wayne's Chief Engineer Slataper submitted detailed plans to the Milwaukee Road and the Alton for review. A day later, the Burlington announced that it would leave the Illinois Central for the new West Side depot.[6] For its part, the Ft. Wayne won the argument to retain its riverside freight houses by noting that the remaining passenger area was wider than that of the Rock Island depot. That station, of course, serviced two companies' trains, while the new West Side depot was to handle five. Indeed, it was still the goal to handle eight railroads. Slataper stated that, excluding the Adams Street viaduct that split the train shed, his plan created the longest depot in the country, if not the world.[7]

It was not until December 22 that the Ft. Wayne board approved the four-party contract to build and operate the station together with the related authority for expenditures not to exceed $1 million. By agreement, the Alton reconveyed property that Ft. Wayne sold to the Joliet and Chicago in 1863. This and other land exchanges allowed four tracks on a straighter alignment from the Chicago River bridge. Finally, on New Year's Eve 1879, all the railroads signed an agreement for a new Union Depot. It stipulated that the Ft. Wayne was to construct the depot and that the Alton and the Milwaukee Road would be tenants. The agreement further stated: "It is agreed that the following companies shall be admitted to joint use of said depot . . . in case they so desire: The Chicago, Burlington and Quincy, the Michigan Central, the Pittsburgh, Cincinnati, Chicago and St. Louis (Panhandle) and the Chicago and North Western. No other companies shall be admitted except with the unanimous consent of the parties occupying same."[8]

All winter, rumors swirled about companies changing terminals. The Western Indiana, which had yet to sign contracts with all prospective carriers, toyed with other lines as well. Tenants in existing stations jovially fed the rumor mill, the better to bargain terms. Gossip and speculation intensified, but the North Western broke the ice. On January 7, 1880, it applied to the city for authority to build its own depot on the north bank of the river.

VAN BUREN STREET.

A SECTION OF A PULLMAN VESTIBULED TRAIN.

DEARBORN STATION.
POLK STREET.

GRAND CENTRAL PASSENGER STATION.
HARRISON ST. & FIFTH AVE.

CHICAGO & NORTH-WESTERN DEPOT.

UNION DEPOT.

It sought permission for a Franklin Street viaduct, a desirable (but never built) feature. This, however, sparked agitation for a similar viaduct and bridge over the West Side depot approach at Jackson Street.[9] The Ft. Wayne resolutely countered that it would never build a new depot if the city mandated a Jackson Street viaduct.

There was a sound reason for not having this bridge. It was too close to Adams Street to have both swings open and still leave room for boats to maneuver. For their part, the railroads objected because they needed long stub tracks south of the depot. These tracks ran near Canal Street and this left scant room to build bridge approaches.[10] Boat owners who feared yet another obstruction in the channel supported the railroads by obtaining an injunction. Aldermen approved the North Western's plan, but caved to Ft. Wayne objections without requiring that railroad to announce its intentions.

The trigger for construction of both the North Western and Union depots was the sale by the North Western of its interest in the line along the riverbank, an astonishing decision given both its existing role as interchange track and its conveyance to the Milwaukee Road, a direct competitor. Perhaps it was hard to turn down an appeal by the mighty Pennsylvania Railroad; possibly the price was right or there was other horse trading. And there was another incentive. The C&NW line extended as a straight shot from its former Fond du Lac northwest line through the depot area to the Empire slip and its adjoining privately owned elevator. The North Western's major grain artery was now its former G&CU west line, and Empire-bound cars required switching, which fouled its own station leads, its Chicago River bridge, and the Union Depot. It preferred that this grain went to its own elevators anyway, so it was best to sell this track and exit this business.

BRICK AND MORTAR

The railroad released preliminary plans in late February; they were a Pennsylvania Railroad conception unvetted by tenants.[11] Approval by each company's directors occurred March 12, 1880.[12] Demolition of the old depot actually started a week earlier, taking only two days. Seventeen days after formal approval, the Pennsylvania rented a temporary construction office on the second floor of the Ashland Block at Canal and Randolph Streets, where railroad managers received nearly one hundred bids for various pieces of the work. On April 1, the railroads decided to award one construction contract, including everything except the iron train shed, to Sherburne Bryant of Milwaukee.

Hiring a general contractor empowered to let subcontracts for specialized work was a relatively new concept to both the railroads and the Chicago construction community, but it proved successful. Foundation work for what was called the "General Passenger Station" began on April 19, and brickwork commenced May 15. The Delaware Bridge Company began the shed that fall. By mid-July the north baggage building was nearly complete, and the main passenger house rose to two stories. The railroads lifted the Adams and Van Buren Street viaducts one foot to improve clearances and to install construction better able to resist the vibrations and locomotive exhaust blasting their undersides. Viaducts now admitted four tracks rather than the previous two.[13] During construction, both the Panhandle and the Milwaukee used the Galena's ancient Carroll Street depot.[14] The Ft. Wayne and Alton operated from temporary quarters to the south.

The Michigan Central continued negotiations to use the new depot but delayed commitment. Early in 1880, William Vanderbilt purchased control of the line and dissolved its alliance with the Burlington. Vanderbilt's New York Central already controlled the Lake Shore and Michigan Southern, fierce rival of the Pennsylvania. The Lake Shore co-owned LaSalle Street Station, and while there was a great desire to consolidate the Vanderbilt roads, that site lacked the capacity. Pennsylvania Railroad hostility toward the Vanderbilt lines worked against the Michigan Central's removal to the West Side but not against the Burlington. By going to the West Side depot, inbound Burlington trains no longer crossed the busy Chicago River. Not only was this route easier to operate, but Burlington managers noticed a psychological oddity. Now, when an open bridge delayed travelers en route to the depot and they subsequently missed their train, they blamed either a riverboat or their cab driver. Before, they were already aboard their train and when delayed by an open bridge, they berated the railroad. A West Side location absolved the railroad of public scorn. To reach the new depot, the Burlington had only to build a northward-curving connecting track from a point near its Sixteenth Street roundhouse, a seemingly simple task.

The North Western's new depot on Wells Street north of the Chicago River opened on February 12, 1881, to great acclaim. The West Side depot was well enough along that comparison was possible. One critic noted of the Wells Street edifice,

> Next to the new West Side Union Depot, it is the finest and most commodious in the Western country. The main building fronting Wells Street is a fine specimen of architecture and highly ornate, with a high tower in the center and smaller ones at the corners. The sheds back of the building badly correspond with the surroundings and some disappointment is felt on account of their lack of ornamentation.[15]

This criticism focused on the North Western's economical umbrella sheds over each platform; by contrast, the Pennsylvania opted for a dramatic but flamboyantly expensive balloon shed to arch all tracks.

The West Side Union Depot was ready in April 1881, almost one year to the day after construction commenced. The *Tribune* remarked, "Had it not been for the exceptionally cold winter, it would have been ready for business several months ago."[16]

The general arrangement of the depot grounds appeared little changed. Tracks paralleled the Chicago River, with Canal Street to the west. Ramps continued to connect the warehouses along the river with Van Buren and Madison Streets, which formed the boundaries of the depot. The *Railroad Gazette* stated that the Pennsylvania freight house "is of brick, about 700 feet long and 60 feet wide: all but 80 feet lies north of the Adams Street viaduct, which divided the building into two parts. The short section was moved toward the river about 20 feet last year, to admit more tracks in front."[17]

In fact, to accommodate a new track layout, the railroad bought seven parcels near the depot for $214,000. It then jacked up and relocated the existing freight house to a new location south of Adams Street and added three hundred feet to its length. Similar additions sprang up north of Adams Street. These warehouses handled package deliveries, but the Ft. Wayne moved the switching of carload traffic to expanded freight yards eight miles south. Initially known as the Outer Yard and later as the Fifty-Ninth Street Yard, this eleven-track facility had three and a half miles of track and a twenty-stall engine house.[18] To connect with the depot, a new double-track drawbridge with a 221-foot span was designed, although due to problems with steel delivery it was not in service until a year after the depot opened. With these improvements, the area near downtown became wholly dedicated to passenger, mail, express, and less-than-carload traffic.

The new layout provided through tracks for passenger trains, although in practice trains did not run through the depot. A 1,074-foot-long train shed covered the entire station yard, bisected by the Adams Street Bridge. Wrought-iron arches placed at twenty-five-foot intervals spanned ninety-six feet. Each rested on a masonry pier bolted to a "heavy footing stone."[19] Iron roof arches were connected by pine rafters and sheathing topped with the "best charcoal-tin" plate. The sides of the shed remained open for ventilation. Clear glass glazed the gable ends, while louvered ventilators of ribbed glass ran the length of the shed. Three lines of gas jets housed in glass globes twenty-five feet above the platform provided illumination. These were large Dyott lamps with multiple mantles and a telltale, or pilot light, which allowed ignition from inside the depot offices by turning a control valve.

Commentators bemoaned the lack of electric arc lights, but any light was an improvement. The *Tribune*'s opening description of the depot stated, "Last night the new Union Depot, corner of Madison and Canal Streets, was most brilliantly illuminated for its entire length for the first occasion, thus signaling its completion."[20]

The depot was bounded by the Chicago River and streets on higher elevations; pedestrians entered tracks and train shed through its three redbrick buildings fronting Canal Street. North and south baggage buildings flanked the passenger house, each soaring four floors above track level. Street-side facades, of course, had lower profiles due to the higher Canal Street grade. A wrought-iron embellished veranda extended over the Canal Street sidewalk connecting the structures and spanning Adams Street to reach the south baggage building. The use of dark-red Philadelphia pressed brick with black mortar and Warrensburg stone trim provided a dignified unity to these structures, as did their Peachbottom slate roofs.

The main building measured two hundred by fifty-eight feet, a design requiring the extensive use of load-bearing iron columns. This was not the expensive construction later common in the development of the iron-frame skyscraper. Rather, with one exception, the construction had more in common with cast-iron storefronts where merchants valued space-saving iron interior columns. The massive weight of such commercial buildings continued to be carried by their brick walls. The same was true at the depot, except that the weight of its eastern facade also rested on iron framing. Here an iron colonnade ran along the tracks at ground level. The exterior brick wall was non-load-bearing and it was set back at track level by eighteen feet to allow a wide por-

tico. The iron columns of this porch carried the higher floors, whose facade consisted of masonry veneer.[21] This formed a simple trackside concourse for pedestrian circulation and provided a transformation as depot architecture gave way to the engineer's domain of the train shed.

A wrought-iron gate at the portico's east side controlled pedestrian traffic into the train shed. It controlled the link to a central corridor bisecting the depot's lowest floor from the Canal Street stairwell. On either side were restrooms, a barbershop, a smoking lounge, and the lunchroom supplied by a dumbwaiter from the kitchen above. Each room had marble floors, varnished hardwood trim, and doors with cut-glass panels. The depot master's office, conductor's room, newsroom, and telegraph office were also on the ground floor. The boiler room, however, occupied the greater part of that level. Because of the depot's location adjacent to the river, the water table did not allow construction of a basement. The only excavation, other than the foundation, was a narrow "subway" running the length of the depot complex to provide for water and steam pipes.

Depot Master Charles Case, who had held this position since 1865, was particularly proud of his new charge.[22] The main entrance to the passenger building was a thirty-by-forty-foot vestibule fronting Canal Street. From there, travelers trod down twelve steps to track level or up seven steps to the ticket office and waiting rooms. The handsome design of this entrance, however, probably caused patrons to linger. The frescoed ceiling rose sixty feet, while wainscoting composed of ten contrasting marbles enriched the entryway. Coats of arms from each state served by the depot's railroads decorated the upper walls. The grand staircase was a confection of wrought and cast iron with marble newels topped by brass candelabra. Stained-glass windows set high above the west entrance washed the entire scene with intricate color patterns. Critics proclaimed this rotunda, as the railroad insisted on calling this square vestibule, "a *tout ensemble* pleasing to the eye."[23]

The rotunda and its staircase pierced the center of the second-story waiting room. A 25-foot-high, frescoed ceiling magnified the room's ample 54-by-120-foot dimensions. Here the wainscoting was walnut and cherry wood, while the floor was white and black marble. Warm afternoon sunlight entered from tall windows overlooking Canal Street, each with cathedral glass in its arch. Nine arched windows overlooked the train shed and the tracks. The perfection of this composition received great praise in the perfumed journalism of the period. Fifteen years later, however, an interior decorator hoping to secure a painting contract described the effect differently: "The glasswork is painted in the

opaque manner briefly stylish at the time the depot was built. Walls were painted with dark stencil work and the overall result is rather dull."[24] This décor, however, satisfied the railroads, since they never hired their detractor and actually had the vestibule repainted in the same manner.

North of this main room was the formal dining hall. Hearty meals served on china, silver plate, and crystal spread over crisp white linen rivaled the city's better restaurants. At the opposite end of the waiting room, a six-window ticket office thrust fifteen feet into the main room, fronted by black walnut and cherry wood paneling and a marble countertop. Toward Canal Street was the ladies' waiting room. Here the rich decor became subdued, with delicate colors and designs. A neighboring ladies' lunchroom served light refreshments. To allow gentlewomen unhurried access to the trains, a secluded second staircase connected to the tracks.

The depot's third floor contained the kitchen, supply rooms, and offices. A private elevator connected the kitchen to dining areas below, but the depot had no elevators for public use. An attic in the mansard housed the elevator machinery, a reserve water tank, and storage. The design originally called for electric lighting, but a last-minute decision to illuminate with gas resulted from the owner's belief that the infant science of electrification was not yet sufficient. They feared commitment to an unworkable or uneconomical system.[25] This was the correct conclusion, as the direct-current system originally planned quickly proved obsolete.

Outside on Canal Street, loading docks ran the length of baggage buildings to the north and south. Both had hydraulic elevators to lower baggage, mail, and express to track level. An

The expansive waiting room is shown here after its remodeling by D. H. Burnham & Company.

outside staircase reached top-floor offices of the north building. The comparable floor of the south building held the emigrant rooms. Union Depot was never Chicago's largest transfer point for emigrants. This was a low-profit business with specialized needs that the Pennsylvania somewhat disdained. For example, telegraph messages had to precede each train stating the name and origin of each immigrant. Each nationality had its own protective society, which the railroad had to summon for proper interpreters.[26] Surprisingly, before their new Chicago terminal debuted, the Pennsylvania started a rate war for emigrant business.[27] The facilities, however, likely were dictated by the depot's other tenants. Western railroads viewed emigrants less as a meager, one-time source of passenger revenue than as future farmers who would soon fill freight cars with the bounty of their industry. In particular, this period saw the settlement of Minnesota and the Dakotas, where the Milwaukee Road was a dominant carrier. Because of the extended transit time of their journeys from Europe, emigrants needed spacious washrooms for themselves and their clothes. Limited English-language skills and an overly rosy view of America also made them easy marks for the hucksters and con men common to Chicago. They were therefore segregated from the other patrons for their own protection. Despite precautions, the West Side depot became notorious as a center for sharpsters.

Union Depot's architect of record was Felician Slataper, chief engineer of the Pennsylvania Company.[28] The Trieste-born Slataper had been a Ft. Wayne employee since its beginning, but he gained his reputation with their 1867 Allegheny River bridge. The Chicago depot was a crowning achievement in a career that lasted until 1889.[29] Construction details and design of the train shed and tracks were the work of the Ft. Wayne's operating department under the direction of Robert Trimble, assistant engineer. Both Slataper and Trimble worked in Pittsburgh. Equally important was a young assistant chief engineer, Thomas Rodd. His career intertwined with the Chicago station for four decades, although today he is best known as the architect of the Romanesque Revival–style Union Station in Indianapolis, completed in 1888. Rodd was intimately involved with the site, construction details, and negotiations with tenants. In keeping with Pennsylvania's militaristic management structure, however, the young engineer probably had little autonomy. A rigid chain of command required approval of even minor details, although much of the depot's design and that of the surrounding yards sprang from Rodd's fertile mind.[30] In later years, he claimed that he had been the station's primary architect and this assertion has merit, in part because of a unique arrangement with the railroad, which allowed him an outside architectural practice.

OPEN FOR BUSINESS

Union Depot opened for business on April 4, 1881. The first departure was the 5:55 a.m. stockyards accommodation, and the first inbound was a 7:10 a.m. express, both on the Panhandle. The *Tribune* pontificated:

> For the last twenty years the depot at Madison and Canal streets had been a disgrace to the city—a disgraceful, shambling, broken-down shanty. The railroads appear to have recognized that fact, and to be willing to make amends for the long period of shabbiness by blossoming out now into the extreme of respectability. The new depot is so admirable a building and such an ornament to the locality that citizens will probably pardon the roads on this account for the long years of shabbiness and discomfort.[31]

Newspapers inquired about the cost, but railroad officials simply stated, "There is the depot, ask no more questions." Lacking hard data, the *Tribune* estimated its cost at $800,000. It was a very good guess at out-of-pocket cost, but the depot's total value was higher. Rental agreements dated June 6, 1882, listed the total cost at $1,057,877. This included land but excluded the costs of freight facilities such as the Outer Yard, the Ft. Wayne freight houses, and relocation of the freight tracks near the depot. Initially each tenant paid annual fees of $14,810 for the depot regardless of the volume of their traffic. This quickly devolved to a wheelage charge that spread the actual cost of running the depot over each line's proportionate use.

The Burlington's use of the station began a month after the others, as it awaited the expiration of its Illinois Central lease. The depot became the Burlington's eastern endpoint almost simultaneously with the completion to its westward terminus, a line to Denver that opened for service on June 1, 1882. In Chicago, it required an ordinance allowing a new connecting track. Initially the city stipulated new viaducts at Polk and Twelfth Streets, but when the final ordinance reached the council floor, it required only Polk Street. When various council members questioned the change, two South Side aldermen leapt to the floor shouting their strong support for the bill as written. "That's because you both got $4500," came a quick retort. The chamber echoed with laughter before the bill quickly passed. The Burlington also played hardball with its acceptance of the depot contract, making it conditional upon amendments. It demanded a rotating system of joint agents to run operations and an arbitration system for resolution of disputes. The Ft. Wayne conceded both issues, although not immediately, and its managers controlled all aspects of the depot until October 1882, when a board of management representing all parties took control. In truth, little changed as the Ft. Wayne depot manager, Charles Case, relinquished control to his assistant, Mr. Cropsy.[32]

As operations began, problems became apparent. The biggest issue was the confusing track configuration. Near the riverside freight house, two freight car storage tracks and the main tracks ran through the site. The first passenger track under the shed was incoming passenger track 2. Tracks 1, 3, and 5 also ran through the shed. To the west came a series of stub tracks, which were identically numbered on the north and south sides. Tracks 7 and 9 ran underneath the shed, but 11 and 13 were not covered and

stub ended near the baggage rooms. The asymmetrical layout combined with an illogical track numbering system confused passengers. A more serious issue resulted from the fact that all inbound trains headed into the station and then backed out to their respective coach yards. The station operated as if it were two stub-end terminals even though most tracks did not, in fact, stub end. No bumping posts blocked a train from running past its intended stopping point. More than one dashing commuter was himself dashed on the pilot of an inbound train that overshot the centerline. That imaginary line ran through the middle of the depot's most crowded aisle, a boardwalk that connected the waiting rooms to the various loading platforms.

The depot's other flaw resulted from its narrow site. Baggage and mail wagons loading at the docks along Canal Street blockaded the sidewalks flanking the main entrance.[33] They disrupted pedestrian and street traffic in both directions. The veranda that connected the buildings thus had negligible value, as passengers used the muddy street to get around the congestion. Hapless passengers determined to forego this madness at the baggage buildings soon discovered that it was necessary to lug unchecked bags upstairs to the ticket and waiting areas, only to descend with their load to their train. Neither the track level nor the waiting room had public access other than the main stairway.

Nervous travelers were aggravated by the depot's location across the Chicago River from the business district and by the swing bridges that frequently opened for boats to pass. A study by the Burlington revealed that cab drivers allowed an extra ten minutes for trips to the station. The patterns of streetcar lines reinforced this isolation. While several lines ran past the depot to downtown, none went near Chicago's other railroad stations.

Liveryman Frank Parmelee became wealthy after he established an omnibus line to shuttle passengers between stations. A railway promotional booklet captured the scene near the depot in 1893:

> A jumble of vehicles, a murmur of many sounds swelling to a roar, an all-pervading odor of bituminous smoke, a street corner with an iron canopy high above your head across the sidewalk and a row of picturesque buildings opposite. Some-one reaches forward for the red ticket with its little punched holes that you have in your hand; a voice says: "This way, sir!" The open door of an omnibus appears before you, and you find that you have taken the only vacant seat inside, the door is closed with a slam, that the horses, answering promptly to the snapping of the driver's long black whip, have wheeled sharply to the left, and that your conveyance is picking its way through the riot of wagons, carts, trucks, cabs and street cars. Away you go over a narrow bridge that is swung across an almost equally narrow stream, and a man on your right tells you that you are crossing the Chicago River, which divides the city into its several sections, and which constitutes an essential part of the city harbor. Then you plunge into a canon between huge mountains of stone—a succession of streets overshadowed by mammoth buildings.[4]

A somewhat later and less partisan reviewer saw the scene this way:

The Union Railroad Station, on the banks of the river between Monroe and Adams, was provincial in its proportions, a narrow building of pressed brick with a mansard roof and curious corner dormers, with much yellow tiling on the inside walls and the pungent smell of disinfectant in its rooms. Below, on the riverbank, ran the tracks of the Milwaukee, the Burlington, the Alton, and the Pennsylvania, pouring their thousands into this congested square. On the cobbled streets outside, back against the porch and allowing hardly any room for pedestrians, stood dozens of buses and express wagons. Across Adams Street were the railroad quarters for immigrants and there was Fred Buehler, an energetic, little man in blue uniform and cap, who had charge of the arriving immigrants. There I used to see Poles and Lithuanians arrive with their outlandish togs, bundles and children; there Fred would talk to me about his boy and his poems. For both were his hobbies.[35]

The Ft. Wayne and the Panhandle both had trains to accommodate local traffic, but competition for this business intensified in 1882 when the South Side cable car lines tripled the speed and increased the comfort on previously horse-drawn routes. Chicago soon had the nation's largest cable-car network. This bled short-haul traffic away from the railroads and had a profound impact on regional development.[36] Despite street railway inroads, however, passenger traffic continued to grow faster than the local population. That was quite a feat. In the decade before the depot was built, Chicago's population increased by two-thirds to five hundred thousand. In the next decade, it doubled again.

Population may have grown at a steadily pace, but economic progress was fitful and troublesome times arrived suddenly. In 1883, the Ft. Wayne and the Panhandle were hard hit by a rate war, and their combined net income plunged 55 percent from the prior year. The following year a business depression dampened traffic despite the lower rates. These events combined to saddle the two railroads with an $800,000 loss. Traffic systemwide fell and the Pennsylvania's President Roberts cut all capital expenditures.[37]

Even as business suffered, a notable event occurred at the depot on November 18, 1883. In truth, the same event occurred that day in most US depots. It was the implementation of standard time. At the noon hour Chicago (solar) time, the superintendents, dispatchers, and telegraph operators from each road solemnly gathered. Depot clocks and each individual's pocket watch stopped. Nine minutes and thirty-two seconds later, the telegraph from the Allegheny Observatory sounded the new time. Ft. Wayne trainmen actually reset their watches by twenty-eight minutes, since they had previously kept Columbus time. Trainmen on the road also reset their timepieces to the new noon, while off-duty staff relied on Depot Master Cropsy's chronometer as they reported to work.[38]

Complaints about the depot's inadequacy soon became commonplace. At peak hours, it could barely cope with its traffic. The *Tribune* captured a busy scene in an article entitled only "Local Miscellany":

> It was 2 o'clock in the afternoon and there was a perfect crush and jam at the Union Depot. People of every class thronged the

halls and waiting-rooms. Sealskin and silk worn by the fine lady dusted the humble plaid of the emigrant, and the silk topper of the city "swell" towered over the slouch hat of the countryman. The cold marble clock looked down on a multitude of faces swayed by varying emotions, as the great moving mass pressed its way up the brass-mounted marble stair that leads to the heart of the city. Two strong stern-visaged policemen with clubs in hand stood on either side of the wide-open door as they pressed out into the falling snow. "What does all this mean? Is there any cause for this extra rush today," a reporter asked one of the policemen. "O no, it is only an average day, but this is the hour the Eastern trains get in."

The account that followed narrated the policeman's experience in the ruses used to accost, dupe, and rob newcomers.[39] Said the policeman, "You speak of the country people. Well, if they have any money they soon get robbed of it." If they weren't accosted in the depot, they were often lured to gin joints and brothels west of the depot where the task could better be accomplished. This telling seems in sync with the popular myth of rural maidens lured by promises of employment and being drugged and sold into the flourishing "white slave market" within hours of leaving their train. More common were complaints such as that of the following year, when the paper depicted the depot as "A Foreign Invasion." The article resembled an account from the following June, when the complaint of a "well-known citizen" aired. He accompanied a lady of quality to her Milwaukee-bound train, only to discover their way blocked by a crowd of five hundred "garlic-soaked foreigners." Depot master Cropsy issued an official apology, stating that the depot handled 1600 emigrants that day and a breakdown on the cars caused delays. "Of course it is not right to make the first-class passengers mix with the emigrants," said Cropsy.[40]

Most pedestrians exiting the depot turned north on Canal Street toward the Madison Street bridge. This was about to change as Adams Street began to vie for sidewalk traffic into downtown. In 1881 the Board of Trade moved from LaSalle and Washington Streets south to Jackson and LaSalle. Their new site had been vacant since the Great Fire of 1871 and construction stimulated surrounding land to increase in price from $200 to $1,500 or even $2,000 per front footage. The best office buildings in the city, with a total value of $7 million, were then erected in this quarter. Notable among these was architect William Le-Baron Jenney's Home Insurance Company building at Adams and LaSalle, considered by many to be the world's first steel-skeleton skyscraper.[41] The superior elevator buildings erected in the southern business district attracted the best tenants, and the density of their development materially increased downtown street traffic.

Recovery of the real estate market came equally from an improved national economy and continued in-migration to Chicago. Buildings now reached skyward into the relatively fresh breezes above the city, an immeasurable benefit during the city's hot summers. The skyward building impetus was itself partially the result of railroad land use. In their headlong expansion, the railroads had thrown a corridor of steel completely around the business district. Outlying factories once had their offices on-site, but their executives and salesmen could no longer easily trek into the commercial district. Needing to interact with clients and suppliers, they found difficulty even getting timely telegraph messages at their outlying quarters. Downtown offices became a necessity. Since rail yards limited sprawl, the direction of least resistance for commercial growth was straight up.[42] In 1884, the city had only five buildings nine stories in height, but by 1893 it boasted more than twenty-five buildings over twelve stories. The development of steel-framed skyscrapers proved, however, to be self-limiting, as a Chicago historian noted: "Although twenty-five or thirty buildings from twelve to sixteen stories in height, if bunched together would not have occupied three solid blocks, or seven percent of the main business district, all land in the area was revalued on the basis of what it would produce if occupied by a sixteen-story building."[43] Land prices became so inflated that later buildings never matched the investment returns of the boom's first skyscrapers. Moreover, this initial wave of skyscrapers produced excess office space. Occupancy rates plunged and vacancies plagued the central area for a decade.

Skyscrapers became possible, in part, because cheap mass transport linked central and outlying areas. Land values at both ends of the transit lines increased. The rise in residential neighborhoods took two forms. First, the city witnessed a form of development known as the "flat craze."[44] Rising prices of more distant lots together with cheap, convenient transport increased population density. Renters were happy to have apartments with steam heat, indoor plumbing, and janitor service, while landlords found that a diverse stream of rental payments could better support their mortgage. Second, affluent Chicagoans who could afford more space accelerated the exodus to the suburbs, a process never to abate. The flat craze, suburbanization, and centralization of business downtown combined to push more commuters through Chicago depots.

Heavy commuter traffic was just beginning to develop on the Burlington and the Milwaukee Road. The Milwaukee Road's growth came with the purchase of the Chicago and Pacific Railroad in 1880. This line became the heavily used route known as its "West Line." Extended to Omaha, it also formed a major intercity passenger route. Dedicated commuter service began simultaneously on the Milwaukee's North and West Lines in 1883, with two trains on the latter to Elgin and one on the former to Libertyville. Growth on the West line was immediate, as a train was added to Itasca. An additional two trains then ran to Dunning via a short branch north from Galewood. Yet another train was added, originally going only to Pacific Junction, but gradually extending to Hermosa and later to Cragin. In 1893, three trains went to Elgin, and one each ran to Cragin, Dunning, and Bensenville.

The last line to enter Union Depot was the Chicago & Evanston (the "Evanston"), coinciding with the Milwaukee Road's push into commuter service. Chartered in 1882 as an affiliate of the North Chicago Street Railway, the Evanston quickly fell into the hands of several Milwaukee Road directors. Some historians speculate that the Milwaukee Road wanted a line to parallel its rival, the North Western (North line), along the lake shore, or that its directors wanted to stimulate development of their private real estate holdings on Chicago's North Side. Both were true, but the major reason seems to have been a defensive desire to keep the fledgling line from falling into the hands of a hostile competitor intent on pushing north to the Milwaukee Road's namesake city. The Evanston line left the north side of Union Depot on an improbably awkward alignment. Immediately north of the depot, it crossed the lead tracks for the North Western's Wells Street Depot, then the city's busiest. North Western trains often blocked the crossing as they waited for their swing bridge to close. Their trains had the right of way, so the twenty-eight daily outbound Evanston line trains waited. Once under way, Evanston trains immediately had to contend with their own North Branch swing bridge. Delays seriously impaired operations from the beginning. After various timetable revisions, the majority of Evanston trains actually originated and terminated north of the river at Chicago Avenue with patrons completing their journey by streetcar. The Evanston legally became part of the Milwaukee Road in 1887, although it operated as part of that company for several years prior.

Further south, the Chicago and Western Indiana took six laborious years to push its line northward before it reached its ultimate terminal, the Polk Street Depot (later known as Dearborn Station) in 1885. This was a redbrick Flemish confection by New York architect Cyrus Eidlitz with an imposing clock tower and a multihued slate roof with elaborate dormers. Positioned at the foot of Dearborn Street, now widened and extended to the depot site, its appearance was magnificent, even if the wooden train shed behind the grand facade was an anachronistic carpenter's nightmare. The project shifted the business district further southward, as efficient new office towers lined the new street. This area became "Printers' Row" for the trade that congregated in the area.

COMINGS AND GOINGS

Competition from the five Dearborn Station railroads failed to diminish Union Depot's traffic. Suburban service was the growth market, but intercity travel also prospered. For this business, the number of trains paradoxically grew faster than

The Chicago & Pacific attempted to find its own route into downtown, but after its acquisition by the Milwaukee Road its traffic moved to Union Depot.

MAP OF CHICAGO,
Showing location of the Principal Hotels, Theatres, &c.

The Passenger Depot of the Chicago and Pacific R. R. is corner Chicago Avenue and Larrabee Street.

The Freight Depot is corner North Halsted and North Branch Streets.

General Offices, is Clark Street, next to the Sherman House.

the number of passengers despite a shift toward longer trains pulled by increasingly powerful locomotives. The cause was a proliferation of Pullman sleeping cars, dining cars, and other specialized but low-capacity rolling stock. Chicago Union Depot had been a pioneer in handling these cars, particularly on the Alton. George Pullman operated his first sleeping car over that line in 1858, a remodeled coach for the overnight train to Saint Louis. It had not been the first sleeping car in America, or even into Chicago, but Pullman's finely appointed accommodations and excellent service greatly increased overnight patronage. In 1865, he constructed his first purpose-built sleeper, the Pioneer, also for the Alton. It was so luxurious that its cost was four times that of a typical coach.[45]

Sleeping cars catered to an increasingly affluent population, especially to a legion of traveling salesmen. These "drummers" cemented Chicago's reputation as the heart of the nation's wholesale trade. One dry-goods house alone had two thousand salesmen, each with a large sample trunk, on the road at any given time. Pullman followed the success of his sleeping cars with another innovation in 1868. The Delmonico was the world's first full-fledged dining car, again for the Alton. This car and two sisters were the first to provide a full range of meals cooked on-board for travelers who rode other cars of the train. Dining cars were popular from the start because they eliminated hectic meal stops, but their acceptance required another innovation. This invention, by H. H. Sessions of the Pullman Company, was the passenger-car vestibule. In principle, a vestibule was simply an enclosed walkway that linked cars in order to provide passengers with a safe, all-weather walkway throughout the train. In fact, this obvious expedient that the *Chicago Tribune* called "the latest

triumph in catering to the traveling public"[46] required that all the cars in a train be compatible, each with spring-loaded buffer plates to seal the gap between the cars. Related improvements included stronger construction techniques to mitigate the danger of telescoping cars in the event of a collision, and the rearrangement of stairways and end doors. Older cars could not easily be retrofitted, so the railroads built complete trains of similar cars. The expense of equipping entire trains meant that, at least initially, the railroads reserved this innovation for their best expresses. Bringing complete train sets online at one time posed no problem, for strong demand required steady capacity increases. Open-platform cars, however, remained the rule for mundane local runs.

Sleeping cars caused unique terminal problems. Not only did a Pullman carry far fewer travelers per car than a coach, but night trains increasingly carried dining cars, smoking lounges, and libraries. Each increased the number of cars per train while further diminishing their passenger count. These cars, moreover, required customized switching and servicing. Pullman cars had special cleaning tracks, while dining cars needed to be stocked at their commissaries. While such activities were usually done in yards outside the station, they exponentially increased the complexity of depot switching.

New limited-stop, deluxe trains christened with memorable names featured these opulent specialized cars. To fill them, the railroads developed sophisticated promotional and advertising copy, never lacking hyperbole. The Chicago debut of the vestibuled train came on June 15, 1887, with an inaugural run on the Pennsylvania Railroad's all-Pullman, extra-fare Pennsylvania Limited. This train carried three sleepers and an observation car. It also boasted a full diner, plus a library/smoking car for gentlemen, which included space for an onboard barber. Total capacity was only ninety patrons.

Another specialized car, the Railway Post Office, was also the catalyst for a major increase in depot activity. Most passenger trains handled mail and express. Commuter runs, for example, were the primary means for the distribution of newspapers printed downtown to their outlying audience. An increasingly literate population, falling postal rates, the introduction of rural free delivery, and a general improvement in the quality of postal services caused mail volume to soar. The catalog business, with Chicago as its center, became a major factor in the growth of express and mail traffic. Aaron Montgomery Ward started a mail-order business in 1872 with support from the national Grange movement. By the 1880s, his company became the nation's largest retailer. Catalogue sales at the competitor founded by Richard Sears and Alvah Roebuck were $745,000 in 1895. Four years later Chicago's Sears, Roebuck and Company sold a staggering $10,637,000 in merchandise. The mail and express cars handled through Union Station grew in direct proportion to these retailers' sales.

One of the Union Depot's most famous trains carried no passengers, only mail. The growth in the US post had been astounding, even for this expansive period. When the Ft. Wayne began in 1853, the average person received three letters annually. By 1884 the average was sixty.[47] The best known of these mail trains was Burlington Train 29, the Fast Mail, which first departed the train shed at 3 a.m. on the raw morning of March 11, 1884, for a direct run to Omaha. It was a three-car train carded to beat the time of the best passenger train on that route by nearly four hours. Each Railway Post Office car, or "RPO," was resplendent with white-varnished decor and gold trim, earning the train the nickname of the "White Mail."[48] In later years, it often ran in two sections with up to 25 cars. During the night, the on-board mail clerks sorted their loads into 72 separations for western states, 36 for Missouri, 108 for Nebraska, 204 for Iowa, and even 96 separate zones for the city of Omaha.[49]

Mail traffic peaked during the commuter rush hour as letters picked up during the day made it to the station by early evening. The sorting process used on the Fast Mail duplicated that of many trains, which allowed next-day mail delivery to a substantial portion of the Midwest. Small wonder then that sheet music for a popular rag, "The Fast Mail," sold nationally, or that the train was featured in a booklet entitled, "How the Greyhounds of the Burlington Beat the Rising Sun."[50] The Fast Mail's competitors were RPO runs to Omaha on the North Western, which in 1895 had an average speed of slightly more than forty-three miles an hour, and the Rock Island, whose cars averaged slightly less than forty-three miles per hour. The Burlington train averaged a blistering forty-nine miles per hour to Galesburg despite spending fifteen minutes just to get the three miles from Union Station to Western Avenue. It clipped along at forty-seven miles per hour from Galesburg to Burlington and forty-three miles per hour thereafter.[51] The Burlington mail train may have been noteworthy for speed, but the trains of the Pennsylvania carried the volume. It was, indeed, a fleet of trains, for the tonnage was so heavy that one consist was insufficient from an early date. Although it never sported a name, one of these trains was a true standout. Train 95 from Pittsburgh was one of three sections of Train 99 from New York. Like the Fast Mail, it was a mail and express train, but it

carried so many express packages that many people called it the Railway Express.[52] In fact, the entire mail service for the Midwest depended on the Pennsylvania and the other lines into Union Depot. The station handled half the mail in and out of the city, as well as a proportionate share of mail to connecting trains.

Improvements in passenger cars affected the depot's design and its attendant servicing facilities. For example, the Ft. Wayne improved its coach yard south of the depot in 1890 with continuous planking over nearly its entire surface. This allowed for the easy distribution of parts and supplies. The storage batteries used on electrically lighted trains were recharged in a new brick building. Steam pipes heated standing cars in winter, a real necessity once on-train lavatories and dining cars with water tanks became standard.[53]

Expansion of the railroad network in the early 1880s had been especially beneficial to Chicago. Local industries such as rolling mills, freight car shops, and boiler factories prospered. Meat packers expanded their plants near the stockyards. However, excessive growth begat a stinging business downturn in the spring of 1886 that proved especially painful for the growing ranks of manufacturing workers. Between 1873 and 1884 the number of Chicago industrial workers doubled. As commerce turned sour, employers let workers go, cut wages, or simply failed. Unskilled workers flocked to the Knights of Labor, whose national membership grew from 104,000 in July 1885 to 703,000 a year later. A volatile brew fermented in the streets of Chicago.

The area immediately southwest of Union Depot and its maze of approaching tracks again became the site of violence.

On May 1, 1886, a call arose for McCormick reaper plant workers to strike in support of a radical notion: an eight-hour workday. The idea that workers could walk away from their jobs en masse was itself controversial. Organized labor movements were of untested legality, and the local judiciary openly supported management. Vocal demonstrations erupted within blocks of the Ft. Wayne and Burlington yards. Police sent to suppress the crowds opened fire on strikers and bystanders alike. One week later, labor organizers called for a demonstration by their followers at the Haymarket, a relatively wide and open stretch of Randolph Street adjacent to the Milwaukee Road and Panhandle approach to the Union Depot. Fiery oratory attracted a crowd watched over by a nervous line of policemen. A bomb hurled at the officers killed several, provoking their fellows to reply with a hail of lead that killed four spectators and wounded nearly two hundred. No terrorists were found, but police arrested rally organizers and several were to hang for inciting the violence.

Two years later, in February 1888, labor strife came to the Burlington. Even fellow railroad executives felt the Burlington managers deserved the strike due to their intransigence in labor matters. This feeling intensified in May when a secondary boycott against other lines erupted. The railroads quashed the affair, in part because of an unprecedented legal ruling that resulted in the arrest of nine strikers for contempt of court. Several railroads they picketed were then under court-supervised receivership, and the presiding judge ruled that the strikers were "disrespectful of that federal protection."[54]

The problems of 1886 and 1888, however painful, were of short duration. Manufacturing employment in the city soon rose, and by 1890 it redoubled from its previous peak. That year saw the erection of yet another railroad terminal. Grand Central Depot brought the city total to six. It was the work of the Northern Pacific Railroad, which never came within three hundred miles of Chicago. It did, however, lease the Wisconsin Central, which it pushed southward. Bankruptcy of the parent, however, voided the Wisconsin Central lease and that of the Chicago and Northern Pacific ("C&NP"), a terminal company established to build the station. Grand Central's Norman-style architecture was arguably the best of any depot built in the city. It was the work of Solon S. Beman, an architect of Pullman, Illinois, whose designs also graced many of the rail cars produced there. The Baltimore and Ohio, an unwelcome tenant on the lakefront, and the Chicago Great Western joined the Wisconsin Central (later the "Soo Line") in use of the depot. The C&NP inaugurated an ambitious suburban service, but the station still saw the fewest

trains of any Chicago terminal. That was scant comfort to Union Depot trainmen, for the approach into Grand Central crossed the Alton, Burlington, and Ft. Wayne tracks at grade south of their station.

To facilitate the throngs flooding Union Depot, a new service began in January 1890. Announced in a *Tribune* article entitled, "PEOPLE WHO MAKE THEMSELVES RIDICULOUS WITHOUT KNOWING IT," it elaborated on the new services as, "a Bureau of Information established by the companies for the purpose of telling passengers what they ought to know, but don't."[55] It was only the third information desk in an American depot, modeled after those in New York and Philadelphia. Attendants George McAnky and F. A. Bloomfield sported handlebar mustaches, celluloid collars, and heavy button-at-the-neck suits. While undoubtedly helpful to travelers, they had no qualms about publicly disparaging the sillier questions they received. A common problem involved someone who received a telegram to pick up a relative at the station, but the message failed to state which railroad or depot.

While western lines saw substantial suburban traffic growth, the pillar of the Union Depot's business remained intercity traffic. Here the Pennsylvania Railroad, which operated both the Panhandle and the Ft. Wayne as its "Lines West," was preeminent. In 1891, the Pennsylvania Railroad had 111,000 workers, more than the 95,440 employees of the US Post Office. By 1893 the capitalization of the Pennsylvania Railroad alone was $840 million, only $155 million less than the entire national debt. Chicago's Union Depot was the primary western portal for that system.

WORLD'S FAIR

As the economy rebounded, labor tensions subsided. Chicago celebrated its pick as the host of a mammoth celebration planned for the four-hundredth anniversary of the European discovery of the Americas. The World's Columbian Exposition became a reality, but was a year late due to site selection difficulties. The flood of passengers the Exposition promised impelled local railroads to invest heavily in downtown improvements. The largest expenditure came on the lakefront, where the Illinois Central built Central Station to replace the burnt shell of its original terminal. Its new depot at Eleventh Place and Michigan Avenue was the farthest from the city's heart, an inconvenience tolerable only because the suburban trains continued north to the old terminal. The Exposition itself was built adjacent to the IC tracks in Hyde Park, and the IC's dedicated suburban line from Randolph Street received major enhancements.

Union Depot certainly needed improvement. Only ten years old, it strained to accommodate its existing business. Host to 87 daily trains when built, it now saw 227.[56] Preparations for the Exposition began in January 1891, when the Ft. Wayne rebuilt all approach tracks and signals. To allow trains to run in both directions on all tracks, it installed custom-built interlocking plants on the north and south sides of the depot.[57] An outmoded plant on the south side had been in operation since 1886.[58] This $40,000 improvement greatly expanded capacity without the need for additional real estate. Interlockers are a combination of electrical circuits and mechanical controls that centralize and coordinate signal mechanisms and track switches. Their primary purpose was to provide a fail-safe against collisions. Albro Martin summarized this revolutionary technology: "Because the 'safe' position of a given switch is frequently determined by the particular position of some other switch or switches in the system, . . . the problem was not as simple as it might seem. It was in fact extremely complex. These men, in their ingenious application of primitive scientific knowledge to an unpredictable problem, were the true pioneers of the age of automation."[59]

Union Depot's interlocking plant accommodated a variety of train movements simultaneously, while prohibiting others. It increased station capacity and eliminated a small army of switch tenders and signal passers.

To provide the depot with more land, the Pennsylvania petitioned the US War Department for permission to fill in the river to any extent that did not impede navigation. It is unclear what gain it intended, since freight houses still lined the river. The government denied the application in August, but it is known that it reached President Benjamin Harrison's office for review.[60]

The year 1891 also saw an interesting, if short-lived, improvement to the Panhandle route into Union Depot. Construction of a brick passenger station at Madison and Rockwell Streets served through and suburban trains.[61] On the same east-west street as Union Depot, but three miles from the business district, it underscored the circuitous and time-consuming entry of that line into the city. It remained open as a stop for the line's three express trains until May 1, 1893, and for other intercity trains until July 9, 1893. A better solution was found when the Pennsylvania constructed the South Chicago and Southern, also known as the Bernice Cutoff, a connecting route that allowed Panhandle trains to switch to the Pennsylvania's Ft. Wayne line on the southeast side of Chicago.[62] This allowed Panhandle trains to enter the Union Depot directly from the south, greatly reducing their running time and, as a side benefit, allowing them to stop at Englewood, only three miles from the world's fair. This cure had its own problem, however; it created a traffic imbalance at the depot, with the majority of trains now entering the terminal from the south. Only Milwaukee Road trains and a few Panhandle stockyards commuter trains remained on the northern tracks. At the Exposition's end, many Panhandle trains switched back to their original circuitous route.

The Ft. Wayne continued to own the depot, but all of the roads met monthly for managers' meetings. Stiffly formal, meeting minutes nevertheless show the difficulty everyone had containing their glee over the Exposition's anticipated traffic influx. At the same time, they were anxious about their ability to handle the surge and were unanimously cautious about spending for a temporary event. The tenants were especially conservative, while the owner paradoxically presented a radical and expensive new plan. Developed by Thomas Rodd, the plan dated to January 1891. It increased the passenger waiting room by 241 percent, the area for the freight houses by 278 percent, and the available track space by 35 percent. Rodd's plan extended the depot to Van Buren Street, without added width. He believed the same elevator technology that created Chicago's skyscrapers could provide the needed space by allowing development above the yards. In particular, it allowed multistory freight houses. Street-level freight loading docks would eliminate existing ramps, and he proposed that the space thus conserved be reallocated to the passenger terminal. Rodd noted that any passenger facilities needed at least a four-story building, but that a ten-story block would cost only slightly more. Why not build a tall office tower, he asked, and rent the space? Rodd estimated that the total expense, including the required changes to viaducts and street grades, would not exceed $2.7 million.

Station managers vetoed Rodd's proposal and other major changes. They decided that coordinating their schedules could allow better use of the depot's scarce capacity. To expand space for baggage, they moved the emigrant room to the Ft. Wayne's Adams Street freight house. They disagreed only over the necessity to build temporary commuter stations at Lake and Van Buren Streets, a debate that occupied most of their attention. While everyone understood the need to create capacity for intercity trains under the shed, the only engineering work done was for commuter platforms outside the depot, and even that was deferred. Suburban ticket sales moved to the nearby freight houses. Managers stated that if needed, further additions could be built in two weeks. Delay proved a sound policy, as the depot ably handled the increased traffic.

There were cosmetic improvements, the most noteworthy being the remodeling of the main waiting room. The ticket office, formerly at both its east and south borders, relocated along the east wall. Existing offices became ticketing areas, which added ten feet to the length of the waiting room, provided 200 new seats, and increased the number of ticket counters. Access to the ladies' waiting area also improved, due to the relocation of offices to the baggage buildings. The new ticket counters replicated their predecessors in somewhat cheaper materials, a substitution that prompted Rodd to complain to Daniel Burnham, architect for the remodeling. There was no written reply. Presumably Burnham was too busy, as he was also chief of construction for the World's Columbian Exposition.

Baggage handling received great attention, with both baggage buildings receiving additions along Canal Street. The south building grew to 245 feet in length and the north building was now nearly 275 feet long. At twenty-five feet wide and four stories high, they were designed to hold twenty-five thousand pieces of baggage, any one of which could be retrieved within three minutes from the presentation of a claim check. Even that space was insufficient. Baggage unclaimed after thirty-six hours went to a rented five-story warehouse on South Canal Street that had a capacity of forty-five thousand pieces.[63]

Replacement of the entire steam heating system required moving the boilers to a separate plant at Madison and Canal.[64] Care was taken to match its brick exterior with the depot. Inside, its boiler capacity was sufficient to heat the enlarged buildings and to supply steam lines to several, but not all, of the depot's tracks. These brought heat for sleepers and other set-out cars while they stood in the depot. A separate boiler supplied power

The terminal at the World's Columbian Exposition to the design of Charles Atwood, Daniel Burnham's partner, provided the Beaux-Arts template for railroad terminals large and small, including competing but unbuilt designs for Chicago Union Station.

COURTESY OF THE CHICAGO PUBLIC LIBRARY, HAROLD WASHINGTON LIBRARY SPECIAL COLLECTIONS

for twin dynamos providing a current for 45 arc lights in the train shed and 564 incandescent lights in the station. While great effort was taken to get attractive chandeliers for the waiting rooms, nearly everyone agreed that the result was somewhat wanting. Fixtures were only available in current styles and none matched the station's dated decor. The most time-consuming improvement was the replacement of floors, stair treads, and wainscoting worn from a decade of heavy use. Relocation of the boiler room provided ground-floor space for mail and baggage. The total cost of all these changes was $185,000, with nearly one-third related to the baggage facilities. The improvements proved well timed, for the Columbian Exposition had the expected impact. Before the

world's fair, the Union Depot saw a total of 288 arrivals and departures daily.[65] When the Exposition opened in May, the Pennsylvania lines alone brought 2,967 cars into the station, pulled in 498 trains. A record was set in October when all railroads handled 6,524 cars in 809 trains during a single day.

The world's fair reinvigorated the city's efforts to require grade separation after the Illinois Central agreed to raise its tracks adjacent to the fairgrounds. There was a glaring need for grade separation throughout the city, for it was a rare day in Chicago without a crossing fatality. Previously the city occasionally invoked its police powers to force railroads to build viaducts at their own expense, and it now forced the Panhandle to install pneumatic crossing gates at twenty-eight crossings.[66] Sharing expenses with the parallel Western Indiana, every street crossing between Twenty-Second and Forty-Seventh Street was illuminated by arc lights to prevent accidents. The railroads bore the expense of installation and even generated the required electricity.[67]

As opening day neared, many of the Exposition's attractions and visiting dignitaries moved through Union Depot, nearly always met by great throngs. On April 22, the John Bull, an 1831 locomotive, arrived under its own power, having pulled two vintage coaches of varnished olive green from New Jersey.[68] The train was taken to the Pennsylvania Railroad exhibit the following day. The passage of this venerable relic, actually only sixty-two years old, created a stir in every town along the Pennsylvania Railroad.[69] A similar spectacle was created a week later when the Ft. Wayne carried the Liberty Bell from Philadelphia. From the depot, it made its way in military procession to the State of Pennsylvania Building at the fair.[70] The next day, President Grover Cleveland arrived by special train, accompanied from the state line by Governor John Altgeld of Illinois and Mayor Carter Harrison of Chicago.[71] Perhaps the greatest excitement came from the June reception of the Infanta Maria Eulalia, the sister of the queen of Spain, who arrived with her courtiers to a trackside greeting from Mayor Harrison.[72]

Initial fair attendance was low. The nation entered a severe depression and the fair's signature Ferris wheel was not complete and open for business until midyear. The real break came on June 24, when the railroads announced an excursion fare that allowed a round trip for the one-way price. The effect was instantaneous, and the railroads immediately added extra sections to most trains.[73] Initially, the Ft. Wayne and the Panhan-

dle offered the special rate on alternating days to control the crowds. As word of the extravaganza spread, however, the crush intensified and excursion rates became a daily affair. Through August, the Pennsylvania operated nearly all scheduled trains in two sections averaging ten cars. By the first of September, five special trains a day supplemented the regular schedule, and by September 10 there were seven excursions daily, averaging twelve cars each. The Alton put three to four additional coaches on each of its six regular trains. Burlington trains jumped from seven coaches to thirteen or fourteen, with extra trains run as needed. The Milwaukee Road ran trains in seven sections from Saint Paul and three sections from Omaha.[74] By October, Union Depot handled sixty-five thousand people daily. The Burlington handled one thousand coachloads of passengers in a single day.[75]

The Exposition was wildly successful, due in part to its emphasis on technology. In this machine-crazy age, the tools of industrial production attracted great public interest. For example, the German exhibit demonstrated a process for manufacturing chocolate bars. At the end of the fair, this machinery was purchased by a small-time confectioner named Milton Hershey. The grandest triumph of the Exhibition was the illusion of the fairgrounds as a nearly mythical White City. While not a myth, it was certainly ephemeral, since its major construction material was an impermanent mixture of straw and plaster known as staff. Nevertheless, the fair's neoclassical architecture stood in pristine contrast to sooty American towns. Its remarkably clean grounds resulted from its design as a pedestrian-only district devoid of wagon traffic and the attendant horse pollution. Smoke and soot, the banes of urban life, were minimal due to an unprecedented use of electrical power. The buildings' white hue provided a uniform appearance, but the fair's genius was to effectively magnify the power of thousands of electric lights. By operating at peak levels well into the night, the fair was the harbinger of a new era, when wholesome nocturnal activities would replace the sordid and often dangerous nightlife typical of major cities.

Two nascent technologies featured at the fair were to have profound impacts on local transit. The Intramural Railroad provided internal fairgrounds circulation. It was a prototype for the electric street railways soon to become a national mania. Electric power quickly supplanted horse or cable street railways in most American cities. Trolleys had been developed five years before, but the Intramural Railroad proved that heavy-duty trains, not just small streetcars, were economical for mass transit. Also present, but less conspicuous, were two iconic vehicles. Neither was presented in the illustrious Transportation Building, dominated by displays from the railroads and bicycle manufacturers. The American Storage Battery Company showed an electric automobile built by an Iowa inventor the previous year, while the German pavilion presented a gasoline-powered motorcycle created by Gottlieb Daimler. Both were curiosities unappreciated as valuable innovations.

LABOR AND COMPETITIVE STRIFE

Following the world's fair was another year of stagnation and strife. In early July 1894, a strike initiated against the Pullman Company stopped traffic throughout the nation as workers refused to move trains containing sleeping cars. Violence flared, especially in Chicago's South Side rail yards, where looted and burned freight cars littered the landscape. Burlington and Mil-

waukee Road lines sat well away from the seat of turmoil, and neither their suburban nor through trains had many problems. The Alton ran its trains with difficulty. Both Pennsylvania routes ran through the turbulent South Side, although the Panhandle optimistically had six switch engines working its Western Avenue yard. Officials said, "Whether the trains would get out was another question."[76] As before, railroad workers were responsible for little of the riot damage, but the newspapers nevertheless blamed union subversives. Overall, the railroads were to lose far more money from business foregone than from property damage. Newspaper headlines and the situation on the South Side of Chicago suggested otherwise.

Governor Altgeld refused the railroad companies' request for state militia, but President Cleveland sent troops anyway, ostensibly to protect the mails. By presidential order, Union Depot and forty-nine other local stations were placed under federal guard. Rioting and looting at the Panhandle's Fifty-Ninth Street yard was the nation's most severe, with 729 cars burnt and 42 damaged before violence spilled into the neighborhoods.[77] Chicago's elite had a special reason to be thankful for the twelve thousand troops that kept the violence away from downtown. The ravages of Chicago's Great Fire were within memory and residents feared that class warfare would ignite a similar disaster. River bridges again swung open to thwart the mobs and to form a cordon easily patrolled by the blue-uniformed infantry. They succeeded in isolating the mob miles from the city center. Despite widespread solidarity with the union, the result was its utter defeat, the blacklisting of union employees, and the imprisonment of union leaders. For preventing the delivery of mail, union organizers were found guilty of restraining interstate commerce under the

Sherman Antitrust Act, a law intended to restrain their employers' predatory business practices.

GROWING CITY, GROWING TRAFFIC

After the Pullman strike, Union Depot returned to normal, but it struggled because Chicago's population continued to surge—from 505,185 in 1880 to 1.7 million in 1900. As the Midwestern economy matured, rail traffic continued to grow faster than population. Wholesale businesses attracted streams of buyers into the city and sent legions of drummers out onto the prairie. At the same time, the middle class expanded and more Midwesterners could afford vacations or social visits to other cities.

The burgeoning population and immense commercial opportunities continued to draw rail competitors to Chicago. The ability of conventional railroads to penetrate the urban area was at an end, but specialized rapid transit railways such as the South Side elevated line to the Columbian Exposition proliferated. Naturally, the traffic of a single fair could never justify the expense of erecting a double-track railway atop steel columns its entire length. Elevated lines needed to attract multitudes regularly. They could do so because employment became concentrated in massive industrial plants and in the city center simultaneous with the migration of residential neighborhoods farther from the center. Street railways became increasingly inadequate for the longer commutes now required. Elevated lines, like the cable cars before them, diverted traffic from the railroads. Prior to construction of the Union Loop in 1897, each independent elevated line also had its own downtown depot. The depot of the Lake Street "L," for example, was east of the river at Market and Madison Streets, a location most Union Depot commuters passed daily. This line, however, was not a direct competitor of any Union Depot railroad. Likewise, the Metropolitan West Side elevated spanned the depot's south approach in 1896 en route to its Franklin Street terminal. Branches of that railroad were minor competitors to Burlington and Milwaukee commuter services. Direct competition from the "L" came with the erection in 1908 of a branch line to Chicago's stockyards by the South Side Elevated Company. Stockyards' packing plants were major employers and the high-volume, low-cost "L" wreaked havoc on the Panhandle's patronage.[78]

Suburban service was not stagnant, however. By 1905, Milwaukee Road initiated runs to Hanson Park and Mont Clare. North Line traffic warranted the addition of four trains to Morton (now Morton Grove) in 1892 and four more trains in 1895. Service gradually extended to Glenview and Deerfield. In 1900, the Milwaukee added a line to Madison, Wisconsin, and with it a commuter run to Fox Lake. By July of that year, traffic on that route rose to four trains, in what proved to be a seasonal pattern following the development of summer resorts in that area. Four trains to Deerfield were added in 1905 and four more to Libertyville in 1911.[79]

Early in 1901, Evanston Line passenger service to the Union Depot ceased. A Wilson Avenue connection between the Evanston and the Northwestern Elevated Railway Company now allowed passengers to travel directly into the Loop. Because passengers had to pay two fares, this arrangement proved unpopular, and Union Depot service was reinstituted after a few months. In 1907, however, the Northwestern Elevated Railway Company took over direct service to Evanston and the Union Depot connection ceased.

AT THE UNION DEPOT, MADISON AND CANAL STREETS.
Strikers on the Viaduct watching Railway Officials trying to get out Trains.

Although elevated railroad construction was a local bright spot, the depression at the end of the Columbian Exposition lingered. The downturn had a spectacular impact on real estate values in a city too recently overbuilt in the euphoria preceding the Exposition. Office towers failed to rent and real estate values declined 25 percent per annum for several years. One local sage noted, "real estate is now a liability instead of an asset."[80] By 1893, the city council passed the city's first limit on building height under pressure from real estate speculators who wanted the city to expand outward rather than upward. At 130 feet, the new limit kept new buildings under ten stories.

The flat craze rendered the cheap homes built after the Great Fire unfashionable. By the mid-1890s, the West Division had seven thousand vacant middle-class homes. Said Homer Hoyt: "Such was the specific effect of swifter transportation afforded by cable, steam, elevated, and electric lines that [it] enabled people to hurry past the decayed areas built up by the transit lines of the former generation."[81] No area of the city experienced more adversity than immediately west of the Union Depot. With skyscrapers to the east and developing slums to the west, Union Depot sat squarely on the divide. Assessment records show that the decline in property values as one moved westward from the business district along Madison Street was one of the most dramatic drops in the world—if not the most.

Although shifting transport patterns caused some urban areas to miss out on development, it proved a positive force, stimulating changes that were to lead Chicago out of its doldrums. Downtown department stores and theaters were the most visible of these changes. Ladies living at a considerable distance from the area became convinced that the latest fashions and best prices were to be had downtown. Improved street lighting stimulated the theater and music hall businesses. Railroads responded with the addition of midday and evening commuter runs to cater to these new markets. The depot now handled an almost equal number of suburban and long-distance trains.

The intercity markets for which the depot had been built were hardly ignored. In fact, the ultimate in luxury travel may have been achieved in January of 1898, when the Pennsylvania Limited was reequipped. Its Circassian walnut, English oak, vermilion rosewood, and Santiago mahogany–inlaid interiors were embellished with leaded glass, gilt ornamentation, velvet curtains, and even potted palms. The exterior received great public comment. In the early years of railroading, most trains were drab. The new Limited, however, earned the nickname "The Yellow Kid" because of its pleasing decor of Brewster green and yellow cream, accented by a red-letter board, gilt lettering, and abundant gold scrollwork. The Pennsylvania Limited remained the flagship train to the east, always to receive the newest equipment. It was renamed the Broadway Limited in 1912, and it continued as one of America's premier trains for another sixty years.

The Alton also foreswore the mundane colors of the era's passenger trains by dressing its pride, the Alton Limited, in a striking combination of maroon and crimson with gold trim. Most of its online traffic was relatively short haul, as it was the favorite of Chicago politicians and businessmen going to the capitol in Springfield. As a result, its extra fare patrons occupied not sleeping cars, but parlor cars. The train's three parlors each held only forty-one passengers, compared to eighty-four in coaches. Perhaps reflecting the conservative agrarian areas it served, the best

trains of the Burlington, such as the Chicago-Denver Express, were cloaked in somber green. Travel times in the Trans-Mississippi West were substantial and Burlington trains featured the standard accoutrements, such as buffet smoking cars and Pullman sleepers. Burlington dining cars featured Spanish tangerines, mangoes, and oysters—truly exotic to the flatland farmers and storekeepers who populated its trains. The Milwaukee Road meanwhile combined conservative Midwestern service with its own flamboyant style. Pride of its fleet was the Pioneer Limited, which held down the shortest of seven competitive routes vying for traffic to Saint Paul and the northwest. Although it was re-equipped and given its name in 1898, the service actually dated back to 1872, and its orange and maroon livery was that of an earlier period. These colors remained for eighty years. The Milwaukee was relatively unique in that it operated its own sleeping cars, and despite fearsome competition, its traffic was heavy. In 1914, the regular consist of the Pioneer Limited was fourteen sleepers, which required that the train be operated in two sections. Deluxe

parlor car service also ran throughout the day to Milwaukee on a series of swift trains.

Scheduling at the depot was problematic. By 1912, trains left the south side of the station on three-minute headways between 7 a.m. and 8 a.m. Early evening was the ideal departure time for both mail movements and for sleeping car patrons; unfortunately this overlapped the outbound commuter rush and this drained capacity. By 1927, timetables ironically touted this operational disadvantage as a great event, by advertising the "Burlington Hour," which began at 5:30 p.m. when the Denver Limited departed, followed by the Missouri Limited, Nebraska Limited, and Commercial Limited. Morning schedules were actually more difficult to operate. So-called set-out sleepers arrived during the night, but they had to be switched into the depot the next morning. This allowed passengers to slumber almost until business hours. Unfortunately, this practice devoured precious yard-track space, required extra switch engine movements, and congested the depot during the morning commuter rush.

CHAPTER FOUR
A MOST PUBLIC SERVICE

RAISING THE BAR

Staggering traffic growth dictated that Union Depot expand; Chicagoans constantly complained about the situation, since improvements were meager. However, the civic push for a new Chicago depot was but one front in a larger war over increasing societal expectations toward corporations—especially railway corporations. When the railroad network began, towns and cities saw themselves in competition with neighboring locales. Cities courted railways as their allies in this struggle. Soon, however, citizens realized that just having rail service into town was not enough, because the power to set tariffs conveyed the power to discriminate against cities or even whole regions. Due to its many competing lines, Chicago was the beneficiary of this system. Elsewhere, however, rates for like goods between similar distances varied with origin and destination. Railroads charged what each market could bear. Towns without alternatives viewed this as pure malevolence. Laissez-faire attitudes continued to permeate American legal and social thinking, but as labor, business, and civic groups demanded corporate social responsibility, this philosophy eroded.

Rate reform was a battle with major repercussions for the railroads; even though rates in general had declined for decades, most people, especially farmers, regarded freight tariffs as unfair, even ruinous.[1] The Illinois Granger movement successfully lobbied for state rate regulation, a form of government intercession for businesses organized in the public interest upheld by the US Supreme Court in *Munn v. Illinois* in 1877. Nine years later, however, in *Wabash, St. Louis, and Pacific Railway v. Illinois*, the high court reversed its original decision.[2] That verdict, which denied states the power to regulate rates on interstate traffic, pushed the rate issue into the national limelight. The following year the Interstate Commerce Act became law. The Pennsylvania Railroad was among the minority of major railroads that supported this act, which it believed would rein in ruinous competition. Although the Sherman Antitrust Act of 1890 also addressed corporate abuses, rate regulation was weak until passage of the Elkins and Hepburn Acts, in 1903 and 1906 respectively.[3]

Once started, the populist firestorm spread to campaigns against other abuses, real and perceived, of the railway corporations. Freight rates were undoubtedly important to Chicago's grain brokers, millers, and business interests, but urban reformers had a different focus from their agrarian counterparts. As with most politics, battle lines coalesced around local issues and it hardly helped that the railroads seemed allied to the corrupt

Receiving mail at Union Station Chicago.

urban political system. Reform of the graft-ridden city council was the hot issue of the day, and increased political action stemmed in no small part from a desire to dilute the influence of railroad, streetcar, and elevated transit companies.

The newspapers universally called the most rapacious aldermanic group the "Grey Wolves." This faction rose to power after 1890, and it was somewhat more cohesive than its equally graft-seeking predecessors, the "Big Four" and the "Little Four." This debased cabal, which included saloonkeepers and representatives of the city's illicit gambling interests, controlled enough votes to sell out the public interest at almost every turn.

Deep-seated social injustices also needed redress; it seemed to come as a revelation to the town's upper classes that many fellow Chicagoans lived in abject poverty. The inhumanity they mentally consigned to Dickens's East End London was brought closer to home by Upton Sinclair's *The Jungle*. Unfortunately, political grafters proved better placed than the elite to provide the aid, jobs, and relief needed by the poor. Reformers knew that the railroads, however unwilling, were a major funding source for corrupt politicians.

The Progressive movement found no shortage of causes to champion. Temperance, universal suffrage, expanded sanitation, immigrant settlement, and other pressing social issues competed for attention as a new generation of novelists, journalists, and reformers exposed diverse problems. Muckrakers exposed abuses by large corporations and avaricious capitalists. Progressives soon realized, however, that just as rotten politicians could tap into the staggering financial resources of the railroad corporations, they too could harness those funds for the public good.

A CITY BEAUTIFUL

New to this period was a cry to reform the basic urban fabric and physically remake cities through thoughtful urban planning and architecture. Known as the "City Beautiful" movement, its basic tenet was that the environment shaped human dignity. Radical reshaping of cities had its historic base in the imperial dictates of Europe; the American version had a democratic veneer, but was nevertheless a top-down philosophy that saw the newly rich impose their tastes and beliefs on the city at large. In its most advanced form, City Beautiful sought to replicate the Beaux Arts–inspired magnificence of the World's Columbian Exposition of 1893. Unsurprisingly, Chicago was the movement's epicenter.

Adherents of the City Beautiful movement proclaimed that its application was good for business. In part, their platform derived from the improvements emanating from industrial corporations, then the wellspring of new ideas in engineered efficiency. The scientific management of Frederick Taylor illustrated that improvements could be made even to mundane activities. The application of engineering solutions to business problems had proven effective for the improvement of manufacturing, transport, and communications. Progressives reasoned that the same principles could apply to cities.

It came as no surprise that the movement targeted an obvious need for better train stations, because the railroad network and its local depots sat at the centers of commerce. Due to the nation's rapid economic growth, the concentration of heavy industries in cities, and increased urban population density, American depots staggered from undercapacity and overwork. Moreover, reformers saw their owners, not always correctly, as being receptive to their pressures. Depot owners, more than anyone, incurred congestion-related expenses, they too believed in engineering-driven progress, and they had the financial and organizational resources to effect change. There were few better targets for the City Beautiful movement, and there was a reformist's glee in having giant corporations as an adversary.

Aesthetics aside, legitimate social issues arose from the congestion around Chicago's downtown railroads. Traffic obstructions of epic proportions were the norm on city streets and the train tracks. Poor municipal finances hampered governmental ability to solve these problems, while the prevailing laissez-faire philosophy and common-law legal framework allowed little latitude for intervention into private property issues. Chicago's railroad companies contributed more than their share to congestion on the public ways. The challenge was to find civic means to control those private businesses that impinged on the public welfare.

Because the railroads shouldered more congestion costs than anyone, the first actions to address the problem came from within the industry. Each company had built junctions, sidings, and yards as needed, resulting in a maze of overlapping tracks. Attempting to control the chaos, the railroads established the Chicago Switching District, an administrative device to provide uniform rules within a four-hundred-square-mile area. The district was nearly twice the size of the city itself, containing 5,710 miles of track, 160 freight yards, and 76 freight stations. The latter typically consisted of two warehouse buildings—one for inbound and one for outbound freight. The network strained under a daily barrage of slow coal trains, urgent livestock extras, countless manifest freights, commuter trains, and crack overnight limiteds. Transfer runs connected the yards of more than thirty separate companies, while switchers shifted cars to tens of thousands of online industries. By 1891, one junction on Chicago's lakefront documented 381 trains in a single day. Train operations relied on a network of manually thrown switches marked at night by kerosene lamps. The backbone of this system was a legion of wayside telegraphers. These skilled workers passed written orders to conductors and engineers who relayed them to brakemen and switch tenders by hand or whistle signal. The system barely coped. Rail lines intersected so frequently that a train stopped at one crossing often blocked several others, creating true gridlock. Alleviating this congestion presented complex engineering problems involving grade-separated junctions, elevation of tracks over streets, and improved signaling.[4]

As the railroads expanded, their burden became that of the city as a whole. Enlarging their facilities required them to acquire urban real estate; often the city needed to vacate adjoining streets. As the number of through streets diminished, whole neighborhoods became isolated. This problem was particularly acute immediately south of the business district, where the ever-growing commerce that poured from freight houses teemed through fewer and fewer thoroughfares. After 1890, for example, only four streets ran directly south from the business district. Two of the four southbound streets had railroad freight houses flanking both sides, and another carried the tracks of the city's busiest streetcar lines.[5]

Another railroad-created problem was more lethal. As the railroads modernized their equipment, they ran more, longer, and faster trains. To allow for their passage, street crossings closed for increasing periods. Chicagoans saw grade crossings in terms of public safety, while the railroads continued to view them as problems of traffic management and capital allocation. The public worried, "Could my cable car be pulled into the side of a moving freight, or my horses become frightened and unable to be moved aside for a rocketing express train?" Such horrific events happened often. According to an 1891 estimate, four million people crossed three thousand railroad grade crossings within the city daily. More than three hundred people annually never made it to the other side. A local politician bluntly stated, "The city's railroads yearly killed the population of a small village." He could well have added that thousands more were maimed.

Viaduct construction became a lightning-rod political issue. The city mandated viaducts in return for granting a new right of way across public thoroughfares, but it had little power to force their erection on existing lines. In 1873, the city council passed measures requiring companies to build the structures, while the city would indemnify nearby property owners for the cost of raising their building to the new grades or for any lost value. One act listed twenty viaducts to be constructed immediately, but in the next eight years, the slow economy allowed the erection of only five. With an improved business climate and a growing population, Chicago needed to eliminate even more crossings, so the city council started an annual battle to pay for them from its general fund. Critics wailed that the railroads often agreed to pay for such improvements. While aldermen heard the public outcry for immediate improvements, they never made the railroads build anything. They knew that when a railroad paid for viaducts it hired the workers, whereas public works projects yielded a patronage army. So for years, annual city budgets contained a half-dozen such projects to be built at public expense, usually one per ward. In nearly all cases, city funds proved insufficient to actually do any work.[6]

There was another economic dimension pushing viaduct construction and track elevation. By 1890, property owners near downtown developed a unified campaign to require the elevation or depression of nearby rail lines. They wanted the business district and its high rents to expand in their direction. Railroad lines, they believed, were barriers to expansion. Reformers and planners tried to coerce the railroads into massive investments for track elevation, but their cause was futile until November 30, 1890, when the Supreme Court of Illinois gave the city a powerful weapon. Ironically, the city lost the case, *Legare v. City of Chicago*.[7] The *Legare* decision held that it was not within the powers granted by the state to municipal governments for them to gift

any street to one party to the exclusion of others. The decision terrified the railroads because it challenged titles to existing rights of way. The statute of limitations seemed to allow long-established tracks to remained undisturbed, but even the town's earliest lines regularly added industrial spurs, yard expansions, and branches. Previously, the City Council's only leverage in negotiations had been the threat to disallow future construction. However, siding franchises were such a stable source of graft that the railroads felt little danger to their expansion plans. Political payments may have been distasteful, but in the final analysis they were just another cost. The court's decision now threatened to create an environment of continuous blackmail, because well after the construction of any line the city could selectively target its removal.

Given this radical change in the legal landscape, it was not long before someone attempted to capitalize on the new situation. The city council granted a charter for an upstart company on November 7, 1891. The Chicago Elevated Terminal Company was known as the Torrence Terminal after its founder, General Joseph Torrence, whose political connections and wealth rocketed after his rough dealing with the mob a decade prior.[8] He promised to build entirely new elevated mainline tracks into the city. Designed by a steel magnate, the plan understandably relied on iron trestles similar to those of the proposed elevated transit lines. Cynics sniped. They were unsure whether Torrence hoped to monopolize the rail lines into Chicago or just sought a captive market for his mills.[9] Torrence planned to construct one or more mammoth passenger depots on the South Side near Twelfth and State Streets, a point at the end of his elevated rail network.[10] The Atchison, Topeka and Santa Fe was so enthusiastic about the idea that it conveyed all its Chicago terminal properties to the new scheme. The *Chicago Times* supported the plan by noting, "Rarely has such a valuable charter been extended to a single corporation." Mayor Carter Harrison defended the grant by saying, "I am told on good authority that every railroad now entering the city is obliged to pay on average $100,000 a year in settlement of damages to life and limb, and one road I understand paid $200,000 for this class of injury last year. Looking at it from a humane and lifesaving standpoint, an elevated terminal should not only be demanded but also insisted upon by the public and council for every road entering the city."[11] The *Chicago Tribune* saw city council actions in a different light:

> It is stated that a city paper is about to make an alleged expose of the use of "boodle" in the passage of the Chicago elevated terminal ordinance (the Torrence scheme), and there is a row brewing among the Aldermen who were alleged to have received their "bit" because the money was not distributed properly. The newspaper, it is said, will allege that the Council was divided into three classes as follows: Those members who would vote for the ordinance through conviction that it was a meritorious measure, those who could be obtained through political influence, and those who only vote for the ordinance for a consideration.[12]

Torrence started his plans before the City Beautiful movement captured the public imagination. Like many developers, however, he knew an attractive architectural rendering could galvanize public support. Solon S. Beman, designer of the town of Pullman, devised a plan for what easily would have been the largest building in the world. Although only ten passenger tracks were to enter the depot, it was to have an equal number of freight tracks on a lower level. Office and warehouse space in the building were to have a 2,400-foot frontage on State Street.[13] The arched vault of its waiting room skylight would have been larger than most train sheds. Its Romanesque style, however, was out of step with the Beaux Arts ideals soon to sweep Chicago.

The prospect that track elevation would require staggering outlays prompted the railroads to rethink their strategies. Previously they fought every viaduct proposal, but now they petitioned for viaduct construction. Their hope was that elimination of the worst crossings would slow the calls for a hideously expensive comprehensive solution.[14] Early in 1891, the city council formed the Chicago Railway Terminal Commission to investigate track elevation. Its report the following year, *The Chicago Railway Terminal Problem*, clearly signaled the city's intent to force the railroads to elevate all of their tracks, at least in the areas bordering the business district. It said:

107

The lines of the West Side, North Side and South Side districts so-called, should be excluded from the following boundaries, to wit: on the west, by the line of Canal Street, and on the south by the south line of Twenty-Second Street. The lines of the Southern District, so called, could stop at Twenty-Second Street, and join in the erection of an elevated depot of size, plan and character sufficient to accommodate all of the business that they now have or are likely to have in the future, thus relieving a large amount of property lying north of Twenty-Second Street, now used by them, and which is in demand at the present time for business purposes and relieving the City from the necessity of constructing the extremely high buildings now in the course of construction on the account of the circumscribed area to which business is confined at the present time.[15]

The study's minor theme was a perceived need to unify all downtown passenger stations. Replacement of six downtown depots with one or two promised to ease the problems encountered by out-of-town passengers connecting between trains. By definition, however, that group excluded the constituencies of Chicago's aldermen. In the political realm, that was all that mattered. The political stance had been that the longer travelers took to change trains, the more money they contributed to the Chicago economy. Now, the driver for station consolidation was the need to reduce street congestion.

The idea that it would be cheaper to elevate a few large depots than many scattered lines was new.[16] Despite the great expense, later years saw the elevation of most major tracks through the city. At the time, however, the railroads were unclear whether the report's conclusions represented true municipal goals or just another aldermanic shakedown. Whatever its motivation, the Chicago Railway Terminal Commission study served notice that municipal powers could and would force track elevation.[17] It set the stage for decades of discussion on consolidation schemes, but like studies that followed, it dictated solutions with little input from those paying for the improvements.

All six of Chicago's passenger terminals were within the area proscribed in *The Chicago Railway Terminal Problem*. The report made it official policy to remove these terminals to another location. While the report hinted that the railroad companies would be "compensated" for their land holdings, it neither provided nor suggested funds for that purpose. Rather, it valued the land vacated under the plan. An estimated 11.6 million square feet was thought to have a value of $50 million. Sale of this land would "go far toward defraying all the expenses . . . for the improvements in question."[18]

This emphasis on real estate valuation tipped the city's hand. So long as the land was held for railway use, neither the railroads nor the municipality could tap its perceived value. If it were resold for commercial purposes, the city would reap a tax windfall due to its increased assessed value. Concurrent with the Chicago Terminal Commission report, the city challenged the state's railroad taxation methodology, the overall level of taxation assessed, and the allocation formula. All these challenges were without success, with the last appeal lost in October of 1903.

Populist rhetoric aside, the city was hardly indifferent to the railroads' problems, often helping to alleviate the congestion that strangled train movements into the Union Depot. In 1897, for example, the city council passed an ordinance to widen Stewart Avenue south of the depot. This portion of the "street" never existed as a public thoroughfare except on maps, and its sole improvement was the Ft. Wayne tracks. The council's simple expedient allowed the railroad to widen its right of way and thus increase trackage into the depot without having to go through a time-consuming condemnation proceeding. Adjacent property owners who lost property were uncompensated. But neither the railroads nor the city counted on the irate determination of one such landowner, who filed an expropriation suit that occupied the courts for five years. The Ft. Wayne fully occupied the widened Stewart Avenue with depot tracks. When the court found against the railroad in 1903, the case gained national attention because the heir to the complainant and the substantial beneficiary of the settlement was President Theodore Roosevelt.[19]

During this period, the Ft. Wayne also occupied—without benefit of any ordinance for vacation or transfer—six separate streets and alleys between Twelfth and Eighteenth Streets. It even built a brick building on land platted as a street. When this became public in 1909, the railroad's local counsel noted dryly, "I have been expecting this for a number of years. We will probably have to pay compensation from now on for use of the streets."[20]

City and railroad interests continued to clash on the need for viaducts. Many lines' enabling ordinances required overpass construction, but the law addressed neither their maintenance nor the possible need for their widening if street traffic grew.[21] Roadway upkeep, or lack thereof, caused constant complaints. The city engineer took every opportunity to warn of impending tragedy; on August 3, 1883, it struck. The Polk Street Viaduct, built by the Burlington south of the depot, was only two years old. It was of iron truss construction with a badly worn timber deck. An unfortunate omnibus waited on the viaduct for the swing bridge to close when a locomotive passed underneath. Its exhaust blasted through chinks in the plank paving and red-hot cinders pummeled the underbelly of the bus's horse, causing it to leap forward into the river with its omnibus in tow. Three children in the bus drowned. The finger pointing was immediate, but maintenance responsibilities were never clarified.

The Adams Street viaduct exemplified another issue resulting from street traffic growth. It could not accommodate all the wagons or pedestrians that wished to use it. Built with iron trusses from the Keystone Bridge Company in 1869 and damaged in the Great Fire, it was rebuilt and altered in 1872. Another remodeling in 1879 allowed for more station tracks underneath, and in 1883, it was damaged and closed after a lake freighter collided with the center pier of the adjoining bridge. The city decided to widen the bridge, but the Ft. Wayne refused to pay. A solution was found with the granting of a street railway franchise for Adams Street. The streetcar line paid for a wider street, viaduct, and bridge.[22] The wider 1884 construction, the fourth in the viaduct's twenty-five-year history, unfortunately required the demolition of the decorative veranda that connected the Union Depot with its baggage building south of the street.

NO PLACE TO GROW

Union Depot was barely adequate for its traffic and its owners knew by extrapolation that it was near inundation. In 1901, Thomas Rodd (who had been promoted to chief engineer of the Pennsylvania Company's Lines West in January of that year), together with Acting Chicago Division Superintendent C. S. Sims, internally circulated four options for expansion of the depot. They also studied seven related schemes for freight-house rearrangement.[23] Their common element was recognition that

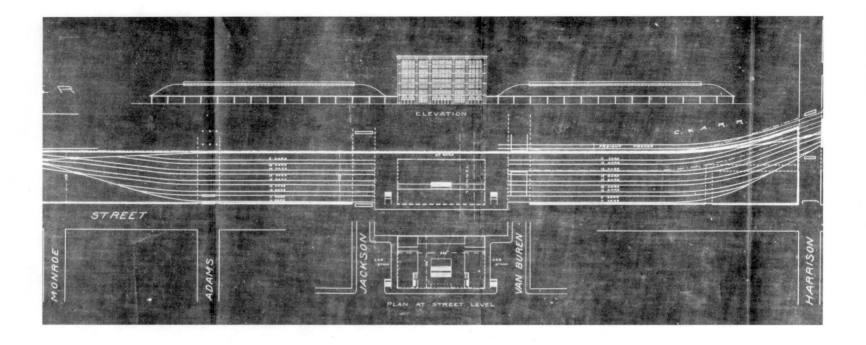

the existing site was too narrow and all alternatives, at first blush, seemed outlandish.

Independent real estate promoter James Galloway presented his own scheme directly to Rodd's superiors.[24] His plan was to buy the "Farwell Plot," a large landholding to be added to the existing Union Depot site. This multiblock tract occupied the blocks bounded by Adams, Madison, and Wells Streets on the east bank of the river opposite Union Depot. The acquisition cost was $11 million. Prodded by home office executives, Rodd developed a scheme that required the construction of a tunnel under the Chicago River connecting what, in essence, were two separate depots. To develop detailed cost estimates for the Farwell Plot, he hired local real estate agent Dunlop Smith and the architectural firm of Holabird and Roche. Otis Elevator Company designed and provided capacity estimates for horizontal funiculars. The plan called for ten pairs of elevatorlike cars moving through the tunnel, with the cars from each pair passing their counterpart midway. The plan also required two new railroad lift bridges crossing the river at Lake Street and at Van Buren Street, for which Pennsylvania engineers made preliminary drawings.

Details of these developments were kept secret by the Pennsylvania because, in Rodd's words, "I feel quite certain that were the Chicago & Alton or the C.B. & Q. [Burlington] to have it brought to their attention, they would step in and get the property, although we could prevent their making a thorough development of it on account of the land we now own."[25]

Rodd had a valid concern, as all three tenants were surreptitiously casting for alternatives. Meanwhile, Rodd drew up plan after plan. One $6 million scheme shifted Canal Street westward to provide more space. Double-deck freight houses would provide for enlargement of the existing yard space. Conventional wisdom among railroad management was that the city council would object to any variation in the street grid, but Rodd felt he could overcome such opposition. His real concern was whether his various schematics created sufficient capacity.

Two of Rodd's plans required that the Chicago River be rechanneled eastward. They varied in detail, but both shifted the east riverbank to Market (now Wacker) Street at a cost of $16 million. Use of the recovered river bottom would have more than doubled the depot's available land. Despite their great cost, these plans remained Rodd's preferred options because they created a simple, easy-to-operate terminal near the business district. Rodd predicated his rechannelization plan on the fact that the river had a new overseer, the Metropolitan Sanitary District. Also known as the Drainage Board, it was not favorably inclined toward railroad interests. Formed in January 1890 by an act of the Illinois legislature, it built one of the great public works projects of the age. Since the town's beginning, sewers dumped directly into the Chicago River, which carried contamination into Lake Michigan, the source of the city's drinking water. The low portage that made the Illinois and Michigan Canal work with few locks solved this problem. By digging a deeper cut linking the Chicago River at Bridgeport to the Des Plaines River at Joliet, the Sanitary District reversed the former river's water flow. Chicago taxpayers, in short, undertook the only project in history to move a continental divide.[26] In the process, they were to excavate more fill than moved for the Suez Canal. The drainage project required the issuance of more bonds than the entire city government was allowed to issue.

Despite obvious benefits to public health, the project had enemies. Downriver towns saw their water sources fouled and city residents feared a sharp increase in property taxes. The railroads sided with the opposition because the plan threatened to create a channel capable of carrying lake boats directly to the Mississippi

basin and allow deeper-draft ships to enter Chicago's harbor. The potential of new competition was only part of the problem. Enabling legislation allowed the district to take three hundred thousand cubic feet of water per minute from Lake Michigan and restricted its flow to three miles per hour.[27] This required a wider channel, a particular problem for the Union Depot landholdings. The already too-narrow site faced possible condemnation of a strip running its entire length. Rodd nevertheless believed that the city or the Metropolitan Sanitary District would pick up $4 million of the cost to move the channel eastward, as this would further two of the District's aims: straightening the river to aid navigation and increasing water flow in the channel.

Construction on the expanded canal started near Lemont in August 1892, but the legal machinery for enlarging the channel was already in full gear. The Sanitary District initiated proceedings to condemn forty-five feet of the west embankment the entire length of the south branch. The Pennsylvania Railroad countered that it too was a public necessity, and thus its land was exempt from condemnation. The railroad lost its final appeal in October 1905, but a few months earlier the Pennsylvania scored a modest victory. The District planned an entirely new channel near Western Avenue. The Panhandle agreed to build a new bridge, but tellingly, it was not required to provide sufficient clearance for lake ships.[28]

The impact of the Metropolitan Sanitary District's project was lost on no one. The *Economist*, a local real estate journal, noted:

> The alienation of this land will take from the roads occupying the Union Passenger Station a large percentage of the space used for their freight business. It is hoped that this event will hasten the time when persons using the facilities of the Union Passenger Station will have better accommodations. It is believed that an emotion in favor of some improvement of the passenger station has at times stirred slightly in the cast-iron breast of the Pennsylvania Railroad system, but when that system thought of the great convenience of those freight terminals and the large profit derived there from it could not make up its mind of taking any of that space for the benefit of passengers. There will be [after the condemnation] so little room left for freight purposes that it will hardly be worthwhile to maintain sheds for dead freight and perhaps human freight may have a chance.

In 1897, the railroad, probably supported by Rodd's engineering, suggested construction of a fifty-foot-wide subterranean river channel under their rail yard, since they only needed the continued use of its surface. Under this proposal, the Sanitary District would pay all expenses, including a new rail yard for the depot. In return, the District would not have to buy the railroad's expensive real estate. The District rejected the idea, in part because it required that the existing streetcar tunnels be lowered.[29] The railroad pressed this solution through 1902.

Thomas Rodd's superiors became unsettled by his continued submission of radical schemes; rather than seek his input they now dictated the options. They ordered him to provide two plans that provided for curving the tracks westward into a stub-end depot set at a right angle to Clinton Street. Senior managers worried about a suit brought by the attorney general claiming the railroads had already illegally filled into the river, so that the amount of land they should surrender was even greater than originally projected.[30] Under duress, the Pennsylvania quoted an asking price for this land, but court proceedings were already under way to determine its value.

Rodd knew that his superiors' dictates were poor options if for no other reason than that all depot tracks would be on curves, a layout that was not conducive to safe operation. At the same time, their plan removed the headhouse from proximity to the center city. He must have protested, for one year later his supervisors commissioned another internal study. This time they brought in C. H. Watson from the Office of the Superintendent of the Pennsylvania's Lines West in Pittsburgh.[31] Watson's economical approach called for a ten-story building that combined the headhouse, an office building, and the freight houses. It was to be built over the tracks, which were laid the entire width of the site between Canal Street and the river. His behemoth would run from Jackson to Adams Streets. He accompanied his proposal with rough architectural drawings, but provided no cost estimate. The design increased the depot from fourteen tracks (seven to the north and seven to the south) to twenty-four tracks

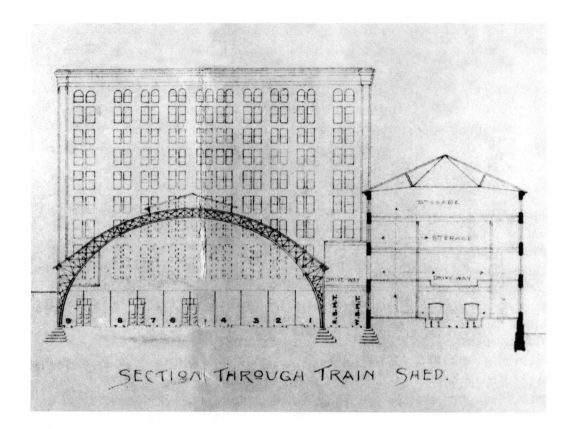

SECTION THROUGH TRAIN SHED.

and swelled station yard capacity to 281 cars from 131. Watson himself described the serious shortcoming of his scheme: "An objection would be that our own trains would stand under the station, where smoke, steam, etc., would be more or less objectionable, and without doubt large suction pipes would have to run up through the building, say at the corners of the waiting-room, to produce an artificial draft."

Nothing came of Watson's plan. When realtors secretly offered yet another piece of property west of Canal Street to the company in 1903, the local terminal superintendent sought guidance from his superiors, stating, "We have so many different plans for Union Station, none of which seem desirable, that I thought it desirable to refer the matter to you. I thought it probable that Mr. Rodd might [already] have some plans showing such a development."[32]

In 1901, the Baltimore and Ohio Railroad came under the control of the Pennsylvania. It was the major tenant of Grand Central Station on the east bank of the Chicago River. The Pennsylvania petitioned the Union Depot's other managers to allow its new subsidiary to switch its trains into the station.[33] The B&O had been a late entrant into the Chicago market and had a circuitous route into town. Using Ft. Wayne tracks to Union Depot would pare nearly an hour from each train's schedule. Union Depot tenants, however, objected. They finally voted to allow the B&O as a tenant after March 1, 1902, but only if the Pennsylvania moved its freight houses to the Grand Central site.[34] Tenants also feared loss of control. The Pennsylvania already had two of five votes on the depot's management committee, one each for the Ft. Wayne and the Panhandle. An additional B&O vote would give the Pennsylvania majority control.

As the B&O sought to vacate Grand Central, the Alton looked in the opposite direction. Financier Edward Harriman controlled the Alton and, to protect his investment, he bought the Peoria and Northern, a line threatening to build a parallel route. Prior to the Alton's purchase, the P&N entered into an onerous lease with the Chicago Terminal Transfer Company, owner of Grand Central Station. The CTT was the cobbled-together lines built by the Chicago and Northern Pacific and the Calumet Terminal, a remnant of General Torrence's rail empire. Harriman quickly discovered that the Alton could not economically move to Grand Central. As the Pennsylvania discovered, freight houses there were entirely inadequate, so the Alton continued to rent the Ft. Wayne tracks across the river.[35] While nothing came of these gyrations, they stoked public ardor for terminal unification, especially after the Rock Island and New York Central accepted a track elevation ordinance that required them to build a new station at LaSalle Street.[36] At the same time, five other lines including the Ft. Wayne agreed to elevate line segments somewhat removed from the center city.

An old issue resurfaced in 1904. Twenty-three years after the Burlington's independence from the Michigan Central, its self-reliance ended when it entered into an alliance with financier Jim Hill's railroads. His lines connected with the Burlington at Minneapolis. The Empire Builder, as Hill was known, had a low regard for railroad passenger service, stating that it was "like a male teat, neither ornamental nor useful." But he also felt strongly that his railroads should be landlords, not tenants. To that end, he attempted to buy the Chicago Terminal Transfer. The Pennsylvania's Chicago Terminal superintendent expressed hope that the Burlington would succeed, as he coveted the space they occupied in Union Depot. The financial consequences of losing a major tenant, however, were not lost on his superiors. At the same time, the Pennsylvania persisted in its efforts to admit the Baltimore and Ohio to Union Depot.[37] An eleventh-hour winning bid by the B&O for the CTT, then renamed the Chicago and Calumet Terminal, thwarted the Burlington's plan.

The B&O's purchase of Grand Central Station renewed speculation that the Union Depot railroads would allow its trains into their station on the condition that, in return, it would relinquish the east bank for them to erect modern freight houses. That, in turn, would release sufficient land west of the river for a passenger depot. Newspapers reported on plans for a union passenger depot to cost $15 million. These speculations seemed well founded,

Newspapers routinely sent photographers to capture celebrity arrivals. Here, Evelyn Nesbit Thaw has been persuaded to pose on a locomotive pilot.

COURTESY OF THE CHICAGO HISTORY MUSEUM, ICHICDN N07887

for the Pennsylvania's local attorney, F. J. Loesch, stated, "A new station has been decided upon, and the freight houses must come down to make room for the handling of passenger traffic of the lines, which increases as fast as the city grows."[38]

The Sanitary District continued to press its claims even as the railroad fought a rearguard action seeking time to build new freight houses. Newspaper speculation escalated. The *Chicago Journal* even published a map of South Side real estate transactions in an attempt to prove that the Pennsylvania intended to build a passenger depot at Twelfth and Dearborn Streets. Picked up as fact by other papers, it was without foundation. Despite scrutiny of its every move, the Pennsylvania covertly purchased six lots at Madison, Canal, and West Water Streets for $1.4 million. The riverbank situation escalated in December of 1907, when the state's attorney claimed illegal encroachment by the railways of an even wider eighty-foot swath of riverbank north of Madison Street.[39] This claim, based on a seventy-year-old deed by the Illinois and Michigan Canal commissioners to the city, was wholly without merit, but it was another indication that the railroads remained populist targets.

The window of opportunity for Grand Central Station as Union Depot's salvation quickly closed when federal antitrust concerns forced the Pennsylvania to sell the B&O. This was accomplished in the fall of 1913 by a trade of shares with the Union Pacific, which had a similar problem with its control of the Southern Pacific Railroad. The following year, the Union Pacific dispersed its B&O stock as a dividend to shareholders, chief among them Edward Harriman. Harriman previously passed on leasing Grand Central when he controlled the Alton, but now he owned the station. He also controlled the Illinois Central, whose own lakefront depot, Central Station, was twenty years old. Harriman thus had the resources to arrange his own terminal consolidation, but that required that he sell freight house land to the other railroads that he needed for his passenger terminal. Declining to part with such a valuable commodity, he lost the easy solution.

OUTSIDE IDEAS

Reformers argued that all six downtown passenger terminals were poorly located and inefficient. But their vague concerns needed tempering by reality. Any reorganization of such vast property holdings presented incredible logistical and technical problems. Nevertheless, the topic became a debate staple among the more liberal members of the engineering community. A paper read before the Western Society of Engineers on May 22, 1901, illustrates their professional interest. R. C. Sattley espoused consolidation of intercity and commuter trains into one complex located east of the Chicago River.[40] Sattley split passenger traffic between a suburban station on the south side of Taylor Street and an intercity depot to the north. He located freight houses south of these stations, with express and mail buildings to the north. Sattley had an engineer's eye for detail. He considered the capacity needed for each railroad's yard and engine facilities, as well as the route each company's trains would follow into his terminal. This approach had considerable merit, but its detail provided his detractors with ammunition to use against him.

With exacting precision, Sattley outlined a scheme for elevating all rail lines entering the city, so that none crossed any other at grade. His paper noted, "In reaching their respective terminals, the railroads form a network of crossings in the heart of the city which the spider would blush to imitate."[41] Diagrams accompanying the proposal detailed Sattley's attempt to best the spider. To give every train an unimpeded journey toward the station, Sattley rerouted many lines, created new junctions and built flyovers well away from downtown. He segregated each company's suburban and intercity tracks from its competitors once in the station. Each depot was to have fifteen sets of dual tracks, one for inbound trains and one for outbound, each of which ran through the depot. An iron fence split each station platform so that inbound travelers never met outgoing passengers. Sattley assigned each company one or more sets of tracks based on their existing traffic. Thus, the Burlington was to occupy two pairs, while four lesser lines shared another pair. Sattley estimated the terminal could "send out a train every twenty seconds for three consecutive hours, and at the same time be capable of receiving a train every thirty seconds."[42] He envisioned discharging suburban and intercity passengers under a train shed 856 feet wide by 750 feet long. For reasons never made entirely clear, a separate 850-by-250-foot suburban station was only for outbound commuters. Whatever its merits, Sattley's plan was inflexible. A broken switch would prohibit a railroad from bringing trains into "its tracks" despite excess capacity nearby.

As an intellectual exercise, Sattley's proposal represented a departure from railroad orthodoxy, and it sparked a public infatuation with obscure planning details. Besides freeing land for expansion of the business district and eliminating grade crossings, Sattley deftly integrated other civic desires into his proposal. Wide streets near the station, for example, increased circulation and provided a ceremonial effect. He redesigned street and rail bridges to promote river commerce. His plan handled mail more economically. Warehouses were to occupy air rights over the coach yards. Sattley even planned new elevated and subway transit lines to connect his station with the city center.

Sattley, a longtime Chicago and North Western employee, presented his findings at several professional meetings and their transcripts capture the intensity he generated. Half a dozen fellow engineers criticized his proposition in detail, seemingly united in their rebuttal. Their discussion, however, covered not just the strengths and weakness of Sattley's proposal, but terminal consolidation in general. Upon questioning, for example, Sattley departed from his prepared text to remark that the IC and C&NW stations could remain in their existing locations for commuter traffic. G. H. Bremner of the Burlington gruffly replied, "If you propose leaving the North Western and Illinois Central stations where they are, I suggest you also leave the other four." Bremner then stated: "According to Mr. Sattley's figures about 72% of the passenger traffic is suburban. Of the remaining 28%, probably 4/5ths or 22 percent is local, leaving only 6 percent, which is exchange business between roads, and of this 6 percent probably one-fourth more is transferred in the same depot in which it arrives, so that on a reasonable estimate about 5 percent of the passenger business would be facilitated, while the remaining 95 percent would be more or less obstructed by the plan under discussion."[43]

Bremner attacked by showing that existing Burlington freight and express facilities were five times larger than Sattley's proposal. J. C. Stuart of the B&O stated simply that Sattley's plan was impossible, and knowingly offered an equally impossible proposition.

If such a scheme could be developed, we would prefer this suggestion to the Union Station: Secure through the State Legislature and City authorities the right to fill in and make sufficient ground in Lake Michigan, on the lakefront, at some convenient location, for the construction of a joint station. Have the railroad companies pay the city of Chicago a sufficient ground rent as to make the franchise a desirable one.

Have the station of right-angular or L-shape: divert all eastern and southern trains to the lakeside at or near South Chicago: permit the Illinois Central railroad right of way to be extended to care for all roads just mentioned, and bring into one of the lines of the right angle just mentioned; then have all the west and northwest lines come in at some point parallel to the main stem of the Chicago River and reach the other line of the angle in the same locality. It would practically take care of the business under two sheds, letting the freight stations, etc., remain as they are now. Then have the Loop line connect with this station so as to make it possible to get to any part of the city over the elevated line. This scheme is, of course, subject to the same criticism as Mr. Sattley's plan, for the reason that we do not believe it would be possible to carry it out.[44]

These animated discussions betrayed the fact that even those who roundly criticized Sattley had been quietly plotting their own consolidation dreams. Despite the attention, nobody present had a solution addressing all of the problems. Widely discussed in the press, Sattley's proposal then languished. However, the topic became a favorite for letters to the editor. Most letters vented frustrations and those few with concrete suggestions seemed more fantastic than practical.

This changed in 1904 when Frederic Delano, former vice president of the Burlington, tackled the terminal issue. Delano stated that he had been working on the problem since 1895, although there is no evidence of this until after he temporarily left railroad employment. Delano envisioned a series of depots along Twelfth Street. He placed new Dearborn, LaSalle, and Grand Central stations east of the Chicago River, with a new Union Depot to the west. Unlike many local reformers, Delano was a patrician, the son of a partner in Russell & Company, the largest China trading firm in New England. That firm was the creation of Edward Russell, a client of William Butler Ogden. One of Delano's father's partners was John Murray Forbes, principal financier of the Chicago, Burlington and Quincy. The Delano family was an early investor in Chicago real estate and owned extensive Pennsylvania coal lands; some relatives, notably nephew Frank-

lin Delano Roosevelt, had political ambitions. Frederic Delano nevertheless had a sterling reputation in railroad engineering circles as a Harvard-educated civil engineer in an era when most railroad men advanced though apprenticeship.

Despite the connections that likely landed him a job on the Burlington, he too started in junior positions. Delano's rise was meteoric, but he took an unusual path to the top of his profession. In an age that exalted engineering works and their creators, Delano's fame rested on a seemingly mundane task; he improved the quality of steel rails. As historian Steven Usselman explains, "Though seemingly the simplest of technologies, rails in fact formed the central component in a complex and expensive technological system."[45] Rather than looking for low bidders on the railroad's largest capital expenditure, Delano conducted tests, set standards, and dictated manufacturing techniques. He preached the doctrine that cheap, poor rail was in fact quite expensive if it failed under a train. At a very young age, he also tackled such issues as the railroad's Chicago stockyards operations. He installed the Burlington's first block signal system, became its Superintendent of Motive Power, and then vice president of one of the nation's largest and most sophisticated railroads.

At his own expense, Delano commissioned architect Daniel Burnham's firm to illustrate a pamphlet outlining his ideas for Chicago's passenger terminal consolidation. In Burnham's elevation drawings, five identical block-wide terminals were to arise, one west of the river and the others east. A widened Twelfth Street provided a broad ceremonial boulevard sufficiently elevated to allow freight tracks underneath to extend northward to existing warehouses. Modern multistory warehouses were to replace the existing single-level facilities. An east-west elevated rapid transit line facilitated interterminal access with stops inside each depot. Similar to the people mover of a modern airport, this line was also to connect with the existing elevated transit system. Delano's plan, like earlier proposals, promised to release land to aid the railroads in recouping expenses. But he told his audience:

> You are expecting too much of the railroads if you are expecting them to do for Chicago as a public spirited act, what the leading citizens of Chicago are unwilling themselves to take up and urge. The railroads are constantly being asked to "pull somebody else's chestnuts out of the fire." The most important fact which leads to a continuation of the existing system is jealousy and self-interest, whereby no interest is willing, or can afford to forego an advantage it now has. Take the case of the Lake Shore and Rock Island [LaSalle] station, which has the best location in the heart of the business section; the men who represent these interests, and who are in a position of Trustees for them, appreciate fully the advantage of their location.[46]

Delano concluded, "public spirited men have an interest which transcends any such selfish view, and the railroads are public spirited." He pointed out that railroads and the municipality shared the expenses of major terminal projects in New York, Philadelphia, and Boston. He estimated the Chicago expense at $75 million. The *Tribune* editorialized, "The advantages of the proposed scheme are obvious."[47] So committed was the Hong Kong–born Delano to the pursuit of his ideal that he reportedly declined an appointment as Ambassador to China. A charismatic after-dinner speaker, Delano had to reprint his pamphlet in 1906. One conspicuous feature of his idea was the straightening of the Chicago River. He may have borrowed this idea from Rodd, although it is uncertain whether he had been privy to the Pennsylvania Railroad's earlier plans and his idea called for a more westerly alignment that subtracted from rather than added to the Pennsylvania's land holdings. Delano preached the gospel of terminal consolidation for over nine years, well after he had moved to the Wabash Railroad as its general manager and later president in 1905.

THE PLAN OF CHICAGO

Reformers like Delano proclaimed the ethos of City Beautiful and other social issues to Chicago's network of social, ethnic, and industry-specific clubs. These groups heartily promoted projects such as manual training schools, park development, and museum placement, but as yet they had shown no interest in comprehensive city planning such as Daniel Burnham developed for Washington, San Francisco, and other cities. Delano changed the model. Daniel Burnham first approached the Commercial Club, a group of thirty-nine leading business leaders formed in 1877 for "advancing by social intercourse and friendly interchange of views the prosperity and growth of the city of Chicago."[48] That group, however, already had other commitments. Delano was an officer in a parallel group, the Merchants Club, formed in 1895 with its membership limited to leaders under age forty-five. On October 19, 1906, the Merchants Club members approved $25,000 to fund the *Plan of Chicago*, a comprehensive proposal for city development by Daniel Burnham and Edward Bennett. The Merchants Club merged into the Commercial Club early the following year, primarily to provide the funds and support needed to execute the project.

In truth, Daniel Burnham pushed plans for massive civic betterments almost from the day the Columbian Exposition

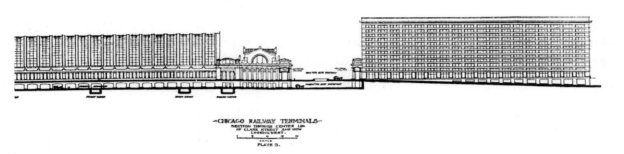

~CHICAGO RAILWAY TERMINALS~
SECTION THROUGH CENTER LINE
OF CLARK STREET AND VIEW
LOOKING WEST.

SCALE
PLATE 3.

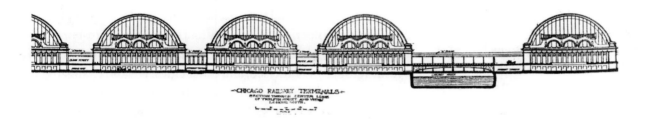

~CHICAGO RAILWAY TERMINALS~
SECTION THROUGH CENTER LINE
OF TWELFTH STREET AND VIEW
LOOKING SOUTH.

Frederic Delano proposed a series of passenger stations fronting a Roosevelt Road viaduct. Tracks would pass underneath to downtown freight houses and team tracks. The wide and ornamental viaduct was built, but except for river straightening, that was the only part executed.

COURTESY OF THE AUTHOR

closed. His major work was to design a lakefront park and parkway system extending for ten miles south from downtown. This and similar plans circulated among progressive groups such as the Civic Federation and the Municipal Improvement League. Burnham had two advantages for this work. First, a single land-owner controlled nearly all of the shoreline needed for this grand scheme. It was a corporation highly motivated to transfer owner-ship to the city. The Illinois Central Railroad saw its 1869 plot to control the lakefront near the center city backfire when the state defensively sued for the removal of its lakefront tracks north of

Fifty-Seventh Street. The US Supreme Court took nearly forty years to rule that the state of Illinois owned the land under the lake but that the railroad could continue to have an easement for its rail line. This ruling definitively conveyed the lakefront back to the people. Burnham's second advantage was the support of John B. Sherman, head of Chicago's South Park Commission, his father-in-law.[49]

In the words of one insider, the relocation of the passenger terminals as part of any comprehensive plan was "the one greatest problem which confronts Mr. Burnham."[50] Even as civic leaders promoted their grandiose urban plan, Chicago newspapers made recurring and authoritative pronouncements that the railroads would soon reveal their own plan for a new Union Depot. The 1907 announcement that the Chicago and North Western would abandon its Wells Street Depot (built simultaneously with Union Depot) fueled this conjecture. As they had done with all of Chicago's railroads, local authorities pressured the C&NW to build a monumental new depot. In this case, the deciding factor came when the city won a verdict requiring either a new elevated terminal or the erection of viaducts over existing Wells Street Station tracks. The North Western's existing site was small and poorly located, so it opted for an elevated depot at a new Madison Street location. Similar pressure forced the Rock Island to build an elevated LaSalle Street station in 1903. Both stations were the work of the architects Charles Sumner Frost and Alfred Hoyt Granger. With two victories in its battle for modern passenger terminals, the public sensed that the Union Depot railroads would soon bow to local demands.

For the railroad terminal portion of the *Plan of Chicago*, Burnham and Bennett predictably drew on their earlier work for Frederic Delano. In one sense, their client was unchanged, since Delano chaired the Commercial Club committee that oversaw the project. The architects routinely consulted Delano on all railroad-related matters, particularly terminal consolidation. They discussed Twelfth Street's place within the overall plan as early as February 1907. By September, Bennett enumerated several principles. Separate grades or levels were established for freight railroads, roadways or streets, and the passenger railroads. Bennett said that the first task was to "push back the passenger depots to a circuit away from the river," while the second task was to "press

back the freight railroads from the center and consequently from the river."[51]

The "circuit" to which Bennett alluded was the idea that a new loop for suburban trains would utilize the existing rights of way of the IC along the lakefront, the C&NW north of the Chicago River, and the St. Charles Airline at Sixteenth Street. Its final leg would be at least one block west of the Union Station line. This new western line worked for two reasons. First, the North Western had already announced that it would bring its trains into a new station along that line, albeit only as far south as Madison Street. Second, the radius at the northwest corner of the suburban train loop would be too sharp if the line dropped southward along the existing Union Depot alignment. One or two blocks further west worked well, at least on paper. The suburban service loop would have multiple depots on its circuit around the business district, including two or three stops west of the river. All inbound trains would be routed back to their original line for outbound movement.

The *Plan of Chicago* directly lifted Delano's original concept for placement of the intercity depots along Twelfth Street east of the river. It relocated Central, LaSalle Street, Dearborn, and Grand Central to monumental depots on land the railroad already owned. That, unfortunately, was not the wish of the Union Depot railroads.[52] Much of the acreage they would need according to the Plan was owned by competitors.

Alone among the railroads, the Pennsylvania got a sneak preview of the proposed terminal layout on March 31, 1908, when Thomas Rodd, his son, and Vice President Turner were shown the plans. Bennett remarked that Turner was "astonished by the magnitude of the scheme and was skeptical. We showed him Paris and convinced him that such things had been done."[53] Bennett overestimated his powers of salesmanship.

A grand meeting of all Chicago railroad executives was held in Daniel Burnham's office on July 14, 1908. No record survives of that meeting, but Bennett distributed detailed track diagrams at a follow-up meeting three months later. He noted that Delano made valuable suggestions, but it appears that input from the other railroad officers was neither sought nor accepted.[54] The *Plan of Chicago* was to incorporate the earlier drawings for Delano, wonderfully recast into bird's-eye perspectives by renderer Fernand Janin and artist Jules Guerin. Publication of the Plan officially occurred on July 4, 1909, although lantern slides of its major illustrations were shown by Burnham as early as January.

SIDETRACKED

The new North Western depot on Madison Street immediately west of the Union Depot train shed opened in 1909 to public acclaim. Its design was by the firm of Frost and Granger, whose principals were sons-in-law of the railroad's president. The project's greatest expense was to snake a block-wide new rail line south from the point where it formerly turned eastward over the North Branch of the Chicago River. For several blocks, it occupied the exact alignment envisioned by Delano and Bennett, but rather than being below grade, it was elevated above street level. It never seemed to occur to Burnham and Bennett that the new North Western Station's massive foundation prohibited the Union Depot railroads from occupying the same alignment below grade.

Meanwhile, public interest took another unusual turn in November 1909 with the publication of an unsolicited plan to coordinate Chicago's railroad stations. Leroy Hunter proposed two depots, both near Sixteenth Street. He located an inbound station east of Clark Street and a station for outbound trains west of that street. Each of these elevated depots was to have two levels of 28 tracks, for a grand total of 112 tracks. The dimensions of each depot were a staggering 1,200 feet by 666 feet, with a fifteen-story office tower to rise 270 feet above. Each tower alone would have been among the world's largest buildings. Hunter estimated that implementation of his plan would cost $120 million. Though employed in the engineering department of the city of Chicago, Hunter promoted his scheme independently. Widely published, his drawings were even exhibited at a major railroad supply convention, but as Hunter freely stated, his plan had little chance of adoption. He timidly remarked, "I hope to be of assistance and help along a subject which is rapidly becoming of increased importance to Chicago."[55]

On March 30, 1912, Chicago architect Jarvis Hunt published his own ideas for a single consolidated station. Like Rodd's and Delano's, Hunt's plan straightened the bend in the Chicago River. His novel proposal funneled all station tracks into a loop to facilitate train movements. The drawback to Hunt's loop was its lavish use of real estate; it was extravagant in both the area it covered and in the expense of the particular parcels he proposed. Not counting the approach tracks, Hunt's plan was to occupy forty-two square blocks. Freight houses would consume an equal area—and Hunt hadn't even provided for commuters. As in the *Plan of Chicago*, Hunt's scheme required a dedicated line for suburban trains that would encircle the entire business district with eight separate stations.

As with Sattley and Hunter, Hunt's proposal received public accolades because it incorporated popular objectives, such as im-

This illustration from the *Plan of Chicago* shows Union Station as designed by the railroads integrated into the broad boulevards leading to the proposed Civic Center. Other drawings and maps show alternate sites and elevations.

COURTESY OF THE AUTHOR

proved street circulation and river navigation. His finely rendered presentation drawings proved to be worth more than a thousand words in capturing the public imagination. His greatest attribute, however, was that he seemed to have the right credentials. His monumental Kansas City Union Station, by many measures the nation's largest, suggested to the public that he was an unquestioned expert in railroad terminal design. In fact, he infuriated the Kansas City railroad men with his expensive tastes and unbendable attitudes. Moreover, railroad engineers found his Chicago ideas unimpressive. They were the ones who knew how to lay tracks and design terminals. In truth, they probably were a bit jealous of the laurels bestowed on the architects, who only designed the buildings that sat atop their massive rail networks.

The engineers knew that in addition to its extravagant use of land, Hunt's plan contained a fatal flaw. Hunt claimed that loop tracks doubled capacity.[56] There was some logic in that idea, since the typical stub-end station required each train to come into the depot, and after it discharged its passengers, to back up to the coach yard. Often a switch engine had to shadow each train into the depot in order to haul its cars back into the yard. Because both incoming and outgoing train movements had to cross multiple tracks along their assigned route, a stub-end layout had inherent bottlenecks. Nevertheless, the use of loop tracks was relatively untested. Only New York City's new Grand Central Station and Boston's South Station featured loops and neither was yet in service. Only certain commuter trains were to use the New York loop, which featured high trackside platforms that allowed these trains to rapidly discharge or load passengers. Moreover, the electric trains that served Grand Central Terminal could easily accelerate around the loop. Detailed studies by the Pennsylvania's engineers determined that arranging tracks in a loop increased capacity per station track by ten percent, not the one hundred percent stated by Hunt. In the minds of the engineers, this advantage was insufficient to warrant purchase of major portions of Chicago's South Side.

The entire *Plan of Chicago* was extensively and tirelessly promoted. Its advocates even adapted it into a 137-page text about city planning taught to a generation of Chicago public school students.[57] As these students became voters, Chicagoans approved dozens of bond issues in the 1910s and 1920s for impressive infrastructure improvements. However, the long-time dream of passenger terminal consolidation remained unrealized.

CHAPTER FIVE

A COLOSSUS OF THE ROADS

HANGING ON

The hangover in Chicago's real estate market following the Columbian Exposition continued through 1902, when office occupancy levels rose enough to fuel a brief downtown building boom. Prosperity stalled in the Panic of 1907 and not until 1918 did business improve sufficiently for the city council to raise the building height limit to 260 feet from 130 feet.[1]

However, the revolution in Chicago real estate was not downtown, but in the neighborhoods. This was the direct result of the street railway matrix that concentrated retail activity at so-called transfer corners. Where major car lines intersected, a new type of retail store opened. F. W. Woolworth Company, S. S. Kresge Corporation, the Walgreen Company, the Great Atlantic and Pacific Tea Company (A&P), United Cigar Stores, and other chains exploited the triple maxim of real estate: location, location, location. Chicagoans no longer had to go downtown for low-cost shopping. There was an even greater transformation in entertainment. Unlike vaudeville or opera houses, a movie theater could make money from neighborhood traffic.[2]

Neighborhood banks also prospered. Prior to 1893, there had been only one bank outside downtown, and it served the drovers who brought their herds to the stockyard. Even that bank was a minor institution, as exemplified by one of the most unusual trains to use the Union Depot. Every weekday, a Panhandle train of one locomotive and two baggage cars ran for the Adams Express Company. Its only riders were the train crew and the armed guards who accompanied the nonstop run of stockyard receipts to downtown banks.[3] The regional economy changed in the following decades, when over one hundred local banks organized. These neighborhood banks offered convenience, but also became powerful advocates for their communities, as they tended to lend near their offices. The result was a wave of teardowns as more old houses gave way to multistory apartments. The resulting population density fueled the economic and political ascendance of the neighborhood. Visionaries such as engineer Bion Arnold predicted that Chicago would have two or three city centers. In reality, nearly one hundred minicenters arose.

It was the industrial development on Chicago's far South Side, however, that paradoxically caused the greatest changes near the Union Depot. Lake Calumet, warily viewed as an alternative port since the earliest days of European settlement, had been progressively improved through dredging and the construction of wharves. This lake and its namesake river became

the center for the steel industry, grain transshipment, and heavy manufacturing. Chicago River tonnage peaked in 1906 and fell ten percent over the next two years. By 1916, the Calumet harbor hosted five times the tonnage of the Chicago River. Notwithstanding the steady stream of boats that kept bridges near Union Depot twirling on their piers, the South Branch's days as a major freight terminal were over.

This should have eased the way for the Ft. Wayne to replace its antiquated swing bridge at Stewart Avenue south of the Union Depot. In 1910, it began work on a new abutment with that intent but was enjoined, because while the new bridge would eliminate the center pier, it provided only a 140-foot channel. A 200-foot width was specified by the Sanitary District. A War Department permit had been issued, but a challenge going all the way to the

US Congress rescinded this permission. The company abandoned $150,000 in completed work.[4] The wider channel would actually require a nearly 300-foot span for a bascule bridge, longer than any yet built. Instead, the railroad contracted with consulting engineers Waddell and Harrington for a vertical lift bridge. The 195-foot towers allowed the single Pratt truss to rise for a 135-foot clearance. At the time, this was the heaviest moveable bridge span in the world. The towers were built first and then the truss was fabricated in its raised position directly over the operational swing span. Once the structure was complete in 1915, engineers quickly floated the old bridge away and lowered the vertical span into its operating position.[5]

Fewer riverboats and the resulting decrease in bridge delays should have been a boon to depot passengers, but they remained an unhappy lot. The winter of 1910 was especially cold and three thousand Burlington commuters petitioned for the Chicago Department of Health to force the railroads to winterize the open downstairs lobby. Stationmaster Glenn confirmed that the wrought-iron gates often confined up to two thousand commuters awaiting their train. The protest was successful, and the station built a three-hundred-foot-long glass partition separating lobby and train shed. Wood decking over the cold concrete provided some insulation, and promises were made to install steam heat.[6]

An attractive new neighbor prompted more complaints about Union Depot's minimal improvements. The Chicago and North Western's massive new headhouse was kitty-corner across Madison and Canal Streets. From there, its newly elevated tracks stretched in three directions. Public pressure on the Pennsylvania Railroad to rebuild became palpable. After all, the C&NW's

Madison Street Station supplanted an old Wells Street Depot exactly the same age as the Union Depot. Only a few years earlier, the C&NW covertly assembled property, and once it announced its intentions, the local company had few issues with city officials. This must have given the Pennsylvania comfort that the required ordinances could easily be procured.[7]

A new Union Station seemed more necessary than ever. The Milwaukee Road extended its main line through the Rocky Mountains to the Pacific Coast in 1909, which generated a new source of depot traffic. The first trains for Seattle and Tacoma to depart Chicago Union Depot over the Milwaukee had been the Olympian and the Columbian, both of whose maiden runs were May 28, 1911. Competing trains to Seattle and Portland left from the same depot because the Burlington now handled the through passenger traffic of both the Great Northern and Northern Pacific railroads from a connection at Saint Paul. Previously these lines used the C&NW and its depot.

The following year the depot saw emergency renovations when a routine inspection discovered irreparable corrosion in thirteen train-shed trusses. Nearly the entire shed roof required replacement. While the balloon-style train shed protected passengers from the elements, it had the flaws typical of such structures. It trapped steam, smoke, and corrosive gases, which discomfited passengers and created maintenance nightmares. No one wanted to spend money on the depot, but they could not ignore the problem. At the same time, advances in illumination resulted in the installation of new train-shed lights, and street lamps along three blocks of Canal Street at railroad expense. The issue of locomotive exhaust corrosion also afflicted the Adams Street viaduct, which was again rebuilt at railroad expense.

Pennsylvania Railroad Pacific-type locomotive 9999 ran on rollers at full throttle to create maximum exhaust. Various materials were then placed over its immobile stack to test viaduct materials for resistance to the corrosive blasts.

An August 1911 ordinance to allow a tunnel under Canal Street revealed the railroads' secret plan for a new station. While details were limited, the newspapers quickly established that the planned headhouse was on the west side of that street between Adams and Jackson. But they incorrectly concluded that, as detailed in the *Plan of Chicago*, the train tracks and platforms would be immediately north and south of that site, with the existing station tracks converted to freight handling. The railroads grudgingly corrected the newspapers a week later, although they did not make the full plan public. Indeed, it was not yet final.

The initial cost estimate was $25 million, of which $14 million was for the land, $4–5 million for the structures, and $5 million for track changes. Separately, the Burlington announced that it would build a $1.5 million office tower. That railroad procured a permit for a nineteen-story structure in anticipation of another decrease in the city's building height limit. It was to be the tallest structure on the West Side.

A month later, the Pennsylvania released the plan for a new elevated freight line and a terminal at Van Buren, Des Plaines, Jefferson, and Congress streets. It had an $8 million price tag.[8] The US Post Office Department immediately threw cold water on this plan when it served notice that it also wanted the site. The government prepared to condemn property before the railroad built its elevated rail line. Local postal officials actually wanted a site at Madison and Canal west of the old depot, but its land was valued at $2.5 million. Congress, however, only appropriated $1.7 million and the Treasury Department could not purchase its preferred site.[9]

MONUMENTAL PLANS

The Post Office relented and agreed to build its facility immediately west of the new Union Station Headhouse, with the two projects linked by an understreet conveyor system. When the Post Office released its plan on August 12, the *Tribune* pieced together enough of the railroads' plan to publish it in detail. Representatives of the various railroads met two days later and decided to "go into the open and make known our plans."[10]

The first step in going public was to inform E. B. Butler, president of Butler Brothers, that the track plan required the demolition of one of his company's relatively new twelve-story ware-

houses north of the depot. The railroads proposed to build him a new building of equal size and value. Butler accepted this generous offer on August 15. The following Monday, Ernest Graham presented the station proposal to the Commercial Club's Committee on the Plan of Chicago, which unanimously endorsed the proposal, perhaps because the presiding chair, E. B. Butler, had just received a buyout from the station company. On Friday, the executive committee of the Chicago Association of Commerce also unanimously gave their approval. A notable feature of the announcement was a pedestrian tunnel under the river at Quincy Street with an entrance pavilion on the east bank.[11]

It surprised no one that the Pennsylvania Railroad engineering department laid out the station, while D. H. Burnham and Company handled the architecture. Daniel Burnham visited Pennsylvania Railroad offices in Philadelphia and Pittsburgh almost monthly for more than a decade as the two firms collaborated on depots in Columbus, Cleveland, Pittsburgh, and Washington. Burnham also knew officers of the Chicago, Burlington and Quincy Railroad. His firm had designed depots in its namesake cities of Burlington (1882) and Quincy (1898) and its general office building in Chicago (1883).[12] As to Union Depot's other tenants, Burnham's firm never designed buildings for them. Both the Alton and the Milwaukee, however, were co-owners with D. H. Burnham & Company in the Railway Exchange Building, where all three firms had their executive offices. Burnham certainly knew the existing Chicago station, which he continued to refer to as the "West Side Depot." Until 1903, his daily commute on the Chicago and Evanston line took him through it to his Rookery Building office. He also had a habit of taking breakfast in the station when his Pullman arrived in town after overnight trips.[13] Perhaps he just enjoyed meals in a dining room he remodeled years earlier.

Burnham, his partner Ernest Graham, and designer Peirce Anderson already had close relationships with nearly a dozen senior officers of the Pennsylvania. Each enjoyed annual company passes for inspecting railroad construction and they often traveled in the office car of the president or chief engineer. Burnham forged an especially close attachment with the Pennsylvania's patrician president, Alexander Cassatt. In 1896, the affable Burnham was close enough to the head of the nation's largest corporation that they vacationed together in Europe and Egypt. Burnham, who had done more than any other designer to redirect the prevailing American building style toward Classical and Renaissance models, was on his first European tour. The imperious Cassatt was more host than fellow traveler, as his childhood and education had been in France and Germany. His sister Mary, the Impressionist painter, lived in Paris. The Cassatt party also included architect Charles McKim, designer of Pennsylvania Station in New York City, and landscaper Frederick Law Olmsted. At the time, Burnham's firm was the largest architectural firm in the world and his journals reveal grand ambitions. As the party traveled up the Nile, the immense scale of the Egyptian ruins set the stage for interesting conversations about art and architecture. After their visit to Giza, Burnham wrote, "The designer who chooses the location and the king who let him do it. They have enabled men forever to feel the greatness of their conception and execution. Would that moderns could follow this example."[14]

The friendship between architect and patron was soon put to a test. In 1901, Burnham received a federal commission to update Pierre L'Enfant's 1791 plan for the District of Columbia. A Penn-

sylvania Railroad subsidiary had its station squarely centered in the Mall. The contract to design its replacement was already Burnham's, but he could not reconcile its site to any reasonable urban plan. This made him the fulcrum of controversy. On the one hand, Cassatt pointedly reminded him that he was "employed to design the station, not locate it."[15] Prominent senators, meanwhile, questioned whether Burnham had a private conflict that impeded his public obligation. Ultimately, Burnham convinced Cassatt to relinquish his line's central site. The new route required expensive tunneling and line relocation, but Burnham skillfully procured a station site adjacent to the US Capitol. He then arranged for the government to contribute $1.5 million for the project. Washington Union Station's highly visible location provided a potent symbol of the railroads' immense power.

Back in 1898, Burnham's firm received the contract for the Pennsylvania Station in Pittsburgh, which it completed in 1902. Pittsburgh was perhaps the key station on the mighty railroad. The company had a near monopoly on traffic in and out of that city. This was no small matter. While small in population, the Steel City generated more freight tonnage than New York, Chicago, and Philadelphia combined. The railroad hauled lime, ore, and coal into town, and steel out. Because of the Pennsylvania's dominance, it charged high rates and in consequence was thoroughly despised. So when Andrew Carnegie and George Gould threatened to break this stranglehold with a new railroad, the local heavyweight invested defensively. A new depot and an office tower were only a portion of its improvements.[16]

Burnham pitched a detailed plan for a new Chicago depot to the Pennsylvania as early as March 1898, although its details are now unknown.[17] He had to wait nearly a decade and a half

The Alton published several chromolithograph advertising books with stories based upon popular plays, in this case Gilbert and Sullivan's Patience. The publisher was in New York, the lithographer was in London, but the scene captured was Chicago's old frame West Side depot.

THE CITY OF CHICAGO.

NEW YORK, PUBLISHED BY CURRIER & IVES, 125 NASSAU ST

This section of an 1869 bird's eye illustration shows the planned but never built depot at Canal and Van Buren Streets near the river. It is shown much larger than the LaSalle Street Station, but we do not know if this representation was based on actual knowledge, an actual architectural plan, or if it is conjecture.

Chicago and Alton

A highly colored young man.
A Pullman Car young man.

WHEN I FIRST PUT THIS UNIFORM ON

Uniformed Alton road conductors and porters
served patrons at the new Union Depot.

Parody of Iolanthe, a send-up of the British judiciary and fairy princesses transposed to Chicago Union Depot, was another of the Alton's promotional books. The illustrations are definitely based upon the Union Depot.

COURTESY OF THE AUTHOR

All of the railroads using Union Depot published color posters,
advertisements, and postcards touting their improved terminal.

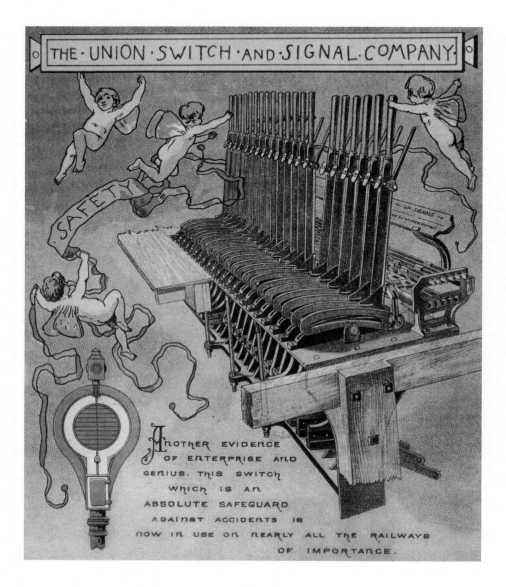

THE · UNION · SWITCH · AND · SIGNAL · COMPANY

SAFETY

Another evidence of enterprise and genius. This switch which is an absolute safeguard against accidents is now in use on nearly all the railways of importance.

(*Left*) The marvels of interlocking technology made good copy for railroad advertising.

COURTESY OF THE AUTHOR

(*Facing, from left to right*) Prosperity of the 1890s is exemplified in the decor of the Alton's smoking car.

COURTESY OF THE AUTHOR

The extra-fare seating in the Alton parlor car was popular with travelers to the state capitol in Springfield and those going to Saint Louis.

COURTESY OF THE AUTHOR

CAFE-LIBRARY-SMOKING CAR

PULLMAN PARLOR CAR

THE UNION DEPOT, CHICAGO—"ALL ABOARD!"

At the "All Aboard" couples and families parted in a scene from the cover of Harper's Weekly.

(*From top*) Depots were a popular postcard subject, signifying a passenger's safe arrival to those back at home.

COURTESY OF THE AUTHOR

The south approach to the depot was difficult due to freight- and express-house tracks. Overhead, the Metropolitan Elevated tracks bridged the yards and adjacent river.

COURTESY OF THE AUTHOR

73. Union Depot, South Canal and Adams Sts., Chicago.
C. B. & Q. RR., M. & St. P., C. & A. RR., Penn. RR.,
C. C. & St. L. RR., P. F. W. & C. RR

Elevated R. R. Viaduct near Adams and South Canal Sts., Chicago.

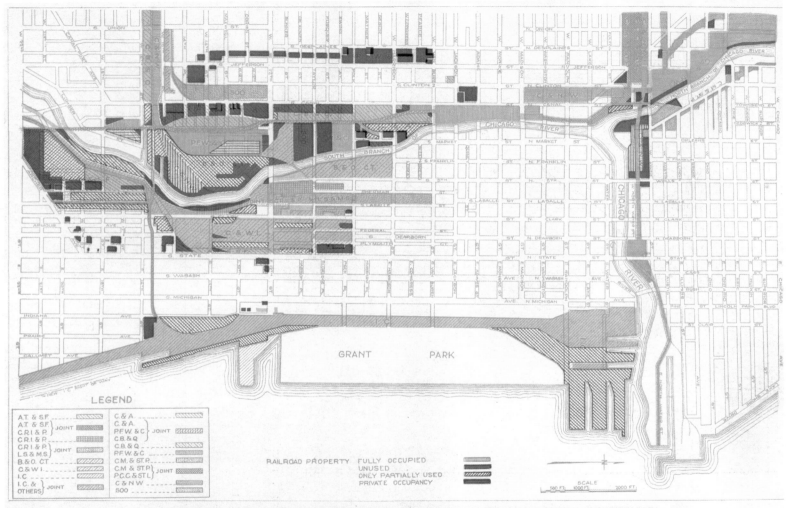

LEGEND

A.T. & S.F.	C. & A.
A.T. & S.F. } JOINT	C. & A. }
C.R.I. & P.	PFW. & C. } JOINT
C.R.I. & P.	C.B. & Q.
C.R.I. & P. } JOINT	C.B. & Q.
L.S. & M.S.	PFW. & C.
B. & O. C.T.	C.M. & ST.P.
C. & W.I.	C.M. & ST.P. } JOINT
I.C.	P.C.C. & ST.L.
I.C. & OTHERS } JOINT	C & N W
	SOO

RAILROAD PROPERTY FULLY OCCUPIED
UNUSED
ONLY PARTIALLY USED
PRIVATE OCCUPANCY

SCALE
500 FT. 1000 FT. 2000 FT.

PLATE 72. MAP SHOWING THE AMOUNT, AND EXTENT OF USE, OF RAILROAD PROPERTY IN CHICAGO'S DOWNTOWN AREA.
(RAILROAD TERMINAL REPORT—BION J. ARNOLD, 1913.)

(*Facing*) The immense extent of railroad landholdings was the major concern of urban planners.

COURTESY OF THE AUTHOR

(*Right*) Frederic Delano's concept of aligning a series of railroad passenger terminals along Twelfth Street was incorporated into the *Plan of Chicago* and later included in a Chicago public school system textbook.

COURTESY OF THE ART INSTITUTE OF CHICAGO

The original 1912 submission of the railroad to the
city called for lunette-style windows.

By 1923 the station plan required an office tower, the post office to
the north, and connections to the North Western station.

COURTESY OF THE AUTHOR

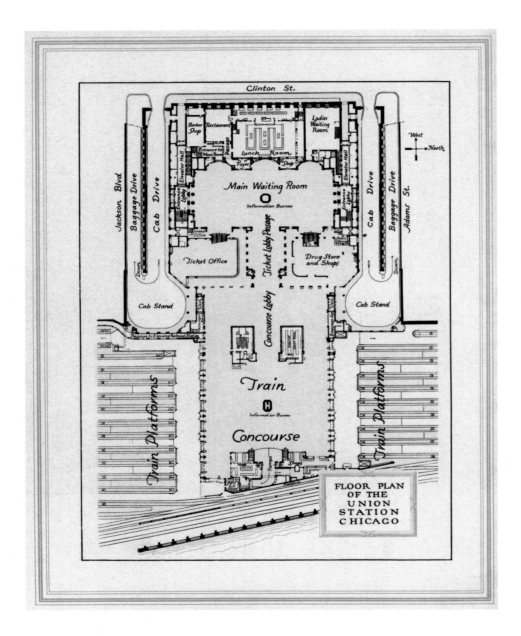

FLOOR PLAN
OF THE
UNION
STATION
CHICAGO

(*Left*) Floor levels of the Concourse and the Headhouse connected under Canal Street, but even this expanse could not contain all services. Restrooms were in the basement and other necessities, such as a small hospital, were located on the mezzanine.

COURTESY OF THE AUTHOR

(*Facing, from left to right*) Concessionaire Fred Harvey & Company hired its own illustrator for a depot guide as well as colorizing sketches supplied by Graham, Anderson, Probst & White.

COURTESY AMTRAK/CHICAGO UNION STATION COMPANY

With some creative coloring and perspective, the ticketing lobby undergoes a majestic transformation. This may be the only time blue sky and clouds were visible from this location.

COURTESY AMTRAK/CHICAGO UNION STATION COMPANY

Canal Street postcard view.

Postcards showing the original conception of the Fred Harvey restaurant and lunchroom circulated for decades even though it was built to a different plan.

UNION STATION
CHICAGO

Burlington
Bulletin

JANUARY-FEBRUARY-MARCH 1969   NUMBER 41

NEW STATION FOR CHICAGO

(*Facing, from left to right*) Visitors to the opening day at the station received a commemorative booklet with this cover illustration.

COURTESY AMTRAK/CHICAGO UNION STATION COMPANY

The Tishman-built tower was touted by the Burlington railroad even though they didn't own the structure.

COURTESY OF THE AUTHOR

(*Right*) A cutaway view of Lucien Lagrange's twin tower redevelopment design only hints at the complexity of constructing modern spaces atop vintage footings.

COURTESY OF LUCIEN LAGRANGE

(*Facing*) Lucien Lagrange's first proposal for the Headhouse envisioned twin towers.

COURTESY OF LUCIEN LAGRANGE

(*Right, from top*) The Union Station Master Plan had short-term and long-term goals. It proposes eventually to house intercity functions under air-rights buildings south of the current station.

COURTESY OF THE CHICAGO DEPARTMENT OF TRANSPORTATION

The West Loop Transportation Center was an ambitious concept to provide through tracks for high-speed trains, a new CTA transit line, and an underground walkway to the Ogilvy Transportation Center.

COURTESY OF THE CHICAGO DEPARTMENT OF TRANSPORTATION

Amtrak trains from due south must navigate with back-up moves from the elevated St. Charles Airline, which materially slows schedules. Commuter trains and Amtrak movements on the ground level BNSF line have a direct route.

The Grand Hall of the Headhouse has rarely been crowded since World War II, but
the 2016 battle of the Chicago Cubs for a World Series title brought standing-room-only
crowds to suburban trains and the station.

Recent renovations have brought two new lounge areas to the station, this being an attractive two-level oasis for sleeping car patrons.

COURTESY AMTRAK/CHICAGO UNION STATION COMPANY

for a contract. During that period, the Pennsylvania Railroad invested $100 million in New York City for the Hudson and East River tunnels and Penn Station. A tunnel and Union Station in Washington and major Pittsburgh improvements were nearly as expensive. Between these points it undertook an almost complete rebuilding of the railroad's physical plant. New bridges and stronger rails were required to carry heavier new locomotives. The Pennsylvania reequipped its trains with steel cars for both passengers and freight. In the process, it revolutionized the railroad business, and with considerable justification called itself "The Standard Railroad of the World." Historians would later call this part of the "Second American Revolution." Albro Martin, for example, noted that the "Progressive era saw a continuation of eager demand for capital, but also a shift away from quick-payoff commitments to more complex, more sophisticated and generally slow payoff investments."[18] The Pennsylvania's many projects required it to issue $375 million in fresh debt between 1896 and 1906. Despite its preeminence, its thirst for capital meant that by the end of this period it paid 5 percent on bonds versus only 3.5 percent at the beginning. With capital scarce and expensive, Chicago waited while other cities received new terminals.

Clearly, Daniel Burnham's personal relationships, as much as his firm's design prowess, won the plum Chicago station contract. Burnham personally oversaw draft designs through the delivery of preliminary blueprints dated January 1, 1912.[19] He sailed for Europe in April, and on June 1, he died in Heidelberg, Germany. It was front-page news, and even President Taft was moved to eulogies. Inside the railroad, the death notice written by Joshua D'Esposito, the Pennsylvania Railroad's liaison with the architects, was terse. It briefly expressed shock and grief, but then bluntly stated, "We will miss the prestige he brought to this project."[20]

D'Esposito's career is itself a fitting representation of the teamwork needed to develop a project of Union Station's scale. Senior draftsman for Pennsylvania Railroad Lines West, he reported to Thomas Rodd. His title gave little hint of his importance to the project, but his office address was notable. He worked in the Railway Exchange Building office suite of D. H. Burnham and Company. Born in Sicily, D'Esposito trained in naval architecture. This honed his considerable analytic prowess, but also reflected a streak of wanderlust, for upon graduation he struck out across the world as a ship's officer. After several years, he decamped for America, where he found jobs in civil engineering. One engagement was for the Pittsburgh street railway, where he attracted the notice of the town's largest employer. He worked only a few years as a draftsman before the Pennsylvania Railroad sent him to Chicago, where he was to spend nearly three decades working on Union Station. As onsite engineer, he was knowledgeable about the railroad's building standards, hierarchy, operating practices, and a host of other details. D'Esposito was in almost daily contact with the senior partner of the architects, Ernest Graham.

Graham handled the business details of the Burnham firm's contracts. He was a builder who learned the trades of carpentry, bricklaying, and construction management from his father. He possessed a liberal arts education from Coe College, but his unique understanding of people's motivations and an innate ability as an overseer served him best. Graham was renowned for his ability to run construction sites populated with uneducated

laborers often lacking rudimentary English-language skills. After he became a partner of Daniel Burnham, the sociable redhead adroitly placed a glossy veneer over his once hard-hewn manners. As a result, he became a remarkable salesman. The sense of rough justice he learned in the construction trade resurfaced with sufficient regularity, however, that a lampoon of Graham remarked,

And he said, If you think that my locks,
Are the only thing like a fox
Remember my guile and you'll see by my smile
That you've got yourself into a box![21]

The chief designer for Chicago Union Station was soft-spoken Peirce Anderson, who earlier had been responsible for Washing-

ton Union Station.[22] As a young man, he succeeded the brilliant Charles Atwood as head of design for D. H. Burnham and Company after Atwood's death at age forty-five. A lifelong bachelor, Anderson's modesty belied his education. After graduating from Harvard in 1892, he gained the notice of Daniel Burnham, who encouraged him to enroll at the École des Beaux-Arts in Paris, from which he graduated in 1899. He quickly joined Burnham's firm; like his boss, he had a natural affinity for the conservative styles appreciated by the firm's blue-chip clientele. As D. H. Burnham and Company grew, Anderson recruited like-minded designers. Their classicism produced a uniform body of work, which assured clients of the highest-quality workmanship in a monumental style.

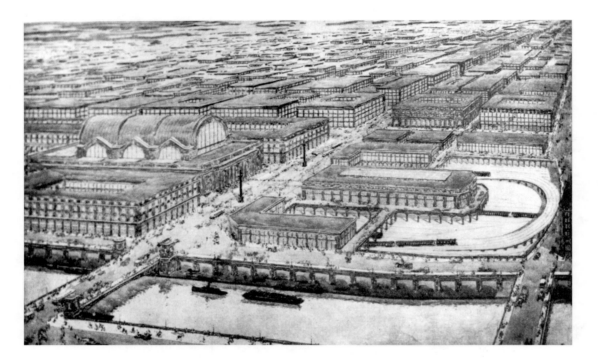

Edward Bennett likely drew this Chicago Plan Commission proposal, which located the depot at Twelfth Street, but it has several unworkable components. The loop for turning trains was unworkable, as it would have required straightening the river prior to station construction, the northern approach would have been under buildings for over a mile, and it required an extravagant use of expensive real estate.

COURTESY OF THE AUTHOR

After Burnham's death, the architectural partnership reorganized, first with his sons as partners in the firm of Graham, Burnham and Company. Subsequently, the Burnham brothers and Edward Bennett left to set up their own firms, while the other partners formed Graham, Anderson, Probst and White. The dissolution agreement between the parties specifically mentioned that the latter firm retained the Chicago Union Station contract. They had, after all, always been the ones with the expertise necessary to design and build such a massive project. Anderson and Graham, moreover, were known in railroad circles. Daniel

Burnham's sons, by contrast, had little contact with Pennsylvania Railroad officials.

At the new firm, Edward Probst oversaw drafting, structural engineering, and plumbing. These details were the responsibility of his staff of two hundred professionals. Probst and Howard White started as draftsmen and both worked their entire adult lives for Burnham or successor firms. White handled contract administration and managed construction. Ernest Graham's administrative assistant, Charles Murphy, seems (for the period during which Union Station was designed) to have provided

Early sketches by Graham, Anderson, Probst & White simply transposed Washington Union Station to a Chicago site, with particular interest in an elaborate concourse.

COURTESY OF THE HAGLEY MUSEUM AND LIBRARY, 97.263

some of the glue that kept the architectural team together, although he later left the partnership.[23] While the firm actively courted and consulted the railroad's senior executives, design-related matters were addressed to Thomas Rodd and increasingly to Joshua D'Esposito.

The Pennsylvania Railroad envisioned a monumental in-kind replacement for its existing depot. Unlike suggested comprehensive plans, it included only companies already using the depot. Thus limited, at first it did not seem to reorder the map of Chicago. Its core, however, was a substantial capacity increase requiring staggering amounts of additional real estate. In particular, it relocated the antiquated freight houses along the river. Rail-to-water transfer had diminished and, since the affected riverfront was controlled by the Ft. Wayne, there was little impediment to the reallocation of that land for passenger service. This partially solved the passenger capacity issue, but created problems elsewhere. A freight house in a new location had to provide for another rapidly growing business. Moreover, the narrow site still seemed to defy the demands for ample passenger waiting and ticketing areas.

Thomas Rodd sketched the solution, at least for the depot itself, in December 1909. On a half sheet of graph paper, he inked a freehand plan to relocate the headhouse and its waiting room west of Canal Street. It called for an understreet passageway connecting these monumental new areas with the concourse in such a manner that the main floor, both east and west of Canal, was level with the station platforms. This arrangement dictated a centrally located concourse flanked north and south by stub-end station tracks. While not a duplication of the original track plan, it was consistent with existing operating practice. Vesti-

gial through tracks adjacent to the river remained for switching mail cars. Rodd's equally rough elevation showed an office tower wrapping in a U shape around the headhouse. Otherwise, it captured the ultimate design of the project, even incorporating the underground taxiway that was one of the plan's major features. This rude sketch, which still survives, was sent to draftsmen and clean blueprints circulated among railroad officials together with a dozen schemes. It prevailed because of its simplicity.

As the Pennsylvania finalized plans and shipped its specifications to Graham, Anderson, Probst and White, it also established new legal underpinnings. July 3, 1913, saw incorporation of the "Union Station Company (Chicago)." No longer would the Ft. Wayne be landlord and the other carriers tenants. Ownership reflected the rising importance of the western lines, as well as the need to spread the staggering cost among multiple owners. The creation of a separate terminal company, however, broke the chain of railway property valuation. When the Ft. Wayne owned all depot grounds, taxes on each parcel reflected a prorated share of the owner's earning power. As a separate company, however, valuation now rested on station company earnings; that is, taxes were calculated on the fees needed to retire a staggering amount of bonded debt for what was now an entirely urban property. Property taxes soared as a result.

The incorporation was not without controversy. The Pennsylvania paid a $50,000 fee to the state of Illinois for the station company charter, even though this may not have been strictly necessary. Until the previous year, the state assessed a fee of $1 per $1,000 of authorized capital for each corporate charter. A new law known as the Landee Act reduced this to a $2.50 filing fee. First to take advantage of the Landee Act had been the

Chicago, Burlington and Quincy, which needed to reincorporate with greater capital. The Act saved it $110,000. When the public learned that Burlington attorneys drafted the Landee Act, however, payoff rumors surfaced. Progressive legislators entered a bill to revoke the Act, but it did not pass until after the Union Station Company presented its charter. To save face (and money) the Burlington tried to negotiate a "good faith" agreement that was to have both it and the depot company pay one-half the old rate. Both reformist politicians and the pragmatic Pennsylvania Railroad rejected this compromise.[24]

OPPOSITION

Peirce Anderson's first elevation drawings for Union Station strongly reflected his Beaux-Arts training. His preliminary sketches were, in fact, simple adaptations of his Washington Union Station design to the Chicago site. The waiting room thrust upward from a base of Corinthian columns, then sprang skyward on great arches forming a coffered barrel vault. This concept went unused, although like the eventual design, it mirrored Thomas Rodd's site plan.

Monumental in scope and innovative in layout, the proposal should have pleased the Chicago establishment. On January 20, 1913, Ernest Graham unveiled detailed elevation drawings and the layout for both the passenger station and a new freight house to the Chicago Plan Commission, including Chairman Charles Wacker and staff architect Edward Bennett. Graham reported to Thomas Rodd that "from all appearances the meeting was a very happy and satisfactory one." Graham, noted for his ability to read and influence men, knew that influential portions of Chicago's establishment already endorsed the plan. He thought their support

unwavering, but he was wrong. The Plan Commission quickly condemned the proposal and enumerated its issues:

1. The proposal impeded the unification of all railroads into a single depot.
2. Relocation of the freight houses while maintaining their proximity to the downtown area presented major difficulties. In particular, the Pennsylvania Railroad planned an elevated freight line to reach a new warehouse complex, but it bisected the spot where the *Plan of Chicago* proposed a new civic center. In addition, the new freight line would block through streets into the business district, an effect opposite to that desired.
3. No land was released for the expansion of the business district. To the contrary, it required that the railroads purchase and occupy additional land.
4. The Union Station proposal continued the railroad's "monopoly" on the riverfront near the business district. The commission thought this aesthetically and commercially unacceptable.
5. Stub-end terminals were poorly suited to suburban traffic. Through-routing trains to coach yards on the other side of town, allowing connections with other suburban lines, had had strong advocates.

Five years earlier the Chicago and North Western's depot plan had raised similar issues without objection. The difference was that Chicago now had a Plan Commission, guardian of Burnham and Bennett's *Plan of Chicago*. The Commission consisted of several hundred prominent citizens plus the head of every major department of city government. It had a diverse constituency, but maintained its focus on long-held municipal objectives. Its

GRAHAM, BURNHAM & CO ARCHTS.

142

quasi-official status as a government planning body allowed it to mobilize powerfully and quickly. A unified civic voice rose to oppose the project. In retrospect, however, the question is, why? The railroads desperately needed increased capacity, and no matter how much operating efficiency improved, that required more land. How then could the railroads also release land for commercial development? That was possible only if the city enacted its decades-old plan to move the railroads out of downtown. The Plan Commission demanded adherence to the letter of the *Plan of Chicago*, but this task was impossible.

In 1913, as in the 1896 proposal to remove the railroads from proximity to the business district, no railroad would unilaterally move to a less competitive location while its rivals remained downtown. The railroads using LaSalle Street and North Western Stations had relatively new depots entered by elevated tracks built at great cost. So there was little possibility of forcing them to move soon. The Plan Commission knew, however, that if it allowed Union Station to remain near downtown, the probability of getting the other railroads to move to Twelfth Street—its real motive—seemed slight. Edward Bennett knew the high stakes, and as he confided in his personal notes, there was a "Risk of throwing discredit on entire plan movement in changing [the

Plan] . . . [We] must connect the problem with whole plan scheme—this is greatest challenge offered to establish prestige of Plan Commission."[25]

The Plan Commission was adamant, and managing director Walter D. Moody expressed its sentiments:

> Mr. Graham yesterday showed you the magnificent terminal that the railroads offer us, that beautiful Roman structure with classical lines. Such a station, in view of the disgraceful conditions in the present west side station, we have a perfect right to expect and a perfect right to demand.
>
> When the Union Station officials appeared before the City Council . . . they stated that their present Union Passenger Station was a disgrace, a menace to life and limb, and wholly inadequate for the current needs. The next day the newspapers published an ultimatum by those railroad officials in which they said that if they could not carry out their proposed plans they would carry out none. Gentlemen, as one citizen of Chicago, I am not prepared to have persons come here from Pittsburgh or anywhere else and tell me to jump through their hoop, and I don't think the rest of the citizens of Chicago are in that frame of mind either.[26]

Opposition coalesced around the Pennsylvania's proposed elevated freight line. Everyone agreed that the only way enough downtown land could be made available for new passenger terminals was to move the freight houses. Still, freight facilities needed proximity to downtown customers and the Pennsylvania's existing trackside sites seemed inadequate. The railroad held steadfastly that it needed an entirely new alignment, but the public saw the proposed elevated freight line as a "Chinese wall" between the West Side and the business district. In truth, it would have closed few streets, but it promised to increase congestion in several already densely packed neighborhoods.

The Pennsylvania's freight line seemed to preclude opening Congress Street as a boulevard, a major component of the *Plan of Chicago*. That processional thoroughfare was to be a grand link between a new civic center and downtown. This pre-expressway solution to traffic circulation problems was crucial; any proposal blocking this vision was politically naive. The Pennsylvania unilaterally declared that the planned civic center had to move two blocks north. There, the railroad stated, its freight houses and warehouse facilities would front this monumental group of public buildings. Chicagoans were insulted and would not consider relocating their proposed city hall, its great dome prominently illustrated in Daniel Burnham's plan, to a warehouse district. The railroads' every statement caused greater indignation, which only swelled when surveyors and engineers combed the West Side while railroad officials demurred on detailing their plans. Stonewalling resulted in their vilification.

In a gesture to local sentiment, Hale Holden, president of the Chicago-based Burlington, replaced Thomas Rodd and other Pennsylvania managers as public spokesman for the Union Station companies. Holden was a Commercial Club member who once sat on the Plan Commission. The "men from Pittsburgh"

publicly retreated, even as they met privately with Bennett and Wacker. Chicagoan Ernest Graham's persuasive powers focused on the commissioners, who included fellow architects and their businessmen clients. He cajoled Bennett, but privately Bennett sneered, "ERG poses as a sympathizer to the Plan of Chicago."[27] What seemed to be a public battle over real estate was a private contest between two men, each of whom inherited half the Burnham legacy. Graham was heir to the lucrative architectural partnership and Chicago Union Station contract, while Bennett got the city planning practice and Chicago Plan Commission contract. Given his distaste for Graham, Bennett was in a bind. Peirce Anderson, who was Graham's partner, executed the station design. He was Bennett's best friend, a gentle man the Bennett children called "Uncle Dandy."

Graham seemed stunned when the Chicago Plan Commission countered with its own proposal. It was a comprehensive arrangement of railroad terminals that borrowed from earlier works, but included more detail on arrangements west of the river. The new plan was the creation of Delano, including multiple terminals at Twelfth Street as had his original proposals. Delano once gave Graham his personal support for the station company's plan; now he abrogated that alliance.[28] From Hunt, the Commission borrowed the idea of loop tracks; like various independent plans, its plan straightened the Chicago River. Two loops oriented south to north replaced Hunt's single east-west loop. Union Depot was to be on a loop west of the river with a sister terminal occupying the opposite east bank. Warehouses north of Twelfth Street eliminated the need for the offensive freight line. Delano provided Bennett a track plan, which suggests the assistance of his Wabash Railroad staff. The

The Plan of Chicago marked the infancy of city planning in America, so it is not surprising that the Plan Commission responded to railroad proposals in an infantile manner. They countered with vitriolic rhetoric and this bird's-eye view that encapsulated their unrealistic demands.

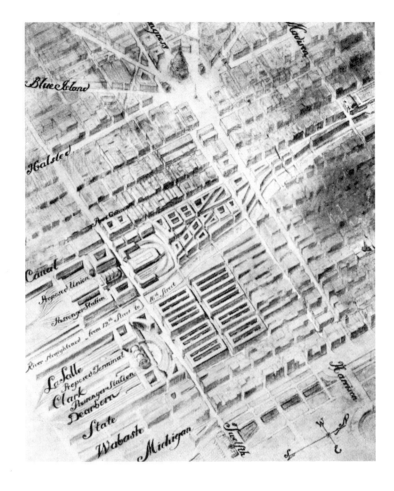

Plan Commission then pressed it on the larger Pennsylvania Railroad.

Perspective drawings by Edward Bennett accompanying the Plan Commission's report had the familiar Burnham look. In fact, elevations show three great semicircular windows piercing the great barrel vault over the station's waiting room. These dramatic lunettes were also known as thermal windows after their origin in the Roman baths of antiquity. The resulting vault was nearly identical to the work Burnham's firm had done for Delano nearly a decade before. Perhaps Bennett's hand executed the early

Delano design. Reused first in the *Plan of Chicago*, Bennett recycled it again.

By the spring of 1913, battle lines were already drawn when Peirce Anderson's detailed elevations for the Chicago Union Station Headhouse debuted. He conformed to his client's site plan, but discarded his original drawings. His new design pierced the barrel vault with lunettes like the Plan Commission design. Anderson's exterior, however, featured a shallow peaked roof, unlike earlier designs in which the rounded vault had clear expression. It bore a striking resemblance to another Pennsylvania Railroad monument, the New York City station designed by McKim, Mead and White that opened three years prior.

Ernest Graham suggested that the planned post office locate west of the station, to allow a direct underground connection from the station baggage room to the post office. Graham noted that 65 percent of the mail entering Chicago passed through the Union Depot. In this respect, Graham struck a conciliatory note with the Plan Commission, which grudgingly added that a post office located directly north rather than west of the proposed headhouse site would also adjoin the C&NW's Madison Street Station.

Adamant for a new freight line, the Pennsylvania plunged into the real estate market even as it began engineering work, finally revealing its plan. The freight terminal was to occupy a plat bounded by Van Buren, Ewing, Jefferson, and Des Plaines Streets about two blocks west and two blocks south of the Union Station Headhouse. It called for a triple-deck terminal with loading docks for outgoing freight below grade, teaming incoming freight at street level, and railroad cars loading and unloading from an elevated freight yard. Details fanned dissent.

Railroad managers came to expect the worst. They knew the notoriously corrupt city council never gave anything away, but they were unsure of Plan Commission intentions. The Commission should have been their ally under the City Beautiful banner, but they feared it was an aldermanic stalking horse put forth to maximize graft. In his 1936 monograph on the history of Union Station, A. B. Olson, valuation attorney for the Chicago Union Station Company, stated: "It seemed at one time that the Station Company would be forced to pay a million dollars to certain politicians in order to secure passage. It is to the everlasting credit of General Counsel Frank J. Loesch that he refused to be a party to any such demands of the politicians, and carried the fight to the general public—who, when aroused, forced its passage."[29]

Olson was likely correct about the demands, as local politicians were hardly timid, but he was wrong about the public's support. The railroads and the public were adversaries, not allies.

Complicating an already tense situation, architect and activist Jarvis Hunt went public with a campaign for his own consolidation plan.[30] Surprisingly candid about his sincere dislike for the Pennsylvania Railroad, Hunt admitted that one experience colored his thoughts. He cited an earlier contract to construct the Keely-Maus Building on Chicago's West Side. A roadway to this building needed to be built over Pennsylvania Railroad tracks, for which Hunt procured a municipal ordinance. The Pennsylvania feared a rival claim to its land and worried about maintenance costs. Pending appeal, it parked trains on the four-track wide construction site. Hunt's client maintained that the land over the tracks was public, while the railroad defended its property.

Hunt expressed his antipathy toward the railroad in the following testimony before a city council committee:

ALDERMAN HEAZLY: "Mr. Hunt, the PRR group, supposing we refuse to grant them the privilege of building a terminal where they have in mind. They would stay where they are, the present Union Depot. What power would force them out?"

JARVIS HUNT: "The people will force them out. Why, that has been done in many different cities."

ALDERMAN HEALY: "Do you mean a boycott?"

JARVIS HUNT: "Now let me tell you what happened in one little city in the south in building a Union Station in Dallas. One of the roads said, 'We won't consider a Union Station.' The merchants in town said, 'Gentlemen, if you don't consider a Union Station, we will tell you what we will do. We won't put any freight on your road.' Did they come in? You bet they did."[31]

Hunt unwittingly committed professional suicide. Railroad companies had been his largest clients and he never worked for them again. He was not alone, however, in his antagonism. In 1913, the Chicago Plan Commission, by its own account, held 420 meetings on the subject of railroad terminals.[32] Most were efforts to jawbone the railroads into a consolidation scheme. The rail companies were intractable—the result was a standoff. Politics, however, abhors a vacuum, and the impasse seemed to create opportunities others could exploit. Local architects independently promoted their own radical schemes to consolidate the city's six depots. The City Club of Chicago held weekly public forums on the subject and eventually discussed nine formal proposals.

Brothers Allen and Irving Pond thought the rapidly growing city required four separate depots. They borrowed from all previous plans to propose that the Illinois Central stay on the lakefront and three other depots be built west of the Chicago River. To reach these West Side depots, their scheme elevated all tracks to create a two-block wide "great rail highway" available to all companies. South- and eastbound trains were to use tracks on the west side of this highway; north- and westbound trains utilizing tracks next to the river. In addition, the scheme elevated approach tracks for miles outward.[33] Within their de-

pots, the tracks were double decked, an expensive proposition in which two upper decks would ride atop one another over miles of viaducts. A series of three interconnected loops ensured that trains from various yards and approach tracks connected smoothly to their correct departure track.[34] The Ponds had even more faith in loop tracks than Hunt. They postulated that loops increased capacity threefold, a claim without merit. Examination of their loops showed that the switches they required were near each loop's point of minimum radius. Since turnouts need an even tighter radius than the loops themselves, no existing rail car would be able to negotiate them. When engineers objected at a public meeting of the Western Society of Engineers, the Pond brothers retorted that the railroads were simply obstructionist.

William Drummond of the firm of Guenzel and Drummond based his plan on an idea that railroad managers perhaps found attractive. He believed downtown freight and passenger terminals were a municipal asset requiring city funding. The city would then lease access to all railways. In return, they would coordinate their facilities. Of the competing ideas, Drummond's plan was the most economical in land use, a goal he accomplished by expanding on the idea of the "great railroad highway." His proposal did away with the loops of Pond and Pond by making

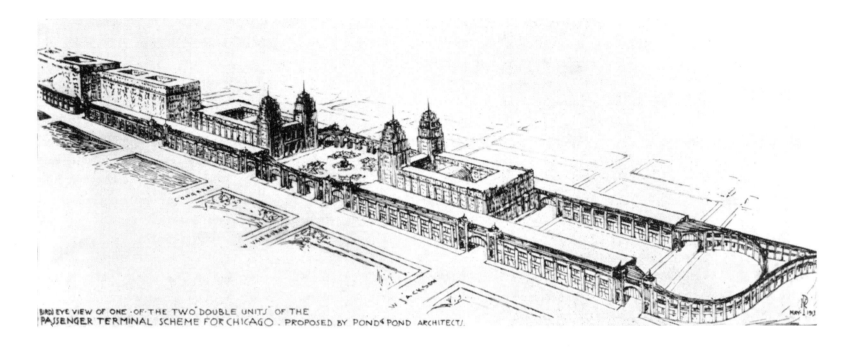

BIRDS EYE VIEW OF ONE · OF · THE · TWO DOUBLE UNITS · OF THE
PASSENGER TERMINAL SCHEME FOR CHICAGO · PROPOSED BY POND & POND ARCHITECTS.

the railroads reorder their various lines entering Chicago and by adding specialized connecting tracks at their junctions. It resembled the West Side placement of the *Plan of Chicago* without the loop for suburban traffic. Edward Bennett sniffed, "Mr. Drummond architect outlined [the] most radical proposals including ideas evolved and discarded during the study of the Chicago Plan."[35] By Drummond's method, traffic entering or departing the downtown area would always face in the proper direction and all stations would operate as through depots, rather than stubended. Drummond's railroad highway, while only one block wide along the river's west bank, required tracks on three levels—all elevated above the streets.[36] This required a mammoth structure

miles long, which Drummond embellished with a uniform facade in the style subsequently called "Prairie School." Four depot towers of uniform design would serve various companies, although commuter trains would stop at all four stations.

The various proposals served mainly to confuse and delay. Pennsylvania engineer Joshua D'Esposito summarized the proceedings by noting, "Sometimes we get involved in difficulties by reason of too ready a belief in attractive presentations of poor projects." George E. Hooker, as an officer of the City Club, presented an overview of train station development domestically and in Europe. The politically connected Hooker already served on an ad hoc city council committee that reorganized the street railways. He became so enamored with the idea of coordinating the transit system that he proposed a similar study of the steam railroads. He succeeded in August 1913 with the formation of the Citizens' Terminal Plan Commission to sift the competing plans. The Commission was entirely separate from the city council, which already had a standing committee to review railroad matters. Hooker's independent organization raised $100,000 by private subscription. It had no legal standing and its directors were self-selected. Unlike the corrupt city government, it had an unimpeachable image. With substantial resources mobilized behind this blue-ribbon panel, its power seemed unstoppable.

The Citizens' Terminal Plan Commission hired nationally prominent consulting engineer Bion Arnold to review the city's needs. Arnold was an electrical engineer, then the pinnacle of technology; as a street railway expert, he was part of Hooker's earlier transit effort.[37] Arnold knew that streetcar lines promoted wide dispersal of commercial activity. As such, he believed that Chicago's growth required multiple business districts. Following this hypothesis, the true need in railroad terminal rearrangement was development of a system allowing passengers to travel through one city center onward to other urban and suburban locations. Similar thinking had been responsible for two seminal European projects revered for their pioneering work in urban planning. The Quai D'Orsay station in Paris and its electrified Orleans line were the model for unobtrusive construction of a railway line in an urban context. The Alexanderplatz station in Berlin and its Stadtbahn and Ringbahn network meanwhile showed great promise as the model for intracity passenger circulation.[38] Arnold's Chicago street railway reorganization instituted a system of universal transfers to promote through traffic.

His steam railroad plan extended this logic. Rather than endorse any existing proposal, Arnold muddied the waters when he outlined not one but three new alternatives.[39]

Government leaders, meanwhile, realized they had a problem. The politicians exercised limited control over Chicago Plan commissioners and now they faced another unbridled rival. Both the politicians and the Plan Commission saw the Citizens' Terminal Plan Commission as a foe. Worse for city officials were the mocking (and true) insinuations that due to recurring municipal graft the citizen reformers held the moral high ground. If Hooker's new group found common cause with the railroads, the wider demands of the Plan Commission and the city government would likely go by the wayside.

In December, Mayor Harrison pushed the railroads and they pushed back. The city publicly called for negotiation, but privately was implacable in its demands. The railroads, led by J. J. Turner of the Pennsylvania, conspicuously walked out while testifying at a city council committee meeting, prompting the mayor to retort, "A bat five miles back in Mammoth Cave could not be blinder than these railroad men." Taking special aim at the Pennsylvania freight line proposal, he added, "Everybody sees, except you railroad men, the monstrosity of the Northwestern [sic] railway station now. If the city council and mayor were to stand for such a station today they would be lynched."[40] This statement ignored the fact that the North Western station was built without opposition and that it continued to be hailed by newspapers and city guidebooks.

In April the city redirected its efforts with the formation of its own dedicated group, the Chicago Railway Terminal Committee, adding to three already standing City Council committees—

This beautiful Prairie School rendering by Guenzel and Drummond illustrated that the architects had not listened to the debate. It featured a "Chinese wall" many times longer and higher than that which scuttled the Pennsylvania freight line.

COURTESY OF THE AUTHOR

one each for railways, track elevation, and railroad electrification. Subcommittees on subways and harbors also debated railway matters. Each was nominally independent of the Chicago Plan Commission, as was this new committee. The mayor's floor leader in the council, alderman Ellis Gage, received his appointment as chairman from the mayor. Unlike council committees composed exclusively of aldermen selected by majority vote, Gage hand-picked the committee's three other representatives and promised each $12,000 for their service. Council committee members here-

tofore never received pay and this gave an appearance that the "fix was in," albeit a fix made with public funds. Once exposed, the Mayor disavowed everything, but the committee appointments remained unchanged.

On May 20, Mayor Carter Harrison II surprised all concerned by endorsing the Union Station Company ordinances and pledging to fight all other proposals. Six days later, three issues came before the council, and despite objections, all were sent to the new committee for discussion. They involved the vacation of streets, the station itself, and the freight facilities. Few details became public until June 23. As opponents argued that a deal was being "jammed through," the hastily convened committee passed all three ordinances. Chairman Gage sent draft ordinances to the full council that afternoon, denying the five other subcommittees deliberating terminal matters any chance to speak. A private session was then held in Mayor Harrison's office with Joseph Wood of the Pennsylvania Railroad. As they conferred, Charles Wacker, chairman of the Plan Commission, and architect Jarvis Hunt cooled their uninvited heels in the mayor's anteroom. They watched in awe as police stopped Frederic Delano at the door and ejected him from the building.[41] Later that afternoon, the council voted against the idea of tying the Union Station ordinance to the consolidation of the other passenger terminals. All other issues were tabled.

With consolidation of the South Side depots still in the balance, the city realized that it needed a professional manager to place its committee on an equal footing with its private-sector rival. On June 30, Mayor Harrison announced that he would release $10,000 "as a starter" to pay such an expert. Committee aldermen met the next day to discuss the issue. The result as described in the *Chicago Daily News* was as follows:

> It happened like the fairy tale of the rich prince looking for a beautiful maiden. Strolling along Jackson Boulevard, they glanced at the Union League Club—and there in the window was John Wallace. He is supposedly one of the busiest consultants in the country. On the day previous, he just happened to leave his New York home for Chicago, he just happened to be lounging in the club window, the aldermen just happened to be strolling along at that moment and it just happened that Mayor Harrison had given them a $10,000 bank roll, and Mr. Wallace agreed to start.[42]

Designer of the World's Columbian Exposition terminal that featured Charles Atwood's iconic Beaux-Arts station building, Wallace had a brilliant career as a railroad engineer. His specialties included such necessities of urban railroad operation as the design of interlocking plants, the installation of signaling systems, and the elevation of tracks. Briefly in charge of building the Panama Canal, he failed miserably during his short stint at that job due to an inordinate fear of tropical diseases. Now his task was to draw up plans to consolidate the railway terminals—excluding, so it was stated, the Union Station and North Western railroads. The mayor's hand-picked committee and their consultant presented a reformist face to the public. Their public facade, however, concealed traditional machinations. In December, Thomas McGuire of the McGuire & White private detective agency admitted under oath that he had been hired to follow opponents of the proposed Union Station site.[43] This intimidation was insufficient, so Mayor Harrison and Alderman Geiger publicly planted rumors that opponents of the plan held options on land near alternate sites. City Hall was playing hardball.

The depot ordinance passed on March 23, 1914, fifteen months after Ernest Graham unveiled his preliminary drawings. The key to passage was the Pennsylvania's abandonment of its elevated freight line and freight house plan. Rather, it would build new freight facilities south of Union Station at Taylor and Canal Streets. The railroads agreed to build viaducts at Sixteenth,

Fourteenth, Twelfth, Taylor, Polk, Harrison, Congress, Van Buren, Jackson, Adams, Monroe, Madison, Randolph, and Lake Streets. They agreed to pay for an elevated roadway at Canal and Kinzie Streets, with a new bridge to the North Side. They would also widen, regrade, and pave Canal Street between Twelfth and Washington Streets. Railroad engineers estimated these improvements would cost $5.86 million. The Panhandle and Milwaukee also agreed to elevate their tracks between Ashland and Curtis Streets. For its part, the city agreed to $1.8 million in related improvements including two bridges, but only after the railroads paid $1.5 million for streets vacated by the city.[44]

The ordinance also elevated the Council Committee on Railway Terminals to commission level to widen its membership and allow for permanent funding. It was to monitor railroad company performance under the Union Station ordinances, but it was destined to work primarily for South Side depot consolidation. The ordinances required that the Chicago Union Station Company agree to straighten the bend in the Chicago River and to pay a proportionate share of the expense.[45] The railroads immediately indicated their willingness to sign all these agreements.

The Citizens' Terminal Plan Commission and the new Chicago Railway Terminal Commission discussed consolidation after the Union Station ordinance passed. Both excluded railroad managers from membership. The railroads, of course, would have to pay for any improvements they demanded. Perhaps the reformers excluded them because they would brook no discussion of cost limitations, but at least now the rival commissions began to cooperate. Rapprochement between zealous reformers and rapacious boodlers was a curiosity, but as one contemporary noted:

Civic pride was high in Chicago. It stung, in particular a few rich men, and these decided that they must have the finest city on the globe. They formed a Plan Commission and gave it money to employ engineers. And although this Commission has never had any authority except that of general public enthusiasm, its edicts have been obeyed as explicitly as Napoleon's were when he commanded Baron Haussman to rebuild Paris. Through shifting administrations and the worst city government on earth, their work has progressed. "How?" I asked. The answer was a wink. "Remember—there is always big graft in letting such huge contracts for improvements."[46]

Their new rapport started with a joint European tour to review state-of-the-art railroad planning. Twenty-two delegates sailed for Liverpool on the RMS *Lusitania* on July 14, 1914, intent on inspecting fifteen cities. The outbreak of war in Europe made it difficult to change money and the threat of imminent hostilities caused railroad sites on the itinerary to be reclassified as military facilities. Local officials did conduct tours for the group in London, Paris, and Brussels, but their visit to the latter coincided with the Belgian mobilization. The Chicagoans wisely curtailed further travel.

European hostilities had enormous repercussions on the American banking system, which required the Union Station Company to ask for a one-year extension to accept the ordinances. It only got a three months' reprieve, and signed the agreements on September 23, starting the clock for project completion. Though this was momentous local news, Chicago's front pages headlined British and German battleships bombarding each other in the North Sea.

154

Union Station, the proposed Post Office, and North Western Station could have made an impressive assemblage on the Near West Side.

ALTERNATING CURRENTS

As politicians and moguls dickered, traffic steadily rose on every rail line, with the greatest increase on the Ft. Wayne. Its Valparaiso commuter service was an off-and-on affair until firmly established in 1906. By 1910, there were five commuter trains to Valparaiso, locally known as "Dummies," with fifteen trains to Gary and twenty-two to East Chicago on branches off the main line. Even service on heavily trafficked freight branches flourished before vanishing in 1919. Intercity train movements actually declined in 1903 due to congestion near Pittsburgh, but the new terminal there eliminated that bottleneck. The November 1907 opening of the Hudson River tunnels into Manhattan improved the Pennsylvania's competitive position and pushed the number of express trains to Chicago to fifteen.[47] The Burlington also saw increased service in June 1912 when it extended its commuter territory from Downers Grove to Aurora. To build traffic, it installed electric lighting in its suburban coaches, reportedly the only commuter trains in the world with that enhancement. There were now forty-three trains in each direction on the line.[48]

On July 20, 1913, a restaurant fire forced another remodeling of the existing depot even as debate raged over its replacement. The fire started on the top floor, spread to the waiting room and offices, and forced the evacuation of the building. The damage was $25,000.[49] The year's biggest expenses, however, resulted from an explosive growth in mail business caused by the U. S. Post Office's inauguration of parcel post service on January 1, 1914. Outsiders may have thought that the increased business would cause unmitigated joy among railroad managers. Mail and express, after all, were the only unfailingly profitable traffic through the depot. But the railroads had previously signed a multiyear contract with the Post Office Department stipulating fixed payments, no matter the tonnage. The government refused to renegotiate despite the unilateral expansion of its traffic. As a result, for years the railroads received no additional payments for this bulky new business.

Parcel post devastated the private express companies. These firms owned their own distribution facilities adjacent to the depots on land leased from the railroads. To handle bulky parcel post, Union Depot vacated three offices and converted parts of its baggage building into space leased to the Chicago postmaster. This was scant compensation for lost express company revenue; several companies went bankrupt because of postal competition. In the first year of parcel post, a daily average of five hundred tons of mail moved through the depot. This equaled the average tonnage of a freight train of the era, and it moved in break-bulk over the same platforms used by passengers. The same was true of an equal tonnage of baggage and express. The stationmaster even tallied 834 cans of milk and cream arriving daily on local trains for city delivery. As the mail carts lumbered past baggage-laden passengers, claims for injuries and torn clothing increased.

From late 1914 and continuing through 1915, poor economic conditions suppressed traffic. Depot managers actually welcomed this since their facility was now wholly inadequate. Construction began on the new terminal, but like many projects, its first impact was to obstruct traffic.

A NEW FOUNDATION

Two years after the Chicago Union Station Company's incorporation, it was necessary to recharter. This was done on May 7, 1915. Reflecting that the terminal would be more expensive than originally contemplated, the new charter allowed a larger capital base. In addition to the stipulated public improvements, the company was still buying property. The most expensive plot was Commonwealth Edison's original Chicago generating plant, for which the company paid $11.3 million. It also negotiated for an eight-story furniture warehouse at Polk Street and a two-story beer warehouse at Harrison.

The charter now delineated the duties imposed by the ordinance and allocated these costs to the individual railroads. The most important change, however, was to drop the Alton as a partner. That railroad had fallen on hard times after acquisition by the Moore-Reid syndicate, a group of bankers ruthless in their financial dealings but inept at day-to-day management. The ailing Alton remained as tenant and welcomed a $4.8 million payment for properties sold to the station company.

Construction of the new passenger terminal awaited relocation of the riverside freight houses. The Burlington moved to a temporary warehouse, but the Alton and the Pennsylvania soldiered on in old facilities. The Alton owned an alternative site for a freight house, but the Pennsylvania had to begin land acquisition anew. The river-straightening plan provided a partial solution. As luck would have it, the Baltimore & Ohio, owner of the required land, had its own need. Its Grand Central Station had to expand, which allowed a land swap. The B&O coach yard moved west, which allowed the transfer of its land to the Pennsylvania.[50]

Building demolition along the southern approach began in February, with two hundred men engaged and the promise that one thousand more would be employed on the Pennsylvania freight house within two weeks. In the first phase of Union

Station's construction, they built sewers, viaducts, and a riverside revetment. In addition, the company lowered the streetcar tunnel under its yard and the river to lower the track grade into its new terminal. Nearby, the city started work on the bridges. Back in June of 1912, Ernest Graham predicted completion in two years if work commenced immediately, but two years elapsed before work even began. The target date was now 1920.

LABOR PAINS

American railroads were the world's largest developers and construction managers. The Pennsylvania Railroad alone employed many times more professionals than any architectural or engineering firm in the nation, a force that included architects, civil engineers, draftsmen, and field personnel. The railroads nevertheless contracted for the design and construction of their Chicago facilities. In the latter case, the primary construction firm was the George A. Fuller Company. Massachusetts native Fuller had worked for the architectural firm of Peabody and Stearns before starting his firm in 1883. He appears to have pioneered, or at least perfected, the use of "cost plus" contracting at an early point in his career.[51] He was an affable salesman, like his occasional golf partner Daniel Burnham, and his firm soon dominated the construction of large buildings in Chicago. Fuller died in 1900, and John D. Rockefeller's real-estate holding corporation, United States Realty, bought his firm. A fellow contractor reflected that Fuller was:

> A new type of contractor, pioneering an administrative revolution in construction. Contractors until now usually had been boss carpenters or masons, men of little capital and foremanship, but generally of no technical education, who exe-

cuted sub-contracts under the supervision of the architects. This was feasible in small enterprises, but as buildings grew in magnitude architects were overwhelmed with a multiplicity of burdens for which many of them had little training and no aptitude. Fuller raised contracting from a limited trade to both an industry and a profession, visualizing the building problems in its [sic] entirety—promotion, finance, engineering, labor and materials.

Fuller's success rested on his firm's administrative abilities, its purchasing power, and its access to capital. The combined work of the Fuller company, the firm of Graham, Anderson, Probst and White, and four of the nation's most powerful railroads, the Union Station project benefited from an unparalleled pool of talent and seemingly limitless resources. However, subcontractors performed the actual work. Some of these, such as the iron and steel fabricators, were themselves substantial, while most others were little removed in social station or management sophistication from the workers they supervised. Of particular importance, the Fuller company and its subcontractors had experience in working with the construction unions that had come to power in Chicago during the preceding decades.

The railroads had signed labor contracts with their own workers for the first time only in the previous decade.[52] These agreements now presented a problem when dealing with local construction unions. Railroad workers insisted that only their organizations could represent those working on railroad projects. Building trade unions were equally adamant that only they represented local workers. These local unions formed among overlapping crafts and along confusing ethnic lines. Before the advent of overarching labor groups like the CIO and AFL, brawls and beatings often settled union differences and it was difficult for employers to determine which group to hire.

Collectively, such groups as the Painters' District Council, the Glaziers Union, the Wood Finishers Union, and the Fixture Hangers Union formed the Chicago Building Trades Council, or BTC. By the 1920s, the BTC represented nearly 100,000 construction workers, or 81 percent of the local building trades' workforce, but when Union Station started that level was still an organizer's dream. In fact, organizers engaged in a brutal business that left little time for dreaming. Each union elected its own business agent, often known as a "walking delegate," a title that described their job of patrolling the various job sites.[53] A collective board of such business agents governed the BTC. They met daily to impose fines on members who violated their rules, to determine the need for strikes or boycotts, and to update the "glass list." The latter contained the names of businesses and contractors who had breached contracts, hired scab labor, paid wages below scale, or made use of nonunion bricks and fixtures. It derived its name from the fact that the unions subjected "unfair firms" to a rain of stones and bricks through their windows. Because representatives of the various unions voted on them, union members viewed BTC actions as democratically controlled. In their minds, the fines and punishments meted out by the BTC were, in some vague sense, legal. Of course, its actions were never upheld in court and its vandalism routinely brought grief to its members.

The Building Trades Council held the railroads responsible for all labor used on their projects, even if it was hired by subcontractors. It demanded the use of BTC members on railroad construction within Cook County. Chicago-area track elevation projects then in progress employed an estimated twenty thousand men, so this was not a trivial request. Contracts had already been awarded, many to nonunion firms, and invalidating them was impossible. Railway unions responded that only *their* members should perform such work. Although the American Federation of Labor eventually disabused the railroad unions of this proposition, these issues deadlocked negotiations for months.

The first strike to affect the station project hit on September 11, 1915, when fifty men driving foundation piles struck for six days. Real problems began when three hundred steel workers building the Pennsylvania's new Polk Street freight house walked off the job on July 11, 1916. Another two hundred men refused to strike, but could not be used to advantage. The stoppage lasted 245 days, until March 12, 1917.

The railroads looked for an ally in the Building Construction Employers Association, an affiliate of the Employers Association of Chicago formed by the Chicago Association of Commerce and Industry in 1903. Frederic Delano had been one of its incorporators when he was at the Burlington.[54] The first test of the group was a 1905 strike of the teamsters, which immediately embroiled the railroads. Freight moved to the great distribution center of Chicago on the rails, but as labor historian Andrew Cohen observed, "Once the boxcars entered the city, they still entered a relatively immodern world of hustling entrepreneurs and craft workers, commission merchants and haulers, freight handlers and teamsters." The stage was set for a donnybrook.

A teamsters' strike on April 6, 1905 precipitated a lockout. It lasted 105 days, left 415 seriously injured, and at least 21 dead. The Employers Association broke the teamsters in part by buying a large drayage company and having association members sign exclusive contracts with this nonunion shop. At the same time, the shippers pressured the railroad companies to turn away any worker wearing a union pin from their freight houses—by force if necessary. A dozen years later, this rough treatment was unforgiven. By this time, the Employers Association had an arbitration agreement with the BTC and could threaten an industry-wide lockout to counter strike threats against its members, which included not only the Chicago Union Station Company but also Fuller Construction and many of its subcontractors. But business was brisk and the Employers' Association had no taste for a citywide lockout. According to notes taken by railroad representatives, it outlined four options relating to Union Station. It bluntly advised that the easiest way to settlement was to bribe officials of the BTC. Failing that, the railroads could formally petition the Association to vote on a citywide lockout to pressure union settlement. It gave little encouragement that this would succeed. Another option was simply to wait the men out, hoping they would need the work. Scab labor was also a possibility, but the trade group did not believe that nonunion contractors could be found for a project of the station's magnitude.

Railroad managers knew that any payoffs would go directly into the pockets of BTC officials even though they suspected that such a quick payment (be it a "fine" or a "fix") would solve their problem. Despite vigorous discussion, they never seriously considered such a payment because of confusion as to the price being asked to avoid a strike. The president of the Employers' Association stated that $50,000 was the demand for labor peace at the freight house. Joshua D'Esposito confirmed that he had heard the same quote "from two sources," but that he was uncertain which trades this covered. Other officials disagreed, suggesting

shakedowns of various amounts. The Burlington was also having difficulty with its temporary freight house and reported that union organizers demanded $7,500 for that project to proceed peacefully.

The Employers' Association's reluctance to support a lockout resulted from its membership base of small contractors, which, unlike the Pennsylvania Railroad and Fuller Construction, could not weather a protracted struggle. Moreover, it was not just a matter of work lost to a lockout. Many contractors were members of the Chicago Masons and Builders Association ("CMBA"), a trade group organized along the same craft lines as the unions that cooperated closely with organized labor. As union business agents visited job sites, they made certain that the pressed brick used by its members was union made. In 1897, the CMBA entered an agreement with the Brick Manufacturers Association, a thirty-seven-firm pool-like cartel that controlled 95 percent of local brick manufacturing. The masons agreed to use only the Manufacturers Association's pressed brick. In return, CMBA members, subcontractors on larger projects, received a kickback of one dollar per thousand bricks. Because the Brick Manufacturers Association was a union shop, the Building Trades Council effectively supported them by striking jobs using the products of its nonunion competitors.

The CMBA distributed payments from manufacturers to its members. The Pennsylvania freight house was to be the largest brick structure in Chicago history; many CMBA members stood to gain from its construction. In all likelihood, the railroads were oblivious to the masons' collusion, but they were acutely aware that their fellow Employers' Association members would not support a lockout.

Railroad reluctance to settle the strike through outright bribery was only partially grounded in high moral principle. Freight house projects were only a piece of their development plan. The thought of making endless blackmail payments for a variety of contracts must have been sobering. Pennsylvania officials also alluded to troubles with a payoff made by the Chicago and North Western during the construction of its nearby Madison Street Station. Large amounts of money apparently changed hands but a strike—albeit rather minor—occurred anyway. Finally (though a matter of lesser concern), bribes were illegal. Chicago newspapers routinely carried stories about "Umbrella Mike" Boyle, business agent for the International Brotherhood of Electrical

Workers.[55] Indeed, Boyle was in court at the time that railroad managers let the freight station contracts. Ultimately, his sentence was a year in prison for corruption regarding telephone contracts. What alarmed employers, however, was the $5,000 fine levied on Warren Ripple, the Western Electric Company officer who bribed Boyle.

Things were going so badly that by September 1917 the mayor's office appointed a special committee to look into Union Station construction problems; a month later both labor and management testified before the Chicago Railway Terminal Commission. To everyone's surprise, the city stated its belief that Fuller Construction provoked the strike in order to be released from its contract. They based their theory on the rapid run-up in inflation the nation experienced the previous year and a fixed-rate portion of Fuller's contract. Upon cross-examination, all parties denied this theory. Then attorney Morton Cressey exhibited his talents for double entendre. "Was it," he asked Robert Trimble of the Pennsylvania, "a hold-up on the part of Simon O'Donnell?" O'Donnell was head of the Building Trades Council. Trimble could only laugh and reply, "I live in Pittsburgh, you live in Chicago, and you ought to know O'Donnell much better than I do." The city decided not to intervene but rumors continued, and five years later, the Illinois legislature convened its own investigation. Again, no proof of wrongdoing surfaced, but everyone knew the problem.

That labor strife lasted so long is surprising, especially if its pivot was a mere $50,000 payoff. Ernest Graham knew how to obtain union cooperation and he had union leaders' respect in settling grievances of the gravest magnitude. Graham's private secretary, Charles F. Murphy, retold an event that illustrated his stature:

There was a long-lasting dispute between the plumbers and the steam fitters—they were mad [about jurisdictional problems between two similar crafts, which eventually merged as the Pipefitters Union]. R.J. Powers was a plumber. He was a great fellow to try to get things settled. He'd bring the troubles over to Graham, and they'd use Graham's office to deliberate. Graham was doing it to keep his jobs going. So, there was a lot of acrimonious language between these two, the steam fitters and the plumbers. I was supposed to be taking down the notes. It was about 2:30 in the morning when they decided to adjourn, and they asked me to go and write up the notes. I think eight lines were all they had written. Every word that was said had to be contested, so Graham said, "All right. We'll meet again after the holiday and start it again and talk about it." So the following Saturday, which was the day after or the second day after, at Pat O'Malley's saloon on State Street across from Marshall Field's, there was a gathering of these birds and a shooting. One man, a business agent, was killed: two others were hurt—shot. The following Monday, the whole tribe of leaders—Simon O'Donnell, Skinny Madden, Shaughnessey of the bricklayers, Mike Boyle—they all came back about ten o'clock in the morning to resume negotiations. Graham met them at the front door, and he said, "No, boys. I won't talk, not while you're doing that sort of thing." And he shut them out. You never hear of anything like that anymore, but it was bad. That one shooting was only one of many.[56]

As labor leader "Big Tim" Murphy explained, "they don't use boxing gloves in the labor movement, they use Smith and Westons [sic]."[57]

As construction progressed haltingly, the station's design remained in flux. Impatient for improvements to begin, City

Hall made it known that upon certain conditions it would allow the vacation of Canal Street for a considerable length. The railroads must have found such a concession tempting, but this eleventh-hour offer would require a complete redesign of their project. The city's tender was too late. The Pennsylvania, in fact, had only recently provided its tenants with details of the station's internal layout. Since each tenant railroad had a well-staffed engineering and architectural department, the result was a blizzard of finely executed counterproposals.[58] The Pennsylvania generally had its way, but as inflation and labor stoppages pushed costs higher, it inevitably scaled back plans. The major departure from the original schematic was the elimination of the escalators intended for the quick movement of commuters from the concourse upward to the Adams and Jackson Street bridges. Ramps were substituted.

Late in 1915, the railroads had misgivings about the viability of their project and considered the erection of an office or hotel tower over the headhouse building. Ernest Graham estimated that the maximum allowable height under the building code would permit construction of either a 750-room hotel or twelve floors of rental offices. The estimated cost of the hotel was $3 million, while offices would cost only $2 million. In addition to the higher cost, the hotel project carried political risk. Given the rocky relations between the railways and the city, the station manager speculated that the city could easily revoke a hotel license if matters were not to its liking. Moreover, Graham felt the West Side market would not support the $2.50 per night room rate needed for profitability. As for offices, the Milwaukee Road could take two floors, but the ability to rent the remaining space remained in doubt. The Pennsylvania settled the matter—for

the time being—by stating, "We have advertised to the world our monumental station. We have published it in full-page advertisements in Chicago papers. We have plans to which we will adhere."[59]

On the labor front, the Pennsylvania held out. The building trades resumed work on March 12, 1917, in time for the summer construction season. Work continued for three-and-a-half months, but on July 1, Mike Boyle's electricians struck. The stoppage lasted seventy-four days, but it only slowed construction since other unions dishonored the picket lines. They deemed the basic issue—that subcontractor Otis Elevator used workers from a different union—not their problem. Despite these issues, the annual manager's report noted good progress on the Pennsylvania and Burlington freight terminals, changes to the grades of Van Buren and Canal Streets, the Monroe Street Bridge, and the relocation of underground utilities. Workers cleared the headhouse block and the site for the relocation of a twelve-story Butler Brothers warehouse. Contracts had been let for the Monroe, Harrison, Polk, and Taylor Street bridges.[60]

Meanwhile, the number of passengers using the existing depot rose despite a modest decline in the number of trains. Powerful modern locomotives pulled more cars per train. In addition, the Milwaukee Road rearranged its schedule to cut unproductive commuter runs. The year also saw another fire, this time burning part of the train shed, which again required extensive repairs.

The US entry into the World War in April of 1917 was bound to retard station construction. By July, the War Industries Board rationed cement and steel, and December saw the nationalization of the railroads under the US Railroad Administration. The USRA declared, in the words of its leader, that its first task was to "swat the Kaiser on the nose."[61] To expand capacity, it controlled all aspects of rail operation. At the same time, to ration war materials, it limited capital expenditures.[62] For a time, the Union Station project remained a priority. Construction continued, although both men and materials became increasingly scarce.

Another strike of Mike Boyle's electricians occurred on January 29, 1918. It coincided with a walkout by the workers lowering the streetcar tunnel under the property. This time the painters, plasterers, and sheet metal workers joined in sympathy. Not all was silent at the work site, however, as the ironworkers continued their tasks despite picketing by other unions. By May 15, things had grown especially ugly, as "slugging crews" of from ten to twenty-five men attacked the teamsters running structural steel to the work site. Casualties from these clashes went unreported, although the site seems to have been protected by thugs who differed little from the attackers. A detective for the Harding Detective Agency riding as a guard on a truck was shot through the leg and at least one driver was injured in the head by a flying brick.

Two days later, the War Department appropriated the Pennsylvania's new Polk Street freight house as a "War Emergency Warehouse" and the Quartermaster Corps of the US Army occupied the partially complete structure. The army threatened to arrest all union members who failed to return to work in the first use of new federal powers granted under the Sabotage Act, which had only passed Congress on April 20. A full company of soldiers of the 40th Infantry dispatched from Fort Sheridan guarded the freight house, and nonunion workers were brought in to finish the elevators. On June 10, the US government released the electricians it employed, and turned work back to the contractors. The strike lasted 108 days; by the time it was over, a total of 486 days had been lost to labor unrest.

As fitful construction resumed, Union Station officials strictly enforced a rule that their project never hire contractors using the "padrone system." This early form of worker exploitation preyed on non-English speakers. They paid upfront to get their job and then made monthly contributions to their padrone. Variations, some of which were throwbacks to indentured servitude, were used by the German, Irish, and Eastern Europeans, but the practice was especially connected with the tight-knit Taylor Street Sicilian community southwest of the depot. The response to the railroads' prohibition was as notable as it was ineffective. On January 18, 1918, the nervous onboard behavior of Linda Jose, a sixteen-year-old girl from Youngstown, Ohio, attracted the attention of a Pullman porter who notified police.

Authorities arrested her as she attempted to exit a Panhandle train in the depot carrying a satchel stuffed with dynamite and blasting caps. While being subdued, she kicked her bag yelling, "If I'd hit it, we'd all be in eternity." During the struggle, she tried to swallow literature from the Industrial Workers of the World, the radical "Wobblies." She was held in police custody for months; Vincenzio DeAngelo, business agent for the Italian Hod Carriers Union, finally made her bail. Only weeks later, DeAngelo was gunned down by assassins waiting outside his home. He

had been walking with his wife, Miss Jose, and his six-year-old son. The lad bravely chased the killers, who escaped.[63]

As the war progressed, it became increasingly difficult for the railroad to complete construction projects. There was hope that the appointment of the Burlington's Ralph Budd as director for capital expenditures for the USRA would assure Union Station construction. He had once been active in the depot's management from his office a block west of the planned train shed; he still commuted daily through the depot. The railroads confidently submitted a request to the USRA to allow the station company to expend $9 million of its own funds for the 1918 construction season. Even though the city of Chicago interceded for the railroads, the USRA denied the expenditures. Construction ceased with minor exceptions in July, only a month after the strike's forcible settlement. Only the completion of the Monroe Bridge, foundation work for the Roosevelt Road viaduct, and temporary restoration of Taylor and Polk Streets proceeded.

WARTIME SHORTAGES

The railroads had better luck in 1919 with the designation of Union Station as a project "of great national significance," a declaration that did not come without a fight. Joshua D'Esposito, now the chief engineer of the Chicago Union Station Company, had to prove to federal managers that no better scheme was available. In January, the USRA allowed the release of $5.35 million for station construction and $2 million for related projects. Work proceeded rapidly. In June, 268 caissons for the headhouse foundation were sunk at a cost of $700,000, and retaining walls around the site arose. The new Butler Brothers warehouse neared completion, and over $5 million in viaduct work progressed during the year. Construction was not easy, as Joshua D'Esposito wrote to his Pittsburgh superiors:

> The labor situation here is rather in worse shape that it was when I wrote you on the 18th, as today the employees of both the Street Railways and the Elevated System went out on strike and this, together with the development of serious race riots throughout the south side of the City, has created a condition of unrest which is far from helpful in settling our own troubles. The cost of living is mounting week by week. I agree with you

that it will take patience and courage and a spirit of fairness in working out a solution, but I do not see the existence of such spirit anywhere around me.

D'Esposito was in full charge of the station, now that Thomas Rodd had retired to St. Augustine, Florida. Rodd remained a consulting engineer to the Union Station Company; once relieved of his other duties in Pittsburgh he briefly increased the time he could devote to Chicago. D'Esposito needed Rodd's help because of the continuing labor problems. Chicago's July 1919 race riot had left 38 dead, 537 wounded, and 1000 homeless, but at the work site, it was August that was particularly difficult. In addition to a brief teamsters strike, the electricians again stopped work for twenty-one days. A week after settlement of that strike, the Employers Association imposed a lockout that lasted nearly a month.

The Plan Commission also kept D'Esposito occupied. The Union Station ordinance required the company to be the primary designer and contractor for the new Roosevelt Road viaduct. This project spanned the tracks leading to Dearborn, LaSalle, Grand Central, and Union stations. Sixteen railroads shared the expense and each demanded oversight. The Plan Commission tried to manage by committee, and over several years, it held 394 conferences on Roosevelt Road alone.[64]

Sluggers and shooters dominated the leadership of union locals; many soon sought better money in a variety of illegal activities. Their shakedowns included selling tickets to benefit galas, popularly known as "rackets" due to their high noise levels. Purchasing tickets was not optional, and the promotional methods later caused Employers Association Secretary Gordon Holster to coin the word "racketeering." Its usage came to describe much more than aggressive salesmanship. As early as 1914, the newspapers routinely called the situation "the Labor War," as Mike Boyle's seventy-thousand-member electrical union emerged as the most powerful and violent of organizations. Umbrella Mike was known to have paid cash for a $300,000 apartment building bought, so he said, from the savings on his $50 per week salary. When pressed to explain this paradox, he said it was possible "due to thrift." Boyle's hangout was Johnson's Saloon, known tongue in cheek as "the Kick Inn," at 333 West Madison near the Union Depot. It was there that Mike acquired his nickname by routinely leaving his umbrella hanging by its handle from the lip of the bar. He usually found it filled with cash upon his return from a private upstairs retreat. Several unions frequented Johnson's Saloon, one of which was the Barbers Union. The Barbers had become experts at bombing nonunion shops. Its business agents developed a lucrative sideline by providing this service to other combatants. One client appears to have been Mike Boyle, who, sworn testimony alleged, dynamited fifteen movie theaters and other buildings.[65]

For various nefarious activities, a federal court indicted Boyle and fifty others in January 1917. The jury found Boyle and ten aides guilty, fined them, and sentenced most to prison. He served a four-month term before he was pardoned by President Woodrow Wilson. Boyle simply controlled too many votes.[66] To obtain the pardon, brokered by Samuel Gompers, Umbrella Mike promised to slow down his activities. Instead, he called a streetcar strike for July 14. For three days, commuters sought any means available to get to and from work. The result, among other things, was the biggest crowds ever packed into Chicago depots. The strike turned out to be a victory for the Chicago Surface Lines, as wage increases were near those management

originally offered.[67] Everyone knew, however, that Mike Boyle was back.

Boyle's action against the street railways had an immediate effect on the depot by creating days of utter chaos as desperate downtown workers pushed onto every available train. Many trains left the depot with passengers riding atop locomotive tender coal heaps. Baggage cars and Pullman sleepers added to commuter trains provided increased space for riders. Suburban trains abandoned schedules, with each railroad dispatching trains for another run as quickly as they could be turned and serviced.

The strike was soon over, but even in normal times, operations were difficult. The plan for the new station required a grade reduction of three to five feet, a complex task given the necessity to maintain schedules through one of the nation's busiest railroad terminals. The bustling train yard and a wartime shortage of skilled workers slowed the task. By providing three new tracks on the former site of the freight houses and then taking successive tracks out of service, work pushed forward.

Just as work on the headhouse caissons finished, the owners decided to make a major design change. In mid-July 1919, as D'Esposito penned his lament about labor conditions, the Post Office Department decided to build its main Chicago facility atop the tracks south of the station. This required revision of the track plan, but did not immediately translate into construction work. That was just as well, for unseen political forces subsequently moved the planned post office site to the north side of the station. In a situation that perhaps only the government could create, the Post Office Department drew up plans for a mammoth terminal north of the station at the same time that it pursued a condemnation suit against the railways to acquire land south of the station.

Development stalled as plans shifted with the political winds. The post office site eventually moved back south but the machinations of federal officials created a managerial morass well after plans for the station needed to gel.

A NEW DIRECTION

Joshua D'Espisito had a bigger problem than the dismal reports on the labor situation. Cash was flying out the door and new funds were difficult to obtain. Interest expense alone rose to $1.7 million per year. The original financial plan called for the capitalization of interest; that is, interest would be paid from the initial bond issuance during construction. Instead, a $10 million, high-interest-rate bond issuance in 1920 was necessary to continue construction, and the original reserve for bond interest payments was depleted. High-cost temporary bank loans paid interest and vendor payments became overdue. The new depot was still years away.

The owners seriously considered abandoning the project. Their engineers surveyed every possible economy, but their reports were disheartening. The sunk costs, such as land acquisition, were enormous, and cancellation would cause forfeiture of a $3 million bond posted with the city. The cost to break various construction contracts and to mothball partially constructed structures proved unpalatable. There seemed no easy way out of escalating problems. Nor were the station's owners in a position to front more money. Each needed all available cash to reconstruct their rail systems after the federal government's abusive treatment of their lines during a wartime period when federal managers pushed tonnage to undreamed-of levels while failing to address routine maintenance. At the same time, the station's existing mortgage holders were restive. They feared that the many delays breached the strict completion requirement of the company's enabling ordinance. They made it known that no new construction funds would be forthcoming and they rattled the sword of foreclosure.

The station company desperately needed to issue more bonds, but market conditions for new issuances became stringent. The newly formed Experience Exchange of the National Association of Building Owners and Managers published a dictate that for new depots incorporated and financed separately from their owner railroads, an office component was necessary to provide a second source of debt service coverage.[68] Without adherence to this guideline, the company could not issue the bonds needed to complete the depot.

The railroad attorneys found a dilemma. The Illinois General Corporations Act of 1872 regulated the actions of incorporated businesses. This statute explicitly prohibited corporations from engaging in real estate development. Clever attorneys had developed financing strategies that allowed Chicago's office towers to rise, but it was unclear whether the depot company could use these loopholes. Partnerships, for example, were not covered by the act, but they did not limit personal or corporate liability. Massachusetts Trusts, the forerunner of today's real estate investment trusts (generally known today as REITs), were common but were of questionable legality. Some firms, notably the Pullman Company, simply stated that they built three times as much space as they occupied because they intended to grow their offices and eventually occupy the entire building. These were legal fictions used to construct office towers, but there was one legitimate exemption in the law. It was for safe-deposit companies. A developer could form a company to construct a building containing offices, each of which held a safe. From a legal standpoint, every office suite, as a whole, was a private viewing area for its safe. As a chartered railroad enterprise, however, the Chicago Union Station Company found itself unable to squeeze through this keyhole.[69]

By 1920, the prohibitions on real estate development contained in Illinois's General Corporations Act abated and its enforcement weakened. Real estate developers generally ignored it. However, the railroads remained populist targets, and because the tax rolls listed the station as railroad property, the railroads could not take aggressive legal positions. Initially then, office space would be limited to the station's owners and ancillary activities.

March of 1920 saw the announcement of the revised headhouse design, but new elevation drawings were released only when interim financing became available, on May 17, 1921. The plan provided for a tower of up to 22 stories over the headhouse. Officially, the owners "concluded that the air rights on the site occupied by this structure were so valuable that it would be unwise to construct a building that would not permit their full development."[70] The owners knew, however, that this was fantasy. Office tenants for the tower were likely to be the railroads, the same corporations who paid station track charges. The expensive design change thus did nothing to diversify revenues. Theoretically, it allowed the building's conversion to other uses, but bondholders would receive little comfort given the enormous cost of building a railroad terminal.[71]

The company issued construction bonds of $6 million on May 27 1921, but like the previous issue, their coupon was 6.5 percent, a rate 50 percent higher than earlier bonds. Moreover, the company neared the debt threshold allowed in its charter even as costs continued to escalate. Few projects were anywhere near completion. Of the company's first $30 million in debt, only $3.5 million had been spent for actual depot construction. Demolition expenses had been sizable and the balance went for land acquisition.[72] The Ft. Wayne, for example, had received $7 million for the depot grounds and $2 million to buy out the existing leases. Land needed to relocate the Butler Brothers warehouse cost $1 million, a major project in itself that obligated the company to spend another $2 million for a replacement building.

The majority of the funds expended for construction went to viaducts and other municipal requirements. Work nevertheless continued on the tracks and the concourse. Foundation work was nearly complete for the headhouse, but the new office tower plan required a sturdier base than that just finished. An additional 192 caissons were sunk, some so close to the old ones as to introduce serious complications.

It was not until September 4, 1923 that the city issued the headhouse building permit. Initially only eight of the planned twenty-two stories would arise, a temporary expedient dictated by the municipal height limit. This truncation compromised the tower's classical design as a tripartite tower with identifiable base, shaft, and capital. Only the base and part of the shaft were built, an incomplete scheme at best. As had been anticipated when the new foundation was laid, the city eventually changed its building height limit, but the revised code required setbacks for taller buildings. Buildings could still only have a rise of 265 feet at the street line, but towers could be higher away from the street. The code's intent was to maintain sunlight along the streets lined by

large new structures. Unfortunately, the headhouse's own quest for sunlight stymied any plan to rise higher. Its hollow rectangle plan provided a skylight for the waiting room, making setbacks for the tower impractical. It could rise no higher.

While architects and owners argued over the headhouse, work progressed on the terminal and tracks to the south. Work on the north side was slower due to the relocation of the Butler Brothers warehouse. The Union Station Company proudly reported that "practically no delays to trains were attributable to construction work; in fact, after the old freight yards had been removed there were more tracks available for passenger station use than were embraced in the old station facilities."[73]

Municipal authorities experienced their own problems with station-related projects. The Sanitary District's move to widen the river and the city's desire to widen the streets leading to the business district caused a flurry of bridge building. The War Department added its own requirement that all center-span swing bridges be removed to aid navigation. Widening the channel was dictated by Chicago's need for massive water flows to dilute the raw sewage it dumped into the river. Since longer bridges were now needed, it was an ideal time to modernize, widen the streets, and replace aging timber and iron center-span swing bridges with

new steel-lift bridges. The Jackson Boulevard span had been built by the Strauss Bascule Bridge Company in 1912. The bridge firm provided its patented design on a trial basis for $3,000. A dozen similar bridges followed without royalty payments before the Strauss Company sued and received a $527,000 judgment.[74]

Later, another court ruling negated the reason for widening the river channel. In June 1920, Judge Kenesaw Mountain Landis ruled on a decade-old suit to limit water flow. It was alleged that increased drainage from Lake Michigan threatened the level of all the Great Lakes. Even Great Britain, on behalf of the Dominion of Canada, joined the suit. Cutting the flow meant that sewage would have to be treated, a project estimated to cost $200 million.[75] Taxpayers received a blow when Landis limited the flow, requiring the Sanitary District to build sewage treatment plants.

Another project going badly was the Roosevelt Road viaduct. The viaduct was seen as a major piece of Burnham and Bennett's *Plan of Chicago*. While the railroads agreed to build its west end, the city had to fund its eastern approach. The project required a bond referendum because its cost exceeded the municipal debt cap, but the vote failed in 1919 and it was not until 1922 that work resumed. Despite the slow start, 1922 also saw Ernest Graham and the Pennsylvania Railroad propose an even more radical roadway project. The River Boulevard was a scheme to cover over the Chicago River with a new roadway by bridging its length rather than its width. Plans were presented to the Army Engineers and local officials, but fortunately, nothing came of this idea, whose motivation seems to have been to improve the value of railroad landholdings.[76]

The US Post Office was also having problems. An appropriation sufficient to solve the desperate chaos of its Chicago operations was unobtainable while Congress struggled with staggering war-induced national debt. The Union Station company agreed in 1920 to build a $6 million parcel post terminal and lease it to the government. The new building could load forty rail cars at once, with drayage on a higher level.[77] The business gained or retained was the reward and rental income seems to have only covered debt service.

A WIDE OPEN CITY

Union Station's construction corresponded with an era of extreme gangsterism in the city. Organized crime, of course, had made its home in Chicago well before the advent of Prohibition. Thuggery became notably intertwined with the labor rackets, although equally rough actions had a long association with ward politics. Organized violence was almost an election-time tradition in Chicago. In February 1915, for example, an Old West–style gunfight developed on Canal Street directly in front of the saloons across from Union Depot. Only the bravery of one mounted policeman who separated the swaggering gunmen of rival candidates prevented casualties.[78] Political racketeering depended on votes, and with workmen supplying the largest electoral blocs in the years prior to women's suffrage, rough campaigning was a natural evolutionary step for corrupt and violent organizers.

In 1920 the Volstead Act moved organized crime into lucrative, if lethal, new directions. Many of the same mobsters who infected the labor organizations branched into the newly illicit business of supplying alcohol. The Chicago Association of Commerce and Industry had already been concerned enough in 1917 to form the Chicago Crime Commission. Frank Loesch, the Pennsylvania Railroad's local legal counsel, joined the crime fighters in 1920. He became Crime Commission's head in 1928 at age seventy-six. Undaunted by threats to his family, and at times almost alone due to his colleagues' fears, he battled the "outfit" of Al Capone and corrupt policemen, politicians, and judges. Among his innovations was a numeric list of public enemies that he called "the Rumpus." Capone was the long-time number one on the list, which predated the famous FBI "Ten Most Wanted"

list.[79] In Congressional testimony, Loesch stated that "fully two-thirds of the unions in Chicago are controlled by, or pay tribute to, Al Capone's terroristic organization."[80] That number may have been overstated, but one thing is certain; prompted by the Capone organization's ethnic composition, Loesch publicly vented his hatred for Sicilians. His statements must have been particularly grating for his Sicilian-born Pennsylvania Railroad colleague, Joshua D'Esposito.

One ambitious labor organizer who branched into overlapping corruption was Nicholas "Big Tim" Murphy, business agent for the Painters and Dyers Union. Murphy's influence had garnered him a seat in the state legislature, but he wanted more. On January 18, 1921, accompanied by three armed lieutenants, he executed a 2:00 a.m. raid on the Union Depot. They made off with ten registered-mail pouches containing $550,000 in cash and securities. Two gun battles, one with fatal injuries to the girlfriend of a suspect, occurred as police rounded up the gang.[81] Convicted, Murphy spent several years in prison. After release, he tried to regain control of the union, but his reward was a fatal barrage of bullets in front of his home in 1928.[82]

Mike Boyle continued to make a name for himself by calling walkouts that turned off traffic signals, kept the bridges into the business district raised in their open position, and even threatened to turn off the water pumping stations. On September 3, 1923, he was caught influencing the jury trying Illinois Governor Len Small for embezzling state funds. The term "influence" was a modest description for bribes, threats, and a kidnapping. It succeeded in getting a jury acquittal of Small, but Boyle had to spend a summer on the lam before he was given a vacation at

Statesville Prison. Governor Small repaid Boyle by commuting his sentence along with that of a coconspirator then serving time for murder.[83] Boyle had been back in office only five months when a gun battle on the floor of a union meeting resulted in one dead and three wounded. Despite hundreds of union men at the event, there were no reported witnesses, nor were arrests made.[84] Boyle meanwhile raised polo ponies and started a professional race car team, financed, as always, by "thrift."

Meanwhile, construction on Union Station progressed. The railroads quietly moved their offices into the office tower in October of 1924, although the Pennsylvania lacked enough space for its freight sales department. As a result, there were immediate calls for construction of additional stories. The architects made cost estimates and $7 million in additional bonds were issued, but the money went to debt service and the tower stayed at eight stories.[85]

On May 15, 1925, Chicago Union Station quietly opened to the public. In the dozen years since its inception, economic prosperity pushed the daily commuter total entering the Loop to over 1.25 million. Railroad commuter and intercity traffic surged, even as autos and buses captured most of the new traffic. Every workday, over twenty-five thousand people used the Madison Street Bridge near the old depot.[86] Finishing touches on the new structure, such as the delivery of statues for the waiting room, were not yet complete. Most of the station was already in use, but the railroads delayed a grand public opening until July. The guest of honor was Pennsylvania Railroad train master W. A. Boatman, who as a young locomotive engineer brought the first train into the old depot in 1881.

CHAPTER SIX

A CITY WITHIN A CITY

THE TERMINAL

When complete, the Chicago Union Station complex stretched nearly twenty blocks south of the station buildings and eight blocks north. Nearly two miles long and at least one block wide, it was the central city's largest real estate holding. A lift bridge that is itself an engineering marvel marked its southern limit. The total complex encompassed impressive station buildings, train yards and sheds, switching towers, and a heating plant large enough for a small city. In addition to the mainline tracks that funneled passenger trains into the depot, it once included connections to bustling freight houses, express buildings, the post office, commercial warehouses, engine service facilities, and coach yards. In the eyes of most observers, however, Chicago Union Station consisted of the two buildings where they arrived, departed, or waited for trains.

THE STATION BUILDINGS

The larger and westernmost of the two main station buildings, the headhouse, was designed as a hollow square allowing the office-block light court to frame the waiting room skylight. A hallmark of D. H. Burnham and Company's standard office design, this layout allowed for light-filled lobbies while providing ventilation for the business spaces above. What under normal circumstances would have been a prosaic office-tower light shaft became, with the stately waiting room, the terminal's grandest feature.

The tower occupied the full block bounded by Canal, Jackson, Clinton, and Adams Streets. It had a four-story base 372 feet long on its east and west sides. Roman-Doric columns 39 feet high marked these facades.[1] On Canal Street nearest the business district, a portico ran the entire length, while on Clinton the outer wall sat flush against the columns. Jackson and Adams Street treatments, respectively the north and south facades, were more severe. Their only distinguishing features, at least for the first four floors, were the windows that afforded ventilation to the taxiway.

Both the headhouse building and its companion, the concourse to the east, had Bedford limestone facing, for a unified, stately appearance. Hardly twins, the buildings had substantially different elevations. As built, the concourse was Anderson's fourth and most elaborate rendering. Its appearance, at least on the outside, was that of a Roman temple smaller than its companion. The headhouse and its office block, by contrast, used classical detailing on a forthright office block of businesslike demeanor. As Anderson worked and reworked his design for

the larger building into progressively more sober forms, he compensated by making its entrance pavilion, the concourse, more flamboyant. Indeed, while the headhouse occupied its block from sidewalk to sidewalk, Anderson used only half the riverside block for the concourse, flanking it on both sides by low train sheds. Train sheds may have been the station's reason for being, but their profile was so low that their roof peaks were below viaduct grade. They occupied nearly six square blocks, a flamboyant use of expensive real estate. Thus the terminal as civic monument was best expressed in its smaller component, the concourse, which rose above this field of low shed roofs.

The concourse, set on an east-west axis with gables at each end, was clearly differentiated from city office towers by its relative absence of windows. Twin Doric columns flanked arched

recesses at each end; on the east end, there was a large clock to define the main entrance. Ramps and monumental terra-cotta and iron staircases descended from these street-level portals.[2] Commuters, the majority of the station's patrons, used less elegant entrances from Jackson and Adams Streets adjacent to the Chicago River bridges. Critic Rexford Newcomb described the concourse: "The great plan area, the division of the two masses, and the adjacent street traffic make it impossible to comprehend a view of the entire structure near at hand. While perhaps not so unified in outline or distinguished in detail as some other American stations of its class, it holds a high place in that class."[3]

Exposed steel truss work supporting the concourse roof dominated its interior. These riveted latticework columns and arches stood in contrast to the classical order of the building's

The Concourse was completed nearly a year before the station officially opened.

exterior. Designer Alfred Shaw admitted that the concourse was "somewhat similar to the design of the Pennsylvania Station on New York expressing frankly the structure and nature of the building." Indeed, in Newcomb's eyes, "Only enough of the classical architecture is introduced to indicate the character of that exterior. This is indeed the high point, the achievement of the Station, artistically speaking. This wonderfully is . . . a joy to those who see in modern materials and construction methods the basis for a vital modern architecture."

The arches ordered the structure into a central nave flanked by two progressively narrower and shorter arched vaults. In traditional American depot design, the concourse was the transition between train shed and headhouse facilitating pedestrian circulation. Circulation certainly was paramount in Chicago Union Station's design, but here the concourse separated two sets of station tracks, with the headhouse to one side. This layout, of Thomas Rodd's creation, was found nowhere else in the world. It functioned especially well at handling pedestrian flows and kept rushing commuters out of the waiting room. In addition, two features defined how different this space was from a traditional concourse. The architects' Bedford stone treatment of the concourse with scant fenestration belied great natural illumination. The delicate iron vaulting provided for a clerestory flanked by windows north and south. The roof itself was almost entirely glass. With pairs of giant windows at either end, the sun shone in as if the concourse were a greenhouse.

Rodd also designed a key feature to enhance circulation, the total segregation of baggage handling from the passenger areas. Baggage moved seamlessly from trackside to areas beneath the main concourse floor. The floor itself consisted of glass blocks, which allowed the sunlight streaming through the skylights to serve double duty by continuing its illuminating journey into the basement. The only baggage area on the main floor was a counter nestled behind stairs that rose to Canal Street. This checkroom was visible only from the passageway that linked the concourse and the main waiting room—the route used by intercity passengers, not by commuters. Commuters nevertheless often went here to retrieve purchases sent from department stores that used a "store check." For one dime, the parcel could be picked up with the store check at the end of the shopping day before riding home to the suburbs with its purchaser.

For inbound traffic, the segregation of people from their baggage actually started at train side. Typical station design arranged tracks in pairs with a platform between each set shared by passengers, baggage, and mail carts. Chicago Union Station, however, dedicated aisles exclusively for mail and baggage running between each track pair. As they neared the concourse, these aisles sloped downward and descended into the basement. A fleet of fourteen battery-powered tractors facilitated this unique and logical arrangement. Built by the Mercury Manufacturing Company of Chicago, each tractor could pull several of the station's three hundred baggage wagons.[4] Baggage trains were common at the previous depot and elsewhere, but Chicago Union Station seems to have been the first depot designed around their use. It was noted shortly after the station's opening that "in the operation of the station up to the present, the baggage handling has been found to be much more efficient than in any layout in operation elsewhere in the country."[5] Historian Carl Condit summarized the baggage facilities at the station: "The baggage-handling facilities of the concourse building constituted another ingenious element of this intricate plan—indeed, it may be argued that they represented the most efficient solution so far developed to this still perplexing problem."[6]

The concourse lobby was the name given to the passage under Canal Street, the connecting link between headhouse and concourse. Its floor sloped to accommodate a two-foot difference in grade. Following Thomas Rodd's original design, cabstands flanked it north and south. While these stands were physically under Canal Street, they actually connected by ramps to Clinton Street. The entrance ramp made a hairpin turn under Canal and turned back and down to the basement level. Skirting the west wall of the headhouse, the drive had an underground intersection with another subterranean alley, which led to the baggage dock. The ramp rose on the north side and with similar turns passed the outbound taxicab stand before returning to Clinton Street. From the first day, the number of patrons entering and exiting the station at the cabstands was second only to the Adams Street entrance of the concourse. Alfred Shaw noted, "This is the first modern building in which a great system of streets for vehicles is contained entirely within the property lines. Ramps for teaming and passenger vehicles, as well as the back-up area and unloading space for cabs, are all in the building, thus obviating the great inconvenience of having vehicles standing at the curb lines on a street, as well as relieving actual street traffic."[7] This elaborate system certainly alleviated a chief complaint levied against its predecessor. Rodd's ingenious design, taking advantage of the inclined adjacent streets, allowed patrons to walk on a single level from taxi to ticket window to waiting room to train.

The majority of depot travelers came from the business district on foot and entered the concourse directly after crossing the Adams or Jackson Street bridges. As they moved westward through the station, they experienced a series of gradually smaller spaces. The sunlit, multistory atrium concourse measured 213 feet by 192 feet on an east-west axis. The concourse lobby was also 192 feet wide, but only 100 feet long and one story high. Next was the ticket lobby, only 90 by 55 feet. Because this room was under Canal Street, it had to have a low ceiling, but this provided the context for use of an established architectural ploy known as "visual compression." The smaller space is, in effect, a setup for the expansive main waiting room. Patrons entering from the east had their visual focus first confined, but then expanded, causing them instinctively to lift their eyes. The skylight, set in a coffered barrel vault, covers nearly the entire waiting room ceiling. Illumination within the five-story vault remained surprisingly diffuse due to the subduing shadows of the light well. An entablature whose Corinthian columns rise 47 feet of the room's 112-foot total height circled the perimeter of the waiting room.

The walls and entablature of the main waiting room were painted in a light buff color scheme by Jules Guerin that coordinated with the soft green of the shallow barrel vaulting.[8] Gold and rose highlighted the coffers and accented the acanthus-leaf capitals. Columns of Italian travertine soared over a belt course of warm gray marble ten feet high that circled the room and further enhanced its richness. The Pennsylvania stipulated that these columns be slightly taller than those the C&NW erected in its neighboring depot, and it sent surveyors to surreptitiously confirm their rival's vital statistics. The room's major design elements consisted of segmental arches along each side, vestigial remnants of the lunettes of Anderson's earlier design.

The Main Waiting Room, meant to impress, was supplemented by a separate women's lounge, stores, and restaurants.

Ornamental screens filled the arches at each end of the waiting room vault. This obscured the office tower while allowing additional natural illumination. This was also true of the smaller arches on each side of the vault. Statues of Day and Night by New York sculptor Henry Hering flanked this entrance. The middle arch on the east side opened into a coffered barrel vault that rose sixty feet above the Ticket Lobby. For symmetry, the corresponding west side arch fronted a coffered half dome.

Surviving sketches show that the double-life-sized statue of a seated goddess in flowing robes was to occupy this niche, but it was never installed.

Besides the grand entrance to the Ticket Lobby with its ticketing windows, offices, and space for passengers to queue, the east side of the headhouse building originally housed a drugstore and two majestic stairways to the level of Canal Street. On the north and south were small shops. The west side of the headhouse had

Fred Harvey store fronts and restaurants together comprised one of America's first major indoor shopping centers.

three distinct uses. The northern portion was the Women's Waiting Room, a fifty-four-by-seventy-foot sanctuary whose walls rose to a forty-foot height. As with the Main Waiting Room, the walls were painted buff, but the coffered ceiling had blue, yellow, and dark red decoration. Velvet hangings on the north and south walls displayed the insignia of each railroad entering the station, woven onto a deep red background. At some point, these were replaced by Jules Guerin murals. Upholstered furniture, overstuffed settees of blue mohair, homey floor lamps, and wooden occasional tables created a relaxing oasis away from the crowds.

Alfred Shaw noted, "The usual smoking room for men was intentionally omitted from the design, perhaps as being unnecessary," but he failed to elaborate on this omission.[9]

Largest of the west side spaces was the lunchroom of Fred Harvey & Company, the firm that rented the majority of the station's retail spaces. Walnut paneling completely wrapped this 85-by-111-foot restaurant. Three green Vermont marble counters served hearty fare, including the company's famously oversized slices of fresh pie. South of the lunchroom was a small formal dining room. Its 42-by-52-foot dimensions gave it a warm, intimate feeling even as the walls soared to the coffered ceiling, here painted in bright greens and brick red. High walnut wainscoting, decorative plasterwork, and antique Italian-pattern furniture reinforced a rich ambience. The grill and prep kitchen for both dining rooms and lunchrooms occupied the far western wall of the headhouse.

Outside, the grades of Jackson and Adams Street inclined to rise over the tracks and river. Because the waiting room floor, which was below Canal Street, was almost even with Clinton Street, Anderson could have built the latter entrance without steps, but did not. The Clinton Street entrances were insignificant, intended primarily as routes to the office tower elevator lobbies. Such diminutive portals were not Anderson's style, and indeed, as the design progressed, Pennsylvania Railroad managers made specific requests to downplay these entrances. Saloons, cheap rooming houses, the garment district, and small furniture manufacturers dominated the neighborhood west of the station. The two modest Clinton Street entrances sent a subtle message that residents of that district were not particularly welcome, although there were separate doorways for the restaurant and barbershop.

In some ways, however, the most ceremonial entrances were the ones used by the fewest patrons. Stairs from the sloping Jackson Street sidewalk led to a comparatively dim grand foyer with a balcony that revealed—through the massive columns—the great daylighted waiting room a story below. Travertine staircases lead down to the floor of the waiting room.

Erection of the station was in full swing when designer Peirce Anderson was diagnosed with cancer in the summer of 1923, from which he died the following February.[10] His successor, Alfred Shaw, introduced a more austere classicism to the architectural designs. Anderson, however, had completed most of the primary and secondary design elements. Even the vegetative designs for floor lamps and other ornamental details seem to indicate the intricate work of the older partner, although their execution likely fell to the architectural firm's legion of anonymous draftsmen.

The key concession contract went to the Fred Harvey hotel chain, including all of the buildings' restaurants, newsstands, and shops. They turned the project over to architect Mary E. J. Colter. Her elegant, upscale interior designs in a complementary Beaux-Arts style were a well-executed departure from the Southwest and Spanish Colonial Revival themes for which she is famous.[11] Colter's purview extended from shop layout, display area design, even to the waitresses' uniforms.

The basement below the waiting-room floor housed additional kitchen space, including a complete bakery, butchery, dishwashing room, and commissary. A cafeteria for the budget-minded was accessible from a stairway from the waiting room. A brace of toilets completed the public areas of the basement. A subterranean driveway connected the teeming concourse and its block-long loading dock to the ramp shared with the taxi stands.

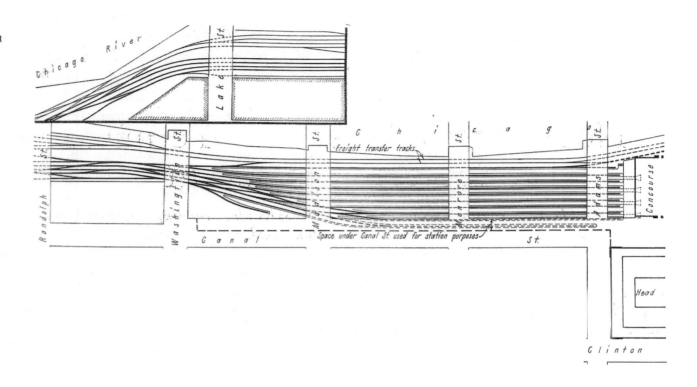

It split the basement and it was so busy that a pedestrian overpass entirely within the basement linked the halves it separated. A favorite stopping point for journalists lucky enough to get the complete tour of the depot was the basement's two-room jail. A similarly sized hospital infirmary was located at street level.

Several facilities typically found in the basement of a Chicago depot were missing. First, there was no boiler room. Rather, the company built a separate heating plant south of the station complex. Nor were express rooms or mail facilities found in the basement. They occupied separate buildings connected to the baggage room by a trucking tunnel. Finally, the immigrant facility was the smallest of the Chicago stations, a reflection of changing times and isolationist immigration laws enacted during the station's construction.

THE TRAIN YARD

The railroad roadbed throughout the terminal needed sufficient elevation above the riverbank to promote drainage. The unstable

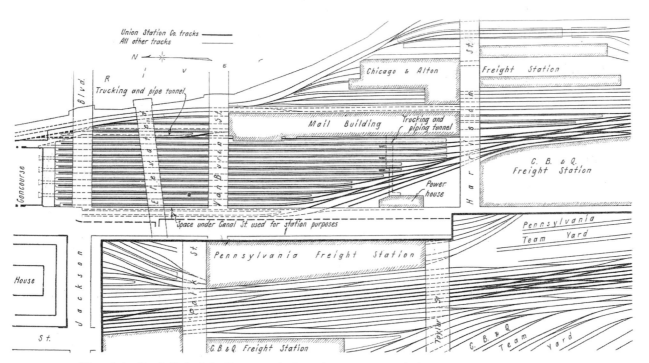

Map of the South End of the New Terminal, the South Approach Being Shown at the Lower Right

bank drained poorly, and as a result the entire yard required an extraordinary foundation. Ten-inch-thick reinforced concrete slabs underlay all 25.6 acres sheltered by the train sheds. At riverside, rusticated concrete piers connected with flattened arches to screen the tracks and create a harmonious embankment. Union Station's predecessors did not have basements, due to the high water table. The new buildings did, thanks to thick concrete walls and the languid nature of the river. Only twice did water rise to threaten the station. The first time, in 1934, actually resulted

from a broken water main. Twenty years later, floodwaters from a spring freshet poured into the basement.[12]

The tracks within the terminal undulated surprisingly, given the gentle Chicago topography, because of conflicting requirements. Track had to be held as high as possible over the river, but overhead clearances were limited to seventeen feet at the viaducts. The most obvious dip in the track was under Madison Street. The street elevation fronting the C&NW terminal did not permit the street grade to rise sufficiently. On the southern approach, a lesser sag allowed clearance under the Van Buren Street viaduct.[13] Track undulations required locomotives to start at least part of their trains on a grade. Due to the press of business into and out of Chicago, locomotives often hauled tonnage near their rated capacity. From their station stop, they had difficulty overcoming the inertia of heavy trains and had to exert themselves mightily under the shed. This resulted in a heavy, sulfurous exhaust from Illinois soft coal. To expel fumes outside the shed, it was decided to use a derivative of the patented Bush train shed.

The basis for the Bush design was a series of low arches covering two tracks, which replaced the traditional balloon sheds that spanned an entire train yard. These impressively broad train sheds had proven expensive to build and even more costly to maintain. They were smoky, dark, and their vertical height overpowered the architecture of the actual station buildings. Inventor Lincoln Bush's innovative shed had a slot built into its low roof over the centerline of each track. Locomotive exhaust pressure forced smoke through the slot to the outside atmosphere. Pennsylvania Railroad engineers, however, complained about the Bush design. Its main drawback was the public space beneath its tar-covered roof, which proved exceedingly dark even on the sunniest day. Moreover, solar energy absorbed by the black roof notched up the ambient heat radiating from the locomotive boilers underneath. With no way to dissipate this energy, in the summer a stroll at train side could be quite uncomfortable. Moreover, Bush demanded a royalty of 7 percent of construction costs, a higher percentage than received by the station architects. At the time, there were seven stations in the US built under Lincoln Bush's patent; Pennsylvania engineers dutifully visited each, including the C&NW's Madison Street depot up the street from Union Station. They also investigated several variations of low-lying sheds. The scheme at Kansas City appeared to hold great promise, but it had been the work of Union Station's nemesis, Jarvis Hunt. As the chief engineer of the Burlington wrote to his colleagues, "As you probably know, these plans were gotten up by our old friend Hunt, here in Chicago. There is no use going to him for copies."

An entirely new design emerged. The Pennsylvania Railroad's engineering department borrowed a modern locomotive and placed it on a specially constructed test stand. As the locomotive labored motionless on rollers, its wheels and piston rods fanned the air while measurements were made of various materials placed over the stack in order to determine their resistance to its corrosive exhaust. Railroad engineers knew that the old balloon sheds allowed rain to mix with sulfurous cinders, which when lodged in their truss work, resulted in sulfuric acid that rotted structural iron. The new low sheds kept moisture out, but their proximity to the locomotives resulted in an abrasive action akin to sandblasting as tiny cinders exploded from each smokestack. The railroad constructed scale models of several types of sheds for study, including some that incorporated high-level platforms for commuter trains and others that could accommodate overhead catenaries to power electric locomotives. One difference from the original Lincoln Bush design was the need at Chicago Union Station to span a greater distance with each archway to clear the depot's unique baggage aisle. The engineers' ingenious solution was to relieve the compression of the arches with overhead cantilevers. The roof over the top of the arches flared upward with the cantilever. This design efficiently handled long spans with a shallow arch. The area under the cantilever, however, was directly over the passenger platform, and the designers wisely gave the cantilever itself a somewhat exaggerated segmental arch to provide increased headroom. This aided in the dispersal of ambient smoke and allowed for a skylight tracing the curve of the cantilever over each walkway. As a result, 40 percent of the roof—the area directly over the passenger platform—was naturally lit.

The track work was impressive. The 130-pound rail used in the station yard was heavier than several of the carriers used on their main lines. *Railway Age* described the train yard:

> The track. . . . alignment has been improved. The primary change was that of providing six tracks in the south approach instead of four, and four tracks in the north approach. Connections between these approaches and the platform tracks were made, in each case, by a single pair of ladder tracks fanning to the west. In most cases the platform tracks are arranged in pairs with a single connection to the ladder track, the parent track of each pair crossing the inner ladder to a connection with the outer ladder and thus providing for simultaneous movements in or out of any two of the platform tracks, except the two tracks of any single pair. To permit direct connection between any approach with any station track, the design included bi-directional double crossovers at the throat of each yard.[14]

The Burlington and Pennsylvania coach yards and engine facilities adjoined the main track of the Union Station Company near Fourteenth Street, while the Alton brought power and rolling stock from Brighton Park some distance away. Milwaukee Road facilities to the west were closer, but also on the railroad's own line.

The Alton and Burlington built modern freight houses at a cost, respectively, of $2 million and $3 million. It was the Polk Street freight house of the Pennsylvania, however, that dominated the landscape. Measuring a staggering 750 feet by 420 feet, it had nineteen stub tracks that could accommodate 199 cars outbound, 176 cars inbound, and over 313 cars stored ready for use. It was a structure so massive that it required six interior light courts.[15] A separate structure along Canal Street served the Railway Express Agency adjacent to the south approach to the passenger station, and indeed the tracks southbound were the busiest from the terminal's first day.

CHAPTER SEVEN

RED INK IN THE WHITE CITY

A WHITE ELEPHANT

Union Station's appearance was that of a great white Roman temple, but in railroad and financial circles it looked more like the proverbial white elephant. Railroad managers knew that investment in plant and equipment equaled $96 million, while total assets reached $101 million.[1] Even this number, three-and-a-half times the original estimate, represented only those expenditures made directly by the station company. Not included were the costs of relocating and replacing coach yards, engine terminals, and freight houses—expenses borne by the individual companies.[2] Nor did the $101 million figure include costs allocated to each railroad for straightening the Chicago River and building the Twelfth Street viaduct.[3]

In 1925, $101 million was a stratospheric sum ($1.45 billion in 2017 dollars).[4] The Bureau of Railway Economics estimated that from 1921 to 1932 the entire railroad industry spent, on average, $727 million annually on capital expenditures. By this measure, Chicago Union Station equaled nearly 14 percent of the entire industry's yearly investment, albeit the amount was spread over a decade and included the cost of land purchased from its owners. During the same period, the value of construction in the city of Chicago averaged $222 million per year. Perhaps embarrassed

by their excess, the railroads publicized the station's cost as $75 million. The true figure was public information, but newspapers and trade journals repeated only this lower amount.

The station was not unique in its extravagance. Railroads nationwide engaged in unprecedented expenditures propelled by ready capital access, demonstrated need, and wildly optimistic growth projections. Architectural historian Carroll L. V. Meeks called this the "phase of Megalomania" in station design and noted, "Opulent dimensions are not functionally necessary: the companies could afford magnificence and enjoyed their munificent role, as princes had in predemocratic ages."[5] Railroad historian Albro Martin echoes his comments: "What a waste, the cynics will say, did say, in fact, in the 1930's when the stewardship of the pre-depression business leaders was so seriously in question. But the only critical point that seems germane to a historical essay is whether the railroad leaders were giving the nation what it demanded. The answer seems to be that they were. The railroads met the demand for grandeur as squarely as they met the challenge of carrying the nation's burden."[6]

Other informed commentary was less charitable. The Interstate Commerce Commission valued the station company property for rate-making purposes at $47 million, half the value on the company books.[7] Estimated replacement cost, including land, track, and the buildings, was $53 million, 55 percent of book value. These discrepancies had several sources. First, the company incurred $16 million in interest expense during construction, the result of the decade-long delay in its completion. Other reasons relate to land. ICC appraisers valued the land at $20 million, while the company paid $47 million. The go-go Chicago real estate market of the era would seem to support the higher value, but the Pennsylvania Railroad also seems to have unloaded its property at a premium. The ICC, moreover, failed to include the cost of buying specific lots from sellers who recognized desperate buyers—as in the need to build an entirely new Butler Brothers warehouse, which never became a station company asset. Payments to the city for vacated streets proved just as costly. Moreover, the station company's purchases included West Side properties acquired for the Pennsylvania's aborted freight terminal. With changed plans, neither the Pennsylvania nor the station company had a use for this land. These lots, collectively called the "Ghetto Property," were written off at a $5.7 million loss in 1928, but the debt funding this purchase remained.[8]

The Pennsylvania, of course, retained a half interest in the station and it received notes as partial payment for land and funds advanced. The revenues to repay all debt, however, came from facility charges. Co-owners Burlington and Milwaukee Road collectively operated the most trains, so indirectly they repaid the most debt. They paid dearly for the "Ghetto Property" never intended for their use. The station sold $66 million in bonds, payable in gold, between 1916 and 1924. The owners jointly and severally guaranteed them, assuring their AAA rating. This negated the need for the office tower previously required for an investment-grade bond rating. Company debt included an additional $26 million in subordinated notes issued to its owners.[9]

The year of Chicago Union Station's completion, 1925, proved to be the pinnacle of intercity railroad passenger travel. The following year also marked the ridership peak on Chicago transit systems. The reason for the subsequent decline is not hard to find. When station planning began in 1912, there were 136 Chicagoans for every registered passenger auto. This number fell to ten people per automobile in 1925. By 1931, the ratio was eight to one.[10] The station's first month also saw the incorporation of the nation's first passenger airline.

Widened bridges and streets accommodating more and faster traffic supported the rising tide of automotive commuting that cannibalized commuter traffic. Equally troublesome was a decline in revenue per passenger that attacked the financial underpinnings of the passenger business. In 1926, the nation's railroads earned an average of 2.94 cents per mile, but this fell to 2.80 cents in 1929. By 1932, the average was 2.20 cents, as fares were cut to induce travel by a Depression-weary public. Thus, even if traffic remained at earlier levels, the depot owners' gross passenger revenue would have fallen 25 percent.

Ridership shrinkage, reduced fares, and a failure to meet inflated expectations exacerbated the station's problems. A study by Carl Condit enumerated its May 1925 train count.[11]

Condit noted that at the station's opening the ratio of trains using the north and south sides of the terminal (160:194) were greater than the ratio of the number of tracks (10:14). According to Condit, traffic density in trains per track per day was somewhat higher in the north-side Milwaukee Road terminal than in the three-road south terminal (16.0 on the north as opposed to 13.9

TABLE 7.1. *CHICAGO, 1910–29: BUILDING, PLANNING, AND URBAN TECHNOLOGY*

Railroad	Through	Suburban	Total
Chicago and Alton	20	2	22
Chicago Burlington and Quincy	28	90	118
Pennsylvania Lines	48	6	54
Total south approach	*96*	*98*	*194*
Chicago Milwaukee and St. Paul—north approach	74	86	160
Total, both approaches	*170*	*184*	*354*

Source: Carl W. Condit, *Chicago, 1910–29: Building, Planning, and Urban Technology*, 298.

on the south). The density was even greater with respect to traffic density on the approaches.

Condit then looked at ensuing decades. The numbers declined even before the Depression—then they plummeted. Only in wartime 1944 did the total number of trains reach four hundred per day. Over the years, the distribution of trains between the north and south sides changed. Traffic density became approximately equal. Condit summarized:

> The great irony in the operation of Union Station is that the spacious facility has seldom been used to more than half its capacity. The track system of the north half can easily and safely accommodate 300 trains per day, and that of the south half 420, while the concourse, waiting room and entrance and exit ways provide sufficient area for the movement of 400,000 passengers a day. As incredible as it seems after years devoted to the formation of merger plans, Union, North Western and the Illinois Central's newly electrified suburban station were all that Chicago railroads needed to handle the city's maximum total of 1,600 daily trains.[12]

The station company remained afloat despite costs that were exasperatingly over budget and operations that failed to reach anything approaching capacity. Threats to solvency were tangible, especially since profitability eluded several of its users/owners to which it had to pass through its expenses. While its monstrous debt burden was never itself sufficient to embarrass its owners, station costs per car (the unit used for charge-back to the railroads) were the highest of any major US depot. A 1939 study shows that net of retail revenues, Chicago Union Station's cost was $8.27, Cincinnati's was $7.01 and New York Grand Central's was $4.70. The average was $2.09. Chicago Union Station's debt service alone was $4.96 per car, more than twice the national average for total expenses. Property taxes lifted the total another $2.37.

The charges were only one component of the station's cost. The layout of yards and engine facilities, union crew agreements, and switching needs all varied by carrier and each contributed to terminal costs. The Pennsylvania had the highest unit costs because it operated intercity trains. The Burlington and the

Milwaukee ran twice as many trains as the Pennsylvania, but their substantial commuter services required little switching. Low fares, however, ensured that even these made no money. A decade after the station opened the average one-way commuter fare was eighteen cents. Even with a full train, possible only during rush hour, the service made no money. In fact, the *Tribune* claimed of Union Station and its railroads that "the cost of operating that monumental white elephant terminal is sixteen cents out of every passenger dollar earned on their entire systems."[13]

The Pennsylvania operated into both sides of the station, which duplicated expenses. Even after its trains moved to the south side, two seniority districts remained segregated because of union agreements made by the Pennsylvania's predecessors. The Panhandle also continued to operate freight houses on its original line.[14]

More costs were to come. The Union Station and the Pennsylvania Freight Terminal Ordinances of 1914 provided for straightening the Chicago River. Infill of the old riverbed exceeded the space excavated for the new channel. This creation and destruction of real estate required the redistribution of hundreds of lots held by inherently hostile competitors. Each was hungry for the additional land. Understandably, the allocation of land and construction costs between the city and the hostile parties proved contentious. Legal maneuvering consumed years; engineering work added several more. It was 1926 before construction commenced.

Simply put, the project widened and straightened the channel of the south branch of the Chicago River between Polk and Eighteenth Streets, but this belies its devilish complexity. The project covered the world's busiest rail yards, junctions daily traversed by hundreds of trains, a major commercial waterway, and developed industrial properties. Included were all of the tracks leading to Grand Central and Dearborn Stations, together with yard tracks for LaSalle Street Station and the freight houses of a dozen major railroads. All needed to remain operational, as did two railroad and three street lift bridges physically relocated by the project.[15]

Completed in 1932, the new channel cost $7.6 million with the railroads shouldering $4.5 million. Over $12.3 million of railroad, municipal, and private property changed hands. Net, the railroads increased their land holdings, the opposite of city planners' intent. Bennett, Delano, Wacker, and others' vision had foreseen the southward expansion of the business district, but that never occurred. Nor were additional streets extended from the Loop to the South Side. The dream of consolidating railroad stations, the reason for the project, remained just that.

The exchange of land attendant to river straightening resulted in one important improvement. Near Sixteenth and Canal streets, the Burlington tracks from the station curved sharply westward, while the Alton and Ft. Wayne continued straight south. Bisecting these busy lines at grade were the tracks leading to Grand Central Station, busy transfer tracks of the St. Charles Airline, and Chicago and North Western tracks serving several of Chicago's largest grain elevators. Thirty-six individual tracks crossed here, and they were used daily by seven hundred train and engine movements. It was the world's busiest rail junction. A three-level crossing replaced this labyrinth with Burlington trains at ground level, Canal Street in the middle and the St. Charles Airline overhead. The total cost of the project was $4 million; it opened for traffic on July 31, 1931.[16]

Straightening the south branch of the Chicago River rivaled better-known engineering works of the era, if only because it required cutting a channel through the busiest rail yards in the world.

COURTESY OF THE AUTHOR

MORE RED INK

During the prosperous 1920s, two Union Station railroads faced financial difficulties. Passengers on the Chicago and Alton could be forgiven if they did not comprehend the company's dire condition. The line reequipped its flagship Alton Limited in 1924, immodestly dubbed "the handsomest train in the world." The railroad's financial statements, however, had a decidedly shabby appearance. The railroad never expanded beyond a Chicago–Saint Louis–Kansas City route, while competitors built greater and ofttimes parallel networks. It found itself unable to garner enough connecting passenger or freight traffic to ensure profitability. Management changed from one group of financiers to another, each seemingly less adept than the last.[17]

If the Alton suffered from failure to grow, the Milwaukee Road had problems of the opposite kind. Its Pacific coast extension in the century's first decade strained its finances. By November 1926, the railroad was sold at a sheriff's sale on the Butte, Montana courthouse steps to satisfy its creditors. In January 1928, a protective committee supposedly representing these creditors received permission from the Interstate Commerce Commission to reorganize in a manner that stood the usual process of bankruptcy on its head. Bondholders were nearly wiped out, while the stockholders—who were now mostly speculators and well-connected bankers—retained ownership of the property.[18] This legal travesty and related chicanery prompted Congress to pass section 77 of the Bankruptcy Act, effective in March of 1933. While some sections of bankruptcy law contemplate the liquidation of a company, section 77 recognized the quasi-public nature of railroads. It provided for the appointment of trustees by the bankruptcy court and the Interstate Commerce Commission to ensure continued operations. It also allowed temporary relief from debt payment requirements pending reorganization. The new bankruptcy act came none too soon; by June of 1935, the Milwaukee again filed for reorganization. It was to remain there until 1945.

In stark contrast to the problems at the Alton and the Milwaukee, Pennsylvania and Burlington securities were the proverbial havens for widows and orphans. These railroads remained solvent, if less profitable. Passenger service, however, had rarely been a paying proposition since early in the century. Worse, rate regulation and truck competition limited the ability of freight to cross subsidize the passenger business.[19]

The railroads pared passenger schedules early in the Depression even as they worked to recapture lost business. The industry cut fares early in 1932, and with fewer freight trains to interfere with express runs, the schedules of the flagship trains actually accelerated. On April 25, 1932, child actor Jackie Cooper cut a ribbon in Chicago Union Station to inaugurate a one-hour reduction in the running time to New York of the Broadway Limited to eighteen hours. By fall, travel increased on a brief uptick in business and optimism.[20] It continued into 1933, with a winning season by the Cubs and the Century of Progress Exposition contributing to the best summer traffic in years. Labor Day saw outbound traffic twice that of the July 4 weekend; the Pennsylvania dusted off one hundred mothballed sleeping cars and coaches for Chicago traffic. A year later it pared an additional fifteen minutes from the schedule of the Broadway Limited and by the following April the run took only seventeen hours. This required an average speed, including stops, of 53 miles per hour and sustained speeds over 70.[21]

One innovative effort speeded schedules at the same time it economized. April 1933 saw the Pennsylvania and Wabash Railroads combine their Chicago-Detroit service using the best parts of both routes. From Union Station, trains ran on the blazingly fast Pennsylvania Railroad to Fort Wayne, where they shifted to Wabash rails. Dearborn Station, Chicago home of the Wabash, lost four trains, in part because the Roosevelt administration pushed for the "elimination of waste."[22]

The flashiest innovations of the Depression years were the near-simultaneous introductions of lightweight, streamlined passenger cars and of the diesel locomotive. The Burlington's Zephyr incorporated both technologies. Delivered in April 1934, this famous train was confined to a Nebraska-and-Missouri run after spending a summer on display at Chicago's Century of Progress Exposition. By the following year, however, the Burlington operated the first streamliners to call Chicago Union Station home. Thousands visited the trains on display in Union Station on April 16 after a ceremonial run to Minneapolis carried eighty-eight pairs of twins as guests of the railroad.[23] The Twin Zephyrs were immediate hits and soon the Burlington hosted a fleet of these stainless steel–clad, diesel-powered speedsters.

The Zephyrs competed for Chicago-to-Minneapolis traffic against the Milwaukee, whose finances precluded innovative investments. Nevertheless, the weaker road's management dug into its pockets for two streamlined steam locomotives and home-built sets of matching orange, gray, and maroon lightweight cars. On a May 15, 1935 demonstration run, the new Hiawatha was clocked at 112 miles per hour, and the press corps faithfully remarked that at top speeds the bar car's glassware did not tremble. In actuality, travel above 90 miles per hour was initially reported as "like moving about on the deck of a ship in a heavy gale."[24] This reveals one secret of all of the famous streamliners. They required substantial investments in track rebuilding combined with ultrahigh maintenance standards. This included reengineering the track with superelevated curves, high-speed turnouts, and an accurate signaling system that allowed the flashy new trains to maintain their blistering pace. On the Hiawatha's first outings, the track work had not been complete. While it later ran glass smooth, it demanded expensive track maintenance standards. At first, these expenses were for the sole benefit of the single train

carrying only 300 people each. Sixteen months later a new lighter-weight train set allowed the same type of locomotive to pull an additional car. A second Hiawatha soon followed.

Speed differentiated the streamliners from bus competition and provided an advantage relative to automobiles. Most intercity highways of the period had no paving, but one of Union Station's users paralleled Route 66, one of the nation's best and busiest roads.[25] The Alton placed a steam-hauled streamliner, the Abraham Lincoln, in service in mid-1935, and locomotion was soon changed to diesel.[26] Two years later, this Chicago–St. Louis train got a diesel-powered companion, the Ann Rutledge. The Alton was also a pioneer in air-conditioning passenger cars. Still a novelty, air-conditioning provided another advantage relative to automobiles and buses in addition to cooling; windows could remain sealed eliminating the soot that had been the rail travelers' curse.

The staid Pennsylvania was a relative laggard in restyling its Chicago trains, in part because solid heavyweight Pullman sleepers were a good fit for its bread-and-butter night trains. A single bullet-nosed bronze-and-gold locomotive styled by Raymond Loewy premiered in 1936, but it primarily represented a public relations reaction to the two-tone gray speedsters designed by Henry Dreyfuss for archcompetitor New York Central. In 1938, however, it unveiled "The Fleet of Modernism," which included a crisp streamlined version of its flagship Broadway Limited, detailed inside and out by Loewy. Despite hard economic times, the onboard barbershop and train stenographer did a brisk business. On the same day, a Dreyfuss-appointed Twentieth Century Limited made its maiden run on a parallel route from New York City to Chicago's LaSalle Street Station.

Observation car of the streamlined Hiawatha in 1943.

Like every other business, Union Station adjusted to the harsh realities of the Great Depression. Its workforce, 1,088 strong in 1926, declined to 564 by 1933, rebounding to 719 by 1939.[27] Of equal financial importance, it successfully protested its property taxes. Beginning in 1929, it withheld its tax payments and by the following year $2.4 million was escrowed. After state review, taxes fell by a quarter. When the Interstate Commerce Commission reduced the value of the station for rate-making purposes, the company again appealed in 1936. Although it finally remitted most of the $250,000 withheld in 1937, some taxes were not fully paid until an appeal was lost in 1942.[28]

The station company's greatest savings came from consecutive refinancing of its bonds at lower rates. First called were $16 million in 6½ percent bonds on March 20, 1935. Although the new bonds carried a 4 percent coupon and sold at a 10 percent premium, recalling the old bonds required a 12½ percent premium. In July 1937, the company called an additional $44 million in bonds bearing 4½ percent and 5 percent coupons by issuing an equal amount of 3¾ percent debt. While the deal saved $9 million over the life of the bonds, it was not without controversy. It needed consent of the Milwaukee Road trustees and the ICC. The ICC objected to the lack of a sinking fund and the use of $730,000 from the company treasury to pay issuance costs. Later in the year, $7 million of 5 percent debt was swapped for 3½ percent bonds. Taken together, annual interest savings on all bonded debt was nearly $850,000.

Another $16 million refunding to garner interest-rate savings in March 1940 was even more controversial. The ICC demanded a competitive auction, rather than the traditional negotiated underwriting, despite the historical refusal of any underwriter to bid competitively on railroad bonds. The company contacted 107 firms, but only one bank tendered a bid and it was rejected on technical grounds. In the end, Kuhn Loeb, Harriman Brothers, and Smith Barney jointly received the commission, but the price negotiated was higher than the earlier rejected bid. ICC Commissioner Claude Porter asked the Pennsylvania's treasurer to testify and asked, "Was it a sort of sit-down strike by capital?" Treasurer George Pabst admitted, "I have heard it described as that."[29] But the deal was done and the ICC failed to investigate. In July 1941, $6.8 million of these 3½ percent bonds became callable, refinanced at rates from 7⁄10 percent to 2.1 percent, for even more savings. Total annual interest savings over the original payments was an impressive $1.1 million or 33 percent.

Capital expenditures at the station, usually the major place to cut in hard times, stayed relatively high. The steam plant required almost complete replacement in 1929, and as detailed below, air rights construction over both the north and south approach tracks required track and signal reconfiguration. In 1935, some station lunch and dining areas were air-conditioned. Prior to this time, cooling came from a moderately successful attempt to use blowers drawing cool air from the freight tunnels underneath the station.

One major series of projects came after July 1936, when a broken thirty-six-inch water main flooded the station and mail terminal. The immediate response to the flood was to run seventeen borrowed fire engines into the train shed on flatcars to remove seven feet of standing water. Several years' engineering work ensured that the problem would not reoccur. The station suffered $250,000 in damage, primarily to its electric generators. They were not replaced; power henceforth came from Commonwealth

Edison. Replacement of all cast-iron water mains under the station resulted from the determination that vibration from heavy trains caused their failure.[30]

AIR RIGHTS AND OTHER DEVELOPMENTS

As steam shovels and trains of dump cars rechanneled the river south of the station, another transformation was underway to the north. Building above the tracks had been an alluring possibility for decades, but economic and legal considerations thwarted such development. Historically, there was little demand for offices, shops, and hotels immediately west of the river. Two office tower developments, the Lyric Opera and the Insurance Exchange Buildings, although located east of the river, pushed business westward toward Union Station.

It was unclear whether a railroad could build and rent office buildings under Illinois law. The construction of Grand Central Station in New York resolved a similar problem by use of a new legal doctrine called "air rights." Air rights were different in two ways from the ground leases common in Chicago. In a ground lease, a landholder simply lets property to a developer who constructs a building on it. The developer mortgages both leasehold and building. Likewise, he pays the property taxes on both. Air rights, however, allow the landowner to occupy part of a property for railroad uses while the developer receives very specific pieces of the ground for the placement of column footings, as well as an undisputed right to build and occupy the airspace overhead. Property owners could either lease or sell air rights. Minor problems developed relative to mortgage valuations, but it was the accurate assessment of property taxes that seemed an insuperable objection. With air rights, both lessor and lessee derived taxable value, a circumstance unique in a century of Illinois tax law. To complicate the issue, Illinois railroad taxes had both a unique basis and a different tax assessor than the lessee. Legislation was necessary to allow tax bills to be split.

There were only three tracts of land suitable for air rights development in the state of Illinois, and each lay adjacent to Chicago's business district. One was the future location of the Merchandise Mart, north of the Chicago River; another was the Illinois Central land bordering the Chicago River and Lake Michigan east of Michigan Avenue; Union Station's land was the third. The necessary legislation thus had narrow political support. An interesting anecdote suggests how the law changed. Ernest Graham told his private secretary Charles F. Murphy, "I want you to go to New York and go to W. C. Potter, the Chairman of the Bankers Trust Company and he'll be expecting you, and you are to get some money there." When Murphy protested that they could get plenty of money from Chicago banks, Graham groused, "What Chicago bankers don't know won't bother them." Upon his arrival in New York, Murphy got $250,000 in $10,000 bills from Potter. Rather than accept a guard and attract suspicion, Murphy hid the money in his shoe and marked time back at his hotel before discreetly boarding the Twentieth Century Limited where he locked himself in a private compartment for the trip to Chicago. Except for one $10,000 bill Graham retained, Murphy took the hoard to Representative Schuyler's office in the state capitol building and the air rights legislation quickly passed.[31]

Once the legal landscape changed, the *Chicago Daily News* chose a site over the tracks at Madison and Canal Streets for its office and printing plant. It executed an air rights lease in 1927 and the following year the station company received a $1.2 million payment for the purchase portion of the contract. That payment covered the sale of land for each column footing. The apparent windfall on this sale is misleading, since the company incurred significant expense to relocate its tracks. In addition to the land purchase, the newspaper continued to lease the space above the tracks. In 1941, it paid $1.45 million to buy out the lease. The station company used the entire sum to pay down debt.[32]

The *Daily News* site proved difficult. The irregularly shaped lot was not in itself a problem. The track layout, however, dictated the tower's column placement. Moreover, the design had to provide ventilation for the steam locomotives running underneath. The site nonetheless had compelling advantages, foremost being its appeal as one of the largest available plots adjacent to the business district. Its location on both railroad and river was a major plus for the delivery of newsprint, while its proximity to both Union and North Western Stations facilitated the suburban distribution of the newspapers. Architects Holabird and Roche found innovative solutions to the site's problems. They placed a plaza along the riverbank flanked by two low arcade buildings.[33] These attractive elements covered the easternmost station tracks. Their construction incorporated a complex system of girders, trusses, and cantilevers that spanned seven tracks without intermediate columns. The office tower was on the site's west edge. The plaza and tower composition also helped solve the problem of smoke dissipation.[34] To address that problem, the architects hired Joshua D'Esposito. His solution was a five-foot-deep "smoke chamber," actually a series of longitudinal vaults, between the tracks and the plaza. This chamber connected to two chimneys inside the twenty-six-story office tower. The natural draft of the chimneys, the exhaust pressure of the locomotives, and several small fans proved sufficient to keep the train shed free of noxious gases.

Many people assume the *Daily News* building, since renamed One Riverside Plaza, is part of the adjacent North Western Station (now Ogilvie Transportation Center). It connects to that station by an enclosed pedestrian walkway over Canal Street. A ramp though the building from its street level entrance near the Madison Street Bridge carries 80 percent of that station's commuters up to the track level of that station. For several decades the building also contained the C&NW corporate offices, whose street address, 400 West Madison, had a resonance with that railroad's fleet of "400" passenger trains. This reinforced the building's link to the North Western despite its location above Union Station property.

A project of even greater scale and importance arose south of the terminal. In 1929, the Post Office finally received authorization for its long-needed expansion. The thirteen-story post office was to be the world's largest, and at $22 million, the most expensive building ever constructed by the US government. It proved every bit as controversial as the original Union Station proposal. The need was obvious, but there were objections to the site. Its two-block-long Chicago River frontage straddled the proposed Congress Street axis of the *Plan of Chicago*. Public response echoed that which greeted the Pennsylvania Railroad's freight line proposal. While the railroad had demurred so as not to hinder Congress Street, the Post Office Department had more leverage. As the Depression's economic winter settled in, the city joyously embraced any construction project as a ray of sunshine. In a compromise never to the liking of the Chicago

202

Plan Commission, the building's third floor included a "slot" to accommodate the yet-to-be-built Congress Street. On paper, this preserved the *Plan of Chicago*, but the post office forever destroyed the majestic tree-lined boulevard envisioned by Daniel Burnham. It was another twenty-one years before Congress Parkway was built—as an express highway unlike Burnham's boulevard.[35]

In addition to the Plan Commission, the US Congress objected to the post office site. Senator John Blaine of Wisconsin was indignant when the Post Office "called the budget bureau at 10 o'clock in the morning and declared that the appropriation had to be approved in two hours, a matter that should have required months to investigate." Upon review, Blaine discovered that in 1926 the Post Office purchased a neighboring site from Marshall Field and Company for $3.9 million. Now the air-rights site required abandonment of the Field plot. Blaine found that Field purchased the site for $2.0 million only two years earlier and that, at the time, an appraiser hired by Field stated that its worth was much less. An investigation ensued. Compliant testimony from a local appraiser fanned the flames by stating that the $3.9 million the railroads asked for rights was $2.0 million more than paid for the Merchandise Mart air rights, which he believed was the superior location. In that instance, Field and Company had been the air rights buyer, not a seller. Blaine decried the deal as "constructive larceny on the part of those who receive and palpable negligence on the part of those who gave." The Senator conveniently failed to make public that the $22 million appropriation also covered the demolition and relocation to Taylor Street of the Union Station power plant, upgraded only a year earlier. Also included in the sale was the Parcel Post Building, then leased from the station company. In the end, the cost would prove even higher than that Blaine found objectionable, but the need for new facilities was too pressing and his investigation died.[36]

Post office construction, which started in 1931, was a major stimulus to the depressed local economy. By this time, Congress paid less attention to facility costs than to the dire plight of postal workers. It held hearings in which local postal officials had to deny that their part-time employees were starving. Although the post office was not a public works project per se, 1,900 workers raced to complete the building by its January 1, 1933 deadline.[37] The project was so large that U.S. Steel estimated that 1,000 workers in its Gary plant would work six months to fill the structural steel order. In all, post office construction created 6,000 jobs.

The choice of Graham, Anderson, Probst, and White as post office architects ensured compatibility with Union Station, but true to form Edward Bennett never embraced the work of his rival, calling the project "Ernest Graham's insult to Congress

Chicago's Main Post Office over the tracks had sixty acres of floor space and the original concept called for an airport on its seven-acre roof.

Street."[38] The location, however, had too many advantages; the site was large, it was adjacent to the business district, and the mail could be conveniently handled from the railway post office cars spotted at basement loading docks.

In 1931 the Union Station Company received $5.5 million from the postal department for land with a book value of $7.1 million.[39] The $1.6 million loss reflected the real estate market's decline, but again the station company was stuck with the original debt. While the purchase was not necessarily an unprofitable venture for the company, tracks had to be relocated at company expense and a new $2.0 million steam plant built. At least the company had a long-term contract to provide steam heat to the post office. The architects retained Joshua D'Esposito, now in private practice, as consulting engineer. Soon after it was built,

however, the postal service discovered a flaw in his design for locomotive exhaust removal. The system was virtually identical with that under the *Daily News* building, but it covered a dramatically larger footprint. There was simply too much smoke to expel. After four years' service, the exhaust chamber accumulated 750 tons of cinders and the weight created structural distortions requiring emergency correction.

THE WILD WEST SIDE

With the ascendance of the automobile and the stringencies of the Depression, long-distance passenger traffic declined faster than suburban services. Union Station increasingly became a portal for office workers, so its destiny was increasingly tied to the downtown real estate market. When the station opened in 1925, Chicago had 17 million square feet of office space, but a

building boom added 10 million square feet in only four years. Office vacancy rates soared during the Depression, with 8 million square feet empty by 1933. While occupied space remained above 20 million square feet, 20 percent more than in 1925, this masked the worst drop in property values of any major city in the United States. The high point had been the year after Union Station's opening. Thereafter, center city values declined 50 percent, forcing record foreclosures.

Union Station, the *Daily News* building, and the Post Office Building seemed to herald a West Side boom, but instead neighborhood land values collapsed. Area warehouses, garment shops, and furniture factories fell to their lowest imaginable fate; the West Side became Chicago's Skid Row.[40] It had not been a viable residential area for decades, but it continued to be dotted with old houses and storefronts. Along Clinton Street were saloons and lunchrooms catering to the district's transient workmen, teamsters, and travelers.[41] Prohibition diminished the need for such storefronts and introduced violent new elements into an already tough neighborhood.

This new lawlessness is illustrated by another Charles F. Murphy story. In 1932 Graham, Anderson, Probst, and White commissioned a luxurious folio to illustrate the company's commissions. New York photographer Robert W. Tebbs came to Chicago and Murphy escorted him on his shoot. After one particularly hot afternoon near the station, Murphy asked Tebbs if he would like a beer, to which the photographer replied, "There's Prohibition, but I'd love it." They drove to a speakeasy at Clinton and Jefferson and as they exited their car, they noticed a man near the saloon lying on the curb, blood issuing from his head. They went in and silently drew on their beers, enjoying them little. Finally, the ashen-faced Tebbs turned to Murphy and said, "My God, I heard about these terrible things in Chicago and Capone running the show." Tebbs again fell silent. On the way back to their car the police briefly detained the pair and they learned that the man had indeed been shot dead.[42]

Aggravating West Side problems was the competition from the period's other Chicago air-rights project. The Merchandise Mart rose over the former site of the Chicago and North Western's Wells Street Depot. Its tenants were the furniture showrooms that continued to dot Chicago's West Side even after

manufacturing moved to low-cost southern states. Their removal to a centralized mart left a void that other commercial tenants failed to fill. Another problem resulted from the construction of Union Station itself. The enabling ordinance required the raising of Canal Street and the widening of Clinton Street at railroad expense south to Twelfth Street. This in turn required the demolition of many older but substantial structures. In the best Chicago tradition, landowners fronting these streets put up cheap buildings, colloquially known as "tax-payers," awaiting an expected West Side real estate boom. Land west of the station, however, was never worth more than one-third the value of like properties a similar distance to the east. Usually it was worth far less. The area deteriorated and became the haunt of transients and alcoholics. Peirce Anderson's design deliberately downplayed its western entrances, a decision that the station's security staff subsequently saw as a blessing.

AUTOS CHANGE THE CITY

As the Jazz Age matured, the Progressive movement waned, but never entirely disappeared. River straightening was complete and the Plan Commission refocused on the consolidation of the Near South depots. Its efforts were too late. Railroad passenger traffic was disappearing and unprofitable. Railroads had more incentive to protect asset values than to invest in a failing line of business. Chicago's streetcar and elevated systems made similar decisions. Historian Paul Barrett studied the situation of the city's transit system, but he could have been addressing the railroads when he observed, "Between 1900 and 1930, city policies helped make Chicago's mass transportation less attractive while increasing the usefulness of the private automobile.

TABLE 7.2. PERCENTAGE OF AREA POPULATION IN THE SUBURBAN RING

YEAR	CHICAGO	NEW YORK	PHILADELPHIA	LOS ANGELES	ALL DETROIT	SMAS
1900	18.8	23.0	31.6	46.1	33.1	38.1
1910	20.6	23.6	31.7	40.7	24.1	35.9
1920	23.3	25.4	32.8	42.2	23.9	34.7
1930	27.8	29.2	37.8	46.8	28.0	36.4
1940	29.6	29.8	39.6	48.8	31.7	38.2
1950	34.1	33.2	43.6	54.6	38.7	42.3

Source: United States Bureau of the Census, Population and Housing Reports, 1900–1950.

This happened because mass transit policy was designed to prevent recurrence of the late 19th century problems, while the difficulties created by wide-spread automobiles were treated pragmatically."[43]

Public promotion of automobile-based transport unwittingly stifled private investment in transit. A 1907 agreement between the city and the local streetcar and rapid transit companies limited fares to a nickel, while giving the city 55 percent of remaining profits. Lacking an adequate return on investment, transit providers virtually eliminated capital improvements.

The *Plan of Chicago* only vaguely anticipated the rising tide of private automobiles and trucks. In 1910, Charles Wacker, chairman of the Chicago Plan Commission, actually stated that the motor truck would forever eliminate traffic congestion on Chicago streets, optimism based on the fact that trucks carried four times the payload in a vehicle only one-third the length of team and wagon. There were fewer than ten thousand automobiles in the city when Wacker made this remark. By 1925, when Union Station opened, Plan Commissioner Eugene Taylor estimated that every Saturday night dealers sold another 1,500 automobiles.[44]

Traffic circulation and wider streets had been pillars of the *Plan of Chicago*. True City Beautiful rhetoric promoted the uplifting benefits of broad parkways to surround the center city. Never intended for intense auto use, these boulevards nevertheless suited the motor age and the Plan Commission quickly encouraged their use as highways. Paul Barrett concludes, "The responsibility of the city to provide facilities for and to regulate the automobile was never seriously contested." In part, Barrett explains, automobile traffic presented the city with a recurrent series of minor, soluble problems; a new traffic signal or revised curb lines were gratefully received as progress. Incremental solutions sufficed for increased automobile traffic, while transit issues, such as the chronic capital shortage and the resulting deferred maintenance, were less easily addressed. Perennial requests by the streetcar operators for fare hikes were political dynamite, while equally insistent public demands for traffic signals and better paving were rarely sensitive enough to tip a close election.[45]

Automobiles increased suburbanization throughout the United States. At the beginning of the twentieth century, Chicago dominated its region to an extent exceeding its metropolitan peers, and by every measure it was the least suburbanized major American city.

However, decentralization was rapid, and thus its need to expand highway capacity was greater than elsewhere. As early as 1928 an estimated 400,000 people daily crossed the city limits by automobile. At that time, a census of automobiles in the downtown area showed that over one in six came from outside the city. This influx clogged the arterial streets designed in an earlier era.

When Burnham wrote his plan, business district congestion was the result of teaming and freight hauling. Two decades later, auto congestion was the issue. The first public proposal for a limited access highway linking downtown with outer areas was the *West Side Superhighway*, a 1929 proposal of the Chicago Plan Commission. The Commission followed in 1933 with a *Comprehensive System of Limited Ways*. These documents languished, but led to the formation of the Department of Subways and Superhighways within city government. It released its *Superhighway Plan for the City of Chicago* in 1939. Despite demonstrated need, the Depression exacerbated the usual financial constraints.[46]

The city was near its state-imposed debt cap and could not levy additional taxes. The state legislature jealously guarded its right to tax gasoline and, although 38 percent of such taxes were collected in Cook County, only 3 percent made it back to the region. The Illinois Municipal Code limited city powers so tightly that it was difficult to find any revenue source other than the property tax. It also limited local regulation of the roadways.[47]

In 1904, for example, when Chicago was home to 1,500 automobiles (nearly the total in the state), a city ordinance required the examination and licensing of drivers. This was found to be unconstitutional, as the Municipal Code granted cities no such authority. The state was not to require a driver's exam until 1935 and even then, it kept all of the revenue.[48]

Just as railroads needed terminals, automobiles needed downtown parking. By the early 1920s, a local editor noted, "For four yards of space along the curb line, the average Chicagoan will every morning and every evening, be willing to exchange most of America's islands in the Pacific."[49] Central district land values made surface lots prohibitive, but demand pushed parking fees high enough to allow construction of some of the nation's first multistory parking structures. Initially off-street parking was the sole province of private enterprise. One of the first parking garages was the Chicago Depository of Automobiles, opened in 1900 on Plymouth Court near Van Buren Street. It started as a stable, but it hired a mechanic to maintain automobiles for its clientele of LaSalle Street bankers. The first building built specifically as a car park was the LaSalle Hotel Garage, erected in 1909. Parking garages became just another type of speculative real estate development. The municipal government, of course, was a de facto provider of parking along its streets. The idea that government could erect buildings and charge parking fees was not yet acceptable. This changed in 1921, when the Chicago Park District opened the first municipally owned surface parking lot near the lakefront at Monroe Street. Larger facilities followed near the Art Institute in 1937 and Soldier Field in 1946. The city was now in direct competition for the commuter traffic lifeblood of Union Station.

THE ALLURE OF PUBLIC FUNDS

Public efforts to consolidate railroad stations continued unabated. With the new channel of the Chicago River complete, its chief benefit—the opening of new streets to the South Side—seemed near reality. The City Council Committee on Railway Terminals presented detailed plans for two new depots in 1931. One was a South Side station at Harrison and Wells Streets, while the other was a lakefront depot at Twelfth Street. Consulting engineer Edward Noonan authored their report.[50]

Local boosters wanted a grand new edifice—maybe two or three. Noonan may have shocked them when he stated, "It is generally conceded that railroads can no longer construct monumental passenger stations. The Interstate Commerce Commission will not permit the issuance of large blocks of securities, the proceeds of which are to be used to construct non-revenue producing facilities."[51]

Noonan created a new plan for a consolidated depot near Randolph and Michigan. Its effect on Union Station should have been minimal, as it was directed at the occupants of Central, Dearborn, LaSalle, and Grand Central Stations. However, it proposed the removal of Alton trains from Union Station to the new depot. The Alton had been purchased by the Baltimore and Ohio, and it actually ran more passengers into the city than its owner. Although it was never assimilated into the larger carrier, at the time everyone assumed that it would become just another B&O division. Thus, even without a consolidated depot, its trains seemed likely to use Grand Central Station.[52]

The public at large paid little heed to what seemed only to be the latest in a never-ending series of plans, but it attracted the attention of Joshua D'Esposito. In private practice since 1927, he was still the acknowledged expert on Chicago terminals. Engineering projects had been in short supply in 1930, however, so he entered politics and won a seat as sanitary district commissioner. His platform stressed his technical competence and he pledged that no political speech would exceed five minutes in length. Even without organized political backing, he waltzed to victory. But D'Esposito could not sit idly when station projects were in play. Borrowing from Delano, he proposed a depot at Roosevelt Road (Twelfth Street). The single station near State Street would replace three older structures. It would connect with the proposed State Street subway and a new diagonal street that would turn northwest to connect with Wacker Drive and the Congress Street extension.[53] D'Esposito's idea never gained traction, in large part because his proposal cost $50 million while Noonan's cost $19 million. In addition, Chairman Simpson seemed to have his own agenda. He sat on the New York Central Railroad board and D'Esposito's plan would have used much of that company's land, rather than freeing it for sale to developers.

The Noonan and D'Esposito terminal plans shared one idea. Both combined traditional methods for infrastructure finance with a call for public monies. Changes were indeed apace in the planning, financing, and ownership of transportation projects.[54] May 19, 1930, saw enactment of a Traction Ordinance in which the city agreed to build two subway lines at its own expense, which it would then lease to the privately owned elevated railways. This arrangement was clearly beyond the city's charter powers, so an act entitled the "Illinois Statute for Subways" passed the state legislature the previous June allowing construction of the State Street and Dearborn Street subway lines together with several underground pedestrian tunnels. In other words, this statute allowed municipal assets to be used by private enterprises.

The subway system was the first Illinois project since canal days to use municipal bonds to finance nonroadway transportation.[55] Bonds whose debt repayment was secured solely by project revenues required passage of specific enabling legislation, and the Illinois constitution specifically prohibited cities from lending to aid private corporations. So it was proposed that the city own the newly constructed subway lines and rent them to the rapid transit lines. The legal argument for this throwback to early Illinois railroad building was notably weak, but it withstood legal challenge. This surprised observers, since precedent pointed in another direction. Chicago tried a similar tactic in 1906, when it authorized the issuance of $75 million in bonds for construction of streetcar lines in developing areas of the city for subsequent lease to the street railway companies. Today, such revenue bonds are an accepted form of finance, but in 1907 the Supreme Court of Illinois held that the so-called Mueller Certificates were municipal debt and thus illegal unless approved by a supermajority of voters in a referendum. The state legislature would not grant Chicago the authority to issue revenue bonds, and while the majority of voters approved of municipal trolley line construction, the measure did not achieve the two-thirds vote required for passage.

Three decades after the Mueller plan died, the Depression was in full force and city and county authorities must have been grateful for one result of the state's restrictive municipal code: a low debt load. Even so, they had trouble servicing their relatively light payments. Tax collections were so poor that officials imposed a property tax moratorium in 1929. To this day, Cook County levies taxes in one year, but collects them in the next.[56]

Remarkably, during this fallow period the city continued to retain Edward Noonan as staff engineer for a project destined to go nowhere. The depressed economy only got worse until December 1936, when a strong holiday season saw the most passenger business through Union Station since 1929. Most lines saw a 20 percent traffic jump and Noonan lost no time dusting off blueprints. The bloom was soon off the boom, however, and new terminal plans withered.[57]

A WAR FOOTING

As an industrial center, Chicago experienced both the worst effects of the Great Depression and a jackrabbit rebound when the nation mobilized for war. The glow of molten steel returned to idle mills, packinghouses added shifts, mothballed tractor factories converted to tank production, and new plants arose to build bombers. With rationing imposed for gasoline and tires, people turned to the rails for most intercity and suburban travel.

Changes at Union Station actually predated US entry into the war. November 1941 saw a new USO canteen operated by the Fred Harvey Company to supply men in uniform with refreshments at "cantonment prices." Six months later, the mezzanine level of the concourse became a USO lounge staffed entirely by volunteer hostesses. The Travelers Aid Society, which originally staffed a booth at the station to help immigrants, retrained its volunteers for the task of arranging accommodations for in-transit servicemen. The society's ten city booths soon handled eleven thousand daily requests for help. A year into the war, the number of women volunteers jumped from 24 to 524. The station company itself hired forty-one female information clerks under manager Marie Griffith to handle requests for transportation information. They received three months' training on timetables and routes and each then handled 350 calls per day. By now janitorial and cleaning crews were mostly women. In late 1942, fifty women even dealt with the hefty work of handling parcel post in the station.[58]

By all accounts, the station ran better than ever and it certainly never saw greater crowds. By war's end employment reached 1,127. A February 1943 account said that all ticket windows were open most of the day and each had five or six patrons in line. There were no seats in the waiting rooms and restaurants, even though more passengers now brought meals from home. Even wall space to lean on was at a premium. "It'll be a couple of hours before any of the big trains pulls out," a white-haired gateman related. "The trains are so crowded nowadays the passengers come here hours ahead of time to make sure they get a seat. Nobody in the railroad

One of the earliest women managers in the railroad industry was Marie Griffith, who ran the Information Bureau.

COURTESY OF THE LIBRARY OF CONGRESS, LC-OSW3-015576-E

business ever saw anything like this." Despite the crowds, the railroads said that anyone needing to make a last-minute trip had "a pretty fair chance" of obtaining a ticket, even if they had to stand part of the way. Wartime freight received priority, but 85 percent of the trains into the station arrived on time.[59]

The inability to get materials or manpower meant few wartime improvements to the station. The major modification was to black out all skylights. In the train shed the platforms became claustrophobic, while the waiting rooms now kept their chandeliers lit twenty-four hours a day. Perhaps the most visible change, however, was decorative. A giant war bond display three months in the making filled the concourse. It was conceived and executed by the Chicago Building Trades Council, whose 225 locals bore the cost. A forty-foot-high mural of the nation's capital proclaimed "Bonds for Us." A block away on the opposing wall was a companion mural of bombs raining on enemy territory labeled "Bombs for Them." In between were suspended 4,500 wooden scale-model bombers. Nearly two thousand apprentice laborers at the Washburn Trade School built the planes. Eight more murals in the waiting room were the donation of the Society of Typographic Arts, which had five hundred volunteers work on the prints.[60]

Union Station's busiest hours came near the war's end or shortly thereafter. Its absolute peak may have been during the Christmas–New Year's rush in 1944. The redeployment of troops from the European theater for the assault on Japan had a different character from the original mobilization. An effort was made to give soldiers and sailors a quick home furlough, rather than running dedicated troop trains from military bases directly to embarkation ports. Thus, traffic poured onto regular trains. At the same time, the War Department enacted a ban on Pullman travel of less than 450 miles. This allowed 895 Pullman cars from Chicago routes to switch to troop train service for the first time. By July 1945, trains like the Milwaukee's North Woods Hiawatha with 700 seats left the station with 340 standees.[61]

Even as the war dragged on, plans to centralize Chicago's stations progressed. A state commission empaneled at the behest of Joshua D'Esposito did the bidding of Mayor Kelly. Heavy wartime traffic may have made the existing facilities seem inadequate, but following the poor maintenance of the Depression, there was little question that all of Chicago's passenger facilities were well worn. In addition, there was a perceived need to coordinate with the planned subways and freeways that surely would follow the war. Under D'Esposito's plan, the city would own rail terminals just as it did at the newly renamed Midway Airport. Asked if his plan would include Union Station, he stated in the affirmative. In fact, a proposed authority would run both airline and rail terminals. It was to have the power to appropriate private property, a power also sought for Mayor Kelly's other major initiative, a slum clearance commission. Kelly's floor leader in the Senate, an ambitious young South Side politician named Richard J. Daley, submitted the bill to provide for these projects.[62]

"Bonds for Us, Bombs for Them" read the patriotic messages decorating the station during wartime.

CHAPTER EIGHT

REMODELING THE DEPOT, REMAKING THE CITY

PLANS FOR A POSTWAR WORLD

Created at the apex of American rail travel, Chicago Union Station fortunately experienced a second peak period during World War II. However, the beleaguered railroad industry misinterpreted an aberration in demand as a glimmer of hope. They thought—wished really—that the public had not entirely deserted the rails. Sleek and speedy trains truly made competitive inroads prior to the war, but the warm glow of postwar optimism magnified what had been rather modest gains. Many railroads nevertheless recycled wartime profits into fleets of modern passenger trains to capture elusive riders.

It should have been the ideal time to consolidate Chicago's terminals. Railroad managers still had faith in a bright future, but even the most optimistic saw no scenario that required existing capacity. Their rosy view stemmed partially from the savings promised by a different investment: the diesel locomotive. Diesel operating savings promised disproportionate gains at terminals. Steam locomotives required a massive infrastructure of roundhouses, coaling stations, repair shops, ash pits, water towers, and storage yards. Diesel locomotives were on the road more and in the shop less than the steamers they replaced. Downsized, consolidated shops could be moved away from the terminals,

releasing expensive city lands for resale. The same was true of nearby freight houses and team tracks. Still busy and important, their profitability declined sharply due to door-to-door truck competition. Freight houses were easier to sell than rail yards since they had street frontage and utilities connections. It seemed time to harvest landholding values, even if that meant the closure of several Chicago depots.

Why did the railroads miss this opportunity? Part of the answer lies in Chicago's real estate market. Office vacancy rates, the driver of real estate value, remained low and the railroads awaited better times.[1] They operated long-obsolete warehouse and shop facilities, but their cost of carry was low. Selling these properties had no effect on debt service, for example, because they were not separately mortgaged. And as railroad property, they carried no separate tax assessment, although once this land was cleared or leased, property taxes became payable. Indeed, citywide tax levies during this period jumped dramatically. Local governments, the city of Chicago in particular, desperately sought revenue to make up for two decades of deferred maintenance. Moreover, New Deal–era social promises proved expensive and the only local revenue source was the ad valorem tax. After World War II, Union Station's assessed valuation declined

The sunlit waiting room was so far from the tracks that directional signage was required.

due to Depression-era tax appeals, but higher tax rates caused its annual levy to increase 69 percent between 1945 and 1950.[2] The station company pushed this cost to the railroads, but rate regulation prevented a pass-through to ticket prices.

Consolidation dreams refused to die, but Union Station was no longer planners' focus. Indeed, the railroads themselves were not a direct concern. Rather, they blocked downtown expansion and congested southbound streets. With a flat office market there was little need to expand the commercial district, but nearby smoke-choked neighborhoods continued their deterioration. Here, in areas wedged between the yards, were the ghettos of marginalized groups such as the Chinese, Eastern European Jews, and African Americans. These poverty-stricken communities suffered within sight of center city office towers; a revived sense of social activism pushed housing issues to center stage. The Chicago Plan Commission noted, "The first impression of a city is the one that usually remains with travelers, and we could hardly present a more dire impression of Chicago's social and economic condition."[3] Unstated was the ghetto landowners' desire to cash in from the expansion of the business district.

Reformers knew poor citizens needed better housing, returning GIs needed any housing, and both interests now seemed compatible with business community sentiment. The combined gaze of these divergent interests focused on trackside properties. Into this mix came radical ideas in planned development under the banner of "urban renewal," a costly program of neighborhood improvement. Urban renewal was explicitly coupled with the modern freeway. Rather than expand multiple streets in the grid, entirely new vehicular arteries addressed congestion. Railroad terminal rationalization became the stepchild of more ambitious reforms.

As the civic focus changed, so did the political landscape. Planning initiatives increasingly came from outside government or mainstream civic groups. Organized outsiders rose to prominence—a seismic shift obscuring who actually wielded power.[4] At its core were the locally focused organizers trained by Chicago radical Saul Alinsky, but larger forces were also at work. The Plan Commission's influence waned as parochial bodies, such

as the South Side Planning Board, garnered business support. Long-standing neighborhood booster groups matured, mastering the process of obtaining grants from governments and charitable trusts. This funding transformation allowed small organizations to hire professional planners. This increased their credibly and ability to court the media.

A 1940 proposal envisioned a new rail terminal at Clark and Congress Streets, the latter being an authorized but yet unbuilt expressway. This latest vision excluded Union and North Western stations, but planners still thought big. The new depot was to have thirty stub tracks, six tracks running through to a LaSalle Street commuter terminal, a 145-by-600 foot waiting room, and parking for three hundred autos. The plan extended Dearborn and Franklin streets southward and freed fifty-five acres for development.[5] The price tag for the depot was $200 million, exclusive of new freight houses. Less than carload lot freight business remained significant enough that the plan called for rebuilding most, but not all, freight houses.

Consolidation calls resurfaced as wartime constraints lifted. Joshua D'Esposito, who continued his private consultation with the city, blasted the four southernmost depots as "slum railway facilities."[6] In December 1947, the South Side Planning Board echoed this with detailed engineering studies proposing replacement of Grand Central, LaSalle Street, Dearborn, and Central Stations' traffic with a facility immediately west of Union Station.[7] Their proposal used the existing waiting room and other facilities, but required a second concourse across Clinton Street. Approach tracks were to parallel Union Station's for several miles, a fatal weakness. They had to cross existing Union Station leads at grade, a prescription for unacceptable congestion.[8] Nor did this plan adequately address the release of property. Previous plans allowed the railroads to benefit from the sale of their land. The new proposal stated that the public, not the railroads, should benefit from consolidation. A new authority would fund construction, but it would also glean profits from the land released.

The board's report, published in late 1948, recommended that a public authority purchase all railroad terminal lands including Union Station. Tax-backed bonds would fund acquisition and construction. The authority would then put in streets, sewers, and other improvements necessary to recoup its investment. However, the assumed beneficiary, the public, resisted the taxes necessary to initiate the projects.[9] At the same time, conditioned by decades of experience as a populist target, railroad managers explicitly branded public ownership of railroad terminals as unacceptable socialism. There were, after all, notable calls to nationalize all railways, as was the European norm. Nor was Mayor Kennelly to be outdone by the upstart South Side Planning Board. He asked the Chicago Plan Commission to issue its own report, which took a year to complete.[10] It proposed a new lakefront Illinois Central Station to accommodate the three South Side stations. Multiple proposals and the railroads' knee-jerk reactions created an industrial-strength stream of newspaper op-ed columns.

MODERNIZATION

The Illinois Central remained bound by a 1919 ordinance to build a lakefront depot capable of accommodating most city passenger trains. That ordinance resolved a bitter controversy over its occupancy of Chicago's lakefront. IC managers now said they could take all South Side railroads except for the Rock Island's

commuter traffic. In their eyes, a new terminal on the site of Central Station would require only a small, modernized headhouse. The other railroads countered with simple renovation plans for their properties. Dearborn, LaSalle, and Grand Central were shopworn from neglect and desperately needed improvement, but their owners reflexively responded with proposals meant to blunt public criticism. They did not rectify any actual problems.

Dearborn Station did receive a complete overhaul. Gutting its Victorian interior enabled its second floor to become a mezzanine, while neon signs and stainless-steel panels provided up-to-date streamline styling. As the result of a 1922 fire, its exterior was already devoid of its builder's Flemish finery. The result was a design that, with the exception of its clock tower, had the flair one might expect from the railroad's bridge and buildings department—in a word, pedestrian. LaSalle Street Station also received improvements, with escalators now lifting passengers to its elevated waiting room. Ancillary retail areas were air conditioned, and neon and brushed steel overlays swathed the ticketing areas. Mercifully, a plan to sheath elegant Grand Central Station in stark white stone went nowhere.

The modernization of LaSalle Street Station, used by the Pennsylvania's archcompetitor, the New York Central, prompted Union Station to dust off renovation plans. A postwar material shortage thwarted a 1946 study to place escalators in the concourse, but that idea still held promise.[11] In 1949 a plan by the Chicago office of Raymond Loewy incorporated earlier concepts into a larger renovation proposal.[12] It centered escalators in the concourse to bring patrons down from the riverside drive, but this placement would dominate the interior space and require a longer journey for commuters rushing to their trains. Loewy also studied the possibility of air conditioning the entire station. Expensive to heat, it came as no surprise that the station was too expansive to economically cool. The compromise was to isolate the Fred Harvey restaurant and shop areas behind glass walls to provide cool in-depot oases. Loewy believed higher retail sales would, in turn, justify higher rents. The income thus generated could pay for the improvements.

Nonpassenger revenues such as the Harvey rentals became increasingly important as intercity passengers, the most desirable type, declined. Long-distance passenger counts fell, but remained the major contributor to passenger revenues. Two Burlington trains, the Twin Zephyrs, each carried only three hundred passengers per day, but produced more revenue than the line's sixteen thousand daily Chicago commuters. They, in turn, brought in more than the Milwaukee's 13,500 commuters, which still used converted sleeping cars and a few antiquated wooden coaches. The Pennsylvania carried only three hundred souls each day on its two commuter runs to Valparaiso.[13] Clearly uneconomical, the Pennsylvania vainly petitioned the Interstate Commerce Commission to double its commuter fares to make its service break even.

Depot losses needed to be staunched. In 1945, even before the postwar decline, surging operating costs combined with the owners' financial decline caused station company bond ratings to fall to A. This downgrade affected existing bondholders rather than costing the company money, but it signaled little investor appetite for the additional bonds needed to finance remodeling. In February 1956, the concourse finally received minor alterations. Flanked by waitresses modeling early Harvey House uniforms, the son of the chain's founder opened a five-thousand-square-foot shopping court in the center of the waiting room.[14] Encircled by glass walls, it carried convenience items needed by commuters and office workers. The increase in retail space came at the expense of public access and circulation, but enough space remained for the diminished crowds still awaiting trains.

PROSPECTS FOR MUNICIPAL FUNDING

Soon after publication of the *Plan of Chicago*, the Chicago Plan Commission had its central role in railway terminal negotiations challenged by ad hoc civic and governmental organizations. Now, thirty years later, urban planning had greater acceptance, but the process fragmented. On one level, the Plan Commission became increasingly entrenched within city bureaucracy, and hence more powerful. By other criteria, however, its role diminished as zoning laws and redevelopment commissions usurped many of its duties. Actions of the city's Zoning Board of Appeals were entirely separate from the Plan Commission until 1954. In truth, zoning continued under aldermanic control, as the granting of variances became the cash cow that traction ordinances had been to earlier aldermen.[15] Merging functions, however, caused the Plan Commission to lose independence and objectivity.

As before, not everyone was comfortable with the city's increased power. One rebel was Daniel Burnham Jr., who organized the Chicago Regional Planning Association in the 1920s to take a wider stance. With engineer Robert Kingery, the Planning Association had a material influence on suburban highway construction. Financed by outlying communities and businesses, its influence within the city was negligible. Its lack of clout partially

The undulating track profile made locomotives exert themselves to move their heavy consists. As a result, exhaust was a significant problem under air-rights buildings.

resulted from its long-term inability to publish an overarching document, *Planning the Region of Chicago*, not released until 1956. This document was meant to foster residential density along rail and transit corridors, but it was too late. The superhighway era supplanted the railway age.

At the same time, other specialized agencies superseded many Plan Commission duties. Development projects, for example, were the responsibility of such agencies as the Illinois Department of Transportation and the Chicago Housing Authority. An organization of particular importance to the neighborhood west of Union Station was the Chicago Land Clearance Commission, formed under the Blighted Areas Redevelopment Act of 1947 to acquire and develop urban slum land. It used condemnation powers to pay the appraised value for real estate parcels and then demolished their blighted buildings.[16] It acquired many small, adjacent properties, assembling them into larger, marketable tracts. It then wrote the land it sought to sell to developers down to appraised value. The Commission's clearance projects covered much of the Near West Side, but results were poor. Lenders hesitated to loan funds for redevelopment, and it proved burdensome to obtain the federal guarantees intended to promote the process. Cleared land often remained garbage-strewn lots for decades.[17]

Local transit issues underwent a similar aggressive transformation, but with better results. Automobile ownership rates continued to rise, of course, precipitating a corresponding fall in transit ridership. Because capital-intensive services like mass transit need to spread their fixed costs, this was a disaster. Fare increases only resulted in further ridership and revenue losses. In response, the state passed the Metropolitan Transit Authority Act on April 12, 1945, to provide a framework for the public purchase of all local streetcar, elevated, and bus lines. Most had been in bankruptcy for a decade and a half. The act, however, provided no funds for purchase or modernization of these properties. Nor was an operating subsidy planned. Since existing operators could not service their debt and revenues continued to plunge, there appeared little promise for a profitable operation, let alone payments on the bonds needed for acquisition.

How then could the new authority, a shell with no staff, history, or purse strings, take over and operate the substantial, but failed, transit operations? The first hurdle was to determine the value of transit system assets. It fell to the courts to decide a sales price. Since local judges were products of the political machine, it came as little surprise when they forced hapless surface and rapid transit company bondholders to lose three-quarters of their investment. However, these investors fared better than the shareholders, who were completely wiped out. An appraisal placed the asset value at only $87 million. Bonds issued in that amount created a new operating company, the Chicago Transit Authority. CTA interest payments were smaller than its predecessor's due to this massive debt reduction, and because as a municipal entity it had access to tax-exempt financing. A relaxed amortization schedule further reduced annual payments. Operating expenses fell too because the new governmental corporation did not pay a franchise tax to the city, nor did it pay property taxes. Together, these changes provided comfort that the fare box could cover operations and retire all bonded debt.

While transit found a solid financial footing, the harsh treatment meted out to its investors sobered railroad executives. Railroad ridership declined in tandem with that of the transit systems, but the railroads soldiered on. Operating losses grew even as they continued to pay the taxes now avoided by their competitor. Worse, the city embarked on new enterprises detrimental to the commuter railroads. A plan in 1949 called for seven multilevel parking garages on the edges of the business district, four on Monroe Street near Union Station. By 1952, the city owned ten facilities in the Loop and thirty-four more nearby. The Chicago Park District reentered the picture in 1954 when it constructed Grant Park Garage, whose 2,359-car capacity made it the largest underground parking facility in the world.[18] It was easier than ever for commuters to forsake the railways and drive to work.

Massive expenditures to improve downtown auto access had the predictable impact on rail ridership. Other projects had a less obvious if similarly toxic effect. Freeways that provided access for commuters, for example, were most economically built next to existing rail corridors. In fact, all the highways punched through Chicago's urban fabric parallel to rail lines. This required the demolition of hundreds of rail-served industries.[19] The economics of urban railroading necessitated dual use of tracks for freight and passengers, but by default these lines became increasingly dedicated to money-losing passenger service.[20] If any freight traffic remained, however, the Interstate Commerce Commission's formula for calculating passenger train expenses as the sum of the operating expenses directly assignable to passenger services did not reflect this harsh new reality. This formula used to justify rate increases failed to capture the railroad's true costs.

Another urban freeway demonstrates the adverse impact of highway construction. Expressways were the result of a 1949 joint venture of the Chicago Department of Public Works and the Cook County Highway Department. The spine of the local system ran parallel to and west of Union Station's tracks.[21] Built

in a cut, it required the demolition of hundreds of structures. Viewed by some as slum relief, it eviscerated the neighborhoods it bisected. Ironically, its southern portion, the Dan Ryan Expressway, occupied nearly the same location as the controversial Pennsylvania Railroad elevated freight line thwarted by the Chicago Plan Commission. City planners once prophesied that the Pennsylvania's rail line would strangle Near West Side neighborhoods; now the expressways fulfilled their worst nightmares by depressing an already down-and-out neighborhood.

Patches of hope remained as the lure of air-rights development over the station tracks continued to tantalize. In mid-1956, the three-year-old Metropolitan Fair and Exposition Authority proposed a convention center above the tracks. The Authority was the result of lobbying by *Chicago Tribune* owner Robert McCormick, who witnessed the ability of the summer-long Chicago Railroad Fair to attract tourists in 1949. Despite the air-rights proposal by its staff, however, the Authority built along the lakeshore at Twenty-Third Street—naming its facility for McCormick.[22]

The Union Station Company itself put forward a plan to build an airline terminal on a new mezzanine level in its concourse. After downtown ticketing and check-in, the plan was for passengers to ride a limo bus to Midway or a planned new airport. Railroad passengers would have to be content with seventeen-foot ceilings in the lower portion of the concourse, while airline patrons could enjoy a spacious terminal above, featuring fifty-three-foot vaults that remained overhead.[23] The North Western, likewise seeking a profitable use for its terminal, countered with a similar offer. Both proposals died quietly.

January 1957 saw the Department of City Planning replacing the Chicago Plan Commission to bring its functions within the city administration. The forces of decentralization that created independent governing bodies and parochial planning groups now found themselves in head-on collision with an immovable object named Richard J. Daley. The new department symbolized the centralization of a resurgent Democratic machine. Mayor Daley suffered no threat to his authority, especially when the stakes included major public works and the jobs they created.[24] The new department released its *Central Area Plan* the following August. Only an outline, it nevertheless designated Union Station as the epicenter for intercity transportation. It sought to consolidate rail lines, bus terminals, airline reservation offices, and a helicopter link to Chicago's proposed new Northwest Side airport. The mayor predictably quoted Daniel Burnham's dictate regarding small plans. Not a reformer in the Progressive tradition, Daley's grand plans rested on a doubly secure base. First, the period saw remarkable amounts of federal money pouring into the city for highways, housing, and social programs. Second, there had been a radical transformation in municipal finance.

Traditional municipal bonds secured by property taxes offered investors a particularly reliable security. In the postwar period, however, optimistic investors willingly took greater risks to reap higher returns than municipal securities historically provided. That is not to say that municipals were less attractive. To the contrary, the appeal of their tax-exempt interest payments increased with soaring income tax rates. A new class of tax sensitive but return-seeking investors emerged. The most significant of these were commercial banks and insurance companies, whose tax-deductible business expenses included the interest paid to attract deposits. They effectively received a double tax deduction for holding municipal bonds. This in turn spawned a generation of portfolio managers more sophisticated than the "widows and orphans" previously seen as bond purchasers. These analysts could independently assess the repayment risks for nontraditional types of municipal loans. They were particularly attracted by the higher coupons of revenue-based bonds used for municipal project finance. These looked to a future revenue stream similar to a business rather than a pledge on the tax base. Municipalities followed the money. They dramatically increased their issuance of such securities and created specialized new municipal agencies to tap this capital.

In step with the changing financial landscape was a new tool for Illinois governments, created by the Illinois Industrial Building Revenue Bond Act. Passed in 1951, the act allowed municipalities to issue tax-exempt bonds for the purchase, construction, or improvement of real estate for the benefit of private industries, without special state legislation. A boon to economic development, such bonds required municipal approval, but were repayable solely by the lease payments from the industry financed. A traditional mortgage provided additional security.[25] In 1959, a variation on this concept provided the city of Chicago with a loophole in the Illinois Municipal Code's debt cap. The new Public Building Commission ("PBC") issued bonds identical, with one exception, to the industrial revenue bonds that the city issued under the 1951 Act. The difference was that the lessees were not industries but other units of local governments—the city of Chicago, the Chicago Board of Education, and related entities. By leasing from the PBC, local governments moved their repayment obligation from a multiyear debt-service tax levy to an operating-fund line item subject to annual appropriation. This circumvented the caps on multiyear obligations, the municipal code's definition of debt, and it effectively skirted the debt ceiling that had constrained municipal finance since 1872.[26]

With these reforms, for the first time the city could borrow funds sufficient for most capital needs. In doing so, it created two classes of debt holders. Traditional investors took comfort that the debt limit remained under the old cap, in effect maintaining the city's underlying credit rating. More aggressive investors took comfort that the new lease-backed bonds had a viable repayment stream from municipal operations.[27] In theory, at least, the city now had the financial tools to support railroad terminal consolidation. Either Industrial Revenue bonds or PBC-backed leases now worked without the need for special legislation. Although a new rail terminal clearly was not the first item on the city's agenda, it rose to prominence due to a connection with another high-visibility project.

THE CAMPUS PLAN

Immediately after the 1958 release of the *Central Area Plan*, the University of Illinois, which had a small ramshackle Chicago operation in converted Navy Pier warehouses, sought to build a new urban campus to accommodate twenty thousand students. The university's challenge was to find a centrally located, several-hundred-acre site. The university's initial idea was to build on a golf course in suburban North Riverside, but Mayor Daley successfully lobbied for an urban site. He proposed a campus on the underutilized rail yards leading to Dearborn, LaSalle, and Grand Central Stations. This required shifting the trains of thirteen lines using these stations to Union Station. The city then hired consulting firm De Leuw, Cather and Company to work out the details.[28]

De Leuw Cather suggested the establishment of a Railroad Terminal Authority, an approach immediately blessed by Mayor Daley. It envisioned Union Station taking most displaced intercity trains, but with the Illinois Central taking Rock Island commuters. So enthusiastic was the Union Station Company about selling itself that it paid half the cost of the comprehensive study. The railroads knew they still had to pay rent, but the possibility of avoiding $1 million in annual property taxes was appealing.[29] There was talk of a $100 million bond issue, but a university appraisal of the terminal lands valued them at only $3.5 million. Disheartening to the landowners, this nevertheless suggested that some funds would be available to repay Union Station bondholders and still make the necessary improvements.

On April 8, 1959, Richard J. Daley won his first reelection with 71 percent of the vote. His twelve-point platform included eight transportation planks (if the university proposal is included). Never again were transportation issues to get such center-stage attention. By May, the mayor announced that the terminal plan, now estimated to cost $158 million, would move all trains to Union Station. Meanwhile, impatient university trustees voted to move their campus to Garfield Park. However, they neglected to discuss this with the Chicago Park District, a unit of government separate from the city but nonetheless controlled by the Daley machine. The plan died quickly.[30] University trustees sued, and after a year in court, they lost. In all likelihood, their intent had been to exert pressure on the city to resolve a problem requiring political intervention.

The Terminal Authority announced a plan on May 24, 1959 to build a train shed and a separate concourse across Jackson Boulevard immediately southwest of Union Station's headhouse to handle trains from the vacated depots. Although the announcement dealt solely with terminal consolidation, its goal was to free 150 acres for development. Unlike previous efforts, the Authority seemed to have a ready buyer in the university for all released property. Mayor Daley "clung stubbornly to the hope that the land vacated . . . could be made available for a campus." Despite an existing lowball appraisal, its value was now set at $30 million, ten times the price of the suburban Riverside alternative. While University trustees griped, politically it was a done deal, with acceptance by the railroad companies constituting the final word.

The railroads should have relished the proposal. The expanded terminal was to cost $158 million, including $50 million to purchase Union Station, a purchase price equal to its outstanding mortgage due in 1963. The remaining $108 million provided track and building improvements. The station company was to accept new forty-year Terminal Authority bonds in payment. Since lease income repaid the new bonds, the city essentially asked the railroads to accept securities backed by their own payments. Presumably, the station company could resell these bonds to the public, but that entailed its own risks.[31] Sale of vacated rail yards to the university was separate from the Terminal Authority transaction, so actually the total cost was $188 million. The proposal essentially meant that some railroads, those selling land to the university, got cash, while others selling their terminal to the new authority, received bonds of questionable worth.

The Terminal Authority Act contained a provision shared with special assessment laws: two-thirds of the property owners had to ratify the agreement. This looked problematic. There was no way to gerrymander the property so that one class of property owners (those who got cash) controlled two-thirds of the votes. The deal killer was the discovery that annual fixed charges on the new terminal would be $3.8 million greater than the combined total of the terminals replaced. This was somewhat offset by assumed operational efficiencies. Still, this greater expense had to be spread over an ever-declining passenger count. From 353 intercity trains per day in 1946 the number fell to 225 in 1959 and the estimate for 1965, when the new terminal would be complete, was 150 per day. Chicago railroads desperately needed lower, not higher terminal costs.

Within a week, the Illinois Central submitted a cost-effective alternative. It called for a stainless steel–clad depot at Twelfth Street, which 95 trains would reach over tracks leased to the authority by the IC. The remaining trains would shift to Union Station. The following day three other lines, the Rock Island, the New York Central, and the B&O, issued their own joint plan to eliminate only Dearborn Station. It shifted these trains to LaSalle, Grand Central, and Union Station, but still created a seventy-five-acre campus—short of what the university required, but enough to start the project. Seemingly capable of immediate execution, this plan received a quick endorsement from the *Chicago Tribune*.[32]

On June 15, 1959, the Chicago Union Station Company counteroffered that its depot could accommodate twelve of the thirteen railroads with modest track expansion. The Rock Island, due to its heavy commuter traffic, would not fit and was to shift to Central Station. The Baltimore and Ohio and the Soo Line would enter the north side of Union Station with the Milwaukee Road.[33] All other railroads would use the south side, after a two-block lengthening of platforms to handle the traffic. Among other

CHICAGO UNION TERMINAL
Looking Southwest

drawbacks, the plan meant that some passengers would alight six city blocks from the concourse.

With competing plans on the table, the consulting engineers again studied the alternatives. Throughout the summer, the Pennsylvania was said to have been especially active in promoting the public acquisition of Union Station. In December, the Terminal Authority surprised everyone when it suggested that a new terminal for Rock Island commuter trains be built on the east bank site of Grand Central. Union Station was to be expanded by four tracks on the southern approach and several new coach yards would be built further away. The Illinois Central was to be frozen out of the plan, in part because the Terminal Authority statute did not allow for the lease of property as proposed by the IC.

LOWERING COSTS

Union Station's ability to handle more trains was not entirely due to declining passenger loadings. There was a dramatic increase in the capacity of each car entering the terminal on September 6, 1950, when the Burlington inaugurated a fleet of bi-level commuter cars. This innovative double-decked rolling stock was called the "gallery car" because its design featured an opening allowing first level trainmen to collect tickets from the higher level without climbing stairs. Seating capacity was 50 percent higher than conventional equipment, so fewer cars entered the station. The relatively affluent Burlington could afford new cars and the diesel locomotives to pull them. Fewer cars required a smaller initial capital outlay, fewer onboard operating personnel, and shorter trains. The cars saved weight, reducing fuel costs. An important ancillary benefit was to reduce the Burlington's "wheelage" into Union Station. Wheelage was the term used to describe the fee paid to spread station-operating expenses to its users on a per car basis. Thus, the Burlington's efficient cars shifted station expenses to other railroads.

With the advent of postwar sprawl, the station's other significant suburban train operator was the Milwaukee Road. It switched to gallery cars years later and under very different circumstances. In 1954, its commuter service lost over $700,000, and it petitioned the Illinois Commerce Commission for a near–100 percent rate increase, a request that was promptly denied. Because some of its trains ran into Wisconsin, the Milwaukee Road then sought and received a 20 percent rate increase from the Interstate Commerce Commission. Its suburban patrons, however, included affluent attorneys and corporate executives. Irritated by

The transition from steam to diesel locomotives changed the passenger experience within the station and had an even greater impact on nearby yards and servicing facilities.

COURTESY OF THE LIBRARY OF CONGRESS, OFFICE OF WAR INFORMATION, LC-OSW3–015584-E

what they considered a rate-making ruse, the passengers formed the Milwaukee Road Commuters' Association and successfully sued. An order from the US Supreme Court in June 1956 forced the Milwaukee back to a hostile Illinois Commerce Commission. In order to obtain a modest fare increase, the railroad agreed to refund excess fares previously collected and to buy a new fleet of passenger coaches. The first of forty new cars entered service on June 19, 1960.

These new cars cost $7 million the railroad could ill afford. Indeed, the Milwaukee's postwar prospects were meager. Reorganized out of bankruptcy in 1944, it was burdened by an obsolescent rural branch network. Midwestern agricultural bounty once poured onto these lines, but they were a liability in an age of automobiles and trucks. Lackluster financial performance caused the Milwaukee to lag in implementing key cost saving innovations, in particular the replacement of steam locomotives with diesels. In 1951, the Milwaukee Road operated 19,596 steam-powered trains into the station, 54 percent of its total. At that time the Pennsylvania, itself considered a laggard, ran 5,333 steam locomotives into the depot, or 19 percent of its total, while the Burlington ran only 2,336, or 6 percent, of its trains with steam. Ironically, the true poor man among the Union Station railroads, the Alton, ran no steam locomotives. The Gulf Mobile and Ohio purchased the line and dieselized all freight and passenger trains shortly after its 1947 merger and resultant entry into Union Station.

Financially weak and genuinely conservative, the Milwaukee Road occasionally mustered the will for risky decisions. Such was its 1955 agreement to run Union Pacific Railroad passenger trains from its Omaha terminus into Chicago. These heavily patronized trains to Colorado, California, and Oregon had operated since the nineteenth century over the rival Chicago and North Western line. When the Union Pacific pushed its traditional partner to buy expensive new equipment, however, C&NW managers balked. The UP approached the Milwaukee Road, whose management knew the additional passenger traffic could never make money. They believed, however, that, aiding its major western connection would garner it a larger share of profitable interline freight. They knew that the Union Pacific interchanged with five lines at Omaha, with the C&NW getting the lion's share. In hopes of attracting that larger cut of freight, they took the bait. Passenger traffic through the north side of Union Station increased, but for the Milwaukee Road, it was a financial disaster. In the first year

under this scheme, system-wide passenger revenues rose 24.1 percent while related losses were unchanged. Freight revenues rose only 1.9 percent. Later years saw greater passenger service deficits—loses larger than the incremental freight profit covered.

Despite a general postwar traffic decline, Union Station Company employment increased. It peaked at 1,440 in 1951, 30 percent higher than that during its top traffic year of 1945. Much of this increase resulted from higher mail and express traffic. Even so, there was little economic justification for a jump of this magnitude, as the company was hardly flush with cash. In the decade following World War II, the station company repaid nearly $10 million in bonds, or 18 percent of its bonded debt. Amounts payable to the parent companies, however, ballooned to $4.3 million. In theory, the company declared dividends each year, but in fact, owners got notes rather than cash. Despite healthy bond amortization, total debt declined only $5.5 million through 1955.

OVER THE TRACKS

The dream to couple railroad station consolidation with a downtown university plan remained high on the political agenda. In January 1960, the city council approved the deal and awaited railroad consent. Speaking for Dearborn Station owners, Louis Evans, president of the Chicago and Eastern Illinois, added "much would depend upon what the city is willing to give" for the cleared site. Sensing the city's zeal to build a twenty-thousand-student campus, however, the railroads failed to realize that the final offer was already on the table. Proprietors of a declining business, the railroads had a legitimate concern over the required forty-year rental commitment. By contrast, in 1959 the airline industry entered nearly identical agreements for a $117 million terminal at the proposed O'Hare airport. A *Tribune* editorial captured the obvious difference when it stated, "A wagon manufacturer would be crazy to borrow money for a new factory after the invention and perfection of the automobile."[34]

In May, the engineers finally quantified projected costs. For the Milwaukee, Burlington, and Pennsylvania, costs per car would climb from the $7.50 to $15.00 range to a new charge between $18.63 and $19.70. The cost for the other railroads would more than double to $14–$15. The good news, if any, was that leases could be for twenty years, rather than forty. As summer turned to fall, Mayor Daley stalled university trustees, but refused to sweeten the pot. Finally, in September 1960, university trustees could wait no longer and settled on a West Side site partially cleared of blighted buildings by the Daley-controlled Chicago Land Clearance Commission.[35] Although the railroads confidently planned for consolidation, the train had, in the greater sense, left the station.

Replacement of the South Side rail terminals with a university campus was not part of the *Central Area Plan* of 1958. The *Plan* did, however, stress that infill of the business district over Union Station air rights would be good for everyone. The idea was hardly an innovation, yet the *Plan*'s imprimatur reflected that the neighborhood seemed ripe for exploitation. In 1959, plans surfaced for a twelve-story office tower directly west of the station at Canal and Jackson Streets to house the headquarters of the Mercantile National Bank and other tenants. The bank served West Side commercial enterprises, but it ran into financial difficulties while its building was under construction. It filed for bankruptcy protection in 1960. Much like the stunted Union Station Headhouse, 550 West Jackson Street rose only four floors.[36]

Nevertheless, it was an indication that the near West Side was attractive to developers.

A meeting between the Milwaukee Road's Chairman Leo Crowley and developer Erwin Wolfson in 1960 bore fruit the following year. A syndicate headed by Wolfson's Diesel Construction Company announced its intent to build a $200 million series of skyscrapers over the tracks. Wolfson's 50 percent partner was City Centre Properties of London, prompting remarks that the project was the largest-ever investment in the city by British capitalists. Wolfson knew all about air rights from his then-in-progress development, the fifty-nine-story Pan Am Building rising over New York's Grand Central Terminal.[37]

Wolfson intended to develop three blocks, with the first tower on Madison Street. He also had options on the blocks immediately north and south of the concourse. Construction was to start in 1961, but he had difficulty landing the lead tenant necessary to secure financing. The firm of Skidmore, Owings & Merrill drew detailed plans, despite a soft office market. Their concept included the extension of the private drive that separated the Union Station Concourse from the river two blocks further north. Ignoring the railways, Wolfson stated, "We have named the area Gateway Center because the recently opened expressway systems have created a new transportation gateway to downtown."[38]

Erwin Wolfson died on June 26, 1962, at a crucial moment. His station air rights option ran personally to him, not to his construction company, and it expired in less than a month. The station company, earnestly wanting a deal, now found their plans encumbered by Wolfson's estate. In quick succession, James Landauer, the new president of Diesel, secured a controlling interest in the options from the Wolfson family and a modest deadline extension from the station company. Within months, however, another suitor arrived. Norman Tishman, a New York competitor to Wolfson, visited the site in August. Tishman Realty and Construction Company entered negotiations immediately and by the end of the year had closed the deal.[39] It was not a great bargain for the railroads. Tishman offered $109,800 per year in rent plus 8 percent of tenant rents, while Wolfson's agreement was for $221,175 plus the premium. Tishman's plans called for a building three stories taller and thus promised higher rental premiums, but the station company took more risk.[40]

Before Tishman could act, yet another depot consolidation scheme surfaced. Charles Snyder, president of the West Metropolitan Area Council, believed all of the city's 604 daily intercity and commuter trains could be accommodated at Union Station. Snyder dubbed his proposal the "new look" and he believed that his plan would work because it would cost "only" $73 million compared to the previous plan's $158 million. Key to Snyder's plan was Union Station's conversion from a double stub-ended station to one with through tracks. The "new look" was to include suburban stops at Twelfth Street (Roosevelt Road) and Randolph Streets, underground moving sidewalks to connect Union Station with the business district, and joint freight terminals south of the depot. Snyder's plan had the same weakness as previous attempts: the need for unwilling participants to sign long-term leases.

Snyder's proposal failed to slow development over Union Station's tracks. Tishman, who was working on a similar air rights development over the former site of New York's Pennsylvania Station, also named his Chicago project Gateway Center. Illinois Commerce Commission approval to lease the air rights at

$440,000 a year was obtained only weeks before the maturity on the station company's bonds. Low-coupon debt issued during the Depression had rates as low as 2 7/8 percent, but now refinancing raised rates to 4 5/8 percent. Air rights income went to higher debt payments.[41]

Construction of the first building, Gateway Center I, northernmost of the series designed by Skidmore, Owings & Merrill, started in 1963 with occupancy in 1965. It cost $20 million, but rents were a modest $4.50 to $5.00 per square foot. This was low for new construction, so low it equaled the average office lease price in 1928, thirty-seven years earlier. Tenants feared the proximity to skid row and disliked the area's lack of shopping. Cheap rents overcame these concerns with difficulty. Construction of a duplicate, Gateway Center II, began in 1965 with only 70 percent of the first building leased. It cost about 15 percent more and its leases cost $5.25 to $5.75 per foot. Tishman Vice President Perry Hurst Jr. explained simply that "those who come later should pay more." Gateway Center II opened in 1967. Erection of the first two buildings was accomplished with little disruption to the terminal's fabric.[42]

The 1969 opening of Gateway Center III departed from the original plan that called for construction south of the Union Station Concourse, tragically requiring the demolition of that handsome building. Two economic forces conspired to change the original plan. First was an obvious need to reduce depot-operating expense. The station company thus embraced the change. Just as important, the concourse site was half the size of the one a block further south. It became apparent that while the first two buildings rented successfully, demand diminished as development moved away from the established business district.

Demolition of the Concourse unfortunately predates modern interests and legislation relating to historic preservation.

COURTESY OF PAUL KROEGER

In practice, even the smaller footprint was subdivided, with the Gateway Center III office tower to the north and a low-rise trading floor to the south.

Little can be said in defense of Skidmore's Gateway Center III's architecture. Even if one ignores the demolition of Peirce Anderson's magnificent concourse, it is bland even by austere Mid-Century Modern architectural standards. Third of the Gateway Center air-rights projects, it was artistically the worst. Ironically, rents were 70 percent higher than in its older siblings. Contrary to initial thoughts that the site was harder to rent, development finally reached the critical mass needed to attract upscale clients. In addition, one client took the southern portion of the site for its own, special-purpose building.

The International Monetary Market ("IMM") was a five-year-old division of the Chicago Mercantile Exchange, a venerable trader in egg and butter futures. The IMM, however, traded currency futures, then a radical notion. This market quickly experienced phenomenal growth. The IMM built an eighty-thousand-square-foot column-free trading floor for its open-outcry trading pits. That firm, together with many of its members, leased office space in the companion tower. The trading floor building was a muscular black box with X-braced trusses to support its clear-span roof. This precluded building floors overhead. When opened on May 16, 1972, the building became ground zero for an explosion in financial derivatives trading. The new trading room proved too small given the IMM's exponential growth; within three years it needed more space. CEO Leo Melamed approached Mayor Daley for the right to cantilever the building ninety feet west, in part over the Canal Street sidewalk. The plan, which would add 40 percent more trading area, was a Skidmore,

Owings & Merrill suggestion, but only once before had the city allowed a structure over a sidewalk. The mayor asked only, "What will it do for the city?" Melamed responded that it would "move the center of gravity of U.S. finance a couple of feet westward of New York."[43] With "His Honor's" blessing, IMM paid the city for sidewalk air rights. They need not have, for the station company actually owned these rights.

Underneath the Gateway Center III tower and the IMM trading floor a cramped maze of exposed concrete and painted cinderblock walls replaced the majestic concourse. While the glass roof, iron trusses, and brass trim of the old buildings were now shopworn and tired, the best finish even attempted with the new construction was sheetrock. In fact, the station company later described its own facility this way:

> The office building effectively decapitated the train facilities, leaving them in the basement of the new building. Consistent with the basement motif, many walls were rough, unfinished masonry, poorly lighted, and totally inappropriate as an entrance to a great city. The concourse was badly designed for the 100,000 persons who use the facility each day. Commuters using Union Station arrive and depart in several directions. The placement of passageways and escalators in the basement facility created massive logjams as crowds of commuters were forced to fight each other to get to their trains.[44]

Cheap construction reflected the cash flow problems of both the station company and its owners. In fact, it was financed by the $7 million sale of the air rights to Gateway I and II. With that transaction, the station company lost the annual lease revenue from a percentage of office tower rentals.[45] Construction took eighteen months. During that period, trains stopped thirty-four feet short of their bumping posts and a temporary walkway routed passengers through the cabstands into the waiting room. This was especially circuitous for commuters, who now outnumbered intercity passengers ten to one. The Boyas Excavating Company demolished the concourse after selling ornamental pieces to some of the 3,500 people who came to the depot to haggle over mementoes. The largest items sold were two clocks, which brought $2,000 each. One difficulty in construction of the new Gateway Center was the need to keep open the through tracks. Tishman maintained, however, that the job was easier than its recent demolition of New York's Pennsylvania Station. Relocated from the concourse to the headhouse waiting room was the Fred Harvey store known as the Isle of Gifts.

Before the old concourse fell, the station's majority owner, the Pennsylvania, merged with its archrival, the New York Central, on February 1, 1968, to form the huge but struggling Penn Central Corporation and its principal subsidiary, the Penn Central Transportation Company. On October 27, 1968, former New York Central trains switched from LaSalle Street to Union Station. Train 27–61, a remnant of what had been the Twentieth Century Limited, was the first of the former Central trains to use the station. The New York Central's Big Four line trains, which relied on Illinois Central tracks to enter Chicago, continued to use Central Station.

It was a dark period for Union Station and its owners, as one businessman recounted in a December 1968 visit:

> Few of the ticket clerks had anything to do and they idly watched [me] move past them into the cavernous Waiting Room. Under the seven-stories-tall Waiting Room ceiling the man quickened his step to avoid the panhandlers and drunks who populated the Station in bad weather. Only a few authentic passengers awaited their trains on the row of hard benches that stretched from one end of the room to the other: from their quaint costumes and beards many were immediately recognizable as Amish families whose religion demanded that they spurn any form of transportation not invented in 1850.[46]

Disaster was narrowly avoided on August 27, 1971, when a twenty-by-forty-foot section of the headhouse ceiling, together with two chandeliers, broke loose and slammed into the unoccupied grand stairway. The toll inflicted by advanced age and deferred maintenance throughout the railroad system was familiar to railroad managers. Accepting reality, but lacking the cash to rectify the problem, the giant Penn Central had written down to salvage value all of its passenger-related assets west of Albany and Pittsburgh at the end of 1969. The $126 million extraordinary recorded loss helped the railroad little. Theoretically, this accounting move could shelter other income from taxes, but the Penn Central already had a $193 million loss.[47] The entire Penn Central Transportation Company, in fact, was a disaster. Only two and one-half years old, it filed for bankruptcy on June 21, 1970. Even relieved of its debts, it continued a dramatic slide. Decades before, the railroads had ceased being America's largest companies, but the Penn Central set one last, if ignominious, record. Its $431 million operating loss and bankruptcy in 1971 entered the *Guinness Book of Records* as the largest business failure in American history. Creditors pressured the Penn Central to sell its real estate, as well as its interests in various subsidiaries, but the complexity of the bankruptcy proceedings blocked immediate sale. With lawyers combing the railroad's books looking for issues to contest, it was best not to draw attention to its Chicago property.

The new concourse, an afterthought stuffed below a mediocre office tower, reopened on January 11, 1972. Tishman claimed, incorrectly, that Chicago Union Station was now the first fully air-conditioned railroad station in the country. As part of their development agreement, Tishman had to reimburse the Fred Harvey organization for key facilities eliminated by construction. It then bought out all of Harvey's leases for $1.5 million. Released from a rail network in obvious decline, Harvey was happy with the cash. Better heating and cooling in the concourse were popular with passengers.[48] Likewise, the replacement of ramps with escalators was appreciated.

Patrons could be forgiven if they waxed nostalgic for the former grandeur of their surroundings, for in the new concourse even the quality of food service dropped. Instead of Fred Harvey, after June 15, 1971 the new concessionaire was Prophet Food Corporation, a subsidiary of bus operator Greyhound Corporation. Mediocre food served in dingy and cramped quarters was the new order of business. Retail sales were leased to Faber, a local convenience store operator. The real tragedy, however, was that the Chicago Union Station Company struck poor bargains in the sale of its air rights. Rental income was approximately $200,000 per year, well below the $440,000 originally negotiated and less than comparable ground leases.[49] New bonds and higher interest on refinanced debt pushed interest expense to nearly $500,000 per year. It was another opportunity lost.

AMTRAK

American intercity rail passenger travel continued its decline in quantity and quality. The introduction of jet aircraft and completion of the interstate highway system accelerated earlier trends.

Many if not most passenger trains were only viable because of mail contracts, but 1966 Post Office actions decimated that traffic. First, the Post Office initiated truck-hauled express mail service in direct competition with the railroad-owned Railway Express Agency. More devastation resulted from the end of railway post office cars that sorted mail en route. That was the inevitable consequence of the enactment of the zip code, the practice of flying the majority of all letters rather than charging extra for airmail, and implementation of regional sorting centers. This pulled mail contracts from 162 trains nationwide, 144 of which departed from Chicago. By September 1967, there were only seventy Chicago railway post office routes and soon there were none.[50]

The railroads attempted to narrow losses by cutting schedules, but regulatory approvals encountered fierce opposition. Unions tried to preserve jobs, online towns resisted service reductions, and the public bemoaned a passing era. The Milwaukee Road, the last company to expand its passenger service, was particularly inept at playing regulatory games. With its partner, the Union Pacific, it gradually consolidated its west coast trains into one daily operation derisively known as the "City of Everywhere." This combined train was split apart in the western states, but when it left Chicago, it often sported thirty or more cars, a length far exceeding station platforms. In 1970, the railroad attempted to curtail even this lone passenger run. Unfortunately, the Milwaukee's chief counsel forgot to provide the required public notice placards at online stations in Illinois.[51] As a result, for nearly a year, the hapless railroad had to run a daily train from Union Station to Savannah, Illinois, a route with few riders.

In February 1969, the Association of American Railroads requested government subsidies for all passenger trains and a government-owned pool of passenger equipment. By July, it had convinced even the Interstate Commerce Commission, the regulatory body that routinely denied many abandonment requests, to support its position. The following February the Nixon administration announced the creation of the National Railroad Passenger Corporation to operate under the trade name "Amtrak." Amtrak legislation allowed railroads that purchased shares in the new company to drop their own intercity trains. The new company was to operate a reduced but coordinated system over tracks now dedicated to freight. The new legislation explicitly excluded the Interstate Commerce Commission from regulating Amtrak. Commuter lines did not become part of Amtrak.

At midnight, May 1, 1971, nearly all American railroads exited the passenger business. On April 30, the Saint Louis–bound Midnight Special, scheduled for an 11:25 p.m. departure, was the last privately owned intercity train to leave Union Station. The first Amtrak train to depart was the 10:45 a.m. Empire Builder. As if to emphasize the change inherent in the new system, this train, which previously departed over the Burlington's southbound tracks, now left over the Milwaukee Road's north side tracks. Long-distance trains that started their journeys prior to the changeover continued their treks and trickled into Chicago for days. The new corporation's birth reduced the daily number of intercity trains into Chicago from 121 to 44. Famous trains that would no longer call Union Station their home included the Midnight Special, the Manhattan Limited, the Admiral, the Varsity, and the Afternoon Zephyr.[52]

So eager was the Milwaukee Road to exit its hemorrhaging operations that it paid $6 million for the privilege of not doing business with passengers. Technically, this was the purchase price of stock in Amtrak, but few believed this investment would provide any return.[53] By formula, the entry fee was equal to about two years' avoidable costs, so at least the railroads capped their losses. The Milwaukee could ill afford the entry price because its freight service lost more money every year. A general decline in traffic resulted from a weakened Midwest industrial base, a malaise compounded by the railroad's poor management and the diversion of interchange traffic due to the consolidation of its competitors. In particular, Union Station co-owner Chicago, Burlington and Quincy merged with two other western lines to form the Burlington Northern on March 2, 1970. The combination successfully shifted freight traffic away from the Milwaukee.

Amtrak attempted to consolidate all Chicago operations at Union Station. Intercity trains immediately ceased using North Western and Dearborn Stations. Grand Central had already ceased operations in 1969, while the bedraggled Rock Island continued to run two intercity trains from LaSalle Street Station. It simply lacked the money necessary to join Amtrak. A year earlier, in April 1969, the Rock Island concluded negotiations to use Union Station for both commuter and long-distance trains, but that effort also failed for want of cash. Of Chicago's other terminals, only Central Station continued to see three daily Amtrak trains. This lasted until March 6, 1972, when a jury-rigged track connection rerouted remaining trains into Union Station. This required several backup maneuvers, which greatly padded schedules. The dream of terminal consolidation, at least for intercity trains, finally arrived, but in a manner predicted by no one.

Amtrak legislation set compensation for the use of all passenger terminals at avoidable costs plus 5 percent, providing little for repair and nothing for improvements. The economics of operating a huge depot were particularly discouraging, especially when the site could be profitably redeveloped. Its location near a business district where developers could charge premium rents seemingly doomed the headhouse. In August 1972, General Manager William Freund remarked:

> We don't know how long the station's waiting room and office building will be around. It might be gone, replaced by an office building above with modern waiting rooms in place of the 110-foot high ceiling building we have now. It [the existing building] might be gone by 1980 or sooner. Railroads are changing, sometimes for the good, sometimes for the not-so-good. I'm inclined to think the railroads are on the threshold of a new era of public acceptance because of Amtrak and improved commuter service.[54]

LOCAL GOVERNMENT SUPPORT

Instead of demolishing it as many observers expected, Amtrak cleaned and repainted the waiting room in July of 1974. It was the first rehabilitation of any extent since 1946. The six-week job cost $45,000, a sum paid entirely by Amtrak. The motivation for this spruce-up may have been that it had a suitor. A governmental agency, the West Suburban Transit District, was a conduit for financing new commuter equipment with tax-exempt funds. Confounding many, it actively sought $54 million in state and federal funds to buy the station. It then announced plans to build a bus and taxi terminal and to put in additional tracks and platforms. A helicopter landing pad was even part of its design. The biggest

surprise was a plan to bring the twenty-five thousand daily Rock Island riders into the station even though that line served none of the communities in the transit district.[55]

Illinois statute had authorized the formation of transit districts since the 1950s, when the Local Mass Transit District Act passed. Dormant for a decade, transit districts were later found to be convenient conduits for federal transit Urban Mass Transit Administration grants, first available in the late 1960s. The West Suburban Transit District was the area's first. Its genesis came from within Burlington management. Sixty percent of the railroad's commuter coaches were not air-conditioned, and as that amenity became available in autos, the railroad thought it had to respond. The price for improving the Burlington fleet was $25 million. Federal funds were available if a match could be found, but no local government stepped forward. The Burlington provided an innovative solution when it donated its existing cars to the Transit District in 1970. The value of this "donated" equipment provided the match. The railroad then leased back both old cars and new equipment.

The Transit District sought to replicate this template to purchase Union Station. A valuation set its worth at $46 million, exclusive of air rights, the headhouse, or the power plant. This valuation was more than enough to retire all outstanding debts and leave the railroads with assets valued at $27 million. The plan required the Transit District to buy out the Tishman retail leases for $9 million, six times their value only a few years before. The plan was thwarted by the city of Chicago, which marshaled congressional support to block the UMTA grant. Ostensibly, it wanted the funds for three of its own projects. These included extension of the "L" to O'Hare airport (successfully built), construction of a subway under Franklin Street (never built), and a bus way on State Street (built, but with disastrous consequences).[56] Underlying this was a clear message; Chicago leaders would never allow their suburban neighbors to own a major city asset.

Another great change in municipal governance and finance was on the horizon. Illinois's constitution was rewritten for its 1970 centennial. Of particular importance to Chicago, cities over twenty-five thousand in population were granted "home rule powers" that exempted them from state-imposed caps on property taxes and bonded indebtedness. Moreover, the constitution explicitly classified transit as an essential public purpose eligible for government support. There was a dire need for public aid, especially for the Chicago Transit Authority. Ironically, an expansion of services precipitated the CTA's financial decline. Federal capital grants funded new routes, but operating them pushed expenses up 24 percent. Ridership grew only one-tenth that amount. Despite the city's newfound financial flexibility any transit fix required cold, hard cash.

It was unrealistic to believe that politicians would raise property taxes to support transit services, especially when an ever-decreasing number of residents rode buses and trains. Sales and gasoline taxes were unavailable, because the state kept these lucrative resources to itself. The situation clearly required new state legislation, especially since demographic changes shifted political power, together with the majority of the area's tax base, to the suburbs. Chicagoans were fortunate that the suburbs had their own transit woes. Privately owned suburban bus systems were on the brink of collapse and the commuter railroads that connected bedroom communities to downtown jobs needed

resuscitation. Deferred maintenance was so acute that commuter railcars occasionally derailed while standing still. For several years, the state forestalled total collapse by appropriating cash to transit providers from gasoline taxes. This funding, however, provided only the requisite 20 percent local match for federal capital funding under the 1970 Urban Mass Transit Act.

Chicago's problems were far from unique. Their solution followed a national trend; public transit everywhere now required governmental operating subsidies. The Illinois legislature created a new special-purpose agency, the Regional Transportation Authority ("RTA"), to act as the umbrella organization for financing all area transit. The template was thus established, but the RTA next had to find money of its own. On March 19, 1974, a public referendum established taxing powers for the RTA. The issue squeaked through with less than 51 percent voter approval, only because of lopsided support from Chicagoans. The vote not only saved commuter service, it arguably saved the city of Chicago. Cook County's property tax assessment system values commercial property at double the rate of residential property. When heavy industry reigned, these highly taxed properties were dispersed throughout the city. Amid rust-belt woes, however, half of all city tax receipts now came from downtown office towers. Without dependable public transit, this tax base would have been dealt a staggering blow.

RTA tax funds and fare revenues were used to contract with railroad and private bus operators. One commuter service to Union Station was ineligible for RTA support. The Penn Central's two trains from Valparaiso, Indiana, served communities outside the RTA's taxing district. Conrail, the government-controlled successor to the Penn Central Transportation Company, began discussions with an Indiana counterpart of the RTA in September 1975 about subsidies, but talks were fruitless. Penn Central and Conrail continued to run seven hundred riders per day on its trains until October 1978, when the service was taken over by Amtrak.[57]

Following the precedent set by Amtrak, the RTA unilaterally set fares without regulatory approval. During the inflationary 1970s, this was a godsend. In 1974, for example, the RTA raised fares 11 percent. By design, however, the RTA did more than just contract for service—it funneled tax revenues and federal grants to capital improvements. Its first distribution of such funds came within months of its formation, with money provided by a small carve-out of state sales taxes collected in the region. It imposed a 5 percent gasoline tax in 1977, but this proved inadequate and unpopular.[58]

The RTA subsidized commuter lines by contracting for service. Well-to-do lines like the Burlington balked at the terms, but the ailing Milwaukee capitulated on December 15, 1975, accepting $4.6 million per year to maintain eighty-eight daily trains that carried fifteen thousand commuters downtown. Ten percent less than the railroad lost on suburban service that year, this amount was one-quarter of the bedraggled company's total operating loss, which plugged a huge shortfall.[59] The two Milwaukee routes were the area's fastest growing, averaging 5.6 percent yearly ridership increases. This caused the RTA to quickly order forty-one new bi-level coaches and seven locomotives.

Six months later, the railroads made a concerted effort to sell Union Station to the RTA. However, the majority of the RTA board represented the city of Chicago. Instead of purchasing the station, they opted to guarantee a $20 million federal grant for two hundred new CTA buses.[60] That is not to say that they were unwilling to acquire commuter assets. On January 1, 1978, the RTA announced its intent to purchase the bankrupt Rock Island's tracks to the southwest suburbs. Trains on that line often crept along at 10 miles per hour. To conserve cash, the RTA only intended to buy the tracks south of Englewood Station, where a connector would take trains to Union Station. The connection was to cost $5 million, but one year later capacity studies of Union Station discovered that without the space afforded by the old concourse these new passengers simply could not be accommodated.[61] Work on the nearly complete Englewood connection was abandoned.

Ink was barely dry on the thwarted study to move Rock Island trains to Union Station when another proposal surfaced. Architect Harry Weese, a favorite of Mayor Jane Byrne, proposed canceling a long-planned CTA subway under Franklin Street and transferring earmarked funds to a $100 million streetcar line running from the near Southwest Side Pilsen neighborhood and then over Union Station's through tracks. Further north it would turn due east toward Navy Pier. The city did cancel the Franklin Street subway, but safety regulations prohibited streetcars incompatible with mainline railway equipment sharing tracks through the station. Weese's plan was stillborn.[62]

RTA service improved, a fact almost unnoticed except by the remaining commuters. December 17, 1977, witnessed the delivery of RTA's first new locomotives. Two days later, however, the Milwaukee Road again filed for bankruptcy. By February 25, 1980, the proud Milwaukee Road was a third its former size and no longer extended to the west coast. But the high interest rates of the period, a decline in the agricultural economy, and the

collapse of Rust Belt industries accelerated the line's financial descent. Nowhere did this tragedy play out with greater force than in the railroad's headquarters in the Union Station Headhouse.

Despite great strides funded by federal grants, the RTA had its own serious financial problems. By July 1981, it owed the railroads and other vendors $106 million despite raising commuter fares. Most commuters saw a 57 percent fare hike, but Milwaukee Road riders were hit with a 75 percent jump resulting in a 22 percent ridership fall. The Burlington, meanwhile, ran afoul of the courts when the RTA ordered it to collect a surcharge on monthly tickets sold before the rate increase. It was unable to increase fares for one month, but thereafter its ridership remained largely unchanged.

The Milwaukee Road tottered while the bankruptcy court worked out the disposition of its assets. Its viable freight-hauling remnants were sought by a smaller rival, the Soo. Although the Milwaukee previously exited the intercity passenger business, Amtrak trains continued to run on its tracks from Union Station, as did commuter trains. The Soo Line forcefully stated that its purchase contract did not include the Chicago station or the commuter passenger business, even if subsidized by the RTA. On October 1, 1982, an RTA subsidiary, the Northeast Illinois

Regional Commuter Rail Corporation, took control of the Milwaukee commuter service and its 360 employees without buying any track. This corporate framework copied that used to acquire the Rock Island commuter lines, although that case included railroad property. Milwaukee riders rejoiced in an immediate 15 percent fare reduction, but a more important and simultaneous change was less obvious; the RTA overhauled its entire organization. The state legislature bailed out the RTA with a $100 million handout, but demanded changes. The RTA became an oversight and funding agency, while rail and suburban bus operations became distinct operating units with their own appointed boards. Metra was the name chosen for the newly separate rail operation. At the same time, suburbanites replaced Chicagoans in control of the RTA board.[63]

The RTA and Soo Line were not alone in coveting Milwaukee Road assets. In January 1984, Amtrak sought to buy the half of Union Station it did not own, having earlier acquired the Penn Central shares. Its motivation may have been the difficulty it experienced negotiating track sharing agreements with Metra. By May 1, it acquired both the Milwaukee Road and Burlington real estate interests for $15 million. Negotiations were difficult. The Milwaukee's attorney noted that Amtrak's initial response to the railroad's overtures was "laughably self-serving." But the economics of a willing buyer meeting a willing seller were strong. Union Station was now one of only two major terminals owned by the passenger corporation, the other being New York's Penn Station. Additional air rights sales allowed the retirement of the station company's 1963 bonds.[64] Amtrak then induced the RTA to enter an operating agreement spelling out cost sharing.[65]

Milwaukee Road corporate offices remained in Union Station until February 19, 1985, when the Soo Line acquired the company. As quickly as possible the new owners eliminated or transferred any remaining staff. As with the now-abandoned Penn Central offices in the building, the space proved too antiquated to re-let. Rotten wooden window sashes rattled in their frames, tattered wiring led to archaic brass fuse boxes, and window air conditioners ceased to function.

HOPE IN THE SHADOWS

As the station decayed into decrepitude, the Pennsylvania coach yard and engine facility proved especially troubling. Heavy snows followed by a severe freeze in January 1977 froze water and fuel lines, cracked a water main, and buried tracks under six inches of ice. Since maintenance on cars occurred outdoors, frozen coaches and locomotives were unrepairable. Amtrak acquired control of the yard, which employed 380 persons, only the year before with the intention to save money by consolidating work once done in three separate yards. This allowed abandonment of the leased Santa Fe and Milwaukee Road coach yards, but the winter's problems caused Amtrak to annul eight routes for weeks while extreme delays rippled system-wide. Within a month, the Amtrak board authorized $6.8 million as the first phase in yard

modernization. An additional $34 million in the fall built a car repair building, a locomotive shop, and an electrical distribution system. The latter provided power to heat and light the passenger cars, which were finally being refurbished. Rebuilt cars eliminated the steam lines that once supplied each car in a train from the boiler of its coal-burning locomotive. Diesel locomotives generate electricity for movement, but they continued to have steam generation units as the source of heating for their train. Amtrak reengineered cars and locomotives for hotel electric power, requiring yard standby power to undergo a similar transformation. The change came twenty years after steam locomotives ceased using the station.

Even as offices above the station closed, a near-tragic event had a rare happy outcome. A 1980 fire in the former Fred Harvey restaurant on the west side of the headhouse caused severe smoke and water damage. Gutted, the ground floor restaurant area never reopened, but this near disaster prompted the repainting and renovation of the waiting room. The Isle of Gifts vanished and mammoth benches returned to the waiting room.[66] The most important renovation was reglazing of the skylight, which lost its wartime blackout paint thirty-five years after the end of hostilities.

In 1981, the city had proposed local landmark status for the headhouse, but the owners requested deferral pending sale or development. Later, when Amtrak purchased the station in 1984 landmark status became moot, because Amtrak has the legal latitude to ignore landmark regulations, even prohibitions on demolition. Amtrak knew, however, that any request for redeveloping the structure could trigger a Commission on Chicago Historical and Architectural Landmarks declaration that the building was a local landmark. While such status contains sanctions that prohibit demolition, Amtrak nevertheless voluntarily complies with local rules.

Amtrak wasted little time once it controlled the property. Within a year, it selected U.S. Equities Realty from a field of ten applicants to plan redevelopment. That developer made its mark on the city with the 1985 development of the LaSalle Street Station site, but its Union Station philosophy was nearly the opposite of its approach to of the destruction of that historic building. Neither Amtrak nor U.S. Equities founder Robert Wislow affirmed or rejected landmark status. Rather, they negotiated with the Landmarks Commission to designate only certain building features. Limited agreements had been struck regarding facades, but the primary feature preserved under this proposal was the waiting room interior. Allowing alteration or elimination of other building features would have been unique, at least in Chicago. As a public-private agreement, no public hearing was required for landmark designation, but this proved controversial. Critics noted that the Landmark Commission lacked authority to grant conditional changes in the architectural fabric of a building. That point was never tested, however, as the pact was never ratified by the city council.

Wislow's work with architect Lucien Lagrange included One Financial Place, home of the Midwest Stock Exchange on the former site of LaSalle Street Station. Where that station's train shed once bridged Congress Parkway, Lagrange created an elegant arched gateway into downtown Chicago that pushed the train tracks one block south. For Union Station, Wislow and Lagrange stated that they would construct a "Daniel Burnham building that didn't get built," meaning the headhouse office tower conceived well after Burnham's death.[67] Lagrange sought to tear away the stunted office portion of the building, but he would retain the waiting room and the exterior's limestone base with its Corinthian columns. Overhead, twin twenty-five-story office towers would replace the existing structure. Unlike most modern buildings, design of these towers used a classical vocabulary that divided them into base, shaft, and capital.

According to U.S. Equities, the waiting room and the Beaux-Arts facade required few changes. But in the words of former Landmarks Preservation Council of Illinois Executive Director Deborah Rosenthal, "they will be saving the elements of the building which don't get in the developer's way." For example, new elevator shafts in the north and south ends of the waiting room required that its columns move inward seven and a half feet. The coffered ceiling, the key to the room's dramatic effect, would have lost about thirty feet on each end. Grand stairways to Canal Street also required relocation, with one dramatic staircase substituting for twins. Union Station's existing foundation and superstructure could support additional floors, but the proposed development did not use them. New towers, it was deemed, required new footings.[68]

While the U.S. Equities plan seemed to endanger the waiting room's majestic architecture, powerful outside forces resolved the issue. The early 1990s real estate market was, in the words of First National Bank of Chicago chairman Barry Sullivan, "in its worst shape since the Great Depression." Office tower prospects dimmed when the prospective tenant, the Maxwell Group, floundered after the shipboard disappearance of its founder and the subsequent dissolution of his media empire. Tower plans were dormant, but architect Walker Jones summed up the threat remaining to Union Station's architectural grandeur: "When they

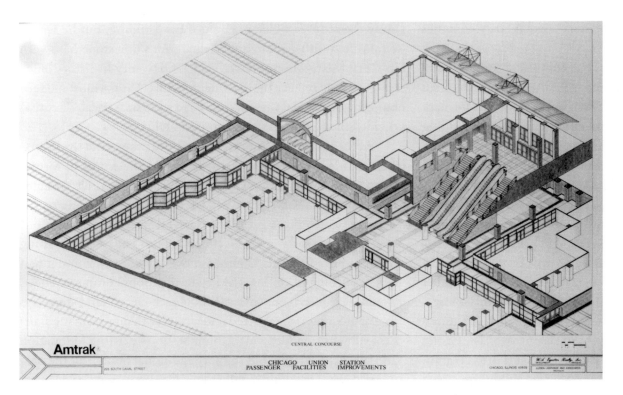

CENTRAL CONCOURSE

Amtrak

CHICAGO UNION STATION
PASSENGER FACILITIES IMPROVEMENTS

tore down the Illinois Central station we all thought, 'Well at least North Western is still standing.' When North Western went, we said, 'Thank God Union Station is still with us.' Now some people look at the plan to alter the place and argue that half a loaf is better than none. Myself, I think we're already down to half a loaf."

Yet critics could take comfort from concourse renovations within the Gateway Center III building, since renamed 222 South Riverside. U.S. Equities was unable to proceed with its office tower plans, but Amtrak took a liking to architect Lucien Lagrange. It commissioned him to revamp the hideous 1970s-era concourse. The redesign is far from perfect, due to Amtrak's limited budget and the constraints imposed by the overhead building's column placement. It nevertheless provided an ambitious and logical redistribution of pedestrian traffic. Elegant execution improved both operating efficiency and overall appearances. Lagrange used two subterranean levels available for depot purposes to advantage. He doubled the size of a mezzanine corridor that barely existed in the old layout. Formerly a staging point between sets of escalators, Lagrange's solution served dual functions. First, it took Metra'a ninety-eight thousand commuters, who walk to and from offices east of the station, efficiently to trackside on the west side of the concourse. Their mezzanine-level walk now carried them over the longer east side tracks used by Amtrak, and escalators lowered them to nearby Metra gates. This allowed the placement of an Amtrak waiting room underneath, near the east side gates used by its 5,600 daily passengers.[69] The mezzanine now provided the retail space that once occupied the concourse floor. A booming food court makes good use of space during the lunch hour when commuter traffic is slack; its rental income secured financing for the project.[70]

On the concourse level, the Amtrak waiting area was split into three sections. Sedate cherrywood panels frame the central Metropolitan Lounge, reserved for sleeping car patrons. Fewer than 1 percent of the station's daily patrons were eligible to use it. Lagrange located airport-style waiting rooms for Amtrak coach passengers adjacent to the north and south gates, separated from the traffic flow by plate-glass walls.[71] A few steps away, Amtrak and Metra ticket counters reflected a luxurious Art Deco style. The predominant material in this new construction was dolomitic Kasota stone with a honey-colored matte finish. Green and black Italian marble and black granite from Zimbabwe combined with bronze and aluminum detailing for a sleek yet comfortable appearance. The overhead office tower precluded monumental treatment similar to the original concourse, but amenities such as a full-length skylight over the escalators descending from Adams Street (the most heavily used entrance) mitigated its previous corseted feel. In the words of Amtrak chairman W. Graham

Claytor, "The existing structure was a rabbit warren of serpentine passages. Renovation of this structure was important because our passenger stations are the first and last contact with our customers."[72] Chicago Union Station President Charles Hayward described the design philosophy as creating a place that ensured a "frictionless voyage." He noted that Metra provided $7 million of the $32 million renovation expense, the remainder being borrowed by the station company. In Hayward's words, "If Union were a person, it would be eligible for Social Security in a few years. But with this renovation, it will be working hard for many years to come."[73]

The prevailing wisdom for reuse of the underutilized headhouse was to create a two-level atrium supporting a 130,000-square-foot shopping and restaurant area, about the space of a moderate suburban shopping mall.[74] This concept was clearly influenced by the successful retail development of Washington Union Station. Cheryl Stein, U.S. Equities vice president, gave her prospects for success: "Chicago Union Station has a leg up on Washington. Within a three-block radius, we have 10 million square feet of office tenants and new residents are continually moving into the West and South Loop area. Consequently Union Station here is sure to draw crowds on weekends."

Grand planning aside, modifications included a new Madison Street entry whose multiple stairways descended directly to the platforms for the northernmost (Milwaukee District of Metra) tracks, opened several months prior to the dedication of other concourse improvements. Harry Weese and Associates designed its entry kiosk, located diagonally across from Metra's North Western Station, now known as the Ogilvie Transportation Center. Metra funded its $2.2 million cost, inasmuch as it cuts several blocks from many patrons' workday trek. Renovation also extended to the old waiting room, renamed the Great Hall—perhaps unsurprisingly because passengers now waited for their trains trackside. This restored area proceeded despite the planned modifications for the office tower then under discussion. The station's chief engineer, Mark Walbrun, was ecstatic about the repairs. He remarked, "When they built the 300-foot long barrel vaulted skylight into the ceiling of the waiting room, they didn't allow for thermal expansion. Every winter the skylight flexed, and every spring it sagged because of changes in the temperature. We used to have as many as 40 buckets catching drips every spring. So we had to redo the whole thing."[75]

Retail development stalled, as did plans for the office tower.[76] Merchants balked because the indoor shopping mall concept, also known as inward-facing retailing, was past its prime. Completion of the last such Chicago-area mall had been four years earlier. Nor were the project's finances all they seemed. Ray Corcoran, Amtrak's project manager, was convicted of pocketing $300,000 in kickbacks and funneling $27,000 to a decorating company he partially owned.[77]

Tracks and platforms at Union Station were also in line for improvement. Restoration of the glass canopies over the six westernmost platforms on the south side admitted welcoming sunlight for the first time in forty years. Ten miles of surplus 132-pound rail to replace worn track in the station came from the Illinois Central main line then being reduced from two tracks to one. The project rebuilt slip switches in the terminal along with the interlocking machines that controlled them. While this phase of the renovation project was less noticeable, its $54 million cost was higher than the concourse renovation.

Union Station was not the only structure showing its age. The Main Post Office could not accept modern electronic sorting equipment and several trucking ramps could not accommodate modern semitrailers. The Post Office Department ignored a locally suggested site and sought to build a new facility where Grand Central Station once stood. City officials secretly feared that if they pressured postal authorities too hard the facility would relocate to the suburbs. To their relief, a March 1990 proclamation announced that the new one-million-square-foot facility would rise immediately south of the existing post office. Portions of the new facility opened in 1994, and almost immediately, high-speed-rail advocates suggested that the vacated building would make a fine new Amtrak station, an idea borrowed from Senator Daniel Patrick Moynihan's idea to replace New York's Penn Station with a terminal rebuilt from the nearby James A. Farley Post Office Building. Parts of what Chicagoans now call the Old Main Post Office were in use until 1998.

Amtrak continued to invest in Chicago Union Station despite its own rocky finances. It purchased a parking garage south of the headhouse and in 1995 connected it via an underground pedway. Providing parking for commuters, the garage's main role, may seem at cross-purposes with the station's use, but it allows Amtrak patrons longer-term parking and provides rental car facilities for incoming rail travelers.

Metra was hardly still during this period. In August 1996 it launched Chicago's first new rail commuter line in a hundred years. Dubbed the "North Central Service," it departs from the ex-Milwaukee tracks on the north side of the station, travels along its West Line, and then diverges onto ex–Soo Line freight tracks to the fast-growing suburbs of Vernon Hills, Buffalo Grove, and

Libertyville. Starting with three round trips, a dozen years later it grew to eleven trains each way. It reflects the infill of the existing suburban grid, away from established rail corridors.[78] As Deborah Stone of the Metropolitan Planning Council summarized, "The region is very different from what it was 20 years ago when the Regional Transportation Authority was created. The population has only grown 4 percent, but we're spread out over about 50 percent more land and jobs are more far-flung, and they're harder to get to on public transit."[79]

WEST SIDE RENAISSANCE

One area that bucked the trend surrounded Union Station. Commercial development came in the late 1970s when several banks built large remittance-processing centers along South Canal Street, on sites once home to freight and express houses. Meanwhile, northwest of the headhouse office towers sprouted. The pioneer development on West Madison was for the Social Security Administration, joined in 1984 by Citicorp Center, a tower on the former site of the North Western's Madison Street Station that incorporated Metra's Ogilvie Transportation Center. Another development of Union Station air rights helped solidify the area's office development even though it was completed just as the real estate market bottomed in 1990. Perkins and Will designed a thirty-six-floor tower for developer Rubiloff Inc. that required massive seventy-ton, seven-and-a-half-foot-high girders spanning the tracks. Placement of these behemoths was accomplished in twenty-minute windows between train operations. It was an adjacent fourteen-story wing; however, that best illustrated the complexity of building over a busy rail yard. Tenant Illinois Bell wanted large floor plates that necessitated placement

of five cantilever trusses on top of the building to carry weight and transfer it to the load-bearing side beams.[80] In a throwback to an earlier age, the confined site required that the caisson boring machines be rail mounted and their spoil was removed in railroad dump cars.

Further west, the former Skid Row became a self-contained business district with more office space than most medium-size cities. The quality of that space is as notable as its quantity. Early developments catered to back-office functions of major downtown corporations seeking cheaper quarters. Now, however, the area includes prestigious law firms, advertising agencies, financial houses, and supporting services. Firms paying premium rents ensures the area's prosperity.

Area residential development is truly impressive, pointing the way to a new urban role for Union Station. Presidential Towers, a self-contained development of four forty-nine-story apartment blocks, was the catalyst for changing opinions about area residential prospects. Built by politically connected developers using tax credits for mixed-income housing, it was ahead of its time. It struggled financially and never fulfilled the requirements of its federal subsidy. But it changed perceptions and the conversion of older multistory warehouses and offices into condominiums and rental apartments soon followed. The trend reached almost manic proportions, with thousands of units being sold or let at once unimaginable prices. The location could not be more convenient for walking to work or for enjoying the cultural and recreational pleasures of big-city life. Turning tradition on its head, residents began a small but noticeable trend in reverse commutation from urban homes to suburban jobs.

Given this development, it seems strange that in 1998, forty-one acres of the near West Side, including most of Union Station, were officially declared "blighted." That designation was required by statute to justify the creation of the Canal/Congress Tax Increment Financing District. TIF districts are powerful development tools that channel the increase in property taxes generated by new construction toward infrastructure and other projects needed to stimulate that growth. The explosive development of the West Side's condos and offices promised massive tax increments. To qualify the district as blighted the city gerrymandered TIF district boundaries around properties already developed. Creative mapmaking aside, in the five years prior to its establishment the district saw 56 percent of its building stock cited for building code violations, five structures demolished, none built, and a 26 percent decrease in assessed valuation. Including the Old Main Post Office and the Union Station Headhouse, the area had nearly 3 million square feet of unoccupied office space.

In the typical TIF district, paving, lighting, and sewer improvements share the spotlight with the assembly of land for large-scale development. The Canal/Congress District, however, set unique goals including promotion of "transit-friendly" developments, creation of small "arrival" places and mini-plazas, extension of the underground pedway system to connect transit centers, promotion of growth in intercity and commuter rail operations, and protection of the track and platform capacity for expanded rail operations, including high-speed rail.[81] The Union Station Headhouse and the Old Main Post Office are prominently mentioned in all TIF documents and their redevelopment was a stated priority. However, private developers were nimble; initial TIF funds subsidized new office construction. The district's

first project was west of Clinton Street where the old Mercantile National Bank of 1960 rose to only four of its planned twelve floors. Now, with lighter modern materials, architects pushed the building at 550 West Jackson to eighteen floors with a $7.5 million subsidy. Rather than detracting from the district's ability to finance station projects, this development ensured a steady tax flow into district coffers. Deals in 2004 included the headquarters buildings for USG Corporation and Quaker Oats Company, cementing the area's corporate credentials. With them, the district assured itself a tax increment income of over $20 million per year through 2022.

Real estate activity near the station put dollar signs in the eyes of Amtrak's board of directors. To cash in they sought to know more about their holdings. The day before Thanksgiving in 2000 Metra and Amtrak jointly solicited bids for a $1 million study of Union Station's capacity. Current usage was known; the terminal daily handled 306 scheduled passenger trains plus 20 freights through adjoining yards. And each day 110,000 passengers filed through the concourse, a number rising about 2 percent per year. The study looked at pedestrian flow, train scheduling, track, and signals to provide a blueprint for future capital investment to find potential capacity and identify ways in which it could be raised.

In 2000, the Chicago Landmark Commission again initiated hearings regarding landmark status for the station. Unlike the earlier unsuccessful landmark attempt, this time the protected elements included the exterior colonnade of the headhouse and the interior of its main waiting room. Chicago's Commissioner of Planning and Development, Chris Hill, expressed his personal interest in the property by relating that his parents first met there.

The abandoned US Post Office also seemed primed for redevelopment, since it has nearly as many square feet of space as the Willis (originally Sears) Tower or McCormick Place, but it was completely empty. In 2008, the postal service agreed to sell its buildings to Walton Street Capital. Initially, Walton was to pay $30 million for the facility, but after an engineering review, the price became only $10.00, with the postal service to provide $9 million for asbestos remediation. With annual security and heating costs of nearly $2 million, this arrangement better reflected the reality of valuing a distressed property. The city of Chicago agreed to a redevelopment project with 300 rental apartments, a 236-room hotel, 300 condos, parking for 825 cars, 480,000 square feet of office space, and substantial retail development. The office space was to be a so-called telecom hotel designed for major users of computer and communications gear. The city promised $51 million in TIF financing for the $310 million project.[82] The deal stalled, however, because the postal service had to comply with federal landmark requirements even though the buildings are not a designated landmark. This requirement was formally suspended in 2002 to allow demolition of the building's center portion over the Congress Expressway, splitting the remainder into two buildings. By the time the legal framework was in place, the telco-hotel market crashed. Walton continued to pitch the project, but there were no takers.[83] Without prospective tenants, financing was unavailable.

2003 saw another opportunity missed. The International Monetary Market vacated the trading floor over the southern portion of the concourse in 1981 as continued growth of its financial derivatives markets outstripped office capacity and prompted it to build larger quarters east of the river. The old building lay dormant, but availability of TIF funds allowed the city to induce investors to reconsider its unique high ceilinged, free-span trading room. The city contributed $2.2 million toward a $13.8 million project to convert it into a health club.[84] The project boosted the building's taxable value and increased area pedestrian traffic. The lingering question, however, is what it could have been. The concourse below remains congested and moving ticketing functions and waiting rooms upstairs would have been logical. The building's high ceilings and open, sunfilled spaces seem tailor made for a passenger terminal, but it was not to be.

Amtrak certainly could use more space at Union Station. The national carrier expanded existing routes, with particular emphasis on no-frills service to Milwaukee. Funding these trains was spearheaded by the state of Wisconsin, whose savvy former governor, Tommy Thompson, was such an enthusiast that he became chairman of Amtrak and the unlikely apostle for Union Station's resurrection. On March 20, 2000, he convened Amtrak's board in the station, a radical departure from their usual Washington meeting. As part of their discussion, they toured the building and the surrounding neighborhood. Thompson knew there was great interest in redevelopment of the headhouse. An August 1997 request for proposal elicited bids by Jones Lang LaSalle Incorporated and Prime Group Realty Trust. Thompson rekindled the process, but after extensive negotiations for an $80 million project, planning died.

Prime Group tried again in early 2002, pushing a $200 million tower designed by Lucien Lagrange. To house 150 luxury condos and a 300-bed Hilton hotel, Lagrange now believed his eighteen-story addition, a single tower unlike his earlier twin tower proposal, did not need new caissons.[85] Landmark Commission and City Council approval delayed the project, by which time prospective tenants disappeared.

The year 2005 saw two proposals, one with Jones Lang LaSalle backing the Lagrange-designed tower and Lincoln Properties pitching a Lohan Caprile Goettsch twin-tower plan. *Chicago Sun-Times* real estate columnist David Roeder noted that "Reality is a hard concept for Amtrak, whose bureaucracy is as slow as its trains." At the end of the year Roeder listed it as one of five development deals that never got off the ground, noting that "the railroad is so dense it probably has no idea why."[86] Management could be forgiven for being distracted. That year the George W. Bush administration again attempted to delete all Amtrak funding from the federal budget. In February, Transportation Secretary Norman Mineta came to Chicago to announce that Metra, not Amtrak should own Union Station. Metra announced that it would be happy to buy the facility if Mineta provided the funds—not what the Secretary had in mind.[87]

In early 2007, Amtrak committed to Jones Lang LaSalle, whose managing director, Hossein Youssefi, was responsible for one of America's best adaptive reuse projects, Washington Union Station. Negotiations with the Commission on Chicago Landmarks finally set city landmark protection for the Great Hall and various exterior features in place. In return, the commission agreed to the addition of a twenty-six-floor tower around the atrium that would continue to daylight the Great Hall. By late spring, the Chicago City Council boosted the project with a pledged $58 million TIF fund subsidy. This too came to naught as America descended into its most serious recession in seven decades.

Chicago Union Station remains the fourth busiest Amtrak station, and counting its commuter trains it is the third most active depot in North America. The station once faced a cloudy future as a passenger terminus, but had sunny prospects as an office development. Now the course is reversed. Given the complexity of multiple users and an owner isolated from typical development pressures, the site has proven so time-consuming to develop that deals cannot be consummated within one economic expansion. Rail passenger service, however, now seems a growth business.

The station's mainstay, commuter traffic, blossomed because Metra improved service quantity and quality. Particular growth came on the route to the southwest suburb of Orland Park and beyond. This service originated on the Wabash Railroad into Dearborn Station, whose abandonment allowed residential development south of the business district. The RTA shifted Dearborn's last remaining train, unofficially known as the Cannonball, to Union Station. Over two decades, service increased from one train to fifteen, but passengers experience considerable delay from the freight trains sharing the tracks. Service expansion to levels approaching the region's other major commuter corridors will require shifting these trains to underutilized LaSalle Street Station.[88] The same may be true for service to Chicago's southeast suburbs if, as planned, trains again run on rails that last saw passengers five decades ago. Union Station no longer has excess capacity on its southern approach. Other clouds lurk on the horizon. In 2009, the state of Illinois borrowed $120 million to paper over a massive RTA revenue shortfall. Imprudent fiscal management, perhaps, but it met immediate needs and demonstrated some level of legislative support.

Even Amtrak traffic is climbing. Amtrak Hiawatha Service to Milwaukee, together with three Metra lines, keeps northbound tracks busy. Meanwhile, three other Metra lines and most Amtrak departures use the station's south side. With state subsidies, additional Amtrak trains now run to Carbondale, Quincy, and Saint Louis. Doubling the number of these departures caused a more than corresponding jump in ridership. Unlike Metra, which depends on a dedicated tax stream, state-funded Amtrak service must rely on an annual appropriation—a yearly political scramble for money. Even in the face of staggering state fiscal problems, however, funding for intercity trains remained steadfast through 2015.

The real future of Chicago Union Station may lie in the redirection of federal policies. Amtrak funding traditionally provokes open warfare in Congress to preserve the status quo. Operating subsidies are perennially precarious and capital spending nearly nonexistent. Nevertheless, studies for a truly high-speed Midwest rail passenger service suggest a renaissance may be imminent. A Midwest Governor's Association proposal for a moderately high-speed system linking Minneapolis, Milwaukee, Detroit, and Saint Louis to Chicago found a willing audience. For the first time since the days of Richard Nixon, a presidential administration, that of Barack Obama, was openly pro–passenger rail. Presiding over a shattered economy, Obama's core policies featured the word "stimulus" and the phrase "shovel-ready."

Because Midwest governors had detailed engineering and environmental plans, routes centering on Chicago Union Station

received $2.2 billion of the $7.9 billion available for high-speed rail under 2009's American Recovery and Reinvestment Act. Further funding for the Chicago-to-Saint Louis route came after several states opted out of federal rail programs. Wisconsin meanwhile pledged $47 million in state funds to purchase two fourteen-car trains capable of 220-mile-per-hour speeds for runs to Milwaukee. A change in governors, however, scuttled this project and related improvements. Track work for 110-mile-per-hour operation still progressed for routes to Detroit and Saint Louis and the state of Illinois briefly planned Amtrak service to the Quad Cities and Rockford. Higher speeds, comfortable rolling stock, and increased frequency would greatly increase Amtrak traffic at the station.

Will Union Station be ready if an American rail renaissance is forthcoming? Like their federal counterparts, local planners see a bright future for passenger rail—with Union Station the region's undisputed centerpiece. In April 2009, Mayor Richard M. Daley announced a $15.5 billion revitalization proposal called the Chicago Central Area Action Plan. It incorporated $1.5 billion for high-speed rail service to both major Chicago airports, supplementing or supplanting CTA elevated train service. At its center was a $2 billion investment in a "West Loop Transportation Center." Planned to run under Clinton Street, it is a massive multilevel tunnel. A pedestrian level would link Union and Ogilvie (formerly North Western) stations. Below them a new CTA transit line would serve the growing office district and allow crosstown commuters to skirt downtown. Further below would be a true high-speed rail terminal, albeit with limited through tracks. Other plans included an underground busway eastward to downtown and the lakefront.[89] A terminal for suburban transit and urban feeder buses immediately south of Union Station's headhouse would be the first project constructed. Together these proposals formed the most ambitious transportation planning since the creation of Chicago's expressways. As often happened, an official proposal prompted community leaders to float other plans. One such was a separate, dedicated high-speed rail terminal using Union Station's tracks but south of the existing concourse.[90] Concurrently, proposals to use the long-vacant Old Main Post Office or a separate riverside site to its east surfaced. Unfortunately, they suffered from particularly bad timing.

The economic malaise some dubbed the Great Recession killed plans for new high-rise towers built over the historic headhouse building, but Amtrak and developer Jones Lange LaSalle continue projects to fulfill the potential of Union Station's vastly underutilized infrastructure. The first and biggest announced project has gone relatively unnoticed. In June 2010, Amtrak initiated a $115 million upgrade of Union Station's yard and train control infrastructure with proceeds of a American Recovery and Reinvestment Act grant, funds incremental to the high-speed-rail awards that underscore the importance of a Chicago hub for next-generation passenger trains.[91] Amtrak found $40 million more in its own budget for building improvements to provide for coach passengers, whose numbers increased 40 percent in a dozen years to over 3 million annually. Concourse boarding areas were to double seating to 950 and new restrooms were to be added. This required moving the Metropolitan Lounge for sleeping car patrons to an area between the concourse and the great hall. Budgeted funds also provided property manager Jones

Lang LaSalle with resources to renovate the existing office block with Amtrak as major tenant. Amtrak previously occupied leased space in another building. Architect Lucien Lagrange was also to modify public spaces to attract street-oriented retail tenants.[92] The problem came with the office space, which required asbestos abatement, heating and air conditioning work, and building code–related upgrades that absorbed the entire budget. The other improvements await implementation.[93]

It was providential that the ambitious 2009 plan for a three-tiered subterranean line failed, for its demise set the stage for a far cheaper plan promising even greater capacity. That scheme was the work of TranSystems engineers working for the Chicago Department of Transportation. Until 2012 Amtrak barely used the original mail and express platforms under buildings to the south. This vacated space, still owned by Amtrak, could be repurposed into a new Amtrak station. The existing concourse would then see only Metra commuters. To allow better access to Metra trains, platforms could be widened by eliminating the long unused between-track baggage runs. Repositioning the tracks would entail demolition of the last of Union Station's original train sheds, but would allow stairway or escalator access to Van Buren Street.

Two below-grade connections could be made. First, examination shows the possibility of constructing a third through track for use of Amtrak Milwaukee-bound trains. This requires cantilevering one track over the river. Studies also indicated that an existing steam and maintenance tunnel could be repurposed as a pedestrian corridor to new Amtrak waiting areas under what is now 300 Riverside Plaza. A new above-ground concourse could be built on Amtrak-owned land west of that building.[94] Some

The Union Station Master Plan condenses platform space to eliminate unused baggage runs and widens passenger passageways.

COURTESY OF DAVID PHILLIPS

of this land has become a dazzling CTA bus loading terminal designed by architects Muller+Muller that connects to an underground station entrance shared with the parking garage.

Renovations continued in 2015 with rebuilding of the elegant stairways leading from Canal Street down to the headhouse's great hall. A restoration of former barbershop and restaurant spaces to near their former appearance opened as an extra-fare club for Amtrak patrons. In February 2016, Amtrak announced more restorations aimed at attracting restaurant and retail occupancy. The former Women's Lounge off the Great Hall became a rental event space after restoration and the former Fred Harvey restaurant will gain street access to Clinton Street, while former

Clinton Street office space will get a makeover. All designs are from architects Goettsch Partners.

Future plans are based on twin tracks for development. A request for proposals again sought a developer to build office towers above the building. Four respondents vied in mid-2016 for development rights of the headhouse and adjacent parcels including land occupied by the Amtrak parking garage. The winning bid was made in May 2017 by Riverside Investment and Development with preliminary designs presented by Goettsch Partners. This development promises to inject over $1 billion in private capital into the equation. Offices and a hotel would occupy the existing headhouse upper floors, a food court would occupy the great hall, and twin residential towers would be built overhead. Two 40–50 story office towers with an elevated plaza covering the new bus terminal would replace the parking garage. Later a major residential tower would rise on air rights over the only track space remaining for development. Perennially cash-starved Amtrak clearly sought a deal with the largest payout rather than the best conceptual design. It is unclear, however, how much it will have to plow back into Union Station. The scheme and accompanying architectural renderings were widely panned, with *Tribune* columnist Blair Kamin stating, "Almost apologetically, backers of the just-announced plans for redeveloping Chicago's Union Station are characterizing their proposals as preliminary and conceptual. Apologies are indeed in order."[95]

To be fair, privatization of real-estate assets is only half the story. In January 2017 the city requested a $1 billion low-interest loan from the US Department of Transportation. Repayment would be provided by a new transit-oriented tax-increment district far larger than the existing TIF. Funds would be earmarked for passenger terminal–related improvements and municipal costs incidental to redevelopment. After decades of debate, a substantial amount of governmental funding in the form of TIF payments would flow into Union Station. Seemingly, however, the federal loan and local TIF funds would enable Amtrak to transfer a major portion of the developer's payments for use elsewhere. Critics may complain that Chicago taxpayers would subsidize Amtrak operations outside the community, but in reality the railroads serving Chicago Union Station have provided and will continue to provide an engine powering the city's economic growth Indeed, these massive investments signal the greatest improvements to Chicago rail passenger terminals in nearly one hundred years.

Today's city of skyscrapers might amaze Union Station's founders. They nonetheless would immediately comprehend the role their handiwork continues to play in moving people within the region and across the nation. Perhaps Chicagoans of today will set the bar still higher. For generations Chicago Union Station was the center of its neighborhood, its city, and its nation. It is destined to retain this importance for decades to come.

APPENDIX A: CHICAGO'S RAILROAD TERMINALS

AN ALL-TIME LIST OF CHICAGO'S OTHER DOWNTOWN intercity passenger terminals and their users is below. Note that these may not be concurrent users, as the list includes successor companies. Excluded are the railroads using Union Station detailed in this book and the terminals of interurban lines such as the North Shore, South Shore, and Chicago Aurora and Elgin. Also excluded is the Illinois Central's Randolph Street Station, used solely by commuters. Various railroads used temporary terminals outside the scope of this work. The Baltimore and Ohio used several structures on the lakefront; the Nickel Plate and Wabash used south side depots prior to making permanent arrangements; and the Chicago and Pacific had a north side terminal.

NORTH WESTERN AND WELLS STREET STATIONS
Chicago and North Western
Baltimore and Ohio (1970–1972)

CENTRAL AND GREAT CENTRAL STATIONS
Illinois Central
Michigan Central
Minneapolis, St. Paul and Sault Ste. Marie ("Soo Line")
Cleveland, Cincinnati, Chicago & St. Louis ("Big Four")
Chesapeake and Ohio
Illinois Central Gulf
Amtrak

DEARBORN
Chicago and Western Indiana (commuter only)
Chicago and Eastern Illinois
Chicago and Atlantic ("Erie")
Grand Trunk Western
Chicago, Indianapolis and Louisville ("Monon")
Wabash
Atchison, Topeka and Santa Fe
Norfolk and Western (commuter only)

LASALLE STREET
Chicago Rock Island and Pacific
Lake Shore and Michigan Southern
New York Central
New York, Chicago, and St. Louis ("Nickel Plate")

GRAND CENTRAL
Wisconsin Central
Baltimore and Ohio
Minneapolis, St. Paul and Sault Ste. Marie ("Soo Line")
Chicago Great Western

APPENDIX B: NAMING CONVENTIONS

SEVERAL NAMING CONVENTIONS ARE USED IN THIS BOOK. The terms "alderman" and "city council" are used throughout, although the terms "councilman," "trustee," and "board" were also once used. The name *Tribune* is used although the newspaper itself used several variations, such as *Daily Tribune, Chicago Tribune,* and *Sunday Tribune.* The term used for the area around Union Station is *Near West Side.* This term evolved over time. Originally it was the *West Side*, then the *Near West Side*, which now denotes an area further west, and the current usage is *West Loop.*

For consistency, commonly used railroad names are used, as shown in the following chronology with the starting dates for those lines using Union Station.

FT. WAYNE

Ft. Wayne and Chicago Railroad	1851
Pittsburgh, Ft. Wayne and Chicago Railroad	1856
Pittsburgh, Ft. Wayne and Chicago Railway	1869
Pennsylvania Railroad–Lines West	1921
Penn Central Transportation Company	1968
Conrail	1976
CSX	1999–present

PANHANDLE

Cincinnati and Chicago Railway	1856
Cincinnati and Chicago Air-Line Railroad	1861
Chicago and Great Eastern Railway	1865
Columbus, Chicago and Indiana Central Railway	1868
Pittsburg, Cincinnati, Chicago and St. Louis Railway	1869
Pittsburgh, Cincinnati, Chicago and St. Louis Railroad	1871
Pennsylvania Railroad–Lines West	1921
Penn Central Transportation Company	1968
Conrail	1976
Norfolk Southern	1999–present

ALTON

Joliet and Chicago	1856
Chicago and Mississippi Railroad	1852
Chicago, Alton and St. Louis Railway	1855
St. Louis, Alton and Chicago Railroad	1856
Chicago and Alton Railway	1861
Chicago and Alton Railroad	1900
Alton Railroad	1931
Gulf Mobile and Ohio Railroad	1947

Illinois Central Gulf	1972
Illinois Central	1988
Canadian National	1998–present
Metra—Heritage Corridor passenger service operator	1975–present

BURLINGTON

Aurora Branch	1849
Chicago and Burlington	1852
Chicago, Burlington and Quincy Railroad	1855
Chicago, Burlington and Quincy Rail Road	1856
Chicago, Burlington and Quincy Railroad	1864
Burlington Northern	1970

Burlington Northern Santa Fe	1996–present
Metra—Burlington Line passenger service operator	

MILWAUKEE

Milwaukee and Mississippi Railroad	1847
Chicago, Milwaukee and St. Paul	1874
Chicago and Pacific	1874
Chicago and Evanston	1882
Chicago, Milwaukee, St. Paul and Pacific	1928
Soo Line Railroad	1985
Metra—Milwaukee West line, Milwaukee North lines	1982

NOTES

CHAPTER 1

[1] William Cronon, *Nature's Metropolis: Chicago and the Great West* (New York: W.W. Norton & Company, 1991), 32.

[2] Jack Harpster, *The Railroad Tycoon Who Built Chicago: A Biography of William B. Ogden* (Carbondale: Southern Illinois University Press, 2009), 31.

[3] Ibid., 40–41.

[4] Municipal corporations such as towns are political subdivisions of their state, and thus the products of its constitution. Under the US Constitution, the federal government retained only enumerated powers and all other privileges fell to its subdivisions, the individual states. State constitutions, however, take the opposite approach. The Illinois constitution, for example, reserves all governmental powers to the state unless the legislature grants specific authority to municipal governments. Today, these underlying political subdivisions are controlled by the overarching Illinois Municipal Code, but early in the state's history each town had its own unique charter. The state legislature granted specific powers to each city or town in a process replete with the lobbying, negotiation, and horse trading common to most legislation. As a result, some towns had more latitude in their statutory powers than similar towns with less political clout.

[5] This act had a loophole sometimes used to promote private enterprises: it specified the required public use of bond proceeds, but was silent as to the investment of unused proceeds. Local governments had the power to invest surplus funds, allowing them to purchase corporate bonds at par with proceeds of their own bond sale. Everyone understood these were poor investments, since by definition the starry-eyed community had purchased the debt of an unbuilt, risky enterprise, but they may have been just as good as deposits in the shaky banks of the era. Nevertheless, most other bondholders purchased bonds at a discount or only supplied part of the required purchase price up front. In practice this meant that without taking a loss on the investment, bonds held by a local government were unmarketable.

[6] Robin L. Einhorn, *Property Rules: Political Economy in Chicago, 1833–1872* (Chicago: University of Chicago Press, 2001), 102.

[7] New York had issued bonds as early as 1811, but they were privately placed. The development of easily transferable securities fueled the growth of the municipal market. In addition to an exchange that facilitated bond trading, it required a system of underwriters and independent paying agents.

[8] For consistency, the term "alderman" is used throughout this text, although the terms "councilman" and "trustee" were at times the official titles.

[9] John Carbutt, *Biographical Sketches of the Leading Men of Chicago* (Chicago: Wilson & St. Clair, 1868), 20.

[10] William H. Stennett, *Yesterday and Today: A History of the Chicago and North Western Railway System* (Chicago: Chicago Chapter, Railway and Locomotive Historical Society, 1981), 13.

[11] The author examined an extant G&CU depot at the Illinois Railway Museum to determine the construction method used.

[12] The city limit was then at Western Avenue, where the railroad built its locomotive shop and yard tracks would allow locomotive power to be switched to horse power. This yard remains today as one of the city's largest passenger coach yards.

[13] William Butler Ogden to Edward Russell, August 24, 1853, Ogden Jones and Company letter book. William Butler Ogden papers, Chicago History Museum.

[14] Ogden to Russell, September 5, 1854, Ogden Jones and Company letter book. William Butler Ogden papers, Chicago History Museum.

[15] Graydon M. Meints, "Race to Chicago," *Railroad History* 183 (Autumn 2000), 7–29.

[16] William J. Watt, *The Pennsylvania Railroad in Indiana* (Bloomington: Indiana University Press, 1999), 24. The Ft. Wayne, as the line was known from its earliest days, had been discussed in its namesake city since 1852. But it was the 1854 completion of the Ohio and Indiana Railroad, with its connection to Cincinnati, that truly spurred discussion. In fact, the Ft. Wayne began construction in June 1854, three months before the O&I reached Fort Wayne.

[17] *Chicago Tribune*, December 10, 1852.

[18] *Chicago Tribune*, December 15, 1852.

[19] Ogden provided services for various members of the Samuel Russell family of Middletown, Connecticut. Russell & Company was the most important

American China trading firm and its partners included John Murray Forbes, who controlled the Michigan Central and the Chicago, Burlington and Quincy railroads. Another partner was Warren Delano, whose son Frederic was to play a major role in the history of Union Station.

20 Ogden was undoubtedly introduced to Ft. Wayne business circles by Charles Butler, who was Trustee of the Wabash and Erie Canal.

21 *Chicago Tribune*, February 16, 1854.

22 *Chicago Tribune*, February 27, 1854.

23 *Chicago Tribune*, February 5, 1855.

24 Gurdon Hubbard was a principal backer of the Airline. A dozen years earlier Hubbard controlled the charter of the Galena and Chicago Union, but he built less than a mile of track. The charter lapsed, which erased Hubbard's investment. When William Butler Ogden revived the charter, Hubbard was incensed. Ogden had been Hubbard's attorney in the earlier effort, but the latter was later effectively locked out of the enterprise. The Airline directly paralleled Ogden's Galena road, an alignment that may have had as much to do with spite as with economic necessity.

25 *Chicago Tribune*, May 5, 1860. As part of the transaction, Galena allegedly pledged neutrality towards the two Michigan firms.

26 *Chicago Tribune*, November 12, 1855.

27 Charles Butler, untitled monograph, New York, December 17, 1881, 21. William Butler Ogden papers, Chicago History Museum.

28 *Chicago Tribune*, July 8, 1857, and August 4, 1856.

29 *Chicago Tribune*, April 30, 1857.

30 *Chicago Tribune*, October 3, 1857.

31 Cronon, *Nature's Metropolis*, 112. Cronon notes that with the advent of the elevator, grain handling became inexpensive; grain could be funneled as if it were a liquid, whereas bagged grain had to be treated as a series of solid objects.

32 This elevator was located on land the Ft. Wayne sold the Burlington. One of the biggest shippers in Chicago, it was located next to the south throat of Union Depot, but was not accessible to the eastern lines.

33 Cronon, *Nature's Metropolis*, 120.

34 Carroll L. V. Meeks, *The Railroad Station: An Architectural History* (New Haven, CT: Yale University Press, 1956), 170.

35 George Rogers Taylor and Irene D. Neu, *The American Railroad Network: 1861–1890* (Cambridge, MA: Harvard University Press, 1956), 32. Shortly after the Ft. Wayne reached Chicago, it began service with cars equipped with "compromise" wheels whose flanges were set for the narrower, standard-gauge track, but had extra-wide treads that allowed them to run on four-foot-ten-inch track. This solution was never entirely satisfactory. Eastern lines used compromise wheels on specialized express cars run in fast freight service. In passenger service, an 1868 Ft. Wayne advertisement mentions their use on sleeping cars.

36 Alfred Dupont Chandler, *The Visible Hand: The Managerial Revolution in American Business* (Cambridge, MA: The Belknap Press of Harvard University Press, 1977), 125. By nature, railroads have high fixed charges but low variable costs. Unless competitors agreed on rates, individual managers had every incentive to chase business by pushing rates ever lower in search of marginal revenue. Any incremental revenue would help to cover the immense capital charges incurred in construction. That is, carrying an additional passenger cost almost nothing, so any tariff, however low, contributed cash.

37 *Chicago Tribune*, May 8, 1859.

38 I. T. Palmatary, *A Bird's-Eye View of Chicago* (Chicago: n.p., 1857).

39 Homer Hoyt, *One Hundred Years of Land Values in Chicago* (Chicago: University of Chicago Press, 1933), 66.

40 *American Railroad Journal* 2 (1853), 230.

41 *Chicago Tribune*, February 12, 1858, and July 10, 1858.

42 Gene Glendinning, *The Chicago and Alton Railroad: The Only Way* (DeKalb: Northern Illinois University Press, 2002), 33. The ability to move trains over the lines of several railroads illustrates an important feature about the network of lines that radiated from Chicago. Somewhat by coincidence, nearly all of the local railroad companies used the same track gauge. The gauge (the distance between the rails) was not yet standard, and the near uniformity of Chicago's tracks was relatively unique. During this early period, even where like-gauge tracks met, however, little carload freight was transferred. The innovation that leveraged Chicago's advantage of compatible railroad lines was actually administrative. Through-waybills and the accounting system that supported them were an innovation of the late 1850s, but once they were developed, Chicago dominated the business of interchanging freight cars.

43 *Chicago Tribune*, May 9, 1857. The article stated that it was the intent to lease the Joliet immediately upon completion to the Alton.

44 John J. Flinn, *Hand-Book of Chicago Biography* (Chicago: Standard Guide, 1893), 58.

45 D. W. Yungmeyer, "An Excursion into the Early History of the Chicago and Alton Railroad." Paper presented to the Illinois State Historical Society, October 6, 1944.

46 *Chicago Democratic Press*, July 15, 1865.

47 The purchase of an interest in the bridge likely resulted from a need to lay standard-gauge track across the span in addition to the Ft. Wayne's Ohio-gauge line.

48 Glendinning, *The Chicago and Alton Railroad*, 53.

49 *Chicago Tribune*, April 2, 1858.

50 *Chicago Tribune*, September 7, 1858.

51 Ibid.

52 *Chicago Tribune*, May 12, 1857.

53 There were few local beds of alluvial gravel; the stone came from pits near Western and Madison Streets or from Lockport or Joliet area quarries.

54 Alfred T. Andreas, *History of Chicago from the Earliest Period to the Present Time* (Chicago: A. T. Andreas), 148.

55 Ibid., 198; *Chicago Tribune*, July 1, 1858.

56 Peck and Wentworth were both close to Lincoln and both served as directors of the Galena road (although never at the same time). The original Galena charter had, in fact, been signed in Peck's law office.

57 Engineers certainly used the term, as in the case of the B&O's Carrollton Viaduct of 1829 and the Thomas Viaduct of 1835. As with Boston's Canton Viaduct of 1835, however, these structures carried the railroad, with road traffic below.

58 The result was vehicular traffic on three levels. It was, of course, common to have streets or towpaths under bridges, but this may have been the first legislatively created, grade-separated land corridor in the United States

59 *Chicago Tribune*, August 6, and August 14, 1858. No mention of the word "viaduct" occurred in any discussion, although that certainly is what the word "tunnel" meant.

60 *Chicago Tribune*, July 20, 1858.

61 *Chicago Tribune*, August 12, 1858 and August 16, 1858. Only two companies were named in the ordinance. However, the Chicago and Milwaukee and the St. Louis, Alton and Chicago were known to be part of the scheme. The Ft. Wayne was clearly the leader. A letter dated August 10 from J. Edgar Thomson, president of the Pennsylvania Railroad and the Ft. Wayne, urging quick passage of the ordinance was widely circulated.

62 White, John R., "Chicago Locomotive Builders," *Railroad History* 122 (April 1970), 52–60.

63 *Chicago Tribune*, September 1 and 20, 1858.

64 Hoyt, *Land Values*, 63. The statistics are for 1854. See also *Chicago Tribune* July 23, 1860.

65 D. C. Prescott, *Early Day Railroading from Chicago: A Narration with Some Observations* (Chicago: David B. Clarkson Company, 1910), 213–216.

66 *Chicago Tribune*, October 20, 1858. The lots to the north could be had for $600,000 and those to the south for $360,000. By comparison, the price difference could purchase, build, and equip a twenty-mile right of way in the open prairie.

67 *Chicago Tribune*, November 8, 1858.

68 Albert Holmes Bodman, *Bodman's Hand-Book of Chicago* (Chicago: Charles Shober, 1854).

69 *American Railroad Journal*, June 11, 1864, 580.

70 Butler, untitled monograph, 21.

71 George H. Burgess and Miles C. Kennedy, *Centennial History of the Pennsylvania Railroad Company* (Philadelphia: Pennsylvania Railroad Company, 1949), 178.

72 Ibid.

73 H. Roger Grant, *The North Western: A History of the Chicago & North Western Railway System* (DeKalb: Northern Illinois University Press, 1996), 26–27.

74 PFC Henry Miller, diary, ca. 1861, Chicago History Museum.

75 *Chicago Tribune*, October 1, 1860, and November 1, 1860. The steam coach was one of three for the Ft. Wayne that were likely the handiwork of Marrick, Hanna and Company. They and a similar car from the Pacific Railroad of Missouri were commandeered by the Army in 1863 to serve as pay cars.

76 *Chicago Tribune*, November 22 and 29, 1860.

77 *Chicago Tribune*, January 12, 1860.

78 The Panhandle name originally applied only to the Pittsburgh-Columbus section. Lines west of Columbus were not united by common leases until 1868, not by common Pennsylvania Railroad ownership until 1883, and not by actual merger into one company until 1890.

79 *Chicago Tribune*, January 21, 1861.

80 *Chicago Tribune*, September 16, 1859.

81 *Chicago Tribune*, March 20, 1861.

82 *Chicago Tribune*, April 17, 1861.

83 *Chicago Tribune*, June 19, 1861.

84 *Chicago Tribune*, November 9, 1861.

85 *Chicago Tribune*, May 21, 1861.

86 Hoyt, *Land Values*, 76.

87 *Chicago Tribune*, July 8, 1861.

88 *Chicago Tribune*, October 17, 1861.

89 *Chicago Tribune*, November 14, 1861.

90 *Chicago Tribune*, June 1, 1860.

91 *Chicago Tribune*, June 4, 1879.

92 Andreas, *History of Chicago*, 148.

93 Chicago and Alton Railroad Company, *Third Annual Report of the President and Directors for the Year Ended December 31, 1865*.

94 *Chicago Tribune*, August 29, 1862. An accident exactly two years earlier reveals the nature of the neighborhood immediately south of the depot. An Alton train jumped the track at Twelfth Street, tore off the side of an adjacent barn, and severely injured a cow.

95 *Chicago Tribune*, June 17, 1863.

96 Watt, *The Pennsylvania Railroad in Indiana*, 37.

97 *Chicago Tribune*, January 22, 1865.

98 *Chicago Tribune*, June 3, 1864.

99 Glendinning, *The Chicago and Alton Railroad*, 70–72; Charles Long, "The Pioneer and the Lincoln Funeral Train," *Railroad History* 186 (Spring 2002), 88–100. Long states that C&A #58 pulled the funeral train rather than #57, and that the Pullman cars left on a regularly scheduled 7:30 p.m. train.

100 Ida Hinman, *Biography of Timothy B. Blackstone* (New York: Methodist Book Press, 1917).

101 Sanborn Fire Insurance Map of Chicago (Teaneck, NJ: Sandborn Map Company, 1869).

102 Pittsburgh, Ft. Wayne, and Chicago Railway Company, *Annual Report* (Pittsburgh: Pittsburgh Ft. Wayne and Chicago Railway, 1867).

103 *Chicago Railway Review*, February 3, 1870. William Ogden owned Michigan iron mines and a Brady's Bend, Pennsylvania, iron smelter and rolling mill. Allegations made in an unsigned letter to the *Chicago Tribune* on February 16, 1867 stated that he forced his inferior iron on railroads he controlled. It

is more likely that the high wear associated with this compromise track resulted from the wheel hunting associated with slightly different-gauge trains using the same track.

[104] Steven W. Usselman, *Regulating Railroad Innovation: Business, Technology, and Politics in America, 1840–1920* (Cambridge: Cambridge University Press, 2002), 80.

[105] *Chicago Tribune*, October 31, 1864. The C&GE eminent domain suit caused great anguish to the

managers of several roads. There is some evidence to suggest that the outlying freight yards constructed at this time arose due to this issue. Although there was a great need for this capacity, it was also prudent to occupy the complete width of one's right of way in order to prevent a competitor's claim on any unused strip of land.

[106] *Chicago Tribune*, October 6 and 10, 1866.

[107] Burgess and Kennedy, *Centennial Hisotry*, 200. That company's nickname, the "Panhandle," came

from the portion of its route that bisected the similarly named section of West Virginia. The Columbus, Chicago & Indiana Central Railway became the Chicago, St. Louis & Pittsburgh Railroad in 1883 when shareholders often antagonistic to the Pennsylvania Railroad (mostly New Yorkers) were bought out, and was merged with the Pittsburgh, Cincinnati & St. Louis Railway in 1890 to create the Pittsburgh, Cincinnati, Chicago & St. Louis Railway.

CHAPTER 2

[1] Barnet Hodes, *Essays in Illinois Taxation* (Chicago: Reilly & Lee, 1935), 83–84.

[2] Ibid., 85. The 1870 constitution also standardized corporate regulation. Railroads no longer had to petition the legislature individually for a charter, making it easier to form for new corporations.

[3] The new constitution limited local autonomy, although the extent of the restraints was not determined until the Comprehensive Cities and Villages Act was passed in 1872. Because various provisions of the act were untested in court and amendments were still pending in the legislature, the immediate post-Fire period was one of legal limbo.

[4] Valuation, and hence taxes, was now to be based on the earnings power of the railroad as a whole. Each local area was then assigned a percentage of the total based on its pro rata share of each company's mileage within its jurisdiction. Interestingly, the statute stated that "side tracks and all station houses, depots and other buildings shall be taxed in the jurisdiction in which they are located." Sidestepping the philosophical question of whether buildings also contributed to earnings, the new methodology divorced the taxation of depots from that of the tracks needed to serve them.

[5] *Chicago Railway Review*, August 5, 1869.

[6] Ogden seems to have maintained some influence. In 1871 his nephew, James Ogden, acted as attorney for the Ft. Wayne in the subdivision and sale of lands which had comprised its original Van Buren Street terminal. The sale represented the last time the Ogden name was linked to the Union Depot. These lots would be repurchased years later at considerably greater expense.

[7] Richard T. Wallis, *The Pennsylvania Railroad at Bay: William Riley McKeen and the Terre Haute & Indianapolis Railroad* (Bloomington: Indiana University Press, 2001), 27. J. Edgar Thomson put a great strain on the Pennsylvania's relationship with its key western connection in 1866, when he raised capital by selling the Pennsylvania Railway's stock in the Ft. Wayne and using the proceeds to invest in an upstart rival, the Panhandle. The mighty eastern line's original strategy was to provide seed capital, but not to control or enter into formal alliances with its feeders quickly proved unstable.

[8] George H. Burgess and Miles C. Kennedy, *Centennial History of the Pennsylvania Railroad Company* (Philadelphia: Pennsylvania Railroad Company, 1949), 198–199.

[9] Ibid., 198.

[10] Wallis, *The Pennsylvania Railroad at Bay*. In 1874 the administration of the Ft. Wayne and Panhandle,

or "Lines West" (west of Pittsburgh), were legally consolidated into the Pennsylvania *Company*, a subsidiary of the Pennsylvania *Railroad*.

[11] William J. Watt, *The Pennsylvania Railroad in Indiana* (Bloomington: Indiana University Press, 1999), 52. Per correspondence with Christopher Baer, Librarian of the Hagley Museum and Library, Silver Palace sleepers were run by the Central Transportation Company using Woodruff and Knight patents. Pullman leased the company in 1870 and substituted its own cars. They originally ran to New York via the Allentown route (Reading-LV-CNJ), starting in 1867.

[12] *New York Times*, July 23, 1867.

[13] Wallis, *The Pennsylvania Railroad at Bay*, 6. The reference to internal bleeding Wallis described the railroad as "internally bleeding," and it is quite appropriate. From the outside, the Pennsylvania system appeared vigorous. It had grown rapidly to become the largest corporation outside of the British East India Company. But its component parts suffered, in part because even within the system there were duplicate routes and redundancies.

[14] Gene Glendinning, *The Chicago and Alton Railroad: The Only Way* (DeKalb: Northern Illinois University Press, 2002), 93.

[15] Ibid., 94.

[16] James E. White, *A Life Span and Reminiscence of Railway Mail Service* (Philadelphia: Deemer & Jaisohn, 1910), 21.

[17] The Illinois Constitution of 1870 proved to be an impediment to Chicago recovery. The act limiting city debt to a percentage of its property value was set below Chicago's existing debt level, so the city had no ability to issue bonds to replace its burnt assets. The act also listed activities in which a city government could not engage and the courts embellished it to prohibit nearly all unspecified endeavors. (For example, it was once deemed necessary for the city to petition the legislature for permission to sell popcorn on municipal property.) Despite these limitations, a reconstruction boom of mammoth proportions occurred, but it was fueled by real estate speculators and developers, not by local government actions.

[18] Bessie Louise Pierce, *A History of Chicago* (New York: Alfred A. Knopf, 1940), 2:15. The bonds had been issued for the deepening of the channel and to aid sewage disposal, not for the canal's original construction. The state also limited the use of proceeds to infrastructure replacement and debt service.

[19] Herton and Leonard, *New Chicago: A Review of the Work of Reconstruction* (Chicago: Chicago Times, 1872), 85.

[20] *Chicago Tribune*, December 3, 1871. Ogden's comments were somewhat belated because he spent five weeks after the fire in Peshtigo, Wisconsin, the sawmill town and port that hosted Ogden's Peshtigo Lumber Company. That town and the surrounding timberlands burned the same day as the Great Chicago Fire, with even greater loss of life.

[21] *Chicago Tribune*, December 1, 1872.

[22] *Chicago Tribune*, December 6, 1874.

[23] C. E. Perkins, Memorandum, July 8, 1878, CB&Q Collection, Newberry Library.

[24] *Chicago Tribune*, April 7, 1872, and June 2, 1872.

[25] *Chicago Tribune*, February 1, 1873, and February 7, 1873.

[26] William B. Strong to James Joy, November 28, 1874, CB&Q Collection, Newberry Library.

[27] William B. Strong to Charles Perkins, April 29, 1875, CB&Q Collection, Newberry Library.

[28] *Chicago Tribune*, April 18, 1877.

[29] *Chicago Tribune*, April 7, 1877, and April 24, 1877.

[30] Gerald G. Eggert, *Railroad Labor Disputes: The Beginning of Federal Strike Policy* (Ann Arbor: University of Michigan Press, 1967), 1–31.

[31] *New York Times*, March 16, 1864, and May 2, 1865.

[32] Allan Pinkerton, *Mass Violence in America: Strikers, Communists, Tramps and Detectives* (1878; repr., New York: Arno Press, 1969), 387.

[33] David O. Stowell, *Streets, Railroads and the Great Strike of 1877* (Chicago: University of Chicago Press, 1999).

[34] The strike accomplished little. Suspected agitators were blacklisted and never again worked for the railroads. Chicago built a new fortress-like armory at Sixteenth Street to command the southern approach to the business district. By subscription from leading citizens, the city purchased six cannon, a ten-barreled Gatling gun, 296 Springfield rifles and 60,000 rounds of ammunition.

[35] Stowell, *Streets, Railroads and the Great Strike.*

[36] *Chicago Tribune*, February 15, 1879.

[37] The slow negotiations also appear to reflect the divergent managerial styles that made it difficult to reach a consensus. The Alton, with its president Timothy Blackstone, retained its original organization. The company was dominated by its founders, who continued in the active management of their investment. The Milwaukee Road was a company that had come under the control of financiers and bankers. Such companies were governed in a "line and staff" manner in which reporting flowed within functional departments. Departments interacted primarily at senior levels and these upper-level managers were typically financial and accounting professionals. Ownership of the Pennsylvania, in contrast, had always been diverse. For decades its senior managers had been engineers who had risen by merit through the ranks. Its organization relied on strong, self-contained operating divisions. Correspondence from the period suggests that the Pennsylvania Railroad's divisional headquarters in Pittsburgh made most of the decisions about the new station, and in the end the other railroads were forced to yield to its wishes.

[38] Scott suffered a stroke at his desk in 1878 and took a temporary rest. While he returned to work, he was forced to retire effective June 1, 1880. He suffered another stroke, this time fatal, in 1881.

CHAPTER 3

[1] *Chicago Tribune*, October 29, 1879.

[2] James Reed Golden, *Investment Behavior by U.S. Railroads, 1870–1914* (New York: Arno Press, 1975), 12. The fact that it took the resources of five lines pooled together to engage in the expensive proposition of penetrating the expanded city is only part of the story. While the Western Indiana needed to reach center city to attract passenger traffic, it is also important to realize that the attraction of a Chicago terminal lay primarily in the interchange of freight. As Golden states for the period 1870–1893, "Spurts in track extension into new regions, partially stimulated by high grain prices, were followed by reductions in grain prices, falling profit levels and an evaporation of financial capital" (12). One such drop in grain prices occurred in 1882 as the Western Indiana was pushed to completion.

[3] William T. Stead, *If Christ Came to Chicago* (Chicago: Laird and Lee, 1894), 173.

[4] Ibid., 180–181. The unnamed alderman was Cullerton of the Big Four.

[5] Fred Ash, "A Lakefront Excursion," *Rail and Wire* (Illinois Railway Museum), 193 (January 2002), 9–12.

[6] *Chicago Tribune*, November 26 and 27, 1879.

[7] *Chicago Tribune*, November 29, 1879.

[8] Agreement between the Pennsylvania Railroad, Chicago and Alton Railroad, and the Chicago Milwaukee and St. Paul Railway, December 31, 1879.

[9] *Chicago Tribune*, January 8, 1880.

[10] *Chicago Tribune*, January 1 and 12, 1880.

[11] *Chicago Tribune*, February 27, 1880.

[12] A relatively detailed plan appeared in the *Chicago Tribune* on February 27, 1880.

[13] *Chicago Tribune*, July 7, 1880, and September 22, 1880.

[14] After a short period of use as a railroad YMCA it was torn down. The two known photographs of the depot date from this period.

[15] *Chicago Tribune*, February 13, 1881.

[16] *Chicago Tribune*, April 3, 1881.

[17] *Railroad Gazette*, May 15, 1881, 257.

[18] The Panhandle made a similar move to what became the Fifty-Fifth Street Yard.

[19] No description has survived of the use of tie rods, often used in train shed construction to constrain the lateral thrust of the arch.

[20] *Chicago Tribune*, April 5, 1881.

[21] No description of the footings for these columns has survived, and thus we cannot determine the distribution of the load between walls and columns.

[22] *Chicago Tribune*, April 5, 1881.

[23] *Railway Gazette*, May 13, 1881, 258.

[24] Chicago Union Station files, Hagley Museum and Library, Pennsylvania Railroad collection.

[25] *Railway Gazette*, May 13, 1881.

[26] Perry R. Duis and Glen E. Holt, "The Midwestern Gate to the New World," *Chicago*, May 1981, 191–196.

The nonethnic League for the Protection of Immigrants began in 1908.

[27] *Chicago Tribune*, December 30, 1880.

[28] *Chicago Tribune*, February 27, 1880. The Pennsylvania Company was a holding company for various subsidiaries of the Pennsylvania Railroad.

[29] Unpublished research by Christopher T. Baer, Assistant Curator, Manuscripts and Archives, Hagley Museum and Library.

[30] In later years, W. W. Boyington, Chicago's most prolific architect, occasionally received credit for the architecture of the Union Depot. His participation was never publicly noted and there are no records of work by him. Perhaps Chicago's architectural chauvinism could not permit the belief that one of the city's major buildings did not have a local architect. Nevertheless, Boyington probably influenced the design. Boyington had previously designed LaSalle Street Depot, a three-towered edifice with a mansard roof whose profile was vaguely similar to Union Depot. Concurrent with the erection of the Union Depot, Boyington designed the Wells Street Depot for the Chicago and North Western. Boyington's Wells Street design used a Queen Anne style markedly different from Slataper's Union Depot, but they shared a split-level design with waiting rooms above and track level below.

[31] *Chicago Tribune*, April 5, 1881.

[32] *Chicago Tribune*, September 22, 1880, and October 8, 1882.

[33] To back up a horse-drawn dray was an awkward and time-consuming task because horse collars harness only the forward motion of a horse. To compensate for this problem, the profile of Canal Street near the dock had a prominent arch to allow gravity to assist backing. Even experienced teamsters had difficulty spotting their wagons.

[34] Cited in Pennsylvania Railroad, *Pennsylvania Railroad Company to the Columbian Exposition* (Chicago: Pennsylvania Railroad, 1893).

[35] Harry Hansen, *The Chicago*, The Rivers of America (New York: Farrar and Rhinehart, 1942), 11–12.

[36] The geographic basis of the city and the suburbs centered on the discrete neighborhoods that coalesced around their local depot. Street railways, however, stimulated the linear development of the real estate along their routes. Once people left for these new neighborhoods, they no longer had to live conveniently next to their local depot. Steam railroads never recovered their original dominance of local transit. Ironically, Chicago's massive investment in cable car lines caused it to lag in the formation of electric trolley lines in the following decades, particularly into the downtown district.

[37] Richard T. Wallis, *The Pennsylvania Railroad at Bay: William Riley McKeen and the Terre Haute & Indianapolis Railroad* (Bloomington: Indiana University Press, 2001), 70.

[38] *Chicago Tribune*, November 19, 1883. Many railroads, including the Milwaukee Road, did not convert to the new standard until the following Sunday.

[39] *Chicago Tribune*, January 15, 1884.

[40] "A Foreign Invasion," *Chicago Tribune*, June 4, 1885, and June 5, 1885.

[41] This building did not carry its entire load on the iron frame, and tenants remained leery of higher floors, so the era of the skyscraper had not entirely arrived.

[42] Homer Hoyt, *One Hundred Years of Land Values in Chicago* (Chicago: University of Chicago Press, 1933), 134–136.

[43] Ibid., 152.

[44] Apartment buildings had appeared in Chicago only a decade earlier. Flats were fashionable for renters and profitable for owners because they made better use of expensive land than a house. They offered amenities such as steam heat, gas lighting, and a janitor to superintend the furnace, all of which appealed to the growing middle class.

[45] Gene Glendinning, *The Chicago and Alton Railroad: The Only Way* (DeKalb: Northern Illinois

University Press, 2002), 69. Both the Pioneer and the Delmonico were built in Pullman's shop adjacent to Chicago Union Depot. After Pullman built his model shops and city south of town, the site remained Pullman-owned for use as a repair base for his cars.

[46] *Chicago Tribune*, June 15, 1887.

[47] William J. Watt, *The Pennsylvania Railroad in Indiana* (Bloomington: Indiana University Press, 1999), 61.

[48] RPO cars allowed clerks to sort letters en route, a system developed scarcely twenty years before, but this train carried only white RPOs and mail-storage cars that it received from eastern connections.

[49] David P. Morgan, *Fast Mail: The First 75 Years; Chicago Burlington and Quincy Railroad* (Chicago: Chicago Burlington and Quincy Railroad, 1959).

[50] Chicago, Burlington and Quincy Railroad, *How the Greyhounds of the Burlington Beat the Rising Sun* (Chicago: Chicago Burlington and Quincy Railroad, 1899).

[51] *New York Times*, July 19, 1895.

[52] V. S. Roseman, *Railway Express Agency: An Overview* (Denver: Rocky Mountain Publishing Company, 1992), 20–23.

[53] *Railroad Gazette*, September 12, 1890.

[54] Gerald G. Eggert, *Railroad Labor Disputes: The Beginning of Federal Strike Policy* (Ann Arbor: University of Michigan Press, 1967), 35. Strikers in Chicago may have been in for an especially hard time, since

the presiding federal judge was Thomas S. Drummond, an original promoter of the Galena, among other railroads. It was often said that "God rules in Israel, but Thomas Drummond rules in the Seventh Circuit."

[55] *Chicago Tribune*, January 5, 1890.

[56] Board of Managers, Chicago Union Depot, *Minutes* (September 19, 1892). Of the total, 132 trains were suburban service, as follows: Evanston, 41, Burlington 67, Ft. Wayne 24.

[57] Ibid. (September 27, 1892); ibid. (November 16,1892).

[58] Ibid. (September 18, 1886).

[59] Albro Martin, *Enterprise Denied: Origins of the Decline of American Railroads, 1897–1917* (New York: Columbia University Press, 1971), 71.

[60] *Chicago Tribune*, August 21, 1891.

[61] Pittsburgh, Cincinnati, Chicago and St. Louis Railroad, *Annual Report* (Pittsburgh: Pittsburgh, Cincinnati, Chicago and St. Louis Railroad, 1892).

[62] Pittsburgh, Cincinnati, Chicago and St. Louis Railroad, *Annual Report* (Pittsburgh: Pittsburgh, Cincinnati, Chicago and St. Louis Railroad, 1893).

[63] *Chicago Tribune*, January 30, 1893.

[64] Board of Managers, Chicago Union Depot, *Minutes* (January 26, 1892).

[65] *Chicago Tribune*, January 30, 1893.

[66] Pittsburgh, Cincinnati, Chicago and St. Louis Railroad, *Annual Report* (Pittsburgh: Pittsburgh, Cincinnati, Chicago and St. Louis Railroad, 1890).

[67] *Chicago Tribune*, January 22, 1893.

[68] Christopher Baer's research indicates that one of the coaches was restored after having been used as a chicken coop, while the second was a replica. The train was exhibited outdoors by the railroad through July, after which it was moved to the Transportation Building.

[69] *Chicago Tribune*, April 23, 1893.

[70] *Chicago Tribune*, April 28 and 30, 1893.

[71] *Chicago Tribune*, April 30, 1893.

[72] *Chicago Tribune*, June 25, 1893.

[73] *Chicago Tribune*, June 24, 1893. Rate reductions resulted from the economic downturn more than any attempt to promote the fair.

[74] *Chicago Tribune*, September 11, 1893.

[75] *Chicago Tribune*, October 30, 1893. Even if the same car counts on both its inbound and outbound run, that number seems quite unrealistic.

[76] *Chicago Tribune*, July 6, 1894.

[77] Pittsburgh, Cincinnati, Chicago and St. Louis Railroad, *Annual Report* (Pittsburgh: Pittsburgh, Cincinnati, Chicago and St. Louis Railroad, 1894).

[78] Bruce G. Moffat, *The "L"—The Development of Chicago's Rapid Transit System 1888–1932*, Central Electric Railfans' Association, Bulletin 131 (Chicago, 1995), 96.

[79] *High Rail Inspection Trip*, Metra/Milwaukee District (September 31, 1987), 1.

[80] Hoyt, *Land Values*, 181.

[81] Ibid., 180.

CHAPTER 4

[1] Alfred DuPont Chandler, *The Visible Hand: The Managerial Revolution in American Business* (Cambridge, MA: The Belknap Press of Harvard University Press, 1977), 133. Chandler stated that passenger rates

fell 50 percent from 1849 to 1870. They continued to decline in the 1880s and 1890s.

[2] Charles H. Hession and Hyman Sardy, *Ascent to Affluence: A History of American Economic Development* (Boston: Allyn and Bacon, 1969), 482

[3] Ibid., 587.

[4] *Chicago Tribune*, January 31, 1892. The railroad companies initially fought viaduct ordinances, but soon tolerated them as a cheaper solution than track elevation.

[5] *Chicago Tribune*, April 4, 1892. The newspaper stated that the railroads owned 25 percent of the

land bounded by Division, Halsted, and Twenty-Second Streets and the lake.

[6] *Chicago Tribune*, March 19, 1879; November 30, 1879; and December 29, 1880.

[7] *Chicago Times*, November 30, 1890.

[8] Torrence already had built the Chicago and Calumet Terminal Railroad on the south side and had plans to extend to the proposed mammoth "clearing" freight yard proposed in Stickney. The elevated terminal was an extension of his idea for an independent belt line. The first public discussion of the terminal was in the *Chicago Tribune*, August 19, 1890.

[9] It was noted at the time that steel structures, although used in Philadelphia, New York, and London, presented problems. Trestles cost less to construct than an earthen embankment, but annual upkeep was many times higher than a fill enclosed with retaining walls. The higher cost of an embankment was due to the need to purchase land alongside it sufficient to accommodate the fill material's slope. In Chicago, the fill material often was sand, which has a shallow angle of repose. *Chicago Tribune*, August 27, 1891.

[10] *New York Times*, August 1, 1891.

[11] *Chicago Times*, November 8, 1891. The "good authority" was a statement made at the Western Society of Engineers, a reputable group, but nonetheless a statement unsupported by statistics.

[12] *Chicago Tribune*, November 7, 1891.

[13] *Chicago Tribune*, December 13, 1891.

[14] *Chicago Tribune*, January 31, 1892. Although cheaper than elevation, viaducts were not universally popular, since their long approach ramps affected neighboring property values. Torrence's scheme reinvigorated the call for track elevation, since it seemed to claim that elevation was financially feasible. Torrence, however, disbanded his company in September 1885 for lack of financing. He died on October 31,

1896 after a long illness believed to have been Bright's disease.

[15] Chicago Railway Terminal Commission, *The Chicago Railway Terminal Problem*, 189. (Chicago: Chicago Railway Terminal Commission, 1892), 30.

[16] As time passed, the railroads faced increasing economic pressure to elevate their tracks. In particular, passenger schedules were speeded due to competitive pressures around 1900 and congested tracks were an impediment. Crew and fuel costs also soared as trains inched between junction points. Finally, legal settlement costs leapt as liability shifted from trespassers, employees, and pedestrians to the "negligent" railroads.

[17] *Railroad Gazette*, July 22, 1892, p. 565.

[18] *The Chicago Railway Terminal Problem*, 31.

[19] *Chicago Examiner*, June 2, 1904 and *Pittsburgh Dispatch*, May 9, 1093. The president's share was $42,425.

[20] W. H. Scriven, General Agent letter to A. M. Schoyer, General Superintendent, July 8, 1909, Union Station Files, Hagley Museum and Library, Pennsylvania Railroad collection.

[21] *Chicago Tribune*, August 3, 1883.

[22] *Chicago Tribune*, December 29, 1880; September 29, 1883; and September 16, 1894.

[23] Dunlap Smith and C. S. Sims, memorandum of conversation Mr. July 15, 1901, Hagley Museum and Library, Pennsylvania Railroad collection

[24] Galloway also approached the Chicago and North Western, a line whose burgeoning commuter traffic required it to seek a new depot.

[25] Thomas Rodd, note to file, Hagley Museum and Library, Pennsylvania Railroad collection.

[26] *Chicago Tribune*, January 19, 1890, and June 13, 1890.

[27] *Chicago Tribune*, April 16, 1891. Opposition to the canal did not endear the railroads to the public, inasmuch as the basic idea was to eliminate the threat of cholera and typhoid epidemics.

[28] *Chicago Tribune*, June 6, 1895. The Panhandle eventually constructed its bascule bridges to allow unlimited clearance, but the lake-to-gulf ship canal proposal died.

[29] *Chicago Tribune*, November 6, 1897, and December 6, 1897. In fact, two smaller "by-passes" were constructed under these terms.

[30] *Chicago Tribune*, May 23, 1902.

[31] C. H. Watson, "Station Development at Chicago that Could be Built on Land Now Owned by This Company" (Pittsburgh: Office of Superintendent Lines West), March 6, 1902.

[32] Union Station files, Hagley Museum and Library, Pennsylvania Railroad collection.

[33] Albro Martin, *Enterprise Denied: Origins of the Decline of American Railroads, 1897–1917* (New York: Columbia University Press), 21. The Pennsylvania was in control of the B&O from 1901. See also *Chicago Tribune*, February 21, 1902.

[34] *Chicago Tribune*, February 21, 1902, and March 1, 1902.

[35] *Chicago Tribune*, January 31, 1901, and April 16, 1901. Harriman also owned the Illinois Central and while their lines easily connected, there is no evidence that he looked for Alton trains to go into Central Station. He simply wanted to get out from under an expensive lease and he succeeded in that effort.

[36] *Chicago Tribune*, July 15, 1901; August 3, 1901; and September 27, 1901.

[37] *Chicago Tribune*, March 1, 1902, and June 25, 1905.

[38] F. J. Loesch, Chicago Union Station files, Hagley Museum and Library, Pennsylvania Railroad collection.

[39] *Chicago Tribune*, November 16, 1907.

[40] R. C. Sattley, "One Central Railway Terminal for Chicago," *Journal of the Western Society of Engineers* (1901), 421–454.

41 Ibid.

42 Ibid.

43 Ibid.

44 Ibid.

45 Steven W. Usselman, *Regulating Railroad Innovation: Business, Technology, and Politics in America, 1840–1920* (Cambridge: Cambridge University Press, 2002), 225–227.

46 Fredric A. Delano, "Address to the Chicago Real Estate Board" (presentation, Chicago Real Estate Board, Chicago, September 10, 1904).

47 *Chicago Tribune*, December 28, 1904.

48 Carl Smith, *The Plan of Chicago: Daniel Burnham and the Remaking of the American City* (Chicago: University of Chicago Press, 2006), 65.

49 Ibid., 26–36.

50 Ibid., 83, quoting Charles Norton, letter to Adolphus Bartlett. Chicago History Museum, Commercial Club of Chicago collection.

51 Edward Bennett, diary, September 14, 1907, Edward Bennett Papers, Burnham Library of the Art Institute of Chicago, Series III, Box 5.

52 Daniel H. Burnham and Edward Bennett, *Plan of Chicago* (Chicago: Commercial Club, 1909), 61–78.

53 Edward Bennett, diary, March 31, 1908, Edward Bennett Papers, Burnham Library of the Art Institute of Chicago, Series III, Box 5.

54 Edward Bennett, diary, October 23, 1908, Edward Bennett Papers, Burnham Library of the Art Institute of Chicago, Series III, Box 5.

55 "Scheme for Chicago Union Passenger Station," *Railway Age Gazette*, March 15, 1910, 577.

56 "The Hunt Project," *Engineering News* 70 (July–December, 1913): 213–214.

57 Walter D. Moody, *Wacker's Manual of the Plan of Chicago* (Chicago: Chicago Plan Commission, 1916).

CHAPTER 5

1 Homer Hoyt, *One Hundred Years of Land Values in Chicago* (Chicago: University of Chicago Press, 1933), 222–241. This was sufficient for construction of approximately twenty-two stories. Three years later, the limit was reduced to 200 feet when overbuilding again appeared to be a problem.

2 Ibid., 231.

3 *Chicago Tribune*, February 1, 1913.

4 *Chicago Tribune*, May 10, 1910; June 25, 1910; and January 4, 1911.

5 Historic American Engineering Record, Pennsylvania Railroad, South Branch Chicago River Bridge, HAER IL-112, available at https://cdn.loc.gov/master/pnp/habshaer/il/i10700/i10706/data/i10706data.pdf

6 *Chicago Tribune*, January 1, 1910.

7 *Chicago Tribune*, September 25, 1910. The C&NW was later tried for jury tampering regarding a condemnation suit for some of the land it acquired. The "bribe" consisted of buying jurors sandwiches during the drawn-out proceedings.

8 *Chicago Tribune*, September 2, 1911.

9 *Chicago Tribune*, October 4, 1910, and August 16 and 23, 1911. The government's plan should have come as no surprise since its details were hashed out in an August 23 meeting in Daniel Burnham's office.

10 Ernest Graham, unpublished diary entry for August 12, 1912, Burnham Library of the Art Institute of Chicago.

11 *Chicago Tribune*, August 12, 1912.

12 Thomas S. Hines, *Burnham of Chicago: Architect and Planner* (Chicago: University of Chicago Press, 1979), Appendix A.

13 Daniel H. Burnham, *Diaries 1895–1912* (Chicago: Art Institute of Chicago, Burnham Library). See also Daniel H. Burnham, Letterpress Books Chicago: Art Institute of Chicago, Burnham Library), vol. 13.

14 Hines, *Burnham of Chicago,* 136.

15 Ibid. . 148.

16 Patricia Talbot Davis, *End of the Line: Alexander J. Cassatt and the Pennsylvania Railroad* (New York: Neale Watson Academic Publications, 1978), 135–148.

17 Daniel H. Burnham, diary, 1898 (Chicago: Art Institute of Chicago, Burnham Library).

18 Albro Martin, *Enterprise Denied: Origins of the Decline of American Railroads, 1897–1917* (New York: Columbia University Press, 1971), 15.

19 The letter conveying the plans was from Ernest Graham to Thomas Rodd, January 30, 1912, Hagley Museum and Library, Pennsylvania Railroad collection. There seem to have been earlier plans that never came to fruition, including the use of a massive rotunda.

20 Joshua D'Esposito to staff, June 3, 1912, Hagley Museum and Library, Pennsylvania Railroad collection.

21 Sally A. Kitt Chappell, *Architecture and Planning of Graham, Anderson, Probst and White, 1912–1936* (Chicago: University of Chicago Press, 1992), 268.

22 Ibid., 32.

23 Correspondence from all these talented individuals was filed by the Pennsylvania Railroad and is now in the collection of the Hagley Museum and Library.

24 *Chicago Tribune*, May 21, 1913.

25 Edward H. Bennett Papers, Burnham Library of the Art Institute of Chicago, Series III, Box 5, undated notes.

26 Walter D. Moody, "Address before the City Club of Chicago," June 4, 1913.

27 Edward H. Bennett Papers, Burnham Library of the Art Institute of Chicago, Series III, Box 5, May 19, 1913.

28 Ernest Graham, diary, November 25,1913.

29 A. B. Olson, *Chicago Union Station Bulletin* 49 (1936), 101–104.

30 City Club of Chicago, *Bulletin* (Chicago: City Club), January 23, 1913.

[31] City Council Committee on Railway Terminals, *Proceedings* (May 12, 1913), 73. The purpose of this meeting was to discuss a proposal requiring all Chicago railroads to electrify their track, but Hunt's testimony brought the Union Station proposal to center stage.

[32] Walter D. Moody, *Wacker's Manual of the Plan of Chicago* (Chicago: Chicago Plan Commission, 1916).

[33] *Chicago Record-Herald*, May 27, 1913.

[34] City Club of Chicago, *The Railway Terminal Problem of Chicago* (Chicago: University of Chicago Press, 1913), 41–55.

[35] Edward H. Bennett Papers, Burnham Library of the Art Institute of Chicago, Series III, Box 5, June 9, 1913.

[36] City Club of Chicago, *The Railway Terminal Problem*, 55–76.

[37] D. W. Yungmeyer,"Bion Joseph Arnold: 1861–1942," *Railway and Locomotive Historical Society* 58 (January 1942), 8–17.

[38] George Ellsworth Hooker, *Through Routes for Chicago's Steam Railroads* (Chicago: City Club, 1914).

[39] Bion Arnold, *Report on the Re-Arrangement and Development of the Steam Railroad Terminals of the City of Chicago* (Chicago: Citizens Terminal Plan Committee of Chicago, November 18, 1913).

[40] *Chicago Tribune*, December 21, 1913.

[41] *Chicago Tribune*, June 24, 1913.

[42] Reprinted in *Chicago Tribune*, December 12, 1913.

[43] *Chicago Tribune* December 12, 1913.

[44] *Chicago Tribune*, March 24, 1914.

[45] Chicago Railway Terminal Commission, preliminary report, March 29, 1915.

[46] Morris Markey, "Chicago's Democratic Approach," in *As Others See Chicago*, edited by Bessie Louise Pierce (Chicago: University of Chicago Press, 1933), 506

[47] Craig Sanders, *Limiteds, Locals and Expresses in Indiana 1838–1971* (Bloomington: Indiana University Press, 2003), 110; Edward M. DeRouin, *The Pennsy in Chicago* (LaFox, IL: Pixels Publishing, 2009), 218–219.

[48] *Chicago Herald*, June 12, 1912

[49] *Chicago Record*, July 21, 1913.

[50] City Council Committee on Railway Terminals, *The Straightening of the Chicago River, Chicago* (Chicago: City Council Committee on Railway Terminals, 1926).

[51] Robert Bruegmann, *The Architects and the City—Holabird and Roche of Chicago, 1880–1918*, (Chicago: The University of Chicago Press), 1997, 484.

[52] Martin, *Enterprise Denied*, 128. The most important of these craft-line unions was the Brotherhood of Locomotive Firemen and Enginemen, which the Pennsylvania recognized in 1910. The power of organized labor presented one half of a very sad equation for the railroads, as Martin states: "The railroads, which in 1906 had lost the power to price their product [due to rate regulation], were rapidly losing by 1910 the power to determine what they would pay for labor, their most important input." These pivotal changes led the railroads into a cycle of ever-weakening returns and, for many companies, into ultimate financial collapse.

[53] Cohen, Andrew Wender, "The Building Trades, Violence, and the Laws in Chicago: 1900–1920," Research Seminar Paper #72, presented at the Center for the History of Business, Technology and Society, Hagely Museum and Library, May 11, 2000.

[54] Cohen, Andrew Wender, *The Racketeers' Progress: Chicago and the Struggle for the Modern American Economy 1900–1940* (Cambridge: Cambridge University Press, 2004), 34.

[55] Boyle's signature umbrella was both a weapon and a cagey way of collecting bribes.

[56] Charles F. Murphy, *Oral History of Charles F. Murphy as Told to Carter Manning* (unpublished manuscript), Burnham Library, Art Institute of Chicago.

[57] Cohen, *The Racketeers' Progress*, 228.

[58] Receipts for plans in the Pennsylvania Railroad archive at the Hagely Museum indicate that the Burlington and the Milwaukee first saw the plans about March 25, 1915. By early July both railroads had responded with separate plans, and by July 29 there had been twenty-two revisions of the headhouse drawings.

[59] Unsigned memorandum, Hagely Museum and Library, Pennsylvania Railroad collection.

[60] *Second Annual Report of the Chicago Union Station Company for the Year Ended December 31, 1917*.

[61] *Chicago Tribune*, June 8, 1917 (quoting William McAdoo).

[62] Aaron Austin Godfrey, *Government Operation of the Railroads: 1918–1920*, (Austin, TX: San Felipe Press, 1974) 97. The Federal Control Act provided that the USRA could order a carrier to provide additions and betterments when "necessary or desirable for war purposes or in the public interest." The government supplied the funding with provisions for its eventual reimbursement.

[63] *Chicago Tribune*, January 19, 1918, and June 28, 1918.

[64] Moody, *Wacker's Manual*. The Twelfth Street viaduct spanned all of the South Side rail yards, including the Ft. Wayne and Alton approaches. This viaduct was a major component in the implementation of the *Plan of Chicago* for two reasons. It was the precursor of the city's freeway system, inasmuch as it provided a broad limited-access roadway south of the business district. Second, it required a referendum for the issuance of city bonds, something that local voters rarely approved. By successfully getting the required vote, it paved the way for future improvements. In fact, the railway companies built one-third of the viaduct at their own expense and the Sanitary District chipped in about 15 percent.

[65] *Chicago Tribune*, May 15, 1917.

66 *Chicago Tribune*, December 4, 1915; February 2, 9, 10, and 20, 1917; and March 23, 1917.

67 *Chicago Tribune*, July 16, 18, and 19, 1920.

68 Chappell, *Architecture and Planning of Graham Anderson Probst & White*, 32.

69 Miles L. Berger, *They Built Chicago: Entrepreneurs Who Shaped A Great City's Architecture* (Chicago: Bonus Books, 1992), 27.

70 Walter S. Lacher, "Noteworthy Passenger Terminal Completed at Chicago," *Railway Age* (July 4, 1925): https://chicagology.com/skyscrapers/skyscraper s044/.

71 Even the station's owners may have viewed track charges as vulnerable since the city still threatened to force the railroads to move into a consolidated depot on the South Side. Interestingly, the office tower was built over the headhouse, a block further from the business district than the Concourse. The Concourse site would have been a better location for development, but there were never plans to encumber it with offices. Locomotive smoke probably would have made that location less hospitable in the summer.

72 *Fourth Annual Report of the Chicago Union Station Company for the Year Ended December 31, 1919.*

73 Chicago Union Station Company, *Annual Report for the Year 1923*. Unpublished internal addendum. Author's collection.

74 *Chicago Tribune*, May 7, 1920.

75 *Chicago Tribune*, June 20, 1920.

76 Ernest Graham, diary, May 10, 1922 and June 9, 1922. The *Plan of Chicago* had, however, called for double-deck drives along both banks of the river. The only one ever built was Wacker Drive, which opened along the south bank of the main branch in 1926, and was extended south to replace the old Market Street in the 1950s. Nonetheless, space for a companion River Drive was left between the Concourse and the riverbank, and later used by buses and rental cars. The later *Daily News* Building and the Merchandise Mart also left room for the never-built roadway.

77 *Chicago Tribune*, October 19, 1920.

78 *Chicago Tribune*, February 13, 1915.

79 *Chicago Tribune*, August 1, 1944.

80 Cohen, *The Racketeers' Progress*, 269.

81 *Chicago Tribune*, January 18 and 21, 1921; May 31, 1925.

82 *Chicago Tribune*, June 27, 1928.

83 *Chicago Tribune*, September 3, 27, 1923, and October 23, 1923.

84 *Chicago Tribune*, April 29, 1924.

85 *Chicago Tribune*, September 5, 1924; November 22, 1924; and December 17, 1924.

86 *Chicago Tribune*, September 2, 1924.

CHAPTER 6

1 Walter S. Lacher, "Noteworthy Passenger Terminal Completed at Chicago," *Railway Age* (July 4, 1925): https://chicagology.com/skyscrapers/sky-scrapers044/. The majority of descriptions, specifications, and dimensions are those contained in this special issue of the railroad industry's premier trade publication. Walter S. Lacher was primary author.

2 Alfred Shaw, "The Chicago Union Station," *Architectural Forum* 44 (February 1926), 87–90.

3 Rexford Newcomb, "The New Chicago Union Station," *Western Architect* 35 (January 1926), 6–7.

4 Mercury Manufacturing Company advertisement, *Railway Age*, July 4, 1925, 52–53. American Express also used its own tractors at Chicago Union Station, supplied by the Elwin-Parker Electric Company.

5 Shaw, "The Chicago Union Station," 88.

6 Carl W. Condit, *Chicago 1910–1929: Building, Planning and Urban Technology* (Chicago: University of Chicago Press, 1973), 279.

7 Shaw, "The Chicago Union Station," 88.

8 Guerin is better known for his watercolor renderings illustrating the *Plan of Chicago* and for the opulent interior of Graham, Anderson, Probst & White's Civic Opera House. The latter included his dynamic and colorful fireproof stage curtain. Guerin had previously executed six murals in New York's Penn Station.

9 Shaw, "The Chicago Union Station," 88.

10 Sally A. Kitt Chappell, *Architecture and Planning of Graham Anderson Probst & White, 1912–1936* (Chicago: University of Chicago Press, 1992), 151.

11 Robert E. Hartley, "A Touch of Class: Fred Harvey's Operation of Chicago Union Station," *Journal of Illinois History* 14:3 (Autumn 2011), 207–224.

12 The latter event occurred after diesel locomotives had replaced steam engines on most passenger trains. For a brief period the depot again felt the forceful hammering of reciprocating engines, because the older steam locomotives could wade through waters fatal to the electrical systems of the new diesel locomotives.

13 E. Weidemann, "Some Features of the Structural Design of the Chicago Union Station," *Journal of the Western Society of Engineers* 30 (December 1925) 501–526.

14 Lacher, "Noteworthy Passenger Terminal Completed at Chicago."

15 *Engineering News Record*, January 25, 1917, 129–132; ibid., May 13, 1919, 528.

CHAPTER 7

[1] Chicago Union Station Company, *Tenth Annual Report for the Year Ended December 31, 1925* (Chicago: Union Station Company, 1926).

[2] The original estimate for the new Burlington, Alton, and the Ft. Wayne freight houses was $8 million, but eventually they required an expenditure of $34 million. The cost of engine terminals, coach yards, and repair facilities is unknown.

[3] The city also demanded an expensive Canal Street bridge over the north branch, but the US War Department deemed it an impediment to navigation and denied authorization for its construction.

[4] US Department of Labor Statistics, CPI Inflation Calculator, available at https://data.bls.gov/cgi-bin/cpicalc.pl

[5] Carroll L. V. Meeks, *The Railroad Station: An Architectural History* (New Haven, CT: Yale University Press, 1956), 133.

[6] Albro Martin, *Enterprise Denied: Origins of the Decline of American Railroads, 1897–1917* (New York: Columbia University Press, 1971). The cynic in question was Thorsten Veblen, who coined the term "honorific waste" for such architectural excesses in his book *The Theory of the Leisure Class*.

[7] *Chicago Tribune*, October 2, 1934. The study set the value as of December 27, 1927, well before the business downturn. The book value of property does not include working capital included in the $101 million total assets.

[8] Chicago Union Station Company, *Thirteenth Annual Report for the Year Ended December 31, 1928* (Chicago: Union Station Company, 1929).

[9] Given the railroads' own appetite for capital during this period, it is interesting that the station company gave its owners notes rather than issuing its own securities, upstreaming cash to the parents. It would appear that Kuhn Loeb and Company advised its client that the market would not support additional bonded debt. In fact, that investment bank held $5.5 million of the last issuance for its own account, bonds that it did not attempt to market. Some of this undoubtedly represented in-kind payment for banking services, but it is unlikely that Kuhn would have willingly held such a large investment. Private investment banks of the period did not have capital structures sufficient to allow sizeable asset holdings. Retention of 8 percent of the issue seems to indicate a failed underwriting of Chicago Union Station's debt. Such market resistance is unusual for AAA-rated debt unless the bonds were mispriced at issuance.

[10] R. Stephen Sennott, "'Forever Inadequate to the Rising Stream': Dream Cities, Automobiles and Urban Street Mobility in Central Chicago." In *Chicago Architecture and Design, 1923–1993*, ed. John Zukowsky (Chicago: Art Institute of Chicago, 1993), 54.

[11] Carl W. Condit, *Chicago 1910–29: Building, Planning and Urban Technology* (Chicago: University of Chicago Press, 1973). A minor failure of Condit's analysis is that at the station's opening, some Pennsylvania trains still used the north side of the depot, although their number was minuscule.

[12] Ibid., 56. Condit's calculus has several limitations. He did not substantiate the number of trains that Union Station could "easily and safely accommodate." Nor did he explain how rush hour congestion entered his calculus. And he looked only at scheduled arrivals and departures when, especially in its early years, multiple sections of the most popular trains were common during peak seasons. Nevertheless, his conclusion seems roughly correct.

[13] *Chicago Tribune*, December 25, 1938.

[14] The 1940 study estimated each railroad's cost per car as $7.22 for the Alton, $5.19 for the Milwaukee Road, $4.97 for the Burlington, and $9.77 for the Pennsylvania.

[15] City Council Committee on Railway Terminals, *The Straightening of the Chicago River*.

[16] "Busiest Railway Crossing is No More," *Railway Age*, (August 15, 1931): 241–251.

[17] Gene V. Glendinning, *The Chicago and Alton Railroad: The Only Way* (DeKalb: Northern Illinois University Press, 2002). Glendinning attributes the financial failure of the Alton to a too-late 1879 expansion of the railroad to Kansas City. Despite owning the premier route between Chicago and Saint Louis, the Alton was already a minor, if not marginal, carrier by 1880 because it preferred paying high dividends to investing in its operations.

[18] Thomas H. Ploss, *The Nation Pays Again: The Demise of the Milwaukee Road 1928–1986* (Chicago: Thomas H. Ploss), 1986, ii.

[19] A contributing problem was a failure of railroad cost accounting to present unambiguous answers as to how much money any specific train lost. High fixed costs meant that even trains that generated no profit when overhead expenses were fully allocated still contributed toward fixed charges. Those who opposed the elimination of a train could therefore muster statistics to support their position. Regulators had a bias toward the provision of public services, so railroad managers were allowed few opportunities for corrective action.

[20] *Chicago Tribune*, April 23, 1932; and September 3, 1932.

[21] *Chicago Tribune*, April 29, 1935.

[22] *Chicago Tribune*, March 29, 1933.

[23] *Chicago Tribune*, March 30, 1935, and April 13, 15, and 16, 1935.

[24] *Chicago Tribune*, May 30, 1935.

[25] Chicago Union Station is actually located in the center of Route 66, with eastbound highway traffic on Jackson Street and westbound traffic on Adams.

[26] *Chicago Tribune*, December 3, 1935. The new train was owned by the Baltimore and Ohio, which had purchased the Alton. The innovative nature of the design was underscored by a equipment-related derailment just south of Union Station within months of its arrival.

[27] Annual reports of the Chicago Union Station Company for the years ended December 31, 1925 and 1942. With the generous help of Elmer Passow of the Illinois Railway Museum, the author obtained copies of annual reports originally owned by A.B. Olson, Valuation Engineer for the company, which contain unpublished statistical addenda.

[28] *Chicago Tribune*, April 24, 1942.

[29] *Chicago Tribune*, March 24, 1940.

[30] *Chicago Tribune*, July 22, 1936.

[31] Charles F. Murphy, *Oral History of Charles F. Murphy as Told to Carter Manning* (unpublished manuscript), Chicago Architects Oral History Project, Burnham Library, Art Institute of Chicago (2003.), 36. Research by Dennis McClendon suggests this event occurred well after the Illinois General Assembly allowed air rights in 1922. The Illinois Commerce Commission approval for air rights came in 1927. Nevertheless, this first-person account is a window into the way business was done during the period.

[32] Chicago Union Station Company, *Annual Report for the Year Ended December 31, 1941* (Chicago: Chicago Union Station Company, 1942).

[33] The original design called for a gigantic sphinx over each of these entrances, but its execution proved to be too expensive.

[34] Carl W. Condit, Chicago *1930–70: Building, Planning and Urban Technology* (Chicago: University of Chicago Press, 1974). 121–122.

[35] *Chicago Tribune*, November 10, 1932, and February 19, 1941. The city was prescient about the Post Office Department's intent. When it attempted to build the Congress Street Bridge in 1941, the Post Office Department formally protested. It had been using the space as truck storage.

[36] *Chicago Tribune*, May 1, 1931, and October 14, 1932. Blaine's main objection was that railroad freight rates were, in theory, determined by allowing a return on the value of their property. Artificial inflation of air-rights values would, in his mind, lead to higher transportation charges.

[37] *Chicago Tribune*, July 10, 1932; September 1, 1932; and November 10, 1932.

[38] Edward Bennett, diary, January 22, 1931.

[39] Annual reports of the Chicago Union Station Company for the years ended December 31, 1930 and 1933.

[40] The decline of the area was hastened by a 1922 fire that destroyed a dozen buildings. The fire's progress was stopped by the Burlington Building, which had seven of its fifteen floors of railroad office consumed. It was rebuilt at the cost of $1 million. Few, if any, of the burnt area's other structures were rebuilt in kind.

[41] Nearly all of these had been so-called tied houses, a saloon that carried only one brand of beer in return for financial guarantees and fixtures provided by the brewer. Guarantees comforted landlords that their tenants could pay the rent. Prohibition did not stop the sale of beer at any of these establishments, although the bar typically moved to a discreet back room. However, the tie between legitimate brewers and the taverns was broken and this eliminated the guarantees enjoyed by the landlords. Because the buildings' income streams were riskier, property values tumbled.

[42] Charles F. Murphy, *Oral History*.

[43] Paul Francis Barrett, *Mass Transit, the Automobile, and Public Policy in Chicago, 1900–1930* (Chicago: University of Illinois at Chicago Circle, 1976), 123–124.

[44] Sennott, "Forever Inadequate," 54.

[45] Barrett, *Mass Transit*.

[46] Sennott, "Forever Inadequate," 60.

[47] The city of Chicago then had more inhabitants than 38 of the 48 states. In terms of annual budget, it was the fourth largest governmental entity after the US government, New York State, and New York City. The State of Illinois (including only expenditures by the state government) ranked thirteenth, but it jealously guarded its control over the city. For example, state legislative districts within the city had twice the population of their downstate counterparts, a deliberate dilution of the one-man-one-vote principle.

[48] Lepawsky, Albert, *Home Rule for Metropolitan Chicago* (Chicago: University of Chicago Press, 1935), 11. By a 1904 amendment to the Illinois Constitution, the state legislature could pass laws specific to the city of Chicago, abrogating many of the powers of the city council.

[49] *Chicago Tribune*, May 23, 1922.

[50] *Chicago Tribune*, July 10, 1931.

[51] City Council Committee on Railway Terminals, *The Railway Passenger Terminal Problem at Chicago*, 108.

[52] Ibid., 59. The Alton actually would have been a disproportionate winner from Noonan's proposal, as it would have gained coach and engine facilities next to the new terminal. Its existing coach yard was 8.66 miles from Union Station, but this new yard would shave the distance to 1.67 miles for a savings of 733 coach miles daily—the greatest savings of any of the thirteen roads to go into the new terminal, despite being fourth in the number of coaches to be operated into the proposed facility. The New York Central operated 26 locomotives and 250 coaches daily on its trains to the Alton's 14 locomotives and 105 coaches, but the former had facilities only 4.0 miles from LaSalle Street. The Nickel Plate had the most remote yard, at 11.35 miles from its terminal.

[53] *Chicago Tribune*, October 10, 1930, and February 4, 1932.

[54] *Chicago Tribune*, May 20, 1932. Noonan proved flexible as to location. Despite detailed plans for a new terminal at Randolph Street, the objection of the Illinois Central caused him to shift the site of the new station to Roosevelt Road and Michigan Avenue, where the IC had an obligation under city ordinance to build a new terminal. Noonan was less sympathetic to the plan of Union Station's Joshua D'Esposito, who

proposed a new joint terminal at Roosevelt between State and Clark Streets.

[55] The city was once again near the debt cap imbedded in the Illinois Municipal Code. Municipal finance principles currently used apply a cap to debt supported by a property tax levy, not to revenue bonds. Debt repaid from project revenues is not an obligation backed by the city's full faith and credit, but this concept was not generally accepted in Illinois until the 1950s. The prohibition on use of debt issued by a local government to aid private enterprises may seem an entirely separate issue, but it relates to which debts are allowable under the cap. In the end, both leases and revenue-supported bonds were not considered debt under the municipal code.

[56] Lepawsky, *Home Rule*, 94. The moratorium kept tens of thousands of Chicagoans from losing their property to a sheriff's sale, but its immediate result was a financial crisis for local government. By 1932 the Chicago Board of Education was so strapped for money that it "paid" its teachers with checks preprinted with "NSF," standing for Not Sufficient Funds. It thus instructed banks not to cash them. The Sanitary District was so desperate that it tried to sell its main channel, including the Chicago River, to the federal government.

[57] *Chicago Tribune*, December 24, 1936, and June 29, 1938. Economic conditions were not consistently depressed and were strong enough in 1937 that railroad workers got a wage boost. The following year the railroads rescinded this increase and more.

[58] *Chicago Tribune*, November 12, 1941; May 17, 1942; January 1 and January 13, 1943. When the depot opened in 1925, there were only five information clerks. Staff grew because a telephone reservation system prompted the closing of numerous outlying city ticket offices.

[59] *Chicago Tribune*, February 13, 1943.

[60] *Chicago Tribune*, June 17, 1942, and September 7, 1942.

[61] *Chicago Tribune*, July 16, 1945.

[62] *Chicago Tribune*, August 13, 1944; February 20, 1945; March 13, 1945; and April 26, 1945

CHAPTER 8

[1] The postwar planning process actually began in October 1946, when a committee of railway officials met Mayor Kelly to discuss options for relocating freight and passenger terminals. They seem to have been more interested in new freight houses, since existing facilities were better suited to teaming than modern trucks. While the newspapers declared the railroads open to three different station plans, they were variants of an enlarged Central Station and a combined Dearborn, LaSalle, and Grand Central depot located south of the loop. See Robert Howard, "New Loop Rail Terminal," *Chicago Daily Tribune*, October 10, 1946.

[2] Albert Lepawsky, *Home Rule for Metropolitan Chicago* (Chicago: University of Chicago Press, 1935). Like taxpayers everywhere, Chicagoans never willingly supported higher levies, but the rates associated with repayment of war debt somewhat inured citizens to rising taxes. The astute reader may well ask how taxes rose dramatically when the Illinois municipal code capped them. Several factors drove taxes higher, but the primary cause was a series of adjustments to the state municipal code that allowed for the escalation. Illinois property tax rates were determined by the Juul Law, an archaic patchwork of legislation. The Juul Law applied a complex algorithm to determine the tax rate used by every fund of every municipality, agency, and governmental unit. In addition, it should be recalled that the tax levy may stay the same, but how it is distributed to property owners is a separate calculation. The decline in downtown commercial property values shifted the tax burden to others, including the station company. Finally, taxes on railroad property were a function of the value of the entire railroad. Since the postwar value of the rail lines was a function of prior years' earning capacity, property tax growth reflected wartime profits.

[3] "Remarks of Chairman Nathaniel Owings," *Chicago Tribune*, January 1, 1950.

[4] As with earlier periods, the plans recounted here represent a fraction of the proposals floated during the period. Depending on how they are tabulated, there were dozens of proposals for terminal consolidations. In some cases they were simply op-ed pieces, the work of architectural sketch clubs, real estate promotions, political diatribes, or similar outsider proposals. In others they were the work of the various railroads, industry merger studies, regulatory discussions, or more ambitious engineering and architectural plans by the interested parties. I have tried to include the most important of these studies as well as to give a flavor of the varying pressures on the station owners.

[5] Chicago Plan Commission, *A Further Report by the Chicago Plan Commission: South Side Railroad Passenger Terminal* (Chicago: Chicago Plan Commission, October 1940). The report stated that "the opportunity for redevelopment south of Van Buren Street exists because . . . in few cities is there such a precipitous descent in land values in a short distance as there is

from the $23,000 assessed value on State at Adams to $500 a front foot at East Balbo Avenue, a distance of five short blocks" (23). While the report suggested that terminal consolidation was the cure for this anomaly, it also noted that "as it stands today there appears to be no further need for new stores, new offices or new wholesale buildings in the Chicago central business district."

[6] "Vast Railroad Improvement Forecast Soon," *Chicago Tribune*, December 17, 1945.

[7] The South Side Planning Board was primarily interested in slum clearance and wanted the land to build housing (or to relocate industries to provide housing elsewhere). Chicago had 1,178,000 families, but only 906,000 units of housing. The SSPB was somewhat ahead of its time, as federal legislation to fund public housing was not passed until July 1949.

[8] *Railway Age*, 128:6 (1950): 39–42.

[9] If the new authority paid market price for its terminal, it actually reversed the proposition. The railroad selling land would be the first to cash out its holdings.

[10] Chicago Plan Commission, *Report on the South Side Consolidated Railroad Terminal Problem* (Chicago: Chicago Plan Commission, September 8, 1949). The IC, for example, revisited its Twelfth Street terminal, showing a twenty-track terminal located on the east side of the tracks fronting Michigan Avenue. Except for a concourse above the tracks, the platforms and tracks would be below grade extending eastward to Lake Shore Drive.

[11] *Chicago Tribune*, January 1, 1946.

[12] Raymond Loewy, *Chicago Union Station Company: Proposed Modernization of Fred Harvey Concessions and Station Facilities* (Chicago: Raymond Loewy Associates, April 21, 1949). The Pennsylvania Railroad was one of Loewy's largest accounts. He streamlined their steam and electric locomotives, provided tasteful decor for the interior or their trains, and applied his stylistic touch to items as mundane as garbage cans.

[13] "ICC Suspends Pennsy Plea for Rate Hike," *Chicago Tribune*, January 28, 1946. The IC carried 145,000 commuters; the C&NW 65,000. Even the North Shore, which used the loop "L" line, carried 50,000, considerably more than all Union Station carriers.

[14] "Harvey Opens Union Station Shop Center," *Chicago Tribune*, February 21, 1956.

[15] The city of Chicago first gained the ability to zone property by state legislation passed in 1921. April 16, 1923 saw a comprehensive zoning ordinance enacted by the city. The ordinance categorized all land within the city by permitted building types, but it was not drafted with particular care. By 1942, when it was rewritten, zoning regulations had been amended over 1,400 times, a number over and above the thousands of individual variances allowed.

[16] If readers have difficulty distinguishing between "market rate" and "fair use value," they pinpoint a major flaw in this program.

[17] Ross Miller, *Here's the Deal: the Buying and Selling of a Great American City* (New York: Alfred A. Knopf, 1996), 56.

[18] R. Stephen Sennott, "'Forever Inadequate to the Rising Stream': Dream Cities, Automobiles and Urban Street Mobility in Central Chicago," in *Chicago Architecture and Design, 1923–1993*, ed. John Zukowsky (Chicago: Art Institute of Chicago, 1993), 53–74. Like the city, the park district was limited in the amount of debt it could incur, and the taxes it could levy to support debt were capped. While parking lots on existing landholding required less expenditure, garages were financed by municipal revenue bonds authorized under specific state statutes. Such facilities had to be supported by parking fees, which underscored their similarity to and competition with privately financed garages even if the competitive linkage to commuter rail was less obvious. Nevertheless, those fees were a subsidy to a competing mode that was concentrated in the downtown area, the district best served by radiating commuter lines.

[19] The city's desire to place its expressways along rail lines may have been more than an attempt to use existing transportation corridors. As suggested by Cohen and Taylor, the expressway system in Chicago was used to reinforce existing racial and ethnic boundaries between neighborhoods. Adam Cohen and Elizabeth Taylor, *American Pharaoh: Mayor Richard J. Daley* (Boston: Back Bay Books, 2001).

[20] Between 1945 and 1970 the Chicago area increased its industrial capacity, but growth was confined to the suburbs, where land for single-story factories was plentiful and taxes were lower. While this era is often rightfully regarded as the genesis of suburbia, suburbanization actually began with an opposite trend. The population of the city of Chicago grew by 224,000 between 1940 and 1950, nearly the entire population of such cities as Syracuse (221,000), Dayton (224,000), Omaha (251,000), or Miami (249,000). Since the city boundaries were unchanged, population density increased by 1,100 persons per square mile. The rise was highly concentrated, however, with nearly all gains registered in the black ghettos in the southern and western parts of the city. Restrictive housing practices pushed density levels in those areas to unprecedented heights. The movement of the white population of Chicago outward to cheaper, attractive tract housing near their relocated factory jobs occurred with something of a delay. Whites continued to dominate the clerical jobs of the business district, and because they were the primary suburban population they remained the primary users of Union Station. Thus, the change in the city's racial composition was not reflected in

suburban train ridership during the 1950s. To a great extent, racial divisions between city and suburb remain fifty years later.

21 The first expressway segment actually completed was on Chicago's far South Side between 159th Street and the Indiana state line, but its November 1, 1950 opening had little impact on downtown Chicago. The first open segment of the Eden Expressway stretched from the northwest side of Chicago to the border of Cook and Lake Counties. It opened in September 1952; the Congress Expressway was already under construction. These projects predated the 1956 passage of the Interstate Highway Act.

22 "Fair Authority Hears Foes of Lake Front Site: Plan for Union Station Air Rights," *Chicago Tribune*, July 3, 1956; "Realtors Urge Union Station Exposition Site," *Chicago Tribune*, August 2, 1956.

23 "Union Station Offers Space to Airlines," *Chicago Tribune*, December 13, 1956; "Site for an Air Terminal," *Chicago Tribune*, December 15, 1956.

24 Cohen and Taylor, *American Pharaoh*, 92. Daley, then head of Chicago's Democratic Central Committee, won election against the reform minded but ineffectual Martin Kennelly in 1955. Kennelly had eliminated twelve thousand patronage jobs by instituting civil service reforms; Daley set to work bringing all power back to the Machine. In this, he was extremely successful; the pinnacle of Machine power came in the late 1950s.

25 Tax-exempt industrial revenue bonds became attractive as corporate income tax rates rose. While the city is only a conduit for financing, its participation at an early stage in the financing of projects allows it to work with the developer on project details that would otherwise be outside its purview.

26 The annual appropriation feature is the key, since the right of future legislators not to pay the lease makes it short term in nature under state statute. None of the local entities has failed to appropriate,

however, since one default would effectively close the door on this type of finance for the lessee.

27 Complete independence for the city had to await the 1970 rewriting of the Illinois constitution, when all cities in the state with more than 25,000 in population were given "home rule powers." Among other things, this removed nearly all limitations on the issuance of debt or the implementation of taxes.

28 "Council Group Backs U. of I. City Branch," *Chicago Tribune*, March 23, 1959; *Chicago Tribune*, May 25, 1959.

29 "Depot Merger Plan Moves Ahead," *Chicago Tribune*, September 4, 1958.

30 "Symes Plan Backer Cites Need," *Chicago Tribune*, April 9, 1956; "Expressway Expand Zone of Commuting," *Chicago Tribune*, May 15, 1958.

31 "Sweeping Redevelopment of Railroads," *Chicago American*, March 26, 1959; *Chicago Tribune*, May 25, 26, and 27, 1959.

32 *Chicago Tribune*, May 27 and 28, 1959, and June 2, 1959.

33 *Chicago Tribune*, July 10, 1959, and December 5, 1959.

34 *Chicago Tribune*, March 3, 1960.

35 *Chicago Tribune*, May 2, 1960, and September 24 and 28, 1960

36 City of Chicago, Department of Planning and Development, *Community Development Commission Staff Report* (Chicago: Department of Planning and Development) February 29, 2000.

37 *Chicago Tribune*, July 19 and 20, 1961; November 17, 1961; and January 14, 1962

38 *Chicago Tribune*, March 5, 1962.

39 Development was helped by a decline in commercial property tax rates initiated by railroad tax attorneys. Because they owned so much property in so many cities, counties, and townships, the railroads retained specialized and skilled legal service to fight their tax bills. By contesting the tax caps as well as

the assessed value of the property, the railroads kept everyone's tax bill down. For one brief moment, the railroads had their revenge on the tax collectors. In 1964, John Crane of the Cook County Clerk's Office died unexpectedly. For forty years, he had maintained the Juul Law tax calculations on pasteboard cards in his office. His successor lacked the experience to reconstruct the proper calculations, and the principal attorney who handled railroad tax claims in Cook County was hired to use his firm's records to provide guidance for all major funds of Cook County municipalities. It should not have been a surprise, but the new calculations yielded much lower taxes throughout Cook County.

40 Memo from S. J. Cooley, September 20, 1969, John Barriger Collection, St. Louis Mercantile Library, File 107.7.

41 *Chicago Tribune*, April 30, 1963, and May 16, 1963.

42 Carl Condit, Carl, Chicago *1930–70: Building, Planning and Urban Technology* (Chicago: University of Chicago Press, 1974), 90.

43 Tom Maday and Sam Lander, *Great Chicago Stories* (Chicago: Two Press Publishing, 1994), 44–46.

44 Chicago Union Station Company, press release, 1991.

45 Letter from EJS to R. F. Kratochiwill, September 3, 1970, John Barriger Collection, St. Louis Mercantile Library, File 107.7.

46 Thomas H. Ploss, *The Nation Pays Again: The Demise of the Milwaukee Road 1928–1986* (Chicago: Thomas H. Ploss, 1986), 1.

47 Joseph R. Daughen and Peter Binzen, *The Wreck of the Penn Central* (New York: Mentor, 1973), 213.

48 Contract between Chicago Union Station Company and Prophet Foods, John Barriger Collection, St. Louis Mercantile Library, File 107.7.

49 Chicago Union Station Company, *Annual Reports*, December 31, 1965, to December 31, 1967.

Bonded debt had declined another $17 million dollars; still, the company had $45 million in bonds and another $21 million due to its owners.

[50] *Chicago Tribune*, July 10, 1966; September 11, 1967; and October 1, 1967.

[51] Ploss, *The Nation Pays Again* 85.

[52] Harold A. Edmondson, ed., *Journey to Amtrak: The Year History Rode the Passenger Train* (Milwaukee: Kalmbach Books, 1972).

[53] The federal government was also given voting stock equal to its aggregate subsidies. This ensured that railroad voting rights in the company would be minor and that they would get smaller with each succeeding year.

[54] *Chicago Tribune*, April 24, 1972.

[55] *Chicago Tribune*, April 20, 1974.

[56] Unsigned memorandum, February 9, 1979. John Barriger Papers Collection, St. Louis Mercantile Library, File 107.7.

[57] *Chicago Tribune*, September 7, 1975, and September 30, 1978.

[58] Two commuter trains into Union Station never benefited from Regional Transportation Authority subsidies. The Penn Central Transportation Company ran two trains a day for the forty-four miles to and from Valparaiso, Indiana. As an interstate operation, the RTA could not support it, but its operations were belatedly and briefly assumed by Amtrak until 1990, when the last run occurred.

[59] *Chicago Tribune*, December 19, 1975.

[60] *Chicago Tribune*, June 3, 1976.

[61] *Chicago Tribune* January 1, 1978, and February 26, 1980.

[62] *Chicago Tribune*, June 29, 1980.

[63] *Chicago Tribune*, August 21, 1982, and September 3 and 16, 1982.

[64] Letter from Isham, Lincoln and Beale, June 27, 1983. John Barriger Library Milwaukee Road Collection, St. Louis Mercantile Library, Box B6–467.

[65] *Chicago Tribune*, January 13, 1984, and May 6, 1984.

[66] An unsolicited call from the Field Museum said that it had been donated former waiting room benches from the station years before. Amtrak reacquired them for its renovation project. However, they did not match Union Station's other benches. It is not certain which depot they originally graced, but Amtrak now uses them in a Florida waiting room.

[67] Burnham, of course, had died a decade before the genesis of Union Station as an office tower. Wislow and Lagrange's deliberate misattribution of Peirce Anderson's design reflected the power of Daniel Burnham as a brand name.

[68] Because modern building techniques use considerably lighter materials than those originally envisioned for this site, the expensive new caissons system this called for would seem excessive. The watchdog Landmarks Preservation Council of Illinois took its criticism of the development plan seriously enough to present an alternative designed to save the waiting room from vivisection. However, the cantilevered construction required by this plan would be expensive and the resulting office tower would have a floor layout somewhat at variance with rental standards. Since the Chicago Landmark Commission had already struck a deal with the developer, at the time there seemed little the not-for-profit preservation group could do to intervene.

[69] *Crain's Chicago Business*, April 16, 1990.

[70] More to the point, the restaurants' income stream secured the loan used to reconstruct this portion of the station. The only criticism of this space is that patrons can only reach it by escalator. Elevators serving the mezzanine were available for freight, but not passengers. This oversight was later corrected. Had the renovation been completed a year later, it would have had to comply with the Americans with Disabilities Act and access would have had to be greatly improved.

[71] The rationale for this arrangement was pointed out by Charles Luna, an Amtrak board member and chairman of United Transportation Union. He believed that passengers need the reassurance of actually seeing the departure gate. In the previous arrangement expectant riders queued next to their departure gate, fearing that they would miss announcements made over the notoriously echoing public address system.

[72] *Chicago Tribune*, March 27, 1988.

[73] *Chicago Tribune*, September 26, 1900.

[74] *Chicago Tribune*, September 26, 1990.

[75] *Chicago Tribune*, July 31, 1994.

[76] Additional projects were also proposed to increase access to Union Station. A major project known as the "downtown circulator" trolley system would have included a station on Canal Street accessible from the interior of the depot. After extensive and expensive engineering development, the light rail system was stillborn, the victim of political infighting between Chicago's Mayor Richard M. Daley and Illinois' Governor Jim Edgar. Another plan, an underground pedestrian walkway that would have used an old streetcar tunnel under the Chicago River to connect with the Sears Tower, has been abandoned for lack of funding.

[77] *Chicago Tribune*, January 22, 1999.

[78] *Chicago Tribune*, August 3, 1994

[79] *Chicago Tribune*, September 29, 2004.

[80] *Engineering News Record*, August 31, 1989, 34–35.

[81] City of Chicago, *The Canal/Congress Tax Increment Financing Redevelopment Project and Plan* (Chicago: City of Chicago, August 11, 1998), 24.

[82] Community Development Commission of the City of Chicago, Resolution 07-CDC-41.

[83] *Chicago Tribune*, April 19, 2007, and June 3, 2007

[84] Chicago Department of Planning and Development, *Redevelopment Agreement for 444 W. Jackson* (Chicago: Department of Planning and Development), 11.

85 *Chicago Sun Times*, February 8, 2002, and July 25, 2002.

86 *Chicago Sun Times*, August 2, 2005, and December 28, 2005.

87 *Chicago Sun Times*, February 15, 2005.

88 LaSalle Street Station's headhouse, the last of the near South Side depots, was demolished in the 1970s but its tracks continue to be used for suburban train service. Removing the southwest service to this location will require the construction of a new connecting track.

89 Chicago Department of Planning and Development, *Central Area Action Plan* (Chicago: Department of Planning and Development), 2, 2–24.

90 *Chicago Journal*, March 18, 2010.

91 Amtrak, news release, June 16, 2010.

92 *Chicago Tribune*, August 7, 2010.

93 Jeffery Sriver, Chicago Department of Transportation, interviewed by the author, March 13, 2015.

94 David Phillips TranSystems, interviewed by the author, February 4, 2015; Union Station Master Plan, unionstationmp.org.

95 Blair Kamin, "Union Station Plans Fail to Live up to Lofty Rhetoric," *Chicago Tribune*, May 25, 2017.

BIBLIOGRAPHY

MANUSCRIPT COLLECTIONS

Bion Arnold Papers. New York Public Library.

Chicago City Council, Chicago Municipal Reference Collection of the Chicago Public Library. Harold Washington Library.

Chicago City Council Proceedings. Illinois State Archives at Northeastern Illinois University Library, Chicago.

Chicago, Burlington and Quincy Archives. Newberry Library, Chicago.

Chicago, Milwaukee, St. Paul and Pacific Collection. John Barriger Collection. St. Louis Mercantile Library.

Daniel H. Burnham. Diaries. Burnham Library. Art Institute of Chicago.

D. H. Burnham and Company. Letterpress Books. Burnham Library. Art Institute of Chicago.

Edward H. Bennett Papers. Burnham Library. Art Institute of Chicago.

Graff Collection. Newberry Library. Chicago.

Illinois Central Railroad Archives. Newberry Library. Chicago.

Pennsylvania Railroad Archives. Hagely Museum and Library. Wilmington, DE.

William Butler Ogden Papers. Chicago Historical Society.

BOOKS, ARTICLES, AND MANUSCRIPTS

Abbot, Carl. *The Location of Railroad Passenger Depots in Chicago and St. Louis.* Bulletin 120. Railway and Locomotive Historical Society, April 1969, 31–47.

Andreas, Alfred T. *History of Chicago from the Earliest Period to the Present Time.* Chicago: A. T. Andreas, 1885.

Arnold, Bion J. *Report on the Re-Arrangement and Development of the Steam Railroad Terminals of the City of Chicago.* Chicago: Citizens' Terminal Plan Committee of Chicago, November 18, 1913.

Ash, Fred. "A Lakefront Excursion." *Rail and Wire* (Illinois Railway Museum), 193 (January 2002).

Atwood, Darwin. Diary. Chicago Historical Society. Briggs and Mitchell Family Papers, 1863.

Bailey, Robert F., ed. *Chicago City Council Proceedings, 1833–1871: An Inventory.* Springfield: Illinois State Archives, 1987.

Barrett, Paul Francis. *Mass Transit, the Automobile, and Public Policy in Chicago, 1900–1930.* Chicago: University of Illinois at Chicago Circle Press, 1976.

Bennett, Edward. Papers. Burnham Library of the Art Institute of Chicago.

Berger, Miles L. *They Built Chicago: Entrepreneurs Who Shaped A Great City's Architecture.* Chicago: Bonus Books, 1992.

Bilas, Myron M. *Hub City: A Look at Chicago's Intercity Passenger Train Operation in the Mid-1940's* Chicago: Chicago Chapter National Railway Historical Society, 1993.

Bodman, Albert Holmes. *Bodman's Hand-Book of Chicago.* Chicago: Charles Shober, 1854.

Bruegmann, Robert. *The Architects and the City—Holabird and Roche of Chicago, 1880–1918.* Chicago: University of Chicago Press, 1997.

Bruns, James H. *Mail on the Move* Polos, IL: Transportation Trails, 1992.

Burgess, George H. and Kennedy, Miles C., *Centennial History of the Pennsylvania Railroad Company.* Philadelphia: Pennsylvania Railroad Company, 1949.

Burnham, Daniel H. and Bennett, Edward. *Plan of Chicago.* Chicago: Commercial Club, 1909.

"Busiest Railway Crossing is No More." *Railway Age* (August 15, 1931): 241–251

Butler, Charles. Unpublished monograph. William Butler Ogden papers, Chicago History Museum.

Carbutt, John. *Biographical Sketch of the Leading Men of Chicago.* Chicago: Wilson & St. Clair, 1868.

Cary, John W. *The Organization and History of The Chicago, Milwaukee & St. Paul Railway Company.* Milwaukee: Cramer, Aikens, & Cramer, 1892.

Chandler, Alfred Dupont. *The Visible Hand: The Managerial Revolution in American Business.* Cambridge, MA: The Belknap Press of Harvard University Press, 1977.

Chappell, Sally A. Kitt. *Architecture and Planning of Graham Anderson Probst & White, 1912–1936.* Chicago: University of Chicago Press, 1992.

———. "Railroad Terminals and Urban Life: Examples in the Work of Graham, Anderson, Probst & White," *Threshold: Journal of the School of Architecture.* Chicago: University of Illinois at Chicago, 1985, 36–49.

Chicago and Alton Railroad Company. *Third Annual Report of the President and Directors for the Year Ended December 31, 1865.* Chicago: Chicago and Alton Railroad Company, 1866.

Chicago & Pacific Railroad. Bulletin 113, Railway and Locomotive Historical Society, October 1965, 83–85.

Chicago Area Transportation Study. *Downtown Commuter Station Access.* Chicago: Chicago Area Transportation Study, December 1989.

Chicago Association of Commerce. *Report of the Committee of Investigation on Smoke Abatement and Electrification of Railway Terminals.* Chicago: Chicago Association of Commerce, 1915.

Chicago Burlington and Quincy Railroad. *How the Greyhounds of the Burlington Beat the Rising Sun.* Chicago: Chicago Burlington and Quincy Railroad, 1899.

Chicago Home Rule Commission. *Modernizing a City Government.* Chicago: University of Chicago Press, 1915.

Chicago Plan Commission. *A Further Report by the Chicago Plan Commission: South Side Railroad Passenger Terminal.* Chicago: Chicago Plan Commission, October 1940.

———. *Report on the South Side Consolidated Railroad Terminal Problem.* Chicago: Chicago Plan Commission, September 8, 1949.

Chicago Railway Terminal Commission, *The Chicago Railway Terminal Problem, 1892.* Chicago: Chicago Railway Terminal Commission, 1892.

———. *Report of John F. Wallace, Chairman.* Chicago: Chicago Railway Terminal Commission, 1921.

Chicago Times. *New Chicago: A Full Review of Reconstruction, for the Year.* Chicago: Horton and Leonard, 1872.

Churella, Albert. *The Pennsylvania Railroad: Building an Empire, 1846–1917.* Vol. I. Philadelphia: University of Pennsylvania Press, 2013.

City Club of Chicago. *The Railway Terminal Problem of Chicago.* Chicago: University of Chicago Press, 1913.

City Council Committee on Coordination of Chicago Terminals. *The Freight Traffic of the Chicago Terminal District.* Chicago: City of Chicago, 1927.

City Council Committee on Railway Terminals. *Preliminary Report.* Chicago: City Council Committee on Railway Terminals, March 29, 1915.

———. *The Railway Passenger Terminal Problem at Chicago.* Chicago: City Council Committee on Railway Terminals, 1933.

———. *The Straightening of the Chicago River, Chicago.* Chicago: City Council Committee on Railway Terminals, 1926.

City of Chicago Department of Planning and Development. *Community Development Commission Staff Report.* Chicago: Department of Planning and Development, February 29, 2000.

———. *The Canal/Congress Tax Increment Financing Redevelopment Project Plan*, Chicago: Department of Planning and Development, August 11, 1998.

Cohen, Adam and Taylor, Elizabeth. *American Pharaoh: Mayor Richard J. Daley.* Boston: Back Bay Books, 2001.

Cohen, Andrew Wender, "*The Building Trades, Violence, and the Laws in Chicago: 1900–1920,*" Research Seminar Paper #72, presented at the Center for the History of Business, Technology and Society, Hagely Museum and Library, May 11, 2000.

———. *The Racketeers' Progress: Chicago and the Struggle for the Modern American Economy 1900–1940.* Cambridge: Cambridge University Press, 2004.

Committee on Local Transportation of the City Council. *Electrification of Railway Terminals* Chicago: Committee on Local Transportation of the City Council, 1908

Condit, Carl W. *The Chicago School of Architecture.* Chicago: University of Chicago Press, 1964.

———. *Chicago 1910–29: Building, Planning and Urban Technology.* Chicago University of Chicago Press, 1973.

———. *Chicago 1930–70: Building, Planning and Urban Technology.* Chicago: University of Chicago Press, 1974.

———. *American Building: Materials and Techniques from the Beginning of the Colonial Settlements to the Present.* Chicago: University of Chicago Press, 1969.

Corporate History of the Chicago Union Station Company: 1913–1916. Chicago: Chicago Union Station Company, 1925.

Cronon, William. *Nature's Metropolis: Chicago and the Great West*. New York: W.W. Norton & Company, 1991.

Currey, J. Seymore. *Manufacturing and Wholesale Industries of Chicago*. Chicago: Poole Brothers, 1918.

Daughen, Joseph R. and Binzen, Peter. *The Wreck of the Penn Central*. New York: Mentor, 1973.

Davis, Patricia Talbot. *End of the Line: Alexander J. Cassatt and the Pennsylvania Railroad*. New York: Neale Watson Academic Publications, 1978.

Delano, Frederic A. "Address to the Chicago Real Estate Board." Presentation to the Chicago Real Estate Board, Chicago, September 10, 1904.

———. *Chicago Railway Terminals: A Suggested Solution of the Problems*. Chicago: R. R. Donnelley and Sons, 1904.

Derleth, August. *The Milwaukee Road: Its First Hundred Years*. New York: Creative Age Press, 1948.

DeRouin, Edward M.. *Chicago Union Station: A Look at its History and Operations Before Amtrak*. Elmhurst, IL: Pixels Publishing, 2003.

———. *The Pennsy in Chicago*. LaFox, IL: Pixels Publishing, 2009.

D'Esposito, Joshua. "Foundation Tests by the Chicago Union Station Company." *Journal of the Western Society of Engineers* 29 (February 1924), 33–44.

Donovan, Frank P. "Chicago's Stations: Gates to Everywhere." *Trains* (August 1948): 24–25.

Droege, John A. *Passenger Terminals and Trains*. Milwaukee: Kalmbach Publications, 1969.

Duis, Perry R. *Challenging Chicago: Coping with Everyday Life, 1837–1920*. Urbana: University of Illinois Press, 1998.

Duis, Perry R. and Holt, Glen E. "The Midwestern Gate to the New World." *Chicago* (May 1981).

Edmondson, Harold A., ed. *Journey to Amtrak: The Year History Rode the Passenger Train*. Milwaukee: Kalmbach Books, 1972.

Eggert, Gerald G. *Railroad Labor Disputes: The Beginning of Federal Strike Policy*. Ann Arbor: University of Michigan Press, 1967.

Einhorn, Robin L. *Property Rules: Political Economy in Chicago, 1833–1872*. Chicago: University of Chicago Press, 2001.

Fisher, Glenn W. and Fairbanks, Robert P. *Illinois Municipal Finance: A Political and Economic Analysis*. Urbana: University of Illinois Press, 1968.

Flinn, John H. The Handbook of *Chicago Biography*. Chicago. The Standard Guide, 1893.

———. *History of the Chicago Police*. Montclair, NJ: Patterson Smith, 1973.

Gartner, Michael, ed., *Riding the Pennsy to Ruin*. Princeton, NJ: Dow Jones Books, 1971,

Glendinning, Gene. *The Chicago and Alton Railroad: The Only Way*. DeKalb: Northern Illinois University Press, 2002.

Godfrey, Aaron Austin. *Government Operation of the Railroads: 1918–1920*. Austin, TX: San Felipe Press, 1974.

Golden, James Reed. *Investment Behavior by United States Railroads, 1870–1914*. New York: Arno Press, 1975.

Graham, Anderson, Probst & White. *The Architectural Work of Graham Anderson Probst & White*. London: B.T. Batsford, 1933.

———. *Specifications for the Union Station at Chicago*. Chicago, June 1919.

———. *Specifications for the Completion of the Headhouse and Concourse of the Union Station at Chicago*, Chicago, April 1923.

Graham, Ernest. unpublished diary, Burnham Library of the Art Institute of Chicago.

Grant, H. Roger. *The North Western: A History of the Chicago & North Western Railway System*. DeKalb: Northern Illinois University Press, 1996.

Hansen, Harry. *The Chicago*. The Rivers of America. New York: Farrar and Rhinehart, 1942.

Hapster, Jack, *The Railroad Tycoon Who Built Chicago:A Biography of William B. Ogden*. Carbondale, Southern Illinois University Press, 2009.

Hartley, Robert E. "A Touch of Class: Fred Harvey's Operation at Chicago Union Station." *Journal of Illinois History*, 14:3 (Autumn 2011), 207–224.

Helms, E. A. "Illinois Municipal History since 1870." *Illinois Municipal Review*. 8:1(1928), 9–11.

Hession, Charles H. and Sardy, Hyman. *Ascent to Affluence: A History of American Economic Development*. Boston: Allyn and Bacon, 1969.

Hines, Thomas S. *Burnham of Chicago: Architect and Planner*. Chicago: University of Chicago Press, 1979.

Hinman, Ida. *Biography of Timothy B. Blackstone*. New York: Methodist Book Press, 1917.

Hodes, Barnet. *Essays in Illinois Taxation*. Chicago: Reilly & Lee, 1935. .

Hooker, George Ellsworth. "Through Routes for Chicago's Steam Railroads." Chicago: City Club of Chicago, 1914.

Howe, Frederic C. "The Remaking of the American City," *Harpers Monthly*, July 1913, 186–197.

Hoyt, Homer. *One Hundred Years of Land Values in Chicago*. Chicago: University of Chicago Press, 1933.

"The Hunt Project." *Engineering News* 70 (July–December, 1913): 213–214.

Interstate Commerce Commission. *Railways in the United States in 1902, Part V: State Taxation of Railways.* Washington, DC: Government Printing Office, 1903.

Johnston, Bob. "Chicago's Union Station—Rebirth of a Classic." *Passenger Train Journal* 166 (October 1991), 17–27.

Karamanski, Theodore T. *Rally 'Round the Flag: Chicago and the Civil War.* Chicago: Nelson-Hall Publishers, 1993

Klein, Maury. *Union Pacific: The Rebirth 1894–1969.* New York: Doubleday, 1989.

Lacher, Walter S. "Noteworthy Passenger Terminal Completed at Chicago," *Railway Age,* July 4, 1925.

LaGrange, Lucien. *Union Station Redevelopment.* Chicago: Jones Lang LaSalle, 2006.

Lepawsky, Albert. *Home Rule for Metropolitan Chicago.* Chicago: University of Chicago Press, 1935.

Lind, Alan R. *Chicago Surface Lines: An Illustrated History.* Park Forest, IL: Transport History Press, 1974.

Loewy, Raymond. *Chicago Union Station Company: Proposed Modernization of Fred Harvey Concessions and Station Facilities.* Chicago: Raymond Loewy Associates, April 21, 1949.

Lohan, Dirk and LaMotte, John. *Chicago's Post Office: A Common Sense Proposal for a Tight City Budget.* Chicago: Lohan Associates, January 1992.

Long, Charles. "The Pioneer and the Lincoln Funeral Train." *Railroad History* 186 (Spring 2002). 88–99.

Maday, Tom. *Great Chicago Stories.* Chicago: Two Press Publishing, 1994.

Martin, Albro. *Enterprise Denied: Origins of the Decline of American Railroads, 1897–1917.* New York: Columbia University Press, 1971.

Mayer, Harold M. *Chicago: City of Decisions.* Chicago: Geographic Society of Chicago, 1954.

McIlvaine, Mabel. *Reminiscences of Chicago During the Civil War.* New York: Citadel Press, 1967.

McLear, Patrick E. "William Butler Ogden: A Chicago Promoter in the Speculative Era and the Panic of 1837." *Journal of the Illinois State Historical Society* 70 (1977), 283–291.

Meeks, Carroll L. V. *The Railroad Station: An Architectural History.* New Haven, CT: Yale University Press, 1956.

Meints, Graydon. "Race to Chicago." *Railroad History* 183 (Autumn 2000): 7–29.

Merriner, James L. *Grafters and Goo Goos: Corruption and Reform in Chicago.* Carbondale: Southern Illinois University Press, 2008.

Metropolitan Planning Council. *A Light-Rail Transit System for Chicago's Central Area.* Chicago: Metropolitan Planning Council, December 1989.

Miller, Ross. *Here's the Deal: The Buying and Selling of a Great American City.* New York: Alfred A. Knopf, 1996.

Moffat, Bruce G. *The Chicago Tunnel Story: Exploring the Railroad "Forty Feet Below,"* Bulletin 135. Chicago: Central Electric Railfans' Association, 2001.

———. *The "L"—The Development of Chicago's Rapid Transit System 1888–1932.* Bulletin 131. Chicago: Central Electric Railfans' Association, 1995.

Moody, Walter D. *Wacker's Manual of the Plan of Chicago.* Chicago: Chicago Plan Commission, 1916.

Morgan, David P. *Fast Mail: The First 75 Years; Chicago Burlington and Quincy Railroad.* Chicago: Chicago Burlington and Quincy Railroad, 1959.

Mottier, C. H. "Statement Addressed to the City Planning Advisory Board." September 26, 1946. Chicago Public Library, Municipal Library collection.

Murphy, Charles F. *Oral History of Charles F. Murphy as Told to Carter Manning.* Unpublished manuscript. Chicago Architects Oral History Project, 2003. Burnham Library, Art Institute of Chicago.

Newcomb, Rexford. "The New Chicago Union Station." *Western Architect* 35 (January 1926): 4.

Noonan, Edward J., "Chicago Terminal Situation." *Journal of the Western Society of Engineers* 16 (May 1919), 282–303.

Noonan, Edward J. "Engineer." *Illinois Quest* 1:2, (June 1937), 23–24.

Northeast Illinois Railroad Corporation. *Metra Board Members Inspection Trip of Milwaukee District* (September 30, 1987).

Olson, A. B., *Chicago Union Station Bulletin* 49. Railway and Locomotive Historical Society.

Overton, Richard C.. *Burlington West: A Colonization History of the Burlington Railroad.* Cambridge, MA: Harvard University Press, 1941.

Palmatary, I. T. *A Bird's-Eye View of Chicago.* Chicago: 1857.

Pierce, Bessie Louise. *A History of Chicago.* New York: Alfred A. Knopf, 1940. Vol. 2.

Pinkerton, Allan. *Mass Violence in America: Strikers, Communists, Tramps and Detectives,* 1878. Reprint, New York: Arno Press, 1969.

Ploss, Thomas H. *The Nation Pays Again: The Demise of the Milwaukee Road 1928–1986.* Chicago: Thomas H. Ploss, 1986.

Potter, Janet Green. *Great American Railroad Stations.* New York: John Wiley and Sons, 1996.

Prescott, D. C. *Early Day Railroading From Chicago: A Narration with Some Observations.* Chicago: David B. Clarkson, 1887.

Randall, Frank A. *History of the Development of Building Construction in Chicago.* Urbana: University of Illinois Press, 1949.

Reed, Robert C.. *The Streamline Era.* San Marino, CA: Golden West Books, 1975.

Rennwald, Henry. "Chicago Union Station." *Trains* (March 1944), 4–12.

Roseman, V. S. *Railway Express Agency: An Overview.* Denver: Rocky Mountain Publishing Company, 1992.

Sandborn Fire Insurance Map of Chicago. Teaneck, NJ: Sandborn Map Company, 1869.

Sanders, Craig. *Limiteds, Locals, and Expresses in Indiana 1837–1971.* Bloomington: Indiana University Press, 2003.

Sattley, R. C. "One Central Railway Terminal for Chicago." *Journal of the Western Society of Engineers* (May 1901), 421–454.

Sawislak, Karen. *Smoldering City: Chicagoans and the Great Fire, 1871–1874.* Chicago: University of Chicago Press, 1995.

Schweiterman, Joseph P. *Terminal Town: An Illustrated Guide to Chicago's Airports, Bus Depots, Train Stations, and Steamship Landings 1939–Present.* Lake Forest, IL: Lake Forest College Press, 2014.

Schweiterman, Joseph P. and Caspall, Dana M. *The Politics of Place: A History of Zoning in Chicago.* Chicago: Lake Claremont Press, 2006.

Sennott, R. Stephen. "'Forever Inadequate to the Rising Stream': Dream Cities, Automobiles and Urban Street Mobility in Central Chicago." In *Chicago Architecture and Design, 1923–1993,* edited by John Zukowsky, 53–74. Chicago: Art Institute of Chicago, 1993.

———. "But We Are Not in France: Early Competitions From the Chicago Architectural Sketch Club." *Chicago Architectural Journal* 8 (1989): 12–19.

Smith, Carl. *The Plan of Chicago: Daniel Burnham and the Remaking of the American City.* Chicago: University of Chicago Press, 2006.

Stead, William T. *If Christ Came to Chicago.* Chicago: Laird and Lee, 1894.

Stennett, William H. *Yesterday and Today, A History of the Chicago and North Western Railway System.* Chicago: Chicago Chapter, Railway and Locomotive Historical Society, 1981.

Stowell, David O. *Streets, Railroads and the Great Strike of 1877.* Chicago: University of Chicago Press, 1999.

Strandling, David and Tarr, Joel A. "Environmental Activism and Corporate Response: The Case of the Pennsylvania Railroad and Chicago Smoke Control." *Business History Review* 73 (Winter 1999), 677–704.

Tallmadge, Thomas Eddy. *Architecture in Old Chicago.* Chicago: University of Chicago Press, 1941.

Taylor, George Rogers and Neu, Irene D. *The American Railroad Network: 1861–1890.* Cambridge, MA: Harvard University Press, 1956.

Thompson, J. S. *Chicago, a Strangers and Tourist Guide.* Chicago: Religious Philosophical Publishing Association, 1866.

Usselman, Steven W. *Regulating Railroad Innovation: Business, Technology, and Politics in America, 1840–1920.* Cambridge: Cambridge University Press, 2002.

Wallace, Barbara J. "The Chicago Pneumatic Post." *Illinois Postal Historian* 1:3 (November 1980), 9–19.

Wallace, John F., *Preliminary Report of the Chicago Railway Terminal Commission.* Chicago: Chicago Railway Terminal Commission (March 19, 1915).

Wallis, Richard T. *The Pennsylvania Railroad at Bay: William Riley McKeen and the Terre Haute & Indianapolis Railroad.* Bloomington: Indiana University Press, 2001.

Walker, Samuel C. "Railroad Strike of 1877 in Altoona." *Railway and Locomotive Historical Society Bulletin* 117 (1967) 18–25.

Watt, William J. *The Pennsylvania Railroad in Indiana.* Bloomington: Indiana University Press, 1999.

Weidemann, E. "Some Features of the Structural Design of the Chicago Union Station." *Journal of the Western Society of Engineers* 30 (December 1925), 501–526.

White, James E. *A Life Span and Reminiscence of Railway Mail Service.* Philadelphia: Deemer & Jaisohn, 1910.

White, John R. "Chicago Locomotive Builders." *Railroad History* 122 (April 1970), 52–60.

Young, David M. *Chicago Transit: An Illustrated History.* DeKalb: Northern Illinois University Press, 1998.

Yungmeyer, D. W. "Bion Joseph Arnold 1861–1942." *Railway and Locomotive Historical Society* 58 (January 1942) 8–17.

———. "An Excursion into the Early History of the Chicago and Alton Railroad." *Journal of the Illinois State Historical Society (1908–1984)* 38:1 (March 1945), 7–37.

INDEX

suburban traffic, 82, 91, 95, 155, 193, 221
subways, 211

taxation, 45–46, 108, 209, 212, 214–214, 240, 264n4, 274n2, 276n39
tax increment financing, 250–251, 256
Taylor, Frederick, 103
Tebbs, Robert W., 207
Telautograph, 206
Teletype, 206
Thaw, Evelyn Nesbit, 116
Thompson, Tommy, 251
Thomson, J. Edgar, 15, 21, 22, 27–29, 37, 41, 49, 264n7
Tishman, Realty and Construction Company, 232, 236–237, 239
Torrence, Joseph T., 60, 105–107
track elevation, 105, 115, 153, 159
track gauge, 19
transit corners, 129
transit-oriented development, 256
TranSytems, 254
Travelers Aid Society, 212
Trimble, Robert, 76
Turner, J. J., 150
Twelfth Street, 120, 124, 138, 143, 166, 166, 171, 191, 211.
Twentieth Century Limited, 197, 236

Urban Mass Transit Administration, 239–240
urban renewal, 219
United States Railroad Administration, 163, 165–166
Union Depot, act authorizing, 57
Union Pacific, 38, 231, 237
Union Station Master Plan, 255
Union Stock Yard, 40, 95
University of Illinois, 226–228, 231
U.S. Equities Realty, 245, 247
USO Canteen, 212

Van Buren, Martin, 6
Van Buren Street, 24, 29, 34, 53
Van Buren Street depot, 22, 24, 69. See also LaSalle Street Station
Vanderbilt, William, 70
viaducts, 26, 104–105, 109, 152, 171, 188, 263n57, 270n64

Wabash and Erie Canal, 262n20
Wabash Railroad, 65, 121, 144, 196
Wacker, Charles, 141, 152, 208
Waddell and Harrington, 131
Walbrun, Mark, 248
Wallace, John, 152
Walton Street Capital, 251
Ward, Aaron Montgomery, 85

War Department, U.S., 90, 164, 171
Washington Union Station, 134–135, 139, 141
Weese, Harry, 241, 247
Wells Street Station, 68, 69, 70, 124, 207
Wentworth, John, 9, 25, 31
Western Indiana. See Chicago and Western Indiana Railroad
Western Society of Engineers, 117, 148
West Loop Transportation Center, 252
West Metropolitan Area Council, 233
West Side Superhighway, 209
West Suburban Transit District, 239
West Water Street, 26, 28
White, Howard, 138
Wilson, Woodrow, 167
Winslow, Robert, 245
Wisconsin Central, 87
Wolfson, Erwin, 232
Wood, Joseph, 152
World War I, 163
World War II, 212–215
World's Columbian Exposition, 89–95, 103, 152

Youssefi, Hossein, 252

Zephyrs, 197
Zoning Board of Appeals, 221
Zouaves. See Ellsworth's Zouaves

A farewell kiss.

Fred Ash's interest in railroads, especially passenger trains, started as a teenager and intensified when he moved to Chicago after receiving degrees in business and economics. In the urban environment, he developed interests in architecture and city planning. After thirty years as a commercial banker specializing in nonprofit and government finance, he retired to spend time with his wife and daughter and to complete this history, which had been twenty years in gestation.